Understanding
Mental
Retardation

UNDERSTANDING MENTAL RETARDATION

Research Accomplishments and New Frontiers

edited by

JAMES F. KAVANAGH, Ph.D.

Associate Director
Center for Research for
 Mothers and Children
National Institute of Child Health
 and Human Development
National Institutes of Health
Bethesda, Maryland

·P A U L·H·
BROOKES
PUBLISHING CO.

Baltimore • London • Toronto • Sydney

Paul H. Brookes Publishing Co.
P.O. Box 10624
Baltimore, Maryland 21285-0624

Typeset by Harper Graphics, Inc., Waldorf, Maryland.
Manufactured in the United States of America by
The Maple Press Company, York, Pennsylvania.

Library of Congress Cataloging-in-Publication Data
Understanding mental retardation.

  Includes bibliographies and index.
  1. Mental retardation—Congresses.   I. Kavanagh,
James F.
RC569.9.U53   1988   616.85'88   88-2880
ISBN 0-933716-99-0

| Contents

Contributors

Charles A. Alford, M.D.
Professor of Pediatrics and
  Microbiology
Department of Pediatrics
School of Medicine, UAB Station
The University of Alabama at
  Birmingham
Birmingham, AL 35294

Heidelise Als, Ph.D.
Enders Pediatric Research
  Laboratories
Children's Hospital
320 Longwood Avenue
Boston, MA 02115

John G. Borkowski, Ph.D.
Department of Psychology
University of Notre Dame
Notre Dame, IN 46556

Joel D. Bregman, M.D.
Instructor in Child Psychiatry
Child Study Center
Yale University School of Medicine
P.O. Box 333
New Haven, CT 06510

Donna M. Bryant, Ph.D.
Frank Porter Graham Child
  Development Center
CB #8180
University of North Carolina at
  Chapel Hill
Chapel Hill, NC 27599

Michael F. Cataldo, Ph.D.
Director
Department of Behavioral
  Psychology
John F. Kennedy Institute
The Johns Hopkins University
  School of Medicine
707 North Broadway
Baltimore, MD 21205

Deborah L. Coates, Ph.D.
Associate Professor of Psychology
Catholic University of America, *and*
Project Director, The Better Babies
  Project
1507 Benning Road, N.E.
Washington, DC 20002

Donald J. Cohen, M.D.
Director, Irving B. Harris Professor
Child Study Center
Yale University School of Medicine
New Haven, CT 06520

Robert E. Cooke, M.D.
A. Conger Goodyear Professor and
  Chairman
Department of Pediatrics
School of Medicine
State University of New York at
  Buffalo
219 Bryant Street
Buffalo, NY 14222

Barbara Culley, R.N., M.S.N.
Clinical Nurse Specialist
Vanderbilt University
S-4311 Medical Center North
Nashville, TN 37232

Felix de la Cruz, M.D., M.P.H.
Mental Retardation and
  Developmental Disabilities Branch
Center for Research for Mothers
  and Children
National Institutes of Health
National Institute of Child Health
  and Human Development
9000 Rockville Pike
Executive Plaza North, Room 631
Bethesda, MD 20892

Frank H. Duffy, M.D.
BEAM Laboratory
Children's Hospital
300 Longwood Avenue
Boston, MA 02155

Robert B. Edgerton, Ph.D.
Socio-Behavioral Research Group
Mental Retardation Research
  Center
Neuropsychiatric Institute
760 Westwood Plaza
University of California
Los Angeles, CA 90024

Joseph F. Fagan, III, Ph.D.
Department of Psychology
Case Western Reserve University
Cleveland, OH 44106

Tiffany Field, Ph.D.
Department of Pediatrics
Mailman Center for Human
  Development, D-820
University of Miami
P.O. Box 016820
Miami, FL 33101

Janina R. Galler, M.D.
Center for Behavioral Development
  and Mental Retardation
Boston University School of
  Medicine
Suite M-921
85 East Newton Street
Boston, MA 02118

Mitchell S. Golbus, M.D.
Director
Prenatal Detection Program
Department of Obstetrics,
  Gynecology, and Reproductive
  Sciences
Reproductive Genetics Unit, U-262
University of California Medical
  Center
San Francisco, CA 94143

Jens Grogaard, M.D.
Assistant Professor of Pediatrics
Vanderbilt University
School of Medicine
Nashville, TN 37232

H. Carl Haywood, Ph.D.
Department of Psychology and
  Human Development, *and*
Department of Neurology
Vanderbilt University
Nashville, TN 37203

Nancy Haywood, M.A.
Psychologist
8046 Esterbrook Drive
Nashville, TN 37221

John C. Hobbins, M.D.
Professor of Obstetrics, Gynecology,
  and Diagnostic Imaging
Yale University School of Medicine,
  and Director of Obstetrics
Yale–New Haven Hospital
333 Cedar Street
P.O. Box 3333
New Haven, CT 06510

Mary C. Howell, M.D., Ph.D.
Kennedy Aging Project
The Eunice Kennedy Shriver
  Center
200 Trapelo Road
Waltham, MA 02254

Matthew P. Janicki, Ph.D.
Director for Aging Services
New York State Office of Mental
  Retardation and Developmental
  Disabilities
44 Holland Avenue
Albany, NY 12229-1000

Edwin H. Kolodny, M.D.
Director
The Eunice Kennedy Shriver
  Center
200 Trapelo Road
Waltham, MA 02254

Marty Wyngaarden Krauss, Ph.D.
Florence Heller Graduate School
Brandeis University, *and*
The Eunice Kennedy Shriver
  Center
200 Trapelo Road
Waltham, MA 02254

Harvey L. Levy, M.D.
Director for Inborn Errors of
  Metabolism
New England Newborn Screening
  Program
Department of Public Health
305 South Street
Jamaica Plains, MA 02130; *and*
Associate Professor of Neurology
Harvard Medical School
Boston, MA 02130

Daniel P. Lindstrom, Ph.D.
Research Assistant Professor of
  Pediatrics
4128 Vanderbilt University Hospital
Nashville, TN 37232

Jeanne E. Montie, Ph.D.
Research Associate
Infantest Corporation
11000 Cedar Avenue, 4th Floor
Cleveland, OH 44106

Hugo W. Moser, M.D.
President
John F. Kennedy Institute, *and*
Professor of Neurology and
  Pediatrics
The Johns Hopkins University
  School of Medicine
707 North Broadway
Baltimore, MD 21205

Phillip G. Nelson, M.D., Ph.D.
Chief, Laboratory of Developmental
  Neurobiology
National Institute of Child Health
  and Human Development
Building 36, Room 2A21
9000 Rockville Pike
Bethesda, MD 20892

William L. Nyhan, M.D., Ph.D.
Professor of Pediatrics
Department of Pediatrics
University of California, San Diego
LaJolla, CA 92093

Craig T. Ramey, Ph.D.
Frank Porter Graham Child
  Development Center
CB #8180
University of North Carolina at
  Chapel Hill
Chapel Hill, NC 27599

Roy D. Schmickel, M.D.
Department of Human Genetics
University of Pennsylvania
195 Medical Labs Building/G3
Philadelphia, PA 19104

Rachel Schneerson, M.D.
Laboratory of Developmental and
  Molecular Immunity
National Institute of Child Health
  and Human Development
Building 6, Room 1A08
9000 Rockville Pike
Bethesda, MD 20892

Keith G. Scott, Ph.D.
Professor of Psychology and
  Pediatrics
Mailman Center for Child
  Development
University of Miami
P.O. Box 016820
Miami, FL 33101

Mildred T. Stahlman, M.D.
Professor of Pediatrics and
  Pathology, *and* Director
Division of Neonatology
Vanderbilt University
S-4307 Medical Center North
Nashville, TN 37232

Tanya M. Suarez, Ph.D.
Frank Porter Graham Child
  Development Center
CB #8180 NCNB Plaza
University of North Carolina at
  Chapel Hill
Chapel Hill, NC 27514

Lisa A. Turner, Ph.D.
Department of Psychology and
  Human Development
George Peabody College for
  Teachers
Vanderbilt University
Nashville, TN 37203

Joseph J. Volpe, M.D.
Washington University School of
  Medicine
Department of Pediatrics
400 South Kings Highway
P.O. Box 14871
St. Louis, MO 63178

Bernard Weiss, Ph.D.
Environmental Health Sciences
  Center, *and*
Department of Biophysics
University of Rochester Medical
  Center
Rochester, NY 14642

Savio L.C. Woo, Ph.D.
Professor
Department of Cell Biology
Baylor College of Medicine, *and*
  Investigator
Howard Hughes Medical Institute
1200 Moursund Avenue, #M828
Houston, TX 77030

Foreword
Twenty-Five Years of Accomplishments in Mental Retardation

It is a privilege to recognize the world-famous National Institute of Child Health and Human Development, an institute created to fulfill the hopes and dreams of parents for their children. Dr. Alexander, its director, has insisted that the problems of mental retardation remain high on the national agenda; he is a source of strength and encouragement to me personally and to all who are concerned with the mentally retarded people of the world.

My brother, Jack, would be so delighted to witness the commitment and compassion of those in this field, as exemplified by the authors of the chapters in this book, and by their contributions to this Institute he founded 25 years ago. Many of these authors are veterans of the long, difficult struggle against mental retardation. I know the families of individuals with mental retardation are eternally grateful to them for their steadfastness and devotion. It is most gratifying also to note the contributions of so many young men and women—a second and third generation of physicians, scientists, and educators who will carry on this noble work into the next century. Congratulations to all of them!

What lessons do these past 25 years teach us . . . lessons on which we can build the future? First, we have learned that only a few, committed people with a great idea can change the course of history. When my brother wanted to develop health policies for his new administration, he didn't set up a large bureaucracy to engage in endless studies. He chose a very small group to advise him. He picked them for their professional skills, it is true, but also because they had stood up for what they believed in. They had intelligence and experience, yes, but, even more important, they had virtue and vision.

They saw what almost nobody else saw, neither politicians nor professionals. They saw the disgraceful lack of any significant, national attention to the health problems of the great majority of our population: women and children; mothers and their babies. They saw that in all our national health establishments there was almost no ongoing research in human development, nothing on mental retardation, very little on nutrition, on childhood diseases, and on birth defects, and very little on prematurity or obstetrical difficulties.

The National Institutes of Health were organized around individual diseases—heart, lung, cancer, mental illness—diseases that a congress made up of men could understand. There was no interest in the medical problems of the fetus, the infant, or the child, or the women who were bearing and nurturing the future generation of Americans. In fact, there was not one obstetrician in research in the entire federal establishment. When one of the most senior medical administrators was asked why the problems of children were not being studied, he answered, "Children have no major health problems."

Think of how totally hopeless life was for mentally retarded people, how bleak it was for their families. There was no legislation to improve the lives of the mentally retarded, no public policy, no programs, and no resources to deal with the single greatest affliction of young children. Mental retardation was relegated to a dark corner of the world to which young doctors or scientists were not even exposed. Typically, they never even saw a mentally retarded person in all their years of training. That small presidential advisory group decided that this had to change. They recommended the creation of an entire institute devoted to the health problems of children and their development into mature persons, and that was the genesis of the National Institute of Child Health and Human Development.

We, and mentally retarded persons, were lucky then. My brother, Jack, was president and he was personally and politically committed to improving the lives of children, especially mentally retarded children. However, like any chief executive, he demanded facts . . . facts about the connections between low birth weight and mental retardation, prematurity and mental retardation, childhood diseases and genetic birth defects and mental retardation. Fortunately, when my brother asked me for these facts, I was ready for him.

I told him that if we could only focus enough of our resources and our scientific genius on the problems of retardation, we could change the world for millions of Americans born 5, 10, 20 years in the future. My brother stopped. He thought. Then, with clarity and decisiveness, he said, "We'll do it." And, he did. First he set the machinery in motion to pass the legislation needed to establish the NICHD. Then, he set up a Presidential Panel on Mental Retardation to study the problem in all its aspects and recommend a series of actions to be taken. Thus, within a few months of his inauguration, from nothing at all we had two major new enterprises, both brought into being because of mental retardation.

I often ask myself why my brother acted to make life better for mentally retarded persons? Why was he concerned? Was it only because he had a mentally retarded sister? I think not. I think he had a vision larger than that. He asked himself deep and troubling questions about human values. How do we measure human worth? How do we distribute our national resources? And, I believe he asked himself the most difficult question of all: "What are our duties to the powerless if we are to be a just and caring society?" However, he did more than simply ask himself these questions. He truly believed that many things should be done and could be done for all powerless people. He believed a president could change attitudes, that he could influence people to act and care for others.

These historic developments took place almost 25 years ago. Since then, there have been many magnificent achievements worthy of praise and gratitude, many of these due to the contributors to this book and their colleagues. Because of early infant screening programs, phenylketonuria (PKU) no longer threatens the newborn child. I can remember bringing a child with PKU to the White House to see President Kennedy, along with her younger sister, for whom the disease had been diagnosed early enough to save her from PKU-induced retardation. Rh incompatibility has been solved with the development of RhoGAM. We now have vaccines to prevent congenital rubella and measles encephalitis. Meningitis due to *Haemophilus influenzae* has been reduced as a threat, and babies under 2 pounds at birth and those suffering from hyaline membrane disease now have an extraordinarily good chance to survive.

Yes, it is a different world for the mentally retarded. However, these victories of the past, won by many giants of scientific research, some of whom are contributors to this book, do not guarantee public support and national concern in the future. This will depend on these very responders. Beyond their world of laboratories and clinics is their responsibility for political action. I come from a political family so I know about this. The familiar quotation from John Buchan, the great Canadian writer and political leader, is still true today: "The greatest of callings is politics." We need these researchers and clinicians out there, serving in the legislatures, testifying before Congress in the Senate and House, and making a case for what is needed and why it is needed.

I warn them only to have their facts accurate, and to be able to say clearly and simply how what they are doing will influence for good the lives of retarded persons. They should not ask for too much money. Also, they should be sure that what they are asking for is not already being provided in their community or state.

It is not necessary for researchers to spend all their time in the laboratory. When Dr. Robert Guthrie developed the screening test for PKU he didn't just write it up and go on to the next experiment. He went public. He knocked on doors, buttonholed state legislatures, spoke to parents' groups, organized coalitions until every state passed laws mandating PKU screening and country after country adopted the Guthrie test. If other researchers take their cases to the people, they will find that the way has been paved by mentally retarded persons themselves. I urge them to come out of their laboratories and clinics and see how mentally retarded people and their families are keeping alive public interest in their fate—not through lobbying or protest but by their courage and their character.

Come with me to the 7th International Special Olympics Games at South Bend, Indiana. There, you can see mentally retarded athletes like Loretta Claiborne, who has completed the marathon in 3 hours and 9 minutes, or Jose Gonzales, whose record in the mile is 4 minutes and 43 seconds. Or Jack Phillips, whose leap in the high jump would have won the gold medal in the 1904 World Olympics Games! You can see basketball, soccer, baseball, and volleyball played by teams of severely retarded athletes who, experts once said, could never learn to play team sports. Looking across the Notre Dame stadium at opening ceremonies, you can see a special section, a place of honor for the 10,000 parents and family members who have come to cheer their sons and daughters. These are parents who, 25 years ago, would have been embarrassed to admit they had a mentally retarded child.

Come with me to an electrical plant near Seattle. There you can see mentally retarded adults working as a regular unit putting together highly complex electrical components. This is no sheltered workshop. These individuals are a vital part of that plant's work force. They work, play, eat, and take their breaks right alongside their fellow employees. What is most remarkable is that none of them has an IQ of over 40! Applicants with a higher score can't qualify.

Or, come with me to the great hall of the National Academy of Sciences. There, in a ceremony initiated by the Kennedy Foundation and originally presided over by President Kennedy, the Kennedy Foundation International Awards in Mental Retardation are given. Dr. Guthrie and Dr. Herbert Lubs receive awards for their magnificent achievements in science, and others are recognized for their outstanding service and leadership in their work with mentally retarded persons. However, at this awards ceremony something happens that could not have taken place 25 years ago. Two of the Kennedy International Awards go to William Britt and Nancy McDaniel for their contributions in two equally important areas of human endeavor—art and sports. Both of them are mentally retarded.

Today, most of the headlines and most of the money go to those who have tied their careers to the realm of *outer* space. Star Wars, lasers, and missiles capture the imagination and win the support of politicians. Researchers in mental retardation—who explore *inner* space—are embarked on a more silent journey. They rarely make headlines. Their work cannot be justified by the urgency of national defense. However, the challenge of their question is far greater and more worthy than the exploration of the stars. It is they who will someday unlock the secrets of the mind, secrets that hold the key to the humanity we share—not to our power or dominion over others. These secrets are still undisclosed, although our progress has been great.

Fifty years after Ivor Følling we still do not know why PKU causes mental retardation. Forty years after Jerome Lejeune—and 140 years after Down identified the syndrome that bears his name—we don't know why that extra chromosome causes mental retardation. Educators, physicians, psychologists, neurobiologists, even poets have their theories, but we still do not know what intelligence really is and how the conditions that produce mental retardation work to limit intelligence. That is the greatest challenge we face—for if we can unlock the secrets of mind, we can solve not only the riddle of mental retardation, but many of the greatest problems that trouble mankind.

As researchers work to penetrate the heart of this darkness, I implore them to keep in mind those on whose behalf they labor. The special gift of mentally retarded persons is to show us all how similar we are. One of them has a mind that cannot add; one of us has a heart that cannot feel. One of them has legs that stumble; one of us will look away and let him fall. And some of them will reach out to us—and some of us will grasp their hands.

The whispered message of retarded persons is that we may be different in our gifts, but we are equal in our humanity. Although there is much that intellect can do, it is barren and sterile unless its work is done with love. The great philosopher Teilhard de Chardin said it best, "Someday after mastering the winds, the waves, the tides and gravity, we shall harness for God, the energies of love. And then, for the second time in the history of the world, man will have discovered fire."

Eunice Kennedy Shriver, Executive Vice President
The Joseph P. Kennedy, Jr. Foundation

Preface

The conference that served as the launching point for this book holds a very special place in the history of the National Institutes of Health and the National Institute of Child Health and Human Development. More than one hundred years ago, in response to a cholera epidemic, a Laboratory of Hygiene was established in the New York Marine Hospital for research on infectious diseases. From that one-room laboratory has come the entire National Institutes of Health. Its contributions, from biomedical research to treating and preventing disease and disability, have earned it the accolade of 20th century America's major contribution to civilization. In 1987, NIH celebrated its centennial. A national conference, "Mental Retardation: Research Accomplishments and New Frontiers," was one of the opening events for the year-long celebration. It also marked two other anniversaries—the 40th year since the establishment of The Joseph P. Kennedy, Jr. Foundation, and the 25th birthday of the National Institute of Child Health and Human Development, joint sponsors of the conference. It is a pleasure now to have the expert presentations from that exciting conference redrafted for this book.

The subtitle of the book (and conference), *Research Accomplishments and New Frontiers*, is no accident. The words convey the clear link between the Institute and the Kennedy Foundation, between the course of study in the field of mental retardation and the opportunities that lie ahead. President John Kennedy characterized his administration as the New Frontier for good reason. Just as our forebears overcame forbidding obstacles and faced the challenge of an unknown wilderness in pushing back the frontier as they conquered a continent, so President Kennedy committed himself and the resources of the federal government to facing and overcoming new frontiers. The barriers he challenged were no less difficult or important. He challenged the barriers between nations and peoples with new approaches like the Peace Corps. He challenged the barriers of race and prejudice, and broached new frontiers in civil rights. He challenged the barrier of space and put us on a course to a new frontier that led to the moon, the planets, and eventually the stars. He challenged social barriers that kept our mentally retarded and handicapped citizens shut away from view, and opened a new frontier for them as fuller participants in society. And of particular importance for those attending the conference, as well as their fellow researchers, he challenged the barrier of ignorance of the causes of mental retardation, and put us on a course of developing knowledge through research that would lead to a new frontier of hope for preventing and treating that formerly hopeless condition.

Major components of John Kennedy's plan for approaching the new frontier in mental retardation were represented at this commemorative conference. He sponsored and signed the legislation that created the University Affiliated Facilities for services and training in mental retardation. He sponsored and signed the legislation providing federal funds to construct the Mental Retardation Research Centers. And he sponsored and signed the legislation that created a new Institute at the National Institutes of Health—the National Institute of Child Health and Human Development—that would provide the national leadership for the research effort directed against mental retardation.

The results of John Kennedy's initiatives toward some of these frontiers—the successes of the Peace Corps, the enormous progress in civil rights, the achievements in space, and the deinstitutionalization and barrier-free environment movements—are well known. Far less well known is the success that has been achieved by the NICHD and its scientists in pushing back the frontier of ignorance of mental retardation. The conference was an effort to correct that deficit—to show and celebrate the progress over the past 25 years, and to take a look at the frontier ahead and at the ways biomedical and behavioral research will challenge and overcome its barriers. This book extends that mission.

It is appropriate to pause here to acknowledge the contributions of the person who opened the conference and whose remarks stand as the Foreword for this book. Eunice Kennedy Shriver is our most direct link with our past as an Institute and with our role as a part of the New Frontier. Sister of the President, she was there when he proposed and when he signed the legislation that established this Institute. She was a member of the Institute's first National Advisory Council, and during her 4-year term on that council closely observed and mothered the growth of the Institute and its development of the Mental Retardation Research Centers. Today, as Executive Vice President of the Kennedy Foundation, she continues to direct her family's efforts toward pushing back the mental retardation frontier.

By bringing together the papers from this conference and publishing them for a more extended audience, it is hoped that this book will provide not only a historical record of our progress in the past 25 years, but also a source of assistance and inspiration to other scientists and workers in this field.

Duane F. Alexander, M.D., Director
National Institute of Child Health and Human Development

Understanding
Mental
Retardation

INTRODUCTION

Research Challenges and Opportunities in the Next Quarter Century

WILLIAM L. NYHAN

The past 25 years have witnessed exponential progress in research that has had a direct application to human disease and particularly to the definition and prevention of mental retardation. Nevertheless, the tools currently available are so powerful that almost anything I can predict about the brightness of future progress of research is bound to be an underestimate. These should be wonderful years for the National Institute of Child Health and Human Development. The challenge, I think, is going to be to keep up with the enormous momentum of ever-accelerating progress.

I think progress will continue in the identification of genes involved in a wide variety of human diseases, as ultimately the whole human genome is mapped. The processes of regulation will be increasingly understood; there is reasonable optimism that this work will soon begin to answer the important questions in development, so that the level at which regulation is taking place can be determined. The families of genes involved in regulating development will be cloned, and their functions understood. Knowledge of the genomic signals that turn on and off genes should lead to information regarding the manipulation of these processes for preventive and curative purposes.

The next new frontier is probably going to be that of neurobiology. New insights will come as the gap in information between the gene and the surface of the cell begins to close, and the molecular basis of neural connections, tropism, and sprouting are understood down to a physical level. All known receptors will doubtless be cloned and their structure elucidated. Once this information is obtained, insights into the biology of genes will be available about which one can at the moment only speculate.

I would like to turn from this more general discussion to some specific examples of areas in which there is current understanding of clinical problems and insight into the directions of future research.

3

TECHNOLOGICAL PROBLEMS IN PERINATOLOGY

Technological advances with immediate application to cerebral development and to the problem of mental retardation may be expected to be brought to bear on the perinatal period and the neonatal intensive care unit.

The major current problems are still respiratory distress syndrome and, among the tiniest babies, the issues of control of ventilation in which apnea is the rule rather than the exception and support may be needed for a period of weeks, during which time catastrophes such as intraventricular and intracerebral hemorrhage are so common. This will be a major challenge also for obstetrical management. The objective is to learn to keep these babies longer in utero.

Ventilation and Oxygenation

The ultimate control of the problem of apnea may well be pharmacological, with stimulant drugs. For instance, the infusion of doxapram certainly seems to be useful, but research in this area has only begun. The vast majority of babies with cardiorespiratory problems currently, and for the immediate future, are going to need some form of artificial ventilation.

Among the current approaches to artificial ventilation is high-frequency ventilation. This method is clearly better than older methods in the response to air leaks, including pulmonary interstitial emphysema and bronchopleural fistula. High-frequency ventilation is compliance insensitive, and so it tends to ventilate all areas at lower pressures. A comparison of conventional ventilation and high-frequency jet ventilation indicated that there were very different waveforms leading to lower peak pressures and lower mean pressures, and, despite this, improved levels of oxygenation and decreased accumulation of carbon dioxide.

The new oscillators use very small tidal volumes. They are easy to humidify and can be added onto conventional systems so that there are many possibilities for experimental combinations of the technology. A collaborative study funded by the National Institutes of Health is now going on in 10 centers in the United States in which oscillation is being compared with conventional ventilation. I am hopeful that this study will lead to other studies as the technology improves. Furthermore, the follow-up investigation of the babies studied is critical for the assessment of the long-term results of the various modalities.

The current most intensive form of intensive care is extracorporeal membrane oxygenation. This may be the only answer for babies under 28 weeks, whose lungs have no alveoli, or at best only saccules. It is also currently the only answer for babies with pulmonary hypertension. If blood is not going to the lungs, no amount of artificial ventilation is going to permit oxygenation of the brain. Experience already indicates that this mode of therapy is effective, but it is now in its early stages. As research continues there will be better understanding of the problems involved and newer ways to avoid them.

Respiratory Distress Syndrome—Treatment with Surfactant

The respiratory distress syndrome remains a major cause of mortality and long-range morbidity in neonatal intensive care units. It has been recognized for some time that developmental maturity and phospholipid surfactant play important roles in the lowering of surface tension, the promoting of alveolar clearance, and general mature lung function. In the absence of surfactant there is potential for atelectasis at the end of each expiration.

It seemed an obvious approach to obtain surfactant material and to administer it directly to the baby in order to treat or prevent the respiratory distress syndrome. Nevertheless, early studies were not successful for a variety of reasons. Some encouraging results were obtained using bovine surfactant. More recently, in parallel studies in San Diego and in Helsinki it became evident that immediately on instillation of the surfactant obtained from human amniotic fluid there was a change in oxygenation, and concomitantly the X rays of the babies showed remarkable improvement from a complete white-out of severe respiratory distress syndrome prior to treatment to progressive clearing. It became apparent that respiratory distress syndrome could be treated using these techniques.

It remained to undertake a randomized control study. Data obtained by Merritt et al. were published in 1986 in the *New England Journal of Medicine*. This was a randomized controlled study in which there were 31 treated infants and 29 controls. All of them had lecithin:sphingomyelin ratios of less than 2, indicating the probability that their lungs were very deficient in surfactant. The treated group required significantly less oxygen and significantly less airway pressure, and both bronchopulmonary dysplasia and death were significantly reduced in the surfactant-treated group.

These differences were highly significant statistically. In addition, there were significantly fewer complications such as pulmonary interstitial emphysema and pneumothorax. The treatment substantially reduced the period of neonatal intensive care required. These data and those of others indicate clearly that surfactant replacement has real promise in improving the survival of very premature infants and for reducing the sequelae of this important problem.

Human surfactant contains phospholipids and two groups of lipid-associated proteins. One has a molecular weight of 29,000–36,000 and the other 6,000–14,000. The lower molecular weight proteins remain with the lipids after extraction and these proteins are thought to have a role in the surface activity. Future research will focus on these proteins. Experiments have already been carried out on immature rabbit lung (T. A. Merritt, personal communication, 1987) in which surfactant has been instilled. In comparison to the appearance of rabbit lung treated with saline, the alveoli in the surfactant-treated lung opened up well. It was also shown that rabbit lung treated with an artificial surfactant made by mixing pure phospholipid with isolated 6,000-molecular-weight protein had an identical histological appearance.

We can predict what is going to happen with new techniques. A variety of groups have currently undertaken to clone the genes for both of the surfactant-related proteins. It should ultimately be possible, once these genes are cloned, to make very large quantities of synthetic surfactant, in order to eliminate the dependency on harvesting material from animals or from precious human amniotic fluid. With these materials in plentiful supply one could predict that babies diagnosed at birth as having respiratory distress could be treated so that the complications of this disorder are prevented.

Intraventricular Hemorrhage

Probably the number one problem in perinatology that has direct relevance to the integrity of the central nervous system (CNS) is that of intraventricular hemorrhage. The solution of this problem undoubtedly lies in the area of prenatal obstetrical care. Some fascinating observations have been made by R. Bejar (personal communication, 1987), who has been evaluating the CNS by means of ultrasound analysis. He first showed that it was possible, using the baby's fontanelle as a window, to get much more sensitive indices of CNS morphology by ultrasound than by conventional methods such as the computed tomography (CT) scan. More recently, he has found evidence of periventricular leukomalacia next to the thalamus. This finding appears to be the best prognosticator of later problems of CNS development. Ultrasound reveals the very small hemorrhages and cyst formation in the area of leukomalacia, of which large ventricular hemorrhages are the ultimate outcome. Prospective studies starting very early in life as well as histopathological correlations in some babies who have not survived indicate very clearly that this problem is occurring prior to the time of birth. Therefore, advances in its prevention are going to have to be advances in obstetrical management, ideally those that keep the infant longer in utero. These considerations are also relevant to the issue of extracorporeal membrane oxygenation, which is conceptually the treatment of the infant, once delivered, as though it were still a fetus in utero.

NEWER METHODS OF IMAGING

The ultrasonographic findings of Bejar noted above suggest another area in which there has been exciting progress, that of studies on imaging. The visualization of the CNS obtained when CT scanning first became available was extremely impressive. The images obtained with magnetic resonance imaging (MRI) are infinitely more beautiful. Furthermore, this is a technique in which there is no risk associated with the injection of contrast material and there is no issue of radiation dosage. It is already apparent that MRI has much higher sensitivity.

The differential appearance of gray and white matter is striking. In the T_1-weighted image, which is best suited to the delineation of the anatomy, the brain is shown in light color and the cerebrospinal fluid in dark, as are cortical bone and dura. The cerebral sulci are beautifully defined and so is the anatomy of the cerebellum. In the coronal view one can see the temporal lobe gyri, which were never clearly seen with CT scanning. The method has shown itself to be superbly adapted to the detection of even very tiny tumors.

My colleagues and I are just beginning to utilize MRI in our clinical and research work. We have, for instance, observed the appearance of the brain very early in life in the infant with maple syrup urine disease. This technique is probably the most sensitive in indicating degrees of myelination. In diseases of metabolism such as maple syrup urine disease we are seeing now, in vivo, an extraordinary degree of hypodensity of the white matter in the visual image of the delayed myelination that had previously been seen at autopsy in babies who did not survive. More important, in follow-up studies we are able to assess effects of therapy and observe changes with development. Improvement is being seen in these infants, and this is a rewarding experience. We are carrying out sequential studies of imaging, as well as very finely detailed behavioral analyses of learning and language in our patients. I am hopeful that the future will give us meaningful information on the prognostic value of some of these MRI images. They should provide us with the kind of assessments that, along with early diagnosis, should yield improvements in treatment with the aim not only of preserving life but of promoting optimal intellectual development.

The other area that will spin off from this technology, nuclear magnetic resonance (NMR) spectroscopy, has enormous potential. Phosphorus-31 NMR studies of metabolism in muscle have begun.

For example, type V glycogen storage disease of muscle (McArdle disease) can be diagnosed by the failure of muscle phosphocreatine to reappear in recovery from ischemic exercise. As the technology becomes more widely available, the NMR signals improve, and more complex spectra are analyzed, imaging of carbon atoms will be possible, and the use of stable isotopes such as carbon-13 will enable the study of cerebral metabolism.

The other exciting area of imaging is that of positron emission tomography (PET). Many studies of cerebral metabolism using radiolabeled glucose are being done. I was particularly impressed by the incredible picture of the basal ganglia obtained using ^{11}C-labeled methylspiperone (Wong et al., 1984). This technique provided an important opportunity to investigate the patient with Lesch-Nyhan syndrome. The basal ganglia of one of our patients have now been imaged by Wong (personal communication, 1987). The ligand binds preferentially to dopamine receptors in the basal ganglia and is not seen in the rest of the brain.

The importance of the methodology is that one can foresee the development of specific ligands that bind to highly specific receptors in the brain, permitting the imaging of extraordinarily discrete areas of brain function.

NEW TECHNIQUES IN THE STUDY
OF INHERITED METABOLIC DISEASE

The field of inborn errors of metabolism has been very closely intertwined with the development of progress in research in mental retardation, and the past 25 years have witnessed dramatic accomplishments in this field. The early diagnosis of phenylketonuria in now virtually all of the infants born in developed countries of the world has permitted the prevention of severe retardation in a program that is a model for the translation of research into public health. More recently, the focus has shifted to the neonatal intensive care unit as a site in which babies with inborn errors of metabolism are seen. The baby with propionic acidemia exemplifies the presentation of these disorders, with desperate illness in the first days of life. The methodology for the diagnosis and study of babies like this is complex. Our own approach to the analysis of organic acids is a time-consuming column separation of the organic acids, albeit rewarding in a number of instances. A particularly rewarding pattern is that seen in the patient with multiple carboxylase deficiency. The importance of this diagnosis is that patients with multiple carboxylase deficiency are extraordinarily sensitive to treatment with biotin.

The complexity of the methodology is illustrated following the separation of these organic acids on a column by their identification in the gas chromatograph–mass spectrometer. For instance, the identification of methylcitric acid (Ando, Rasmussen, Wright, & Nyhan, 1972) is a critical element in the early diagnosis of both propionic acidemia and multiple carboxylase deficiency. Its versatility was more recently elegantly demonstrated in the definition of mevalonic aciduria, a newly discovered inborn error in the biosynthetic pathway for cholesterol (Hoffman et al., 1986).

Many of the babies who survive the illness that necessitated admission to the neonatal intensive care unit are left with retarded mental development. However, this does not have to be so. There are a variety of therapeutic measures that enable them to progress through infancy and childhood successfully. Use of such measures can be a very rewarding experience, but one must be patient. One of our patients was behaving at a developmental level of 3 months of age when first seen at 13 months. However, she made up her progress through the developmental milestones and at 17 years of age she was continuing to function as a prefectly normal individual.

I anticipate many advances in the field of inborn errors of metabolism. Disorders not now known to be metabolic will be discovered and characterized and their enzymatic defects established. Newer approaches to treatment will be suggested by the nature of the metabolic disorders. The dramatic successes of vitamin B_{12} treatment in some forms of methylmalonic acidemia and particularly of biotin treatment in multiple carboxylase deficiency provide models.

I believe there will also be advances in early diagnosis. Organic acid analysis is currently carried out in only a few institutions, and very few perform it on the rapid service basis necessary if the lives of these infants are to be saved. Furthermore, even in the best hands it takes a number of days to come up with a definitive diagnosis. A novel approach has recently been developed by Lehnert and Hunkler (1986) of the University of Freiburg in the Federal Republic of Germany. It represents the use of high-resolution NMR spectrometry carried out directly on unprocessed urine in the rapid specific diagnosis of disorders of organic acid metabolism. They have demonstrated the effectiveness of the technique, for instance, in the diagnosis of 3-ketothiolase deficiency. This is a particularly good example because in my experience this is the disorder of organic acid metabolism that is most likely to be missed by current methodology (Middleton et al., 1986). The high-resolution instrument is able to detect the characteristic structure of tiglyglycine and also 2-methyl-3-hydroxybutyric acid, the diagnostic combination.

NMR methods have been used in chemistry for many years, but their earliest approaches to clinical diagnosis were not successful because the resolution of the instruments at about 90 MHz was much too low. Lehnert and Hunkler obtained their data with a 250-Mhz instrument, and they recommend a concentrated effort to develop very high-resolution (400–500-MHz) instruments.

The sensitivity of the method can be increased by lyophilizing the urine and dissolving the residue in deuterium oxide, but the real beauty of the methodology is that it can be applied to complex mixtures of native specimens such as urine without making any alterations. This should permit the rapid diagnosis of these desperately ill infants. I predict that, once these instruments are more readily available, this kind of methodology will readily be extrapolated to the newborn screening programs, so that these babies can be detected before they become ill in the first place. Those of us working in the field of organic acid metabolism have been frustrated by the fact that these infants would be among the best candidates for neonatal screening programs, because if they are diagnosed before the initial episode, death and mental retardation can be prevented. Yet the methodology involved has been so time consuming and expensive that those charged with funding screening programs have not even considered screening for metabolic diseases. With a tool like NMR spectroscopy, one could screen for a host of metabolic diseases rapidly and precisely, the only limitation being the initial purchase of the instrumentation.

MOLECULAR BIOLOGY—RECOMBINANT DNA

The most important advances that have the greatest promise for future research have come from molecular biology, and particularly from the recombinant DNA technology. In the most recent McCusick catalog (1986) some 4,000 Mendelian traits have been listed, and a significant number of these have important effects on the CNS. New genetically determined disorders continue to be discovered all the time. Nevertheless diagnosis, and particularly the kind of diagnosis that is useful to the geneticist and those interested in the prevention of mental retardation, has been difficult indeed. The first applications of the new techniques have been in diagnosis. Furthermore, the initial applications of the ability to clone genes in the diagnosis of disorders have been in those in which the abnormal enzyme protein was known. A particularly good example is that of phenylketonuria (PKU), which is caused by an abnormality in the phenylalanine hydroxylase enzyme. The gene for phenylalanine hydroxylase was cloned by Woo et al. (1983). This enzyme is confined to the liver, and is not expressed in peripheral tissues, such as fibroblasts, leukocytes, or amniocytes. Therefore a molecular diagnosis of PKU has been accomplished in only a small number of patients; heterozygote detection was chancy at best and prenatal diagnosis was impossible using conventional techniques of enzymology.

The new approach employs restriction endonuclease cleavage of the DNA at specific sites to yield fragments of specific size dependent on structure. The fragments then are resolved according to size by electrophoresis in agarose or polyacrylamide gels, and visualized by staining. Following denaturation the single-stranded DNA fragments are transferred to nitrocellulose paper and then the DNA fragments of interest are found by subjecting the filter to a solution containing radioactively labeled DNA probes of the cloned phenylalanine hydroxylase gene. The filter is then washed to get rid of unbound probe and autoradiography is used to reveal those fragments that contain sequences of the phenylalanine hydroxylase gene. Unfortunately, when this technology was applied to the study of patients with classic PKU, it did not yield patterns by which the patient with PKU could readily be distinguished from normal individuals. This means that the gene is present in these patients with PKU, and that there are not large deletions, but rather that we are probably dealing with a single base pair substitution in an area so far not detectable by any of the restriction enzymes. This has been the case with the vast majority of genetic disorders that have so far been subjected to this technology. Nevertheless, the techniques have been useful because an enormous amount of polymorphism has been observed. The polymorphic patterns are normal variations, but they are linked so closely to the genes in question that they can be used to follow the gene through a family at risk.

The patterns obtained with the *Msp* I restriction enzyme included a single band at 23,000 base pairs (or 23 kb) and in other individuals a single band at 19 kb. The heterozygote would have both bands. In an illustrative family the proband was a girl with PKU who had only the 19 band. The parents were heterozygous for the 19 and the 23, and the normal sibling was homozygous for the 23. In this way one could see that the mutant gene was linked very closely to the 19. This is the type of linkage analysis that is enormously useful for both prenatal analysis and heterozygote detection.

In some disorders, such as sickle cell disease and some cases of Lesch-Nyhan syndrome, direct analysis of a sizable deletion or other rearrangement is detectable using the cDNA probe, or a smaller synthetic oligonucleotide probe. It is possible given the right probe even to discriminate a 1 base pair mismatch between the oligonucleotide and the allele under study because hybridization would be abolished by the base change. The number of disorders in which the abnormal gene product (the abnormal protein) is known that are susceptible to detection in this fashion is increasing virtually daily (Cooper & Schmidtke, 1986). I think that in the very near future all of the genes whose protein product is known will be cloned, and therefore there will be reagents available for the kind of diagnostic work and genetic analysis of families that was discussed in the case of PKU.

What is even newer is what has come to be referred to as "reverse genetics." This reflects the ability to obtain access to relevant genes for which no protein product has as yet been identified. The pace of this research is very rapid indeed. The first major success was, of course, the localization of the Huntington chorea gene to chromosome 4p, and its further localization, which has permitted the isolation of DNA probes that serve as markers for the gene. Recent examples seem to appear monthly. They include the gene for Duchenne-type muscular dystrophy (Kunkel et al., 1986), the very interesting retinoblastoma gene, and the gene for chronic granulomatous disease (Royer-Pokora et al., 1986).

The strategy involved in this kind of technique is in essence to clone the gene without reference to any specific protein because its position on the chromosome is known. The X chromosome has been particularly useful for these studies because so much of its genome has been mapped. I think that similar knowledge will be developed over the next 25 years for the autosomes. It is not an unrealistic prediction to foresee the mapping of the entire human genome.

In the approach to the chronic granulomatous disease gene (Royer-Pokora et al., 1986), the position was mapped to the p21 area of the X chromosome by the study of patients with deletions and by formal linkage analysis. The next step was to develop messenger RNA transcripts derived from this region, and the availability of cDNA probes from individuals with appropriate deletions permitted the removal of irrelevant transcripts and the enrichment of the messenger that was sought. The relevance of the particular transcripts to the disorder was then investigated by studying affected patients, and the study of these genetic variants provided strong support for the relevance of a given transcript to the locus. This was conclusively shown by the study of an individual who had a very tiny interstitial deletion.

Once the cDNA was available it was sequenced and its base composition determined. On that basis it is possible not only to use the cDNA in the kind of diagnosis, prenatal diagnosis, and heterozygote detection discussed here, but also to predict the polypeptide for which the gene codes. This promises to be a very interesting area indeed, as structures are developed for proteins that previously were not known to exist and their functions are then considered.

GENE THERAPY

The availability of human genes in plentiful supply has raised the exciting promise of gene therapy. We are most familiar with the work on the hypoxanthine guanine phosphoribosyltransferase (HPRT) gene that was cloned and sequenced by Friedmann and Jolly (Jolly, Esty, Bernard, & Friedmann, 1982). HPRT deficiency is the cause of Lesch-Nyhan syndrome. The phenotype is of extreme motor disability, spastic cerebral palsy, and very striking abnormal self-mutilative behavior.

Once the gene was cloned it was possible to study its insertion into cells in culture. It was first introduced into mouse cells that were HPRT$^-$ and grown in selective media containing aminopterin, which prevents the synthesis of purines de novo but incorporates hypoxanthine so cells containing HPRT will grow normally. Untreated HPRT mouse cells will not grow. When the normal human gene was introduced into these cells they began to function because of the expression of human HPRT. This has now been done with human HPRT$^-$ cells from patients with Lesch-Nyhan disease. At first the inefficiency of the process was very great and this led Friedmann and others to turn to experiments of nature for methods of getting foreign DNA into cells. They employed retroviruses, which in nature are in the business of incorporating DNA into the DNA of host cells. The strategy is to clip out the information that permits retroviruses to cause tumors, leaving the two long terminal repeats (the elements that the virus uses to incorporate the DNA into the cell and get it to express) on either side. The next step is to incorporate the human gene, for example the HPRT cDNA, between the two long terminal repeats. Electrophoretic analysis recorded the appearance of the HPRT enzyme in the treated Lesch-Nyhan cell. These studies have been done in fibroblasts and lymphoblasts derived from Lesch-Nyhan patients (Willis et al., 1984).

The data obtained following transfection varied from a low of 5% of normal activity to a high of 23% of normal activity. All of these cells function phenotypically like HPRT$^+$ cells.

The next important question—and it is the biggest question in this field today—is, "Can nucleic acids used as therapeutic agents function adequately by expressing the gene in vivo?" In one experiment mice were treated with lethal irradiation so that they could only survive if they received exogenous bone marrow, but the bone marrow to be tested was first removed and then subjected in vitro to the HPRT vector. Thus these mice were surviving containing bone marrow stem cells that had been transfected with HPRT. It is possible to see expression of the human enzyme in the presence of the mouse enzyme because the two have different electrophoretic patterns. The good news is that it is in fact possible to put these genes into bone marrow stem cells and put them back into the patient. The bad news is that the level of expression is at the moment very poor.

The strategy for this kind of technique in the treatment of human patients is to remove marrow from the patient, to transfect these cells in vitro with the normal human gene, and then put the transfected cells back into the patient. It has been my hope that the Lesch-Nyhan patient would continue to serve as a model for this, largely because of the importance of this enzyme in developing the techniques. Once the techniques have been developed, they should be applicable to any gene that can be cloned. Thus the potential for curing diseases like PKU is very encouraging indeed. I think there is no question that within the next 25 years nucleic acids will be used as therapeutic agents. The current model approach is promising, but there are still major technical problems to be solved.

Encouraging data have been reported indicating the scope of the things that are possible in experimental animals. Constantini, Chada, and Magram (1986) have studied mice with inherited thalassemia. The mouse model is a good one for the human. In this phenotype the major β-thalassemia gene is entirely deleted, and the animals have a hemolytic anemia similar to that of human thalassemia. The affected mice are anemic and tiny; they grow poorly and die early. In these experiments the cloned human β-globin gene was inserted by microinjection into fertile mouse eggs and the eggs transferred to foster mothers. These transgenic progeny were then able to make enough normal β-globin chains from the foreign gene that they and their progeny failed to express the initial genetically determined thalassemia. They were pink, and had adequate numbers of hemoglobin-containing erythrocytes so that they appeared quite normal.

No one is planning human experiments involving germlines such as these, but the data from the animal work are extraordinarily encouraging because they indicate that even in something as complicated as hemoglobin synthesis, the β-globin gene itself, assuming that this is all that is missing, contains enough information to reverse the abnormality.

DIRECT APPROACHES TO THE BRAIN

Those persons working in the field of mental retardation have been enormously encouraged by the advances of the past 25 years. The model provided by the diagnosis and treatment of PKU has been enormously encouraging about the possibility that one can influence the CNS by manipulation of the peripheral metabolism, and doubtless there will be further advances of this type. However, I think it is realistic to say that a primary focus on mental retardation has to be a focus on the brain itself. A number of diseases are never going to be amenable to therapies that cannot be delivered directly to the brain, and I cannot even hope to predict all of the future approaches to technology in targeting the nervous system.

One that I have discussed with Dr. Gage (personal communication, 1986) of the University of California at San Diego involves transplantations into the CNS. His strategy has been to employ fetal brain. The cells were isolated following dissection and made into a suspension. This is then directly injected into specific areas of the brain of another animal. It is clear from the literature from Mexico, China, and Sweden on homograft transplantation of adrenal tissue into adults with Parkinson disease that this approach has not been working. It does not work in experimental animals either, but experiments in which fetal tissue is employed have repeatedly been successful in experimental animals. Gage (personal communication, 1986) has demonstrated very dramatically the bright yellow–staining catecholamine histofluorescence indicating the presence of transplanted fetal dopaminergic cells surviving in the brain of an older animal and sending out processes. One can imagine the possibilities of this kind of technology, particularly under situations in which there was reason for the dissemination of a neurotransmitter or a hormone in patients lacking those modalities. The methodology is in its infancy, but it is clear that quite a variety of cell types is transplantable. Experiences are beginning with the transplantation of specific primary cell types such as glial cells, which transplant nicely. This is an exciting area of research and one in which I expect to see interesting progress.

REFERENCES

Ando, T., Rasmussen, K., Wright, J.M., & Nyhan, W.L. (1972). Isolation and identification of methylcitrate, a major metabolic product of propionate in patients with propionic acidemia. *Journal of Biological Chemistry, 247,* 2200.

Cooper, D.N., & Schmidtke, J. (1986). Diagnosis of genetic disease using recombinant DNA. *Human Genetics, 73,* 1.

Constantini, F., Chada, K., & Magram, J. (1986). Correction of murine β-thalassemia by gene transfer into the germ line. *Science, 233,* 1192.

Hoffman, G., Gibson, K.M., Brandt, I.K., Bader, P.I., Wappner, R.S., & Sweetman, L. (1986). Mevalonic aciduria—An inborn error of cholesterol and nonsterol isoprene biosynthesis. *New England Journal of Medicine, 314,* 1610.

Jolly, D.J., Esty, A.C., Bernard, H.U., & Friedmann, T. (1982). Isolation of a genomic clone encoding human hypoxanthine guanine phosphoribosyl transferase. *Proceedings of the National Academy of Sciences (U.S.A.), 79*, 5038.

Kunkel, L.M., Hejtmancik, J.F., Caskey, C.Th., Speer, A., Monaco, A.P., Middlesworth, W., Colletti, C.A., Bertelson, C., Müller, U., Bresnan, M., Shapiro, F., Tantravahi, U., Speer, J., Latt, S.A., Bartlett, R., Pericak-Vance, M.A., Roses, A.D., Ray, P.N., Worton, R.G., Fischbeck, K.H., Gallano, P., Coulon, M., Duros, C., Boue, J., Junien, C., Chelly, J., Hamard, G., Jean-pierre, M., Lambert, M., Kaplan, J.-C., Emery, A., Dorkins, H., Arveiler, B., Lemaire, C., Morgan, G.J., Denton, M.J., Amos, J., Bobrow, M., Ben-ham, F., Boswinkel, E., Cole, C., Dubowitz, V., Hart, K., Hodgson, S., Johnson, L., Walker, A., Roncuzzi, L., Ferlini, A., Nobile, C., Romeo, G., Wilcox, D.E., Affara, N.A., Ferguson-Smith, M.A., Lindlof, M., Kaariainen, H., de la Chapelle, A., Ionasescu, V., Searby, Ch., Ionasescu, R., Bakker, E., van Ommen, G-J.B., Pearson, P.L., Greenberg, C.R., Hamerton, J.L., Wrogemann, K., Doherty, R.A., Polakowska, R., Hyser, C., Quirk, S., Thomas, N., Harper, J.F., Darras, B.T., & Francke, U. (1986). Analysis of deletions in DNA from patients with Becker and Duchenne muscular dystrophy. *Nature, 322*, 73.

Lehnert, W., & Hunkler, D. (1986). Possibilities of selective screening for inborn errors of metabolism using high-resolution ^{1}H-FT-NMR spectro-metry. *European Journal of Pediatrics, 145*, 260.

McKusick, V.A. (1986). *Mendelian inheritance in man* (7th ed.). Baltimore: The Johns Hopkins University Press.

Merritt, T.A., Hallman, M., Bloom, B.T., Berry, C., Benirschke, K., Sahn, D., Key, T., Edwards, D., Jarvenpaa, A.-L., Pohjavuori, M., Kankaanpaa, K., Kunnas, M., Paatero, H., Rapola, J., & Jaaskelainen, J. (1986). Pro-phylactic treatment of very premature infants with human surfactant. *New England Journal of Medicine, 315*, 785.

Middleton, B., Bartlett, K., Romanos, A., Gomez-Vazquez, J., Conde, C., Cannon, R.A., Lipson, M., Sweetman, L., & Nyhan, W.L. (1986). 3-Keto-thiolase deficiency. *European Journal of Pediatrics, 144*, 586.

Royer-Pokora, B., Kunkel, L.M., Monaco, A.P., Goff, S.C., Newburger, P.E., Baehner, R.L., Cole, F.S., Curnutte, J.T., & Orkin, S.H. (1986). Cloning the gene for an inherited human disorder—chronic granulomatous dis-ease—on the basis of its chromosomal location. *Nature, 322*, 32.

Willis, R.C., Jolly, D.J., Miller, A.D., Plent, M.M., Esty, A.C., Anderson, P.J., Chang, H.-C., Jones, O.W., Seegmiller, J.E., & Friedmann, T. (1984). Partial phenotypic correction of human Lesch-Nyhan HPRT-deficient lympho-blasts with a transmissible retroviral vector. *Journal of Biological Chemistry, 259*, 7842.

Wong, D.F., Wagner, H.N., Dannals, R.F., Links, J.M., Frost, J.J., Ravert, H.T., Wilson, A.A., Rosenbaum, A.E., Gjedde, A., Douglass, K.H., Petronis, J.D., Folstein, M.F., Toung, J.K.T., Burns, H.D., & Kuhar, M.J. (1984). Effects of age on dopamine and serotonin receptors measured by positron tomography in the living human brain. *Science, 226*, 1393.

Woo, S.L.C., Lidsky, A.S., Güttler, F., Chandra, T., & Robsin, K.J.H. (1983). Cloned human phenylalanine hydroxylase gene allows prenatal diagnosis and carrier deduction of classical phenylketonuria. *Nature, 306*, 152.

I | ETIOLOGICAL MODELS OF RETARDATION

Overview
ROY D. SCHMICKEL

This 25-year anniversary for the National Institute of Child Health and Human Development offers an important opportunity for reviewing the history of the field of mental retardation and for exploring current trends in research and technology. The chapters in this section discuss various etiological models of mental retardation, especially as they relate to conditions and events prior to conception.

The explanation for the fact that conditions and events prior to conception determine mental retardation is that an individual is the product of a very large computer-like genetic program that originated millions of years ago. The sperm and the ova each contain 6 billion bits of information and this information is responsible for human development. A mistake in a single bit of that information could destine a person for mental retardation. Furthermore, the human fetus develops within a womb that must sustain it throughout pregnancy. Both the condition of the uterus and the genetic information are determined prior to conception.

Twenty-five years ago there was feverish excitement in genetics. The Nobel Prize had just been given to Watson, Crick, and Wilkins for their discovery of the chemical basis of inheritance. In 1961 Marshall Nierenberg had cracked the genetic code and found it was a linear code that could be read and understood in terms of very simple rules. That year the Kennedy Awards honored Tjio, Levan, and LeJeune for their discovery of the chromosomal basis of inheritance. Also during that year, Ford, Jacobs, and others showed that chromosomal abnormalities are responsible for 10% of all mental retardation, and Polani showed that the chromosome defects could be inherited and cause repeated mental retardation in families. Twenty-five years ago there was an interesting book written, entitled *The Metabolic Basis of Inherited Disease*, by Stanbury, Wyngaarden, and Fredrickson. In that book 20 different forms of metabolic rearrangements were described that could cause mental retardation. If these metabolic paths could be changed mental retardation could be prevented.

Where is the field today? Each year almost 1,000 people are prevented from having mental retardation by those pioneering studies that were begun 25 years ago. According to statistical predictions, about 70 people this year do not have mental retardation caused by galactosemia because of screening and diet, 150 people do not have phenylketonuria because of screening and diet, and 700 do not have the severe retardation of cretinism because of screening and treatment. Untold thousands do not have kernicterus and mental retardation caused by neonatal hyperbilirubinemia. All of these cases of dreaded illness have been prevented because of the research that has taken place in the past 25 years.

Since 1961, the cellular causes of mental retardation have been explored at the National Institutes of Health by Neufeld and others. These diseases form the basis of exciting new experiments in gene and enzyme therapy. How many causes of mental retardation will be prevented when these trials succeed?

Twenty-five years ago chromosomes were poorly defined entities. I began my research studying these nondescript things. At that time only seven different kinds of human chromosomes could be seen, and they looked like little black smudges. Within each group it was not possible to tell one from any of the others, so they were labeled according to their groups—for instance, Down syndrome was said to be caused by a G-group abnormality, 13-trisomy by a D-group abnormality, and so on. Now we can identify at least 850 bands along these chromosomes and know the exact location of about 3,700 genes. This is the modern map of the chromosome and this information is merging with the information about the molecular structure of genes themselves. As William Nyhan has stated (Introduction), if the genetic location of a disease is known, the DNA can be isolated and the cause determined. The journey from the smudges examined 25 years ago to the finely mapped and intricate pattern of chromosome bands has been a long trip and a successful exploration, so successful that the question now asked is "Should we spend the necessary resources to decode the entire 6 billion bits of genetic information contained in our chromosomes?" It is only a matter of time and money to decode the entire body of genetic information, because all of the techniques have been developed. This kind of question would have met with derision only 10 years ago. Now it is a serious question.

Where is progress being made in preventing mental retardation? It should be remembered that sometimes prevention of mental retardation has nothing to do with science. For example, in 1986 there were 1,300 fewer children born with Down syndrome than there were in 1960, because many women over 35 years of age have chosen not to have children (there were 250,000 fewer mothers over 35 years of age in 1986 than in 1960). These kinds of changes in behavior patterns change the incidence of chromosomal abnormalities dramatically.

An epidemiological study could be valuable in the efforts to prevent mental retardation by identifying the underlying etiological mechanisms. Dr. Keith Scott illustrates the need for a multiple risk factor approach to such a study by examining three of the more common etiological patterns—low birth weight, Down syndrome, and fetal alcohol syndrome—in Chapter 1. He contends that the traditional division of mental retardation into that of biological and that of psychosocial origin is of little use in developing public health plans, and should be replaced by a biosocial perspective that reflects the interactive complexity of the risk factors comprising the various etiological patterns.

Dr. Janina Galler discusses another little-studied aspect of retardation, the long-term effects of malnutrition on mental function. As noted in Chapter 2, intergenerational malnutrition is an important and widespread factor in delayed mental development. Dr. Galler's research in both animal and human populations has shown that, whereas physical growth responds well to dietary rehabilitation, mental development is sensitive to the effects of malnutrition and does not recover completely. Therefore, subtle deficits in brain function may continue over generations, a possibility that should be taken into account in future research.

Advances in molecular genetics have opened new vistas in the etiology and treatment of mental retardation. Using phenylketonuria as a model, Dr. Savio Woo presents the most recent results in research on inherited metabolic disorders. Chapter 3 covers gene isolation and characterization, prenatal diagnosis, mutation identification and population genetics, carrier detection, correlation of clinical phenotype with genotype, and the potential for somatic gene therapy. The ability to examine the genetics of inherited syndromes involving mental retardation at the molecular level has changed the nature of prenatal diagnosis: testing procedures have been refined sufficiently to allow diagnosis of carriers without prior identification of a proband. The identification of the various genotypes and their correlation with epidemiological data allows prenatal prediction of clinical phenotype and appropriate early treatment intervention when possible. The most exciting advances, however, are in the area of genetic therapy—once the molecular structure of the genetic deficit is known, use of recombinant DNA techniques could produce altered cells capable of compensating for the deficit. Injection of these cells into patients could prevent, mitigate, or possibly reverse the adverse effects that usually accompany inherited metabolic disorders.

Another etiological model of mental retardation that is often underappreciated is the presence of toxins in the environment, as described in Chapter 4 by Dr. Bernard Weiss. Many of these toxins have adverse impacts on behavioral and cognitive development, but their impact is masked by the very fact that these developmental deficits are subtle, and their sources difficult to document. In many cases the presence of a toxin is revealed only after its effects have become magnified by level of exposure, as with the tremors associated with mercury vapors, or when its effects are physicially evident, as with the cerebral palsy and retardation associated with methyl mercury ingestion. Research has shown that the impact of such toxins as heavy metals is more severe on the fetus than on an adult. Also, chemical compounds not particularly considered as toxins can have significant behavioral effects; Dr. Weiss cites the work of Feingold in showing the connection between hyperactivity and certain food additives. The sobering aspect of Dr. Weiss' statistics is the enormity of the problem: although (in fact, because) the effects of most environmental toxins are so subtle that they are easy to ignore, each of the hundreds of chemicals released into our environment is capable of adding to the numbers of persons with mental retardation and behavioral disorders, and thus altering the composition of the population relative to intellectual capabilities.

1 | Theoretical Epidemiology
Environment and Life-Style
KEITH G. SCOTT

During the last decade or so, there has been a rapid development in theoretical epidemiology of methodology appropriate to the study of disorders that have multiple causes that are probabilistic and may act in combination (Mausner & Kramer, 1985). This methodology has been used in particular to elucidate the etiologies of cardiovascular disease and of cancer. Although multiple risk factor epidemiology has in the main been applied to the study of these chronic disorders, it is applicable to most afflictions of human populations, chronic or acute, biomedical and sociogenic. Indeed, it is the combination of biomedical and behavioral information that has been so powerful in an improved understanding of cardiovascular disease and in the mounting of effective programs of prevention.

In this chapter I consider the etiology of mental retardation from the perspective of modern epidemiology. To achieve this, current understanding of some of the causes of mental retardation is reviewed and an outline presented of some needed programs for future research on the epidemiology of mental retardation (Scott & Carran, 1987).

The model I propose is a *multiple risk factor* approach. The risk factors are indicators of statistical identifiers that may direct more basic research toward the discovery of underlying etiological mechanisms. It is a public health approach that should lead to rational plans for the prevention of mental retardation.

In mental retardation we have arbitrarily divided the field into two major etiological entities: mental retardation of biological origin and that of sociofamilial origin. I would argue that from a public health perspective this makes no sense. I will illustrate this by taking three etiological patterns of mental retardation, low birth weight, Down syndrome, and fetal alcohol syndrome, and briefly reviewing the current state of knowledge. These are among the most prevalent conditions associated with the occurrence of mental retardation.

LOW BIRTH WEIGHT

Figure 1 provides simplified diagrams to illustrate the parallels between some well-known risk factors for cardiovascular disease and those for mental retardation associated with low birth weight.

The risk factors for low birth weight (LBW), which has generally been thought of as a biological cause of mental retardation, are similar to those generally associated with school failure, much of which has been thought of as sociogenic, as can be seen in Table 1. The clear association between LBW and mental retardation can be gauged from Figure 2, which is based on estimates from some data from the Collaborative Perinatal Study (Scott & Massi, 1979). LBW children are about 2.5 times as likely to be mildly or moderately retarded and about 5 times as likely to be severely retarded as are normal birth weight peers of similar ethnicity and socioeconomic status. However, social factors are very major predictors of the occurrence of LBW. This is dramatically illustrated by vital statistics from birth certificate data available from the National Center for Health Statistics and based on the 52 states and the District of Columbia.

Some of the data from this source are well known. For instance, women who have no prenatal care are at much greater risk than those who receive it by the last trimester of pregnancy. Less well understood are the risks associated with ethnicity, maternal age, and maternal

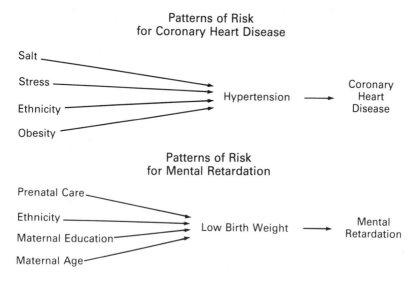

Figure 1. A comparison of risk factors for coronary heart disease and mental retardation.

Table 1. Risk factors for low birth weight and for school failure

Risk factors for LBW	Risk factors for school failure (Ramey et al., 1978)
Race	Birth order
Maternal education	Race
Maternal age	Maternal education
Nativity of mother	Prenatal care
Prenatal care	Survivorship of sibs
Legitimacy	Legitimacy

education. They are shown in Figure 3A and 3B for black and white women, respectively. There are a number of striking results that can be seen from these data. First, the increase in risk associated with

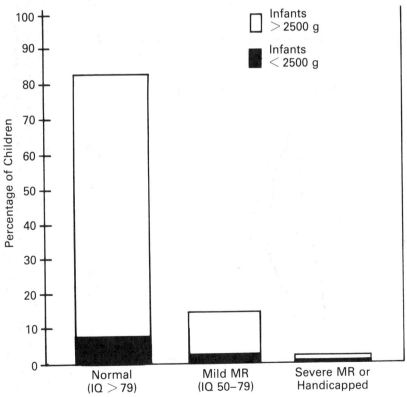

Figure 2. The percentage of children, according to birth weight, who are likely to become mentally retarded. Based on estimates made by Scott and Massi (1979).

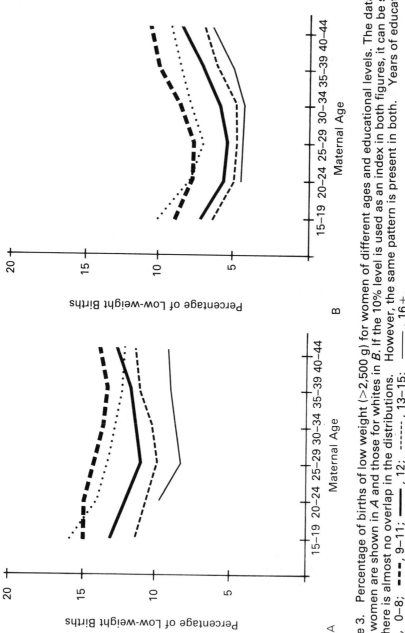

Figure 3. Percentage of births of low weight (>2,500 g) for women of different ages and educational levels. The data for black women are shown in *A* and those for whites in *B*. If the 10% level is used as an index in both figures, it can be seen that there is almost no overlap in the distributions. However, the same pattern is present in both. Years of education: ...., 0–8; ▬ ▬, 9–11; ▬▬, 12; ----, 13–15; ——, 16+.

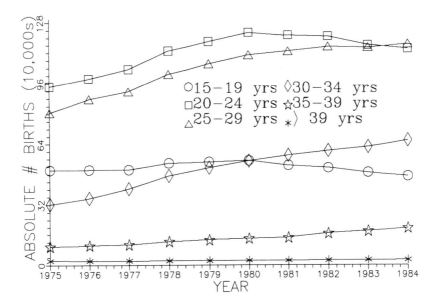

Figure 4. The number of births to women of different ages from 1977 to 1984.

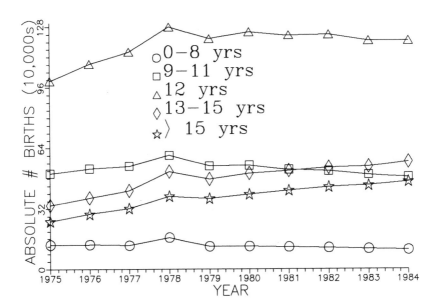

Figure 5. The number of births to women who have different amounts of education from 1977 to 1984.

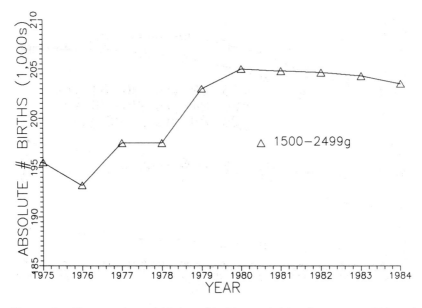

Figure 6. The number of births of babies weighing between 1,500 and 2,499 g for the years between 1975 and 1984.

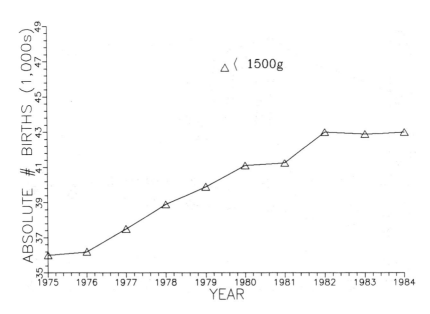

Figure 7. The number of births of babies weighing less than 1,500 g between 1975 and 1984.

maternal age is markedly reduced for women with advanced education. Note that women with a college degree (16+ years of education) are at below-median risk for their ethnic group even when they are 40–44 years of age. Note also that the pattern is true for both whites and blacks, but the two distributions hardly overlap. That is, even the most educated black women are at greater risk than are the least educated whites. The further importance of these data for the prevalence of retardation can be seen in Figures 4 and 5, which show the number of births to women in the United Sates from 1975 to 1984 as a function of age and of education. As can be seen, there is a trend for women to have infants at later ages, apparently after completing their own education. One interpretation of these data is that these women are at low risk, leading to a leveling off or drop in the rate of low-weight births. Figure 6 presents these data for infants between 1,500 and 2,500 g (3.3–5.5 lb), and Figure 7 suggests that improvements in neonatal care are leading to increased rates of survival for those below 1,500 g. It should be noted that births of babies weighing below 1,500 g still account for less than 20% of these high-risk births.

It can be shown that these data are not due to ethnicity, prenatal care, or other risk indicators in the birth certificate data set. What can be stated is that some aspects of life-style and environment are implicated in improved pregnancy outcome as measured by incidence of LBW. Maternal education is a major indicator of these changes in life-style and environment. It should be noted that social and economic measures may also be predictive, but are not readily available in the published figures. What we do know is that changes in birth rates as a function of maternal characteristics will have a large effect on the incidence of LBW and result in a changing incidence of handicapping conditions.

DOWN SYNDROME

As is well known, the incidence of Down syndrome is directly related to maternal age, with a marked increase in risk being associated with maternal ages over 35 years. It follows that the shift in age-specific birth weights for educated women that was outlined in the previous section, while reducing the incidence of mental retardation associated with LBW, may also lead to an increase in births of infants with Down syndrome. However, the use of prenatal diagnosis, generally more likely in more affluent segments of society, may at least partially offset this outcome. The situation is in fact much more complex than this simple analysis would suggest. The aim of the President's Committee on Mental Retardation (1976) to reduce the prevalence of mental

Table 2. The actual, or predicted, percentage of Down syndrome (DS) births to women over 35 years of age, assuming that no prenatal diagnosis was or is employed[a]

Year	Percent DS births
1920	64
1930	62
1940	51
1950	48
1960	47
1970	25
1980	25
1990	32
2000	35

[a] The estimates are drawn from Huether (1983).

retardation due to biological causes by 50% by the year 2000 is unlikely to be achieved.

The situation is complicated by several major factors. First, the epidemiology of Down syndrome is very incomplete. The effects of maternal age are known, but the strong possibility, given most other health data on aging, that this may be attenuated by social and educational factors has not been investigated. Knowledge about paternal age effects is also limited. In general, major work on the epidemiology of Down syndrome is needed.

In a key paper, Heuther (1983) has provided an analysis of the likely impact of birth rate changes and the utilization of prenatal diagnosis. Births to women over 35 years of age totaled 167,000 in 1981. For the year 2000 it is projected that there will be 246,000 births to women in this age group. Table 2 shows what could be expected if no prenatal diagnosis and elective abortions were available. In Table 3 the consequences of differing utilizations of prenatal diagnosis are shown. Current national levels of utilization, Heuther suggests, are close to Model A in Table 3. As can be seen, a marked decrease in the prevalence of births of infants with Down syndrome seems to be unlikely.

FETAL ALCOHOL SYNDROME

Fetal alcohol syndrome, a condition due to the ingestion of alcohol during pregnancy, is associated with pre- and postnatal growth retardation, facial anomalies, mental retardation, and other central ner-

Table 3. Number of Down syndrome births given various levels of
prenatal diagnosis based on estimates by Heuther (1983)

Model[a]	% Diagnosis			Year		
	<30	30–35	>35	1980	1990	2000
None	0	0	0	4500	5300	5250
A	0	12.5	25.0	4050	4800	4700
B	0	25.0	50.0	3700	4200	4000
C	0	35.0	75.0	3350	3700	3500

[a]Model A shows the expected number of births of Down syndrome infants when
no women under 30 utilize prenatal diagnosis, 12.5% between 30 and 35 years of
age do so, and 25% age 35 or older do so. Models B and C represent higher rates
of utilization of prenatal diagnosis and the corresponding numbers of Down births.
There were 3,835 infants with Down syndrome born in 1975, the lowest prevalence
year.

vous system dysfunction (Abel, 1984). Estimates of its prevalence are
from 0.4 to 3.1 per 1,000 births in the general population and from
24 to 29 per 1,000 births among alcoholic women. Estimates of partial
occurrence of the syndrome are several times higher. It is clearly one
of the more prevalent forms of severe retardation. Table 4 gives a list
of risk factors for fetal alcohol syndrome according to Abel (1984).
As can be seen, the picture that emerges is one of a mixture of biological and social factors. Thus, the incidence cannot be understood
solely in terms of the amount of alcohol consumed, even when this
involves heavy drinking. The etiological pattern is much more complex. Maternal characteristics, including age, are again implicated as
risk factors.

DISCUSSION AND CONCLUSION

In each of these three highly prevalent etiologies that lead to mental
retardation, there is a body of knowledge linking it to biological mech-

Table 4. Risk indicators for
fetal alcohol syndrome births

Level of consumption
Binge drinking
Prepregnancy weight
Genetic susceptibility
Undernutrition
Absence of prenatal care
Parity
Advanced maternal age

anisms. Indeed, in most classifications, these conditions are considered to be syndromes of mental retardation that are of biological origin. However, from the perspective of epidemiology or of public health, these etiologies are not simply biological. Nor are the so-called social-familial forms of retardation mainly social; clearly, they should also be understood in a broad biosocial framework where the biological consequences of poor nutrition and environmental stimulation must be sought and understood. However, when public health plans are made for the prevention of mental retardation the tools of epidemiology must be systematically applied. Doctrinaire distinctions between biological and social factors must be avoided as they are elsewhere in the study of public health. Mental retardation is a major public health problem with high prevalence and enormous public cost. Prevalence is influenced by general trends in social patterns that include birth rate demographics.

For most disorders of comparable impact on the nation, we have extensive epidemiological data on which to base plans for prevention and care, and to suggest important lines of basic research concerned with biological mechanisms. To fill these gaps in knowledge of mental retardation, a number of lines of future research are needed:

1. The cornerstone of a modern risk indicator epidemiology of mental retardation is lacking. A national epidemiological study of mental retardation is needed that would study a sample of children representative of both births and households in the United States. Such a study would need very careful planning by a national group of experts and would require that careful social, psychological, and medical data be collected. I have described this in greater detail elsewhere (Scott, 1987).
2. Extensive epidemiological work is needed to extend the important beginning that has been made in the study of the particular etiological patterns. Those presented here are only examples.
3. Finally and most importantly, the value of modern epidemiological methods in gaining an overall perspective on the prevention of mental retardation must be considered. The arbitrary separation of mental retardation as of biological or of psychosocial origin, which has been traditional and is featured in prominent documents such as the reports of the President's Committee on Mental Retardation (1976), must be replaced by a broad biosocial perspective. To fail to do this is to fly in the face of modern epidemiological knowledge and methodology.

The tools of modern epidemiology have only begun to be applied to this field. Major insights can be expected from their application.

REFERENCES

Abel, E.L. (1984). Prenatal effects of alcohol. *Drug and Alcohol Dependence, 14,* 1–10.

Heuther, C.A. (1983). Projection of Down's syndrome births in the United States 1979–2000, and the potential effects of prenatal diagnosis. *American Journal of Public Health, 73,* 1186–1189.

Mausner, J.S., & Kramer, S. (1985). *Epidemiology—An introductory text.* Philadelphia: W.B. Saunders.

President's Committee on Mental Retardation. (1976). *Mental retardation: Century of decision* (Library of Congress catalogue No. 75-42615). Washington, DC: U.S. Government Printing Office.

Ramey, C.T., Stedman, J.J., Borders-Patterson A., & Mengel, W. (1978). Predicting school failure from information available at birth. *American Journal of Mental Deficiency, 82,* 525–534.

Scott, K.G. (1987). The need for a national epidemiological study. In J. Stark, F.J. Menolascino, M. Albarelli, & V. Gray (Eds.), *Mental retardation and mental health: classification, diagnosis, treatment, services* (pp. 50–54). New York: Springer-Verlag.

Scott, K.G., & Carran, D. (1987). The epidemiology and prevention of mental retardation. *American Psychologist, 42,* 801–804.

Scott, K.G., & Massi, W. (1979). The outcome from and utility of registers of risk. In T. Field (Ed.), *Infants born at risk* (pp. 485–496). New York: SP Medical & Scientific Books.

2 | Intergenerational Effects of Undernutrition

JANINA R. GALLER

There are only a limited number of studies available on the social causes of delayed mental development, which are widely present in the United States and elsewhere. One important factor to consider in conjunction with other social factors is the high prevalence of undernutrition that afflicts children throughout the world. Recent World Health Organization statistics showed that 40–60% of the world's population of children suffer from mild to moderate undernutrition. These statistics are not limited to developing countries of the world, but are also present in subpopulations in the United States. For example, at our own institution, Boston City Hospital, up to 50% of pediatric admissions have some form of primary or secondary undernutrition, although the child may be hospitalized for unrelated reasons.

When malnutrition has been present for long periods of time and across generations, as is the primary way that this condition is present in underprivileged populations, the risk for disturbance of mental function is great. Some important early studies that underlined this were performed in Aberdeen, Scotland, where Sir Dugald Baird and his colleagues carefully documented a cohort of women who were short in stature and who were demonstrated to have an increased number of birth complications during their pregnancies, presumably related to a history of undernutrition during their own childhoods (Baird, 1959; Thompson, 1959; Thompson & Billewicz, 1963). This outcome pointed very clearly toward the importance of the role of nutrition prior to conception and from one generation to the next one. There have been other studies, such as those of Ounstead, Scott, and Ounstead (1986) and Hackman, Emanual, VanBell, and Daling (1983), indicating that women who themselves were of low birth weight were more likely to have offspring who were of low birth weight, thus continuing the intergenerational process.

ANIMAL STUDIES OF
INTERGENERATIONAL MALNUTRITION

In our own studies, my colleagues and I examined the relationships between nutrition and mental development using both animal models and a human population. The animal model consisted of rats who were provided with a low-protein diet for up to 25 generations. A parallel colony of animals was provided with an adequate-protein diet for the same number of generations. A third group of rats was derived from the low-protein group, cross-fostered at birth to healthy mothers and provided with adequate nutrition for up to four subsequent generations. The intent of these studies was to determine the long-term consequences of intergenerational malnutrition and the extent to which these could be reversed following nutritional rehabilitation. This colony was originated in England by R. J. C. Stewart and, in its 12th generation, was transferred to my laboratory in the United States.

With respect to physical growth and development, animals maintained for one or multiple generations on the low-protein diet were stunted in size. In fact, they were almost half the size of animals maintained on the control diet. However, within one generation of consuming an adequate diet, the animals' physical growth quickly recovered to normal levels, in contrast to animals who were maintained on the low-protein diet (Galler & Propert, 1981a). Thus, physical growth was impaired following intergenerational malnutrition, but recovered completely and in very short order after dietary rehabilitation.

In contrast to the effects on physical growth and development, delays in the mental development of these animals were much more striking and permanent. We tested the animals on a wide range of behavioral and learning tests, one of which was the Lashley jump stand test, administered at 3 months of age (Galler, 1981). On this test, animals were provided with tasks of increasing difficulty, and were required to discriminate between black and white, between horizontal and vertical stripes, and between a circle and a square.

Our Lashley test demonstrated performance deficits among animals with intergenerational malnutrition or a single generation of malnutrition. Animals with chronic intergenerational malnutrition were significantly more impaired than animals exposed to a single generation of malnutrition. Following rehabilitation on the adequate-protein diet, there was some recovery of function, but this was incomplete among animals with a history of intergenerational malnutrition. Following two generations of dietary rehabilitation, we documented recovery among the females, whereas the males did not recover. These findings are important because most cited experiments have been restricted to brief periods of malnutrition. We are here pointing to the lasting impact of long-term, intergenerational malnutrition.

In addition to these studies, we performed a wide range of tests of development and learning, which included home-orienting behavior during the suckling period (Galler & Seelig, 1981) and mother-pup interaction (Galler & Propert, 1981b, 1981c). These behaviors remained aberrant up to four generations after rehabilitation, suggesting one mechanism whereby the effects of malnutrition may perpetuate across generations.

In summary, in our studies of the long-term impact on mental functioning of intergenerational malnutrition, physical growth was found to be relatively insensitive to malnutrition since it responds fully to dietary rehabilitation. In contrast, the nervous system was more sensitive to the effects of malnutrition and did not recover completely.

HUMAN STUDIES OF EARLY MALNUTRITION

We have supplemented our animal research with human studies of the consequences of early malnutrition. Clearly, human studies are eminently more difficult to undertake than are animal studies. Multivariate approaches taking into account the multiple environmental factors that coexist with malnutrition are necessary. Our study in Barbados followed a group of children who were malnourished in the first year of life up to 18 years of age (Galler, 1984, 1986). Comprehensive assessments, including tests of cognitive and mental function, school performance, and physical growth, were performed at three points in time during their school years. Socioeconomic conditions as well as factors in the home environment were carefully evaluated as factors in the outcome.

The children in this study fell into one of two categories. One hundred twenty-nine had suffered from severe protein-energy malnutrition (marasmus) in the first year of life, and 56 suffered from protein malnutrition (kwashiorkor). These children were compared with 129 children who were classmates from the same socioeconomic background. It should be pointed out that these categories of undernutrition are not restricted to developing countries, but are subsumed in developed countries under the classification of "failure to thrive." All children in our population were followed from the time of illness by the National Nutritional Centre of Barbados, which provided them with maximal nutritional support, health care, and routine home visits by community health sisters. Thus, the children were protected against continued malnutrition.

Results emerged that were similar to those of the animal model. Despite catch-up in physical growth, we were able to demonstrate deficits in school performance. A large percentage of the previously malnourished children did not perform adequately on the common entrance examination at age 11. This test is administered annually to all children in Barbardos in order to classify them for type of high school training. The poorer performance by our index children was therefore of great concern to educators in the country. This corresponded to our study of academic performance, which also demonstrated a deficit among both boys and girls with malnutrition in grades achieved on all major academic subjects (Galler, Ramsey, & Solimano, 1984).

In order to identify the cause of these deficits, we examined the intellectual performance and classroom behavior of the children (Galler, Ramsey, Salt, & Forde, 1987; Galler, Ramsey, Solimano, & Lowell, 1983). Here we found moderate but significant differences between the groups. There was a deficit of 12 points in IQ scores for the previously malnourished groups. It should be pointed out that these results were based on an IQ test that was modified specifically for children in Barbados and included local exemplars.

We also evaluated the classroom behavior of the children. The most striking finding in both cohorts of children with previous malnutrition was the fourfold increase in symptoms associated with an attention deficit disorder: impaired attention, poor school performance, poor memory, and distractibility. In our comparison population, 15% of the children presented with an attentional deficit. However, 60% of children with previous malnutrition of either type presented with an attention deficit disorder syndrome. When these children were retested at later times up to 18 years of age, we continued to document increased distractibility and symptoms of attentional problems in the previously malnourished cohort that were significantly associated with reduced school performance and high dropout rates.

Extensive review of socioeconomic background in the children led us to conclude that the environmental factors played only a small role in the delayed mental and physical development of children with histories of malnutrition.

Finally, we have recently expanded our studies by examining endocrine function in these children. Some of the deficits associated with the early episode of malnutrition did not present until later. We demonstrated that menarche in girls with histories of previous malnutrition was delayed by about a year and a half compared to that in girls who did not have this history. Although adult size was indistinguishable between the groups (Galler, Ramsey, Salt, & Archer, 1987), we found that serum levels of somatomedin-C/intrauterine growth factor-1 were not correlated with other measures of physical growth in boys and girls with histories of previous malnutrition. In healthy comparison children, these relationships were highly correlated. These findings are of importance because they suggest that undernutrition not only may have concurrent effects that present early in life, but also may have delayed late physical effects that do not present until later during the adolescent growth spurt.

Thus, the endocrine and mental effects can be attributed to early brain damage at the time of the episode of malnutrition, excluding environmental factors. As in the case of the animal model, these findings may have consequences extending into subsequent generations. We are currently planning a study of the offspring of our sample to determine the extent to which nutrition may be a factor in mental development in the next generation of children.

SUGGESTIONS FOR FUTURE RESEARCH

In view of the findings of animal and human studies noted in this chapter, the following research directions are recommended:

1. Animal models should be developed to study the range of deficits in brain and behavioral capacities during recovery from chronic malnutrition. This work should emphasize state-of-the-art approaches to nervous system function.
2. Human populations at risk for chronic malnutrition, including those in developed countries, should be monitored for more subtle deficits in brain function.
3. Studies should not be limited to very young children, but should also include school-age children and women during the reproductive years, extending into the subsequent generation.

REFERENCES

Baird, D. (1959). The contribution of obstetrical factors to serious physical and mental handicap in children. *Journal of Obstetrics and Gynaecology of the British Empire, 66*, 743–747.

Galler, J.R. (1981). Visual discrimination in rats: The effects of rehabilitation following intergenerational malnutrition. *Developmental Psychobiology, 14*, 229–236.

Galler, J.R. (1984). The behavioral consequences of malnutrition in early life. In: J.R. Galler (Ed.), *Human Nutrition: A Comprehensive Treatise, Vol. V: Nutrition and Behavior* (pp. 63–117). New York: Plenum Press.

Galler, J.R. (1986). Malnutrition: A neglected cause of learning failure. *Postgraduate Medicine, 80*(5), 225–230.

Galler, J.R., & Propert, K.J. (1981a). The effect of protein deficiency on weight gain and body composition in the developing rat. *Nutrition Reports International, 24,* 885–892.

Galler, J.R., & Propert, K. (1981b). Maternal behavior following rehabilitation of rats with intergenerational malnutrition: I) Persistent changes in lactation-related behaviors. *Journal of Nutrition, 111,* 1330–1336.

Galler, J.R., & Propert, K. (1981c). Maternal behavior following rehabilitation of rats with intergenerational malnutrition: II) Contribution of mothers and pups to deficits in lactation-related behaviors. *Journal of Nutrition, 111,* 1337–1342.

Galler, J.R., Ramsey, F., Salt, P., & Archer, E. (1987). The long term effects of early kwashiorkor compared with marasmus. I) Physical growth and sexual maturation. *Journal of Pediatric Gastroenterology and Nutrition 6,* 841–846.

Galler, J.R., Ramsey, F., Salt, P., & Forde, V. (1987). The long term effects of early kwashiorkor compared with marasmus. II) Intellectual performance. *Journal of Pediatric Gastroenterology and Nutrition, 6,* 847–854.

Galler, J.R., Ramsey, F., & Solimano, G. (1984). The influence of early malnutrition on subsequent behavioral development. III) Learning disabilities as a sequel to malnutrition. *Pediatric Research, 18,* 309–313.

Galler, J.R., Ramsey, F., Solimano, G., & Lowell, W.E. (1983). The influence of early malnutrition on subsequent behavioral development. II) Classroom behavior. *Journal of the American Academy of Child Psychiatry, 22,* 16–22.

Galler, J.R., & Seelig, C. (1981). Home-orienting behavior in rat pups: The effects of two and three generations of rehabilitation following intergenerational malnutrition. *Developmental Psychobiology, 14,* 541–548.

Hackman, Y., Emanuel, I., VanBell, G., & Daling, J. (1983). Maternal birth weight and subsequent pregnancy outcome. *Journal of the American Medical Association, 150,* 2016–2019.

Ounstead, M., Scott, A., & Ounstead, C. (1986). Transmission through the female line of a mechanism constraining human fetal growth. *Annals of Human Biology, 13,* 143–151.

Thomson, A.M. (1959). Maternal stature and reproductive efficiency. *Eugenics Review, 51,* 157–162.

Thomson, A.M., & Billewicz, W.Z. (1963). Nutritional status, physique and reproductive efficiency. *Proceedings of the Nutrition Society, 22,* 55–60.

3 | Molecular Biology
Phenylketonuria as a Model
SAVIO L.C. WOO

Phenylketonuria (PKU) is a metabolic disorder due to an inborn error of amino acid metabolism. Pathologically there is inadequate myelination in the central nervous system, and the clinical symptom is severe mental retardation in untreated children. The biochemical lesion of the disorder is the deficiency of hepatic phenylalanine hydroxylase (PAH). Genetically PKU is transmitted as an autosomal recessive trait. It has a prevalence of about 1 in 10,000 among Caucasians, with a carrier frequency of about 1 in 50 (for reviews see Scriver & Clow, 1980a, 1980b).

There are several landmarks in the history of PKU research (Table 1). Obviously the first is the discovery of the disease by Følling in 1934. Thirteen years after that, Gervis discovered the enzyme deficiency involved in the disease. Seven years after that, Bickel successfully implemented the first dietary treatment of this particular disease and in 1963 Guthrie developed the "Guthrie test" (Guthrie & Susi, 1963), which is currently used for PKU screening of all newborn infants in Western countries. In the 1970s Seymour Kaufman at the National Institutes of Health elucidated the aromatic amino acid hydroxylation system, which is relatively complex.

This paper discusses the molecular genetics of PKU. The following six topics are covered: 1) gene isolation and characterization, 2) prenatal diagnosis by restriction fragment length polymorphism (RFLP) analysis, 3) mutation identification and population genetics, 4) carrier detection without a proband, 5) correlation of clinical phenotype with genotype, and 6) potential somatic gene therapy of PKU. Because of space limitations, many conclusions based on research conducted in these areas by my colleagues and I are presented without some of their supporting data.

The work described in this chapter was supported by the National Institute of Child Health and Human Development.

Table 1.   Landmarks in the history of PKU research

Discovery	Følling, 1934
Biochemical defect	Jervis, 1947
Dietary treatment	Bickel, 1954
Neonatal screening	Guthrie, 1963
Hydroxylation system	Kaufman, 1970s

GENE ISOLATION AND CHARACTERIZATION

Several years ago, Dr. Kathryn Robson was successful in the construction of a PAH cDNA clone from the rat liver (Robson, Chandra, MacGillivray, & Woo, 1982). The full-length human PAH cDNA is about 2,400 base pairs (2.4 kb) in length and contains an open reading frame encoding 451 amino acid residues (Figure 1). From the DNA sequence, the primary structure of the enzyme was deduced (Kwok, Ledley, DiLella, Robson, & Woo, 1985).

The human PAH gene can be detected in genomic DNA using the cDNA as a hybridization probe. This opens up the possibility of actually using the polymorphism analysis to trace the transmission of PAH genes in the offspring of PKU families (Woo, Lidsky, Güttler, & Robson, 1983).

In addition, quite a few enzymes have been identified that show polymorphism (Lidsky, Ledley, et al., 1985). For instance, the enzyme

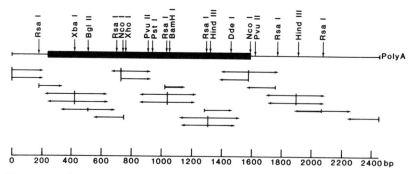

Figure 1.   A schematic representation of a full-length human phenylalanine hydroxylase cDNA clone. The black box represents an open reading frame that encodes 451 amino acid residues. The symbols above the box represent different restriction enzyme recognition sequences. The arrows under the box represent the strategy of determining the nucleotide sequence of the entire cDNA clone. (From Kwok, S.C.M., Ledley, F.D., DiLella, A.G., Robson, K.J.H., & Woo, S.L.C. [1985]. Nucleotide sequence of a full length cDNA clone and amino acid sequence of human phenylalanine hydroxylase. *Biochemistry, 24*, 556–561; reprinted by permission.)

Hin dIII detects two different genetic alleles: bands 4.0 and 4.2. Figure 2 shows a radioautogram (left) in which control individual I/I is homozygous for a 4.2 band and control individual II/II is homozygous for a 4.0 band. These are normal individuals, and this kind of polymorphism has nothing to do with the mutation that causes PKU. Nevertheless, these bands can be used to trace the transmission of mutation genes in PKU families, as shown on the right in Figure 2.

In this particular family, both parents are heterozygotes for the 4.2 and 4.0 bands. The affected child (proband) in this family is homozygous for the 4.0 band. Therefore, we could conclude that the 4.0 bands in both parents must be derived from the mutated genes, and the 4.2 bands must be derived from the normal genes. This is the case because PKU is an autosomal recessive disorder and both parents are obligate carriers. There was also a pregnancy at risk in this family. We performed prenatal diagnosis by DNA analysis and found the fetus also to be homozygous for the 4.0 band. Therefore the fetus must have inherited both mutant alleles from the two parents

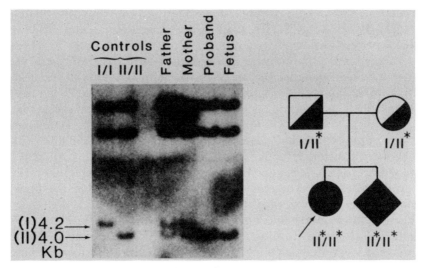

Figure 2. Prenatal diagnosis of PKU by *Hind* III polymorphism in a PKU family. *Left*, radioautogram of a hybridization experiment using the cloned phenylalanine hydroxylase cDNA to hybridize with genomic DNA isolated from two normal individuals shown in the two left-hand lanes (controls), as well as those isolated from a PKU family with a pregnancy at risk, shown on the four right-hand lanes. *Right*, Schematic panel representing the transmission of two mutant alleles to the fetus as determined by the RFLP analysis. (From Lidsky, A.S., Güttler, F., & Woo, S.L.C. [1985]. Prenatal diagnosis of classical phenylketonuria by DNA analysis. *Lancet, 1*, 549–551; reprinted by permission.)

and should be an affected individual. This prenatal diagnosis was confirmed by the neonate's phenotype after the pregnancy was carried to term (Lidsky, Güttler, & Woo, 1985). This is the first case of prenatal diagnosis of PKU since its discovery some 50 years ago by Dr. Følling.

This kind of analysis, however, has one severe limitation: There must be a proband in the family before one can perform the analysis. Without a proband, one could look at the fetal DNA of a homozygous 4.0 individual and not know whether this individual has inherited any normal or mutant genes at all. In order to extend this type of analysis to families without prior PKU history, RFLP haplotyping analysis is necessary.

PRENATAL DIAGNOSIS BY RFLP ANALYSIS

On one portion of the PAH gene there are two *Hin* dIII recognition sites that give a 4.2 or 4.0 band. On the same chromosome, there are two other enzyme recognition sites for *Sph* I that are 9.7 or 7.0 kb apart. The two *Hin* dIII alleles crossed with the two *Sph* I alleles give a total of four possible combinations (Figure 3), or four RFLP haplotypes. Basically a RFLP haplotype is just a combination of individual RFLP patterns using single enzymes.

This kind of haplotyping analysis has been carried out in a relatively isolated genetic area, in this case Denmark. My collaborator, Dr. Güttler, has collected samples from about 90% of all PKU families there. RFLP haplotyping analysis has been performed and the results are shown in Table 2. Knowing that the numbers of these haplotypes can increase exponentially, theoretically one could expect to find over a thousand different haplotypes. The fact that only 12 haplotypes were detected would suggest that there must be linkage disequilibrium between these different polymorphic sites, meaning that the polymorphisms group together as units (Chakraborty et al., 1987).

The most important information derived from this study is presented in the last two columns of Table 2. When counting the haplotypes, it was noted that haplotypes 1 and 4 are most prevalent among the normal chromosomes, and haplotypes 2 and 3 are relatively rare. Yet among the PKU chromosomes, haplotypes 1, 2, 3, and 4 are the most common ones. Together they made up more than 90% of all the PKU chromosomes in that particular population.

Kazazian and Orkin have demonstrated that there are specific mutations associated with various RFLP haplotypes of the human β-globin gene in β-thalassemia. It was of interest to determine whether these four RFLP haplotypes were associated with four different mutations in the PAH gene. If such associations exist, then specific tests

RFLP Haplotypes in the
Human Phenylalanine Hydroxylase Gene

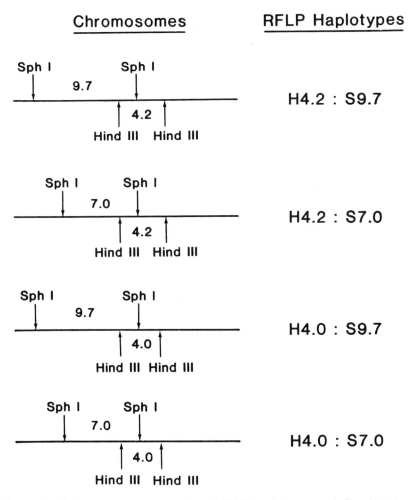

Figure 3.   Schematic representation of RFLP haplotypes as defined by the composite profiles of two independent restriction fragment length polymorphisms.

Table 2. RFLP haplotypes of the phenylalanine hydroxylase genes in PKU families from Denmark[a]

Haplotypes	Phenylalanine hydroxylase genes[b]								Number of genes	
	Pvu IIa	Bgl II	Pvu IIb	Eco RI	Xmn I	Msp I	Hin dIII	Eco RV	Normal	PKU
1	+	−	−	−	−	+	−	−	23	12
2	+	−	−	−	−	+	+	+	3	13
3	+	−	−	+	+	−	−	−	2	25
4	+	−	−	+	+	−	+	+	21	9
5	−	+	+	+	−	+	−	+	7	0
6	−	+	+	+	−	+	−	−	0	2
7	−	+	−	+	+	−	−	−	7	1
8	+	−	−	+	−	+	−	+	1	0
9	+	+	−	+	−	+	−	+	0	1
10	+	−	−	+	−	+	−	−	1	0
11	−	+	−	+	−	+	−	+	1	1
12	+	−	−	−	−	+	−	+	0	2
									66	66

[a]From Chakraborty, R., Lidsky, A.S., Daiger, S.P., Güttler, F., Sullivan, S., DiLella, A.G., & Woo, S.L.C. (1987). Polymorphic DNA haplotypes at the human phenylalanine hydroxylase locus and their relationship with phenylketonuria. Human Genetics, 76, 40–46; reprinted by permission.

[b]+, gene is present; −, gene is absent.

can be developed for these four mutation alleles and 90% of the PKU chromosomes in the population can be detected. Therefore carrier screening as well as prenatal diagnosis could be performed with or without the availability of a proband.

In order to test this hypothesis, the haplotype 3 mutation chromosome was analyzed since it accounts for about 40% of all the mutation chromosomes in the Danish population. DiLella and Marvit in our laboratory isolated this particular mutation allele from a patient who is homozygous for haplotype 3 and then worked out the structure of the gene (DiLella, Kwok, Ledley, Marvit, & Woo, 1986). The messenger coding region is separated into 13 different parts (exons) sep-

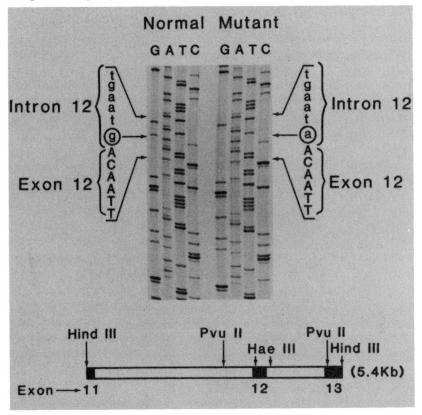

Figure 4. Mutation sequence in a mutant haplotype 3 allele of the humn phenylalanine hydroxylase gene. The single nucleotide substitution from guanine (G) in the normal sequence to adenine (A) in the mutant sequence is shown by circles. (From DiLella, A.G., Marvit, J., Lidsky, A.S., Güttler, F., & Woo, S.L.C. [1986]. Tight linkage between a splicing mutation and a DNA haplotype in phenylketonuria. *Nature, 322,* 799–803; reprinted by permission.)

arated by 12 intervening regions (introns). The entire gene is contained in a total of about 90 kb of DNA.

DiLella et al. found that the sequences of all of the mRNA encoding regions in the mutant gene were identical to those in the normal gene except just after exon 12. At the beginning of intron 12 there is the obligate guanine-thymine base pair (GT) as the donor for RNA splicing (Figure 4). In the mutation chromosome the G has been changed to an adenine (A) so that there is now an AT in the donor splicing site of intron 12 instead (DiLella, Marvit, Lidsky, Güttler, & Woo, 1986).

A number of biochemical characterizations have been carried out to establish the fact that the effect of this particular mutation is to cause the skipping of the previous exon for RNA splicing, resulting in an unstable protein in the cell that gives the PKU phenotype. Unfortunately, I can only give a summary of the data here. We found that there is a GT-to-AT transition at the 5' spliced donor site of intron 12 causing the skipping of exon 12 in the generation of the mature mRNA. This mutated RNA is translated into an unstable protein in the cell, resulting in a total lack of enzymatic activity. This phenotype is therefore mRNA$^+$, CRM$^-$, and activity$^-$ (Marvit et al., 1987).

Having characterized this mutation, we immediately tried to perform genetic analysis. Because the mutation does not change a restriction site, we synthesized two specific oligonucleotide probes: one for the normal and one for the mutant sequence. The two 21-nucleotide-long probes are identical except in the middle, where there is a single nucleotide difference.

The specificity of the probe for detecting the respective alleles is shown in Figure 5. If the cloned normal gene and the mutant gene are put on the gel, they are identical after the restriction enzyme cut using *Prn* II, and the 2-kb band is the one that contains the particular part of the gene that contains the mutation (Figure 5, top left). Using the normal probe, hybridization is seen specifically with the normal gene and very little with the mutant gene (Figure 5, top center). Conversely, using the mutant probe, specific hybridization is detected only with the mutant gene, and not the normal (Figure 5, top right). These autoradiograms were purposely overexposed to show a slight hybridization signal with the wrong allele just to indicate the level of specificity in terms of differential signal, which is in excess of 100-fold.

Using this technology, all of the affected individuals in the Danish population were analyzed, both those patients who have haplotype 3 and those who do not. The results are shown in Figure 6. All of those

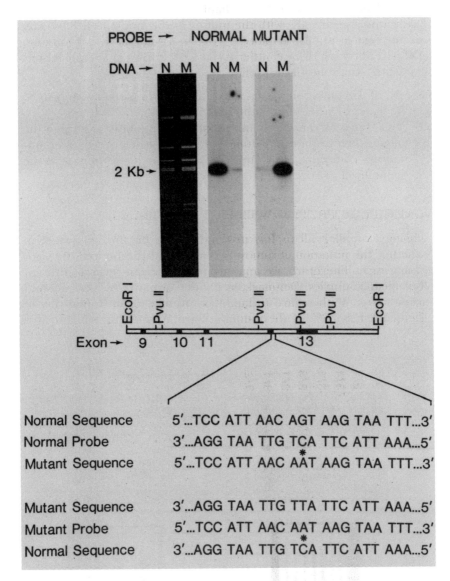

Figure 5. Demonstration of hybridization specificity for detection of exon 12 splicing mutation using a normal and a mutant oligonucleotide as probes to hybridize with cloned normal and mutant human phenylalanine hydroxylase genes. (From DiLella, A.G., Marvit, J., Lidsky, A.S., Güttler, F., & Woo, S.L.C. [1986]. Tight linkage between a splicing mutation and a DNA haplotype in phenylketonuria. *Nature, 322,* 799–803; reprinted by permission.)

affected individuals who bear a haplotype 3 mutant allele show hybridization, specifically with the mutant probe, and all of those who do not bear a mutant haplotype 3 allele do not show hybridization (DiLella, Marvit, Lidsky, Güttler, & Woo, 1986). Two main conclusions can be drawn from these studies:

1. All of the mutation alleles associated with haplotype 3 appear to be caused by the same mutation.
2. PKU must be caused by more than one mutation because in the alleles that are not haplotype 3 we did not detect the same mutation. Therefore, PKU must be a heterogeneous disease at the gene level.

CARRIER DETECTION WITHOUT A PROBAND

Having compiled all of this information, we became interested in whether the mutation chromosome has spread throughout the Caucasian race. Therefore, we analyzed patients from several different European countries: Denmark, Scotland, Germany, Switzerland, and a few more. With regard to haplotype number 3, we found that in Denmark it is 38% of the mutation chromosomes, in Scotland it is

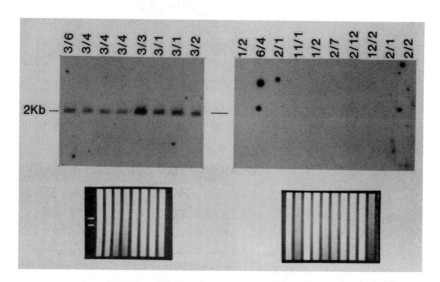

Figure 6. Detection of the splicing mutation in PKU patients bearing a mutant haplotype 3 allele (*left*) and the absence of this particular mutation in patients who do not bear the mutant haplotype 3 allele (*right*). (From DiLella, A.G., Marvit, J., Lidsky, A.S., Güttler, F., & Woo, S.L.C. [1986]. Tight linkage between a splicing mutation and a DNA haplotype in phenylketonuria. *Nature, 322,* 799–803; reprinted by permission.)

33%, in Germany 20%, and in Switzerland, the only place that it is low, about 5%. When all probands in these different countries were analyzed, exactly the same results were obtained. Therefore, we know that the same mutation is associated with a particular haplotype throughout the Caucasian race. What does that mean?

It means that (a) there is a high level of association between certain RFLP haplotypes and specific mutations in the PAH gene; (b) the association, because of linkage disequilibrium, is both inclusive and exclusive; and (c) the distribution of certain mutant genes in the Caucasian population is apparently the result of a "founder effect," a mutation event that occurred on a normal chromosome of haplotype 3 that has been spread throughout the Caucasian race.

We have also characterized mutation alleles of haplotype 2. It is a point mutation in the gene that causes a single amino acid substitution in the enzyme, which results in an unstable protein and gives a PKU phenotype. The genetic analysis is essentially identical to that observed for mutant haplotype 3 (DiLella, Marvit, Brayton, & Woo, 1987). It is also a single-mutation allele that has been spread throughout the Caucasian race.

Thus 50–60% of the mutant alleles in the population can now be detected without the need for a proband. We are looking forward to characterizing haplotypes 1 and 4, which would enable us to detect 90% of the mutant alleles, so that we can achieve our goal of 90% accuracy in carrier detection without prior PKU history.

CORRELATION OF CLINICAL PHENOTYPE WITH GENOTYPE

Güttler (1980) has defined three different classes of hyperphenylalaninemia:

1. *Classical PKU*: a blood phenylalanine level >20 mg/dl; all patients require treatment.
2. *Mild PKU*: a blood phenylalanine level of 10–20 mg/dl; patient treatment is individualized.
3. *Hyperphenylalaninemia*: a blood phenylalanine level <20 mg/dl; patients usually do not require treatment.

These different phenotypes of hyperphenylalaninemia can be associated with different genotypes (Table 3). If an individual is homozygous for haplotype 3, the clinical phenotype is always classical PKU. Similarly, individuals who are homozygous for haplotype 2 always have classical PKU. Individuals who are heterozygous for haplotypes 2 and 3 also have classical PKU. Knowing the mutations associated with haplotypes 2 and 3, it is not surprising to find that all these

Table 3. The parental haplotypes related to the phenotype of their PKU or HPA child[a,b]

	Haplotype 1	Haplotype 2	Haplotype 3	Haplotype 4
Haplotype 1		m	m m m m h	m m h h
Haplotype 2		c c	c c	
Haplotype 3			c c	c
Haplotype 4			h	h

[a]From Güttler, F., et al. (1987). Correlation between polymorphic DNA haplotypes at phenylalanine hydroxylase locus and clinical phenotypes of phenylketonuria. *Journal of Pediatrics*, *110*, 68–71; reprinted by permission.

[b]c = Classical PKU; m = mild PKU; h = hyperphenylalaninemia.

patients exhibit the classical phenotype. In both cases of mutation there will be no stable enzymes in the patient's liver and thus there can be no enzymatic activity at all. Consequently, these patients exhibit the classical phenotype at a clinical level.

Any patient who has a haplotype 1 or 4 mutant allele, however, appears to have either the mild PKU phenotype or the hyperphenylalaninemia phenotype, suggesting that the mutations associated with the haplotype 1 and 4 alleles are less severe. If that is proven to be the case, this correlation of clinical phenotype with genotype can be expanded. This information may be of assistance at the clinical level in prescribing different dietary regimens for the patients.

In summary, these studies have revealed that:

1. There are multiple mutations in the PAH gene that can cause PKU. Some mutations result in zero enzymatic activity; others can give rise to some residual activity.

2. Combinations of various mutant genotypes can lead to different clinical phenotypes. The big question is whether the identification of genotypes in patients can predict the clinical cause of the metabolic disorder. This question cannot be answered yet, but our collaboration with the PKU Collaborative Study Group headquartered in Los Angeles to genotype patients whom they have treated for the past 10–20 years with known clinical courses should help to determine if there is any correlation.

POTENTIAL SOMATIC GENE THERAPY

Phenylketonuria is caused by a lack of the enzyme PAH, which converts phenylalanine to tyrosine in the liver. If the normal gene could be transduced into the liver or any other tissue in the body, some of this enzymatic activity could be restored, perhaps sufficient to convert the PKU phenotype to the asymptomatic hyperphenylalanemia phenotype, this could provide a cure for the deficiency syndrome at the clinical level. Such somatic gene therapy is a distant goal, but one toward which significant progress is being made.

Gene therapy uses retroviral vectors because they are excellent, efficient vehicles for gene transfer into mammalian cells. Figure 7 shows a scheme developed by Dr. Richard Mulligan at the Massachusetts Institute of Technology (Cepko, Roberts, & Mulligan, 1984). Mulligan put a retroviral mouse leukemia virus genome into a mouse NIH3T3 cell. Once in the cell, the virus is capable of inducing the cell to perform all of the viral functions, including reverse transcription and assembly of virus particles with protein coats and RNA cores. The only thing that this viral genome lacks is the signal for packaging of the viral transcript RNA by the viral proteins to produce an infectious virus.

If a recombinant plasmid were made containing human phenylalanine hydroxylase cDNA with the long terminal repeats on both ends and containing the packaging signal, this plasmid could be introduced into the above-mentioned packaging cells, which produce a lot of viral proteins. The packagable RNA transcript from the recombinant would result in a cryptic virus capable of infecting fresh mammalian cells in culture and yet not capable of replication because it lacks all of the other essential viral functions.

Such a cryptic virus was produced in our laboratory and used to infect a mouse hepatoma cell line that is deficient in PAH (obtained from Dr. Gretchen Darlington at Baylor College of Medicine). We obtained hepatoma cells that were infected by the cryptic virus and found that they were capable of producing active PAH in the cyto-

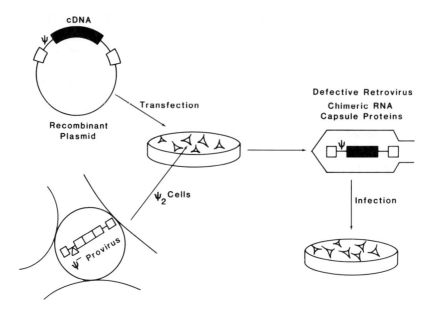

Figure 7. Schematic representation of the construction of cryptic retro-viruses for transduction of human phenylalanine hydroxylase cDNA into cultured mammalian cells via viral infection.

plasm (Ledley, Grenett, McGinnis-Shelnutt, & Woo, 1986). But does that mean the cell will be capable of converting phenylalanine into tyrosine? Ledley, who performed most of these gene transfer analyses, devised a method of testing for this ability. He used a culture medium deficient in tyrosine, which meant the cells could survive only if they could synthesize PAH.

When PAH-deficient hepatoma cells are cultured in this medium they die after a couple of passages (Figure 8). However, PAH-deficient hepatoma cells infected with the retrovirus containing the human PAH gene, after a couple of passages in the same medium, continue to grow well. Thus, the infected cell is not only making active enzyme in the cytoplasm, but it is also capable of surviving in a tyrosine-free medium. It must therefore be able to convert phenylalanine to ty-rosine de novo.

In the future we shall attempt to transduce the active human PAH gene into an experimental animal to determine whether pro-duction of active enzyme could be achieved in the liver or other or-gans. This concept of somatic gene therapy for PKU may serve as a model for other metabolic diseases as well.

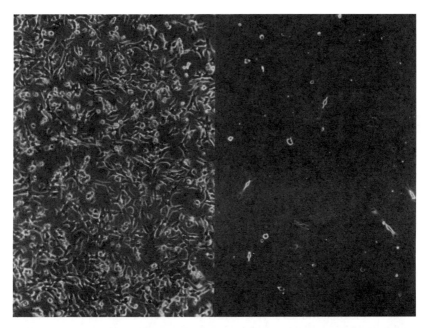

Figure 8. Culture of a phenylalanine hydroxylase–deficient mouse hepatoma cell line in tyrosine-free medium before (*right*) and after (*left*) infection with the cryptic retrovirus containing the full-length human phenylalanine hydroxylase cDNA.

REFERENCES

Cepko, C.L., Roberts, B.E., & Mulligan R.C. (1984). Construction and applications of a highly transmissible murine retrovirus shuttle vector. *Cell*, *37*, 1053–1062.

Chakraborty, R., Lidsky, A.S., Daiger, S.P., Güttler, F., Sullivan, S., DiLella, A.G., & Woo, S.L.C. (1987). Polymorphic DNA haplotypes at the human phenylalanine hydroxylase locus and their relationship with phenylketonuria. *Human Genetics*, *76*, 40–46.

DiLella, A.G., Kwok, S.C.M., Ledley, F.D., Marvit, J., & Woo, S.L.C. (1986). Molecular structure and polymorphic map of the human phenylalanine hydroxylase gene. *Biochemistry*, *25*, 743–749.

DiLella, A.G., Marvit, J., Brayton, K., & Woo, S.L.C. (1987). An amino acid substitution in phenylketonuria is in linkage disequilibrium with DNA haplotype-2. *Nature*, *327*, 333–336.

DiLella, A.G., Marvit, J., Lidsky, A.S., Güttler, F., & Woo, S.L.C. (1986). Tight linkage between a splicing mutation and a DNA haplotype in phenylketonuria. *Nature*, *322*, 799–803.

Guthrie, R., & Susi, A. (1963). A single phenylalanine method for detecting phenylketonuria in large populations of new born infants. *Pediatrics*, *32*, 338–343.

Güttler, F. (1980). Hyperphenylalaninemia: Diagnosis and classification of the various types of phenylalanine hydroxylase deficiency in childhood. *Acta Paediatrica Scandinavica, Suppl. 280*, 1–80.

Kwok, S.C.M., Ledley, F.D., DiLella, A.G., Robson, K.J.H., & Woo, S.L.C. (1985). Nucleotide sequence of a full-length cDNA clone and amino acid sequence of human phenylalanine hydroxylase. *Biochemistry, 24*, 556–561.

Ledley, F.D., Grenett, H.E., McGinnis-Shelnutt, M., & Woo, S.L.C. (1986). Retroviral mediated gene transfer of human phenylalanine hydroxylase into NIH3T3 and hepatoma cells. *Proceedings of the National Academy of Sciences of the U.S.A., 83*, 409–413.

Lidsky, A.S., Güttler, F., & Woo, S.L.C. (1985). Prenatal diagnosis of classical phenylketonuria by DNA analysis. *Lancet, 1*, 549–551.

Lidsky, A.S., Ledley, F.D., DiLella, A.G., Kwok, S.C.M., Diager, S.P., Robson, K.J.H., & Woo, S.L.C. (1985). Molecular genetics of phenylketonuria: Extensive restriction site polymorphisms in the human phenylalanine hydroxylase locus. *American Journal of Human Genetics, 37*, 619–634.

Marvit, J., DiLella, A.G., Brayton, K., Ledley, F.D., Robson, K.J.H., & Woo, S.L.C. (1987). A mutant human phenylalanine hydroxylase cDNA results from an error in messenger RNA processing. *N.A.R., 15*, 5613–5628.

Orkin, S.H., & Kazazian, H.H. (1984). The mutation and polymorphism of the human β-globin gene and its surrounding DNA. *Annual Review of Genetics, 18*, 131–172.

Robson, K., Chandra, T., MacGillivray, R., & Woo, S.L.C. (1982). Polysome immunoprecipitation of phenylalanine hydroxylase mRNA from rat liver and cloning of its cDNA. *Proceedings of the National Academy of Sciences of the U.S.A., 79*, 4701–4705.

Scriver, C.R., & Clow, C.L. (1980a). Phenylketonuria and other phenylalanine hydroxylation mutants in man. *Annual Review of Genetics, 4*, 179–202.

Scriver, C.R., & Clow, C.L. (1980b). Phenylketonuria: Epitome of human biochemicl genetics. *New England Journal of Medicine, 303*, 1336–1343.

Woo, S.L.C., Lidsky, A.S., Güttler, F., & Robson, K. (1983). Cloned human phenylalanine hydroxylase gene allows prenatal diagnosis and carrier detection of classical phenylketonuria. *Nature, 306*, 151–155.

4 | Behavioral Influences of Environmental Toxicants

BERNARD WEISS

It is intriguing that the National Institute of Environmental Health Sciences (NIEHS) is also celebrating an anniversary—its 20th—at the same time as the National Institute of Child Health and Human Development. Its growth coincides with a developing appreciation of the impact of environmental chemicals on health. Toxicology used to be a science, so to speak, embedded in pathology. Substances were defined as toxic if they produced tissue damage. It is now understood that the impact of environmental chemicals can be much more subtle. They can affect behavior; they can impair development.

David Rall, director of NIEHS, once asked the question: "Suppose thalidomide, instead of producing children with missing limbs, had lowered their intellectual potential by ten percent. Would we ever have discovered such an adverse effect?" The probable answer is most disquieting.

The dimensions of this problem pose a challenge. Figure 1 depicts the growth over a 60-year period in the production of synthetic organic chemicals. It is exponential in form. Figure 2 displays the amount of waste that accumulates as a result of chemical production. Note the tremendous increase that would occur over the next 100 years, 13,000 times, if the dumping of chemical waste in the environment was not hindered.

METALS

Many of the metals in the environment, some of which are toxic and some of which are both toxic and essential, have been linked to neurological and behavioral disorders (Weiss, 1983). Table 1 is a partial list of these metals. Some of the signs and symptoms of metal toxicity

Preparation supported in part by grants ESO1247, ESO1248, and ESO3054 from the National Institutes of Health, and by grant DE-FG02-85ERG0282 from the Department of Energy.

Table 1. Metals associated with behavioral toxicity

Aluminum	Mercury
Arsenic	Nickel
Bismuth	Selenium
Boron	Tellurium
Cadmium	Thallium
Lead	Tin
Manganese	Vanadium

appear in Table 2. They range from obvious disabilities such as paralysis to vague, subjective complaints like depression.

Mercury

Mercury is a classic example of a toxic metal with no known biological function. Mercury is extraordinarily volatile; wherever it is spilled and

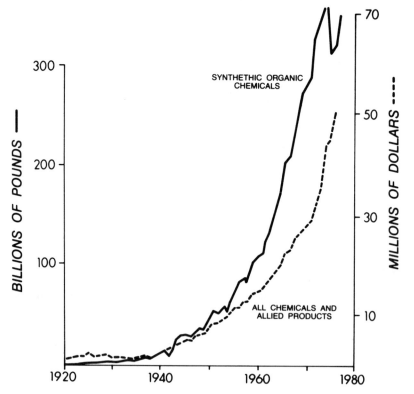

Figure 1. Synthetic organic chemical production over a 60-year period. (Courtesy of T.W. Clarkson.)

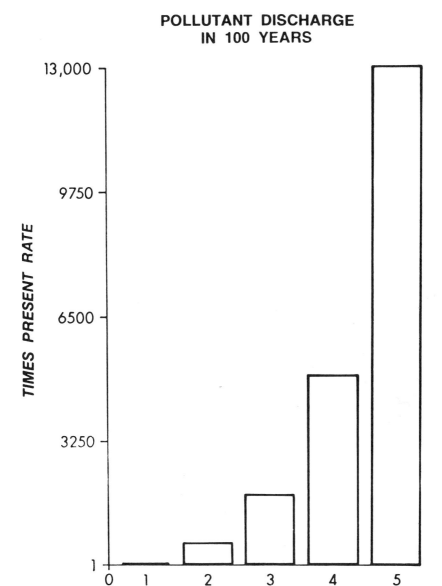

Figure 2.   Increases in environmental discharges of chemicals as a function of projected annual increments. (Courtesy of T.W. Clarkson.)

Table 2. Signs and symptoms ascribed to metal toxicity

Anosmia	Jitteriness, irritability
Appetite loss	Mental retardation
Convulsions	Paralysis
Depression	Paresthesias
Disorientation	Peripheral neuropathy
Dizziness	Polyneuritis
Dysarthria	Psychiatric signs
Fatigue, lethargy	Somnolence
Headache	Tremor
Incoordination, ataxia	Visual disturbances
Insomnia	Weakness

seeps into cracks or carpeting, it slowly evaporates, is inhaled, and is transported to the brain.

Mercury poisoning used to be an occupational hazard to hatters; it was used in the process by which the rough hairs of the fur were converted into a fine mesh that could be molded into hats. Mercury vapor exposure produces a fascinating constellation of signs and symptoms. Its cardinal neurological sign is tremor, and, in the Connecticut hat factories investigated in the 1930s by the Public Health Service, this sign was called hatter's shakes or Danbury shakes because Danbury, Connecticut, was the center of the industry.

In 1970, we encountered several cases of mercury vapor poisoning in a glass factory in upstate New York (Wood, Weiss, & Weiss, 1973). One of the victims, a woman in her 50s, visited physician after physician in the community, complaining she was "not herself." Those physicians, encountering a 50-year-old woman with psychological complaints, prescribed tranquilizers. She finally diagnosed the problem herself. When she came to the University of Rochester Medical Center she was found, indeed, to be suffering from mercury intoxication as revealed by the concentration in her blood.

Not only had the patient been exposed in the glass factory, but the mercury had contaminated her home. She also carried it with her in the folds of her clothing and even in her eyeglass frames. By this time, the amplitude of her tremor was quite high, and visible even on casual observation. Nine months later, without further exposure, the amplitude of the tremor had declined. By quantifying the tremor with a special device, its relationship with blood levels as these returned to normal could be traced.

Even more intriguing than the tremor are the symptoms of erethism (Table 3). Erethism is a classic manifestation of mercury vapor intoxication. It includes a large number of vague, nonspecific complaints.

Table 3. Symptoms of erethism

Hyperirritability
Blushing easily
Labile temperament
Avoidance of friends and public places
Timidity, shyness
Depression, despondency
Insomnia, fatigue

Children may be even more vulnerable to mercury than adults. In the early part of this century, a clinical entity named pink disease was discussed extensively in the medical literature (Weiss & Clarkson, 1982). It takes its name from the erythema displayed by the children who were its victims. Some physicians attributed the condition to infections, other to metabolic disorders. The signs and symptoms of pink disease, or acrodynia (painful limbs), embrace a tremendous number of end points, many of which are neurological and behavioral (Table 4). Only by accident did Warkany and Hubbard (1948) discover the cause: mercurous chloride, or calomel, mainly from teething powders.

Only a small proportion of infants, perhaps as few as 1 in 1,000, suffered the full syndrome. Nobody knows why they were susceptible. Why was mercury added to the teething powders? Nobody knows that either. The reason was probably rooted in tradition; mercury had been viewed as a metal with mysterious powers by ancient and medieval physicians, the latter of whom used it to treat syphilis. That treatment, which is ineffective, persisted even into the 20th century. Once mercurous chloride was removed from teething powders, pink disease fell into obscurity. This history illustrates the difficulties posed in identification of a source of contamination when only a small proportion of the population is susceptible to the toxicant.

Table 4. Pink disease (acrodynia)

Neurotoxicity features	General features
Pain in extremities	Cold, blue fingertips, toes
Numbness, tingling	Reddening of cheeks, nose
Loss of muscle tone	Sloughing of skin
Muscle twitching	Loss or loosening of teeth
Photophobia	Excessive perspiration
Tremor	Elevated blood pressure
Itching, burning sensation	Rash
Diminished reflexes	Loss of appetite

Mercury was first seen to be a threat on a global scale in Minamata, a small fishing village on the southernmost Japanese island of Kyushu. There, in the 1950s, fishermen and their families were afflicted by a mysterious disease they called *kibyo*, whose source was thought to be a viral encephalitis. That hypothesis was not confirmed. Mercury poisoning was eventually suspected, and the source finally was traced to the contamination of Minamata Bay by methyl mercury dumped by a factory that produced acetaldehyde, using mercury as a catalyst. The consequences of consumption of seafood containing high levels of methyl mercury appear in a striking book by the famous photographer Eugene Smith, who visited Minamata in 1972 to document the impact on that population (Smith & Smith, 1975).

Methyl mercury is a powerful central nervous system poison. The events in Minamata first indicated that the fetus might be a great deal more sensitive to its impact than the adult. That hypothesis was confirmed in the winter of 1971–72. The Iraqi government had ordered 80,000 tons of seed grain, mostly wheat and barley, most of it from Mexico, before the planting season. The government had also stipulated that the grain be treated with a methyl mercury fungicide. As a fungicide, methyl mercury dissipates into the soil after planting and poses no danger. But the bags arrived after the planting season, and were distributed to peasants in the countryside who could not read English or Spanish and who did not understand the poison symbols printed on the bags.

Many of the peasants consumed the grain, baking it into bread. In some instances, they washed off the pink dye that labeled the grain as a poison, but washing did not remove the methyl mercury. Some farmers conducted a form of primitive toxicological testing, first feeding the grain to farm animals or, in one case, to a mother-in-law, and observing for any toxic effects. Unfortunately, it takes time both for methyl mercury to penetrate into the brain and then for it to kill enough nerve tissue for those results to be manifested as overt clinical disorders. Ultimately, 5,000 people died, and about 50,000 were seriously affected.

Those most seriously affected were the children exposed as fetuses. Many of them manifested cerebral palsy. Motor retardation, speech retardation, incoordination, and even seizures were the markers of toxicity. In a sequence of studies devoted to the ramifications of this disaster, it became evident that the offspring of mothers who had consumed a large amount of the tainted grain were retarded compared to children whose mothers consumed only a small amount of the grain (Clarkson et al., 1981). The primary estimates of dose

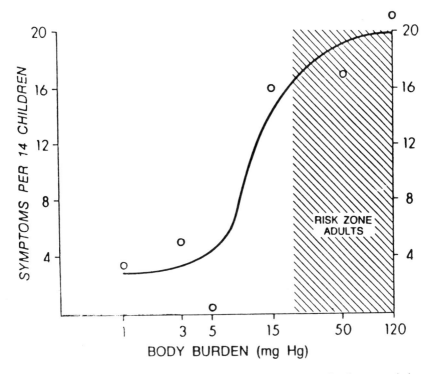

Figure 3. Comparative potency of methyl mercury in the fetus and the adult. A body burden of about 25 mg is the level at which adults begin to complain of symptoms such as paresthesias. Mothers with a body burden of about 2.5 mg place the fetus at elevated risk for developmental disorders. (Courtesy of T.W. Clarkson.)

came from hair analyses. Methyl mercury, fortunately, is about the only contaminant for which such analyses are useful because it is incorporated from blood into the growing hair. Centimeter-long segments of hair can be used to estimate month-to-month blood variations of methyl mercury and trace the patterns of intake and excretion.

An average body burden of 25–30 mg is required for an adult human to manifest the earliest indication of methyl mercury toxicity, consisting of paresthesia (numbness and tingling in the extremities). According to the calculations made on the basis of the Iraq episode, retardation occurs in the offspring of mothers with a body burden perhaps one tenth that amount (Figure 3).

It is not just early development that is hampered by methyl mercury intoxication. Spyker (1975) administered methyl mercury prenatally to mice, then followed the offspring for a lifetime. As they grew older, the mice manifested signs such as discharges from the eyes, skeletal disorders, kyphosis, obesity, and peculiar postures when swimming.

Acid rain has a fascinating relationship with methyl mercury. In Adirondack lakes that have been acidified, the methyl mercury levels in fish flesh are many times higher than the Food and Drug Administration (FDA) action limit of one part per million. Thus, only a few meals of contaminated fish (such as pike) with a flesh level of two parts per million will bring a pregnant woman to the level that seems to pose a danger to the fetus (Table 5). The table shows that a pregnant woman regularly consuming tuna fish, which also contains methyl mercury (0.25 mg/kg), needs only one meal a week of contaminated pike (2.0 mg/kg methyl mercury) to reach a fetotoxic body burden as calculated from the Minamata data.

Lead

Lead is another important toxic metal, widely dispersed in the environment since antiquity, and even more widely distributed since the introduction of leaded gasoline. It poses a threat to adults and children alike, but more to children because they absorb more lead from environmental exposure, partly because of their diet and partly because of immature mechanisms for excreting it.

In 1979, Needleman et al. published a seminal study indicating that, even in suburban children who show no overt signs of lead encephalopathy, high lead levels in deciduous teeth (which accumulate lead, as does bone) were correlated with lowered performance

Table 5. Adult versus fetal toxicity of methyl mercury, based on maternal body burden[a]

Intake source	Average daily CH₃Hg intake (µg)	% Adult toxic dose	% Fetotoxic dose
Tuna,[b] 3 cans/week (630 g)	22.5	9	50
Pike,[c] 1 meal/week (240 g)	68.6	27	150
Tuna + pike	91.1	36	200

[a]Presumed adult toxic threshold-250 µg/day, or steady-state body burden of 25 mg for a 50-kg female.

[b]Assuming CH₃Hg concentration of 0.25 mg/kg of edible flesh.

[c]Assuming CH₃Hg concentration of 2.0 mg/kg of edible flesh.

on various psychological tests and with disturbed classroom behavior. From a series of debates and studies since then, confirmed strikingly by a recent conference in Edinburgh, it now appears that lead levels equivalent to those found in suburban children, and not only the higher levels found in inner city children consuming paint chips, induce small but significant deficits in IQ scores. For example, members of Needleman's group compared children who were assigned to one of three groups on the basis of umbilical cord blood levels of lead, which provided an estimate of prenatal exposure (Bellinger et al., 1987). Even the children in the high lead group manifested lead levels far below the current standard assumed to be the threshold for adverse effects. Yet, at 24 months of age, they scored about 8% below the other two groups on a test of mental development.

To illustrate the significance of these differences, suppose that moderate lead exposure reduces intellectual potential by the equivalent of 5 points on an IQ test, that is, 5%. The assumed distribution of intelligence test scores yields a mean of 100, as in the upper portion of Figure 4. The lower chart shows the distribution with a mean of 95. In a population of 100 million, 2.3 million individuals will score above 130 if the mean is 100. In a population whose mean is 95, that number is reduced to 990,000. I submit that in a technologically competitive world such a reduction in intellectual potential is a societal disaster.

Metal Toxicity and Neurodegenerative Disease

Another provocative instance of possible metal toxicity comes from a long-term study of the distribution of amyotrophic lateral sclerosis (ALS) in the western Pacific. Three communities have been identified: the Kii peninsula in Japan, west New Guinea, and Guam. On Guam, ALS is found in conjunction with a peculiar form of what is called parkinsonism dementia (PD). Scientists are now speculating about the possibility that diseases such as some forms of parkinsonism originate in toxic environmental chemicals. Those speculations were aroused by the finding that a contaminant of illicit drug synthesis, 1-methyl-4-phenyl-1,2,3,6-tetrahydropyridine (MPTP), induces parkinsonism in humans and monkeys. Since Parkinson disease is attributed to a loss of cells in a circumscribed brain area called the substantia nigra, whose cell complement declines with age, chronic exposure to a substance such as MPTP could hasten or underlie this affliction.

Consider the following model. With aging, nerve cells and the ability to synthesize certain neurotransmitters are lost. From about the age of 25 to about the age of 75, 20% of central nervous system capacity is lost, according to calculations made by Kety (1956). The

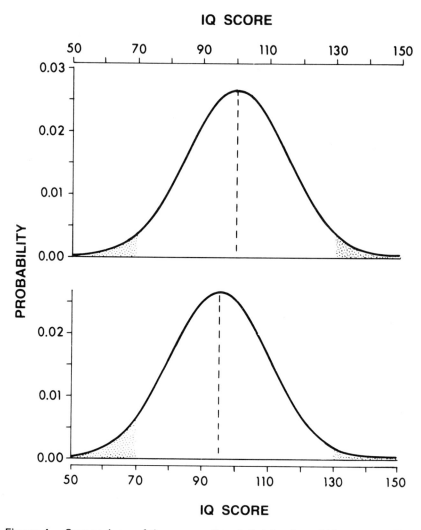

Figure 4. Comparison of the conventional distribution of IQ scores, with a mean at 100 (*top*), and the distribution displaced by 5% (*bottom*), a change produced by moderate elevations of lead tissue levels in children. In a population of 1 million, about 2.3 million individuals will score above 130 if the mean is 100 and the standard deviation is 15 (the empirical value). If the mean is 95, only 990,000 individuals will score above 130.

loss is uneven through the brain. Suppose that exposure to an environmental contaminant accelerates the loss by one-tenth of 1% a year (Weiss & Simon, 1975), a rate that, even with the best current techniques, would be impossible to document. This loss of capacity "ages" the brain by about 15 additional years (Figure 5). Such calculations, crude as they are, hold implications for neurodegenerative diseases, the diseases of the 21st century. Almost nothing is known about the impact of contaminants on aging, and few research efforts are aimed at these questions.

The incidence of ALS/PD on Guam has fallen during the past few decades, perhaps because of the introduction of a more western diet. There seems to be a complex interaction between high levels of certain metals in the environment and diet in the etiology of this peculiar disease. Another etiological hypothesis, also based on an environmental toxin, is gaining support. It asserts that, at least on Guam, ALS is due to the consumption of the seeds of a plant, belonging to the cycad family, that contains a neurotoxic amino acid.

FOOD ADDITIVES

Diet has aroused controversy because of a debate triggered by the huge volume of additives found in foods. Something like 3,000 agents are approved for use in the food supply in many different settings and for many different purposes.

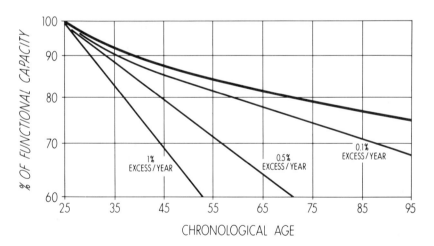

Figure 5. Hypothetical acceleration of brain aging produced by substances incrementing the natural decline in functional capacity represented by the various lines. The thick line is based on values calculated by Kety (1956) to represent normal aging. An acceleration of 0.1% annually will produce a 20% loss by age 60 rather than by age 70. (From Weiss, B., & Simon, W. [1975]. Quantitative perspectives on the long-term toxicity of methylmercury and similar poisons. In B. Weiss & V.G. Laties (Eds.), *Behavioral toxicology* [pp. 429–435]. New York: Plenum.)

Ben Feingold, a pediatric allergist from San Francisco, proposed the hypothesis (Feingold, 1975) that many of the children labeled as hyperkinetic or hyperactive or as suffering from minimal brain dysfunction actually were the victims of a heightened sensitivity to certain constituents of their diets. He singled out synthetic flavors and synthetic colors partly because he assumed that they conferred no nutritional advantage, and partly because they had been identified in the allergy literature as troublesome. As might be expected, Feingold was attacked vigorously by the food industry. His hypothesis and the experimental findings associated with it were also grossly misinterpreted by the biomedical community and by a consensus conference held in 1982. I have reviewed these data in several articles (Weiss, 1982, 1986).

I became involved in a study of the Feingold hypothesis because of my interest in the toxicological question, rather than the therapeutic question, posed by the hypothesis. I collaborated with investigators from Berkeley and from the Kaiser Health Care System in California. The study was conducted with a group of children in the Kaiser system (Weiss et al., 1980). Our experimental design sought to determine whether or not reproducible behavioral disturbances could be elicited in children by administering a blend of food colors at levels we estimated prevailed in the diet.

A double blind study with food colors is not a trivial task. We found that we could make a freeze-dried blend of the seven approved food colors, and match its appearance with caramel coloring; however, a solution of the freeze-dried blend, when a few drops were put on white filter paper, produced a neat red ring, the kind of adventitious chromatography that could break the experimental code. We then undertook a search for other dyes that were not on Feingold's prohibited index.

Grape worked well, but was on Feingold's prohibited list for other reasons. Beet extract worked very well, but made our soda pop vehicle taste like borscht. We finally settled on cranberry coloring. Over an 11-week period, for each of the 22 children in the study, the experimental drink was administered eight times. On all other days, the child drank the control drink.

These 22 yielded two responders. We measured their responses by having the parents sort through a large number of items taken from various behavior rating scales, and then collected into an individualized rating scale those 10 items that seemed to characterize the child most precisely during the times when the parents believed the child had undergone a reaction. We also used a standard measure, the Conners scale. All of the children were maintained on the Feingold diet, that is, a diet that eliminated additives. None were clinically hyperactive. The most spectacular responder was a 34-month-old girl (Figure 6). The hatched bars show the ratings on days when she received the experimental drink, the open bars on days when she did not. For items such as "runs away," "throws and breaks things," and "short attention span," there were enormous differences.

Some critics have complained that, with only a 5% or 10% incidence rate, behavioral responses to food additives do not present a significant problem. Yet, if my favorite hypothetical additive, bilious green, had been developed as a food color, and its manufacturer had sought approval with a claim that only 5% of the children consuming it got cancer, what would have been the response in Congress even had the FDA granted the request?

Food colors, like other additives, typically are tested in 2-year feeding studies in rodents. The tissues are then examined for pathology; weight gain and other indices also are measured during the study. On the basis of the typical 2-year feeding study, allowable daily intakes (ADIs) for these seven colors were calculated as the values in the right-most column of Table 6. The middle column shows the amount of color administered in our blend, which, as best we could calculate, corresponds to what is consumed by children in California.

With behavioral criteria, those levels inducing adverse effects are 50–60 times less than the ADI. If we divide those levels by a safety factor of 10, a standard practice, the difference becomes even more striking. Yet, even pediatricians, to my astonishment, have complained that, if artificial colors were removed from the diet, children could not be induced to eat healthy foods. Somehow, they have neglected a few billion years of evolution.

CONCLUSIONS

We live in a complex world where the positive impact of chemicals on human welfare cannot easily be dismissed, but the risks must be balanced against the benefits, as so cogently put by the late Philip Handler (1979):

> A sensible guide would surely be to reduce exposure to hazard whenever possible, to accept substantial hazard only for great benefit, minor hazard for modest benefit, and no hazard at all when the benefit seems relatively trivial. (p. 24)

Mrs. Shriver's foreword provided a compelling perspective to Dr. Handler's statement. We scientists cannot simply describe the risks and leave the stage. There comes a time when we, too, have to become advocates.

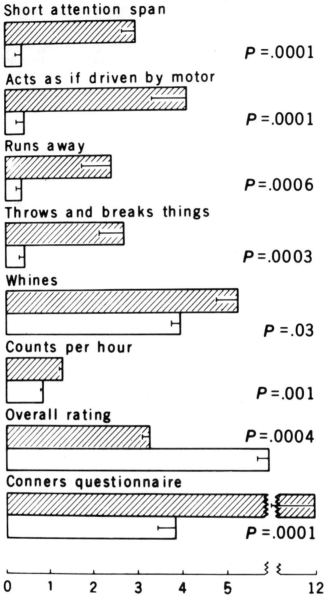

Figure 6.   Behavioral consequences of food dye challenge in a 34-month-old girl. *Hatched bars* represent 7 challenge days interspersed among a 77-day experimental period. Dyes were given in a soft drink vehicle. On placebo days (*open bars*) a matched control drink was consumed. The first five items represent the mother's ratings of individual target behaviors on a scale of 1 to 9 (9 corresponding to severe response). The number of counts per hours was recorded on a wrist counting device worn by the mother. Overall rating is total 24-hour ratings (low rating indicates aversiveness). Conners scale is a 10-item hyperkinesis rating scale; high scores correspond to more hyperkinetic behavior. (Data from Weiss et al., 1980).

Table 6. Food dye consumption estimates in children 1–6 years of age

Color	Consumption (mg/day)	ADI[a]
Yellow No. 5	9.07	300
Yellow No. 6	10.70	300
Red No. 40	13.80	420
Red No. 3	0.57	150
Blue No. 1	0.80	300
Blue No. 2	0.15	37.3
Green No. 3	0.11	150

[a]Acceptable daily intake is based on conventional toxicity testing (see text).

REFERENCES

Bellinger, D., Leviton, A., Waternaux, C., Needleman, H., & Rabinowitz, M. (1987). Longitudinal analyses of prenatal and postnatal lead exposure and early cognitive development. *New England Journal of Medicine, 316,* 1037–1043.

Clarkson, T.W., Cox, C., Marsh, D.O., Myers, G.J., Al-Tikriti, S.K., Amin-Zaki, L., & Dabbagh, A.R. (1981). Dose-response relationships for adult and prenatal exposure to methylmercury. In G.G. Berg & H.D. Maillie (Eds.), *Measurement of risks* (pp. 111–130). New York: Plenum.

Feingold, B.F. (1975). *Why your child is hyperactive.* New York: Random House.

Handler, P. (1979). Some comments on risk. In *The National Research Council in 1979; Current Issues and Studies* (pp. 3–24). Washington, DC: National Academy of Sciences.

Kety, S.S. (1956). Human cerebral blood flow and oxygen consumption as related to aging. *Research Publications of the Association for Nervous and Mental Disease, 35,* 31–45.

Needleman, H.L., Gunnoe, C., Leviton, A., Reed, R., Peresie, H., Maker, C., & Barrett, P. (1979). Deficits in psychologic and classroom performance of children with elevated dentine levels. *New England Journal of Medicine, 300,* 59–65.

Smith, W.E., & Smith, A.M. (1975). *Minamata disease.* New York: Holt, Rinehart, & Winston.

Spyker, J.M. (1975). Behavioral teratology and toxicology. In B. Weiss & V.G. Laties (Eds.), *Behavioral toxicology* (pp. 311–349). New York: Plenum.

Warkany, J., & Hubbard, D.E. (1948). Mercury in the urine of children with acrodynia. *Lancet, 1,* 829–830.

Weiss, B. (1982). Food additives and environmental chemicals as sources of childhood behavior disorders. *Journal of the American Academy of Child Psychiatry, 21,* 144–152.

Weiss, B. (1983). Behavioral toxicology of heavy metals. In I. Dreosti & R. Smith (Eds.), *Neurobiology of the Trace Elements* (Vol. I, pp. 1–50). Clifton, NJ: Humana Press.

Weiss, B. (1986). Food additives as a source of behavioral disturbances in children. *Neurotoxicology, 7,* 197–208.

Weiss, B., & Clarkson, T.W. (1982). Mercury toxicity in children. In *Chemical and radiation hazards to children* (Ross Pediatric Conferences) (pp. 52–58). Columbus, OH: Ross Laboratories.

Weiss, B., & Simon, W. (1975). Quantitative perspectives on the long-term toxicity of methylmercury and similar poisons. In B. Weiss & V.G. Laties (Eds.), *Behavioral toxicology* (pp. 429–435). New York: Plenum.

Weiss, B., Williams, J.H., Margen, S., Abrams, B., Caan, B., Citron, L.J., Cox, C., McKibben, J., Ogar, D., & Schultz, S. (1980). Behavioral responses to artificial food colors. *Science, 207,* 1487–1488.

Wood, R.W., Weiss, A.B., & Weiss, B. (1973). Hand tremor induced by industrial exposure to inorganic mercury. *Archives of Environmental Health, 26,* 249–252.

II | THE PRENATAL PERIOD

Overview
EDWIN H. KOLODNY

Compendia describing mental retardation syndromes are generally organized by causation, that is, chromosomal, metabolic, infectious, errors in morphogenesis, and so forth. This is how, 25 years ago, practitioners would organize their thinking about mental retardation. Perhaps it was because they were just beginning to discover that the common end point, mental subnormality, could result from many causes other than simple perinatal asphyxia and trauma. In contrast, this book primarily focuses on the epochs of life, not only those of infancy, childhood, and adulthood, but also the prenatal period and even the preconceptual period.

This type of structure emphasizes prevention and rehabilitation. These are relatively new concepts to the field of mental retardation. They have gained currency both in the clinic and in the formulation of public policy by a quarter century of remarkable achievements in research. They highlight our progress from the descriptive focus of a generation ago to the proactive stance of today. This section spotlights the tremendous increase in knowledge of the biology of the developing fetus and the ways that this knowledge has been put to work for improving pregnancy outcomes.

In Chapter 5, Dr. Phillip Nelson describes how developmental neurobiological research has begun to elucidate the very, very complex process of human nervous system development. Biological processes involved in early neurodevelopment operate in a strict temporal sequence, and a normal developmental outcome is dependent on a precisely correct interaction between them. Current research in this area is providing interesting information on the mechanisms of action of these processes. For example, the study of developmental regulation of gene expression has revealed that some genes are expressed only transiently, and may be unavailable for study at the time when the effects of their expression are manifested. Also, the process of synapse elimination, which continues several years beyond birth, appears to be influenced by patterns of neural activity imposed by environmental input. Thus this process, which may be abnormal in some forms of mental retardation, may be malleable to some degree. Dr.

Nelson suggests that the molecular basis for pathogenetic processes could be studied with currently available technology if markers could be developed to identify early abortuses as having various retardation syndromes.

The work of Dr. Nelson and others who are studying developmental biology could not really take place were it not for the great advances that have been made in tissue culture techniques. This is one of the great breakthroughs of the present generation and it is a breakthrough that now allows for the diagnosis of Down syndrome and other severe chromosomal anomalies before the 20th week of pregnancy.

The recently developed chorionic villus biopsy procedure enables the time of prenatal diagnosis to be shifted even further back into the first trimester and reduces the waiting time for a diagnosis. Other recent advances in prenatal diagnosis include high-resolution chromosome banding and the recognition of the fragile-X site as a major new cause of retardation.

There has also been a tremendous explosion in knowledge of human biochemistry in the past few decades. Dr. Nyhan mentioned that the biological defects in hundreds of inherited diseases, many of which seriously affect the nervous system, are now known. These diseases can now be detected in the fetus and in certain cases treatment of the affected fetus is even possible by administering corrective factors to the mother.

Another important new development in this field is the ability to detect neural tube defects. Dr. Mitchell Golbus reviews this and other dramatic gains in prenatal diagnosis and treatment in Chapter 6. Measurement of maternal serum levels of α-fetoprotein is increasingly utilized in prenatal diagnosis; high levels indicate the presence of aneuploidy, and low levels are correlated with trisomy 21 in the fetus. Progress in the field of ultrasonography has enabled such sophisticated new diagnostic techniques as umbilical cord blood sampling, fetal liver biopsy, and chorionic villus sampling. All of these efforts are directed toward diagnosing chromosomal and biochemical defects early in fetal development, but they also focus interest on prenatal treatment. Some of these conditions can be treated in utero by medical therapy, administering to the mother substances that can cross the placental barrier and affect the fetus. Other conditions can be treated surgically, either by in utero closed procedures such as urethral catheterization or by ex utero open procedures in which the fetus is temporarily removed from the uterus. Currently hydrocephalus and diaphragmatic hernia are being considered for fetal surgical treatment.

Contemporary developments in diagnostic medicine have also enabled significant advances in a more traditional area—that of assessment of fetal well-being. Dr. John Hobbins reviews the newest assessment techniques in Chapter 7. The fetus with intrauterine growth retardation can now be distinguished by means of ultrasound and magnetic resonance imaging from the fetus that is constitutionally small or is "small" because the mother's menstrual dates were miscalculated. Continuous fetal heart rate monitoring is now used before the mother enters labor in order to identify hypoxic infants at a time when intervention may mitigate the likely neurological sequelae. Also, a "biophysical profile" of the fetus can be constructed using ultrasound to provide a useful adjunct to heart rate monitoring. Dr. Hobbins notes that the ability to sample fetal blood, as described by Dr. Golbus, will enable physicians to determine degree of hypoxia in the third-trimester fetus, thus further refining the ability to monitor fetal progress and intervene as soon as possible or necessary.

The emphasis on the detection of adverse conditions in the fetus, however, must not overshadow the importance of maternal well-being to the health of a fetus. A great deal more is known today about normal placental growth and function, and the proper maternal requirements for calories, vitamins, and minerals. The diets of pregnant women who have phenylketonuria or galactosemia are now modified so that their fetuses are not subjected to toxic amounts of normal metabolites. Women with toxemia and with diabetes are now being better managed than in the past, and we know a lot more now about the harmful effects of alcohol, tobacco, narcotics, and other drugs. It is hoped that the education of mothers-to-be about these particular risks will result in better fetal outcomes.

In addition, several drugs are now recognized as teratogenic to the fetus; therefore, the use of such drugs as aminopterin, methotrexate, phenytoin, coumadin, and trimethadione is avoided during pregnancy. Erythroblastosis fetalis, mentioned by Dr. Golbus, is now being prevented by administering RhoGAM to the Rh-negative mother.

This new emphasis on maternal well-being and behavior quite accurately reflects the dual status of the fetus and the mother as interdependent patients. Dr. Deborah Coates has been concerned with the effects on both the mother and the fetus of such behavioral problems as inadequate nutrition, smoking, alcohol and drug abuse, ignorance of preterm labor symptoms, and social stress. In Chapter 8 she reviews programs designed to modify such maternal behavior in an attempt to reduce the incidence of low birth weight and its associated mortality and morbidity. Most studies of behavioral and medical risk factors have focused on individual factors, and although many factors have been documented, little information has been forthcoming on ways of influencing the mother to alter her behavior in order to lessen the likelihood of a poor pregnancy outcome. As with risk factor studies, intervention designs have also concentrated on individual factors and have been largely effective. However, Dr. Coates proposes that future research and intervention efforts should focus on a multifactor approach; her own research program has illustrated the positive outcomes of a comprehensive services model for prenatal care. Such a model should also take into account the relationship between maternal behavior and pregnancy stage, since a particular risk factor may have a critical influence on outcome if it is present in a particular stage.

Another risk factor for infant mortality and morbidity is that of maternal bacterial infection. The likelihood of permanent damage to the fetus by maternal infection has been greatly reduced through routine immunization for polio and rubella, the availability of immunoglobulin as prophylaxis against hepatitis B virus, and the availability of specific drug therapies for maternal syphilis and tuberculosis. However, less success has been achieved in the case of some bacteria that cause long-term central nervous system damage as well as short-term acute disease. In Chapter 9, Dr. Charles Alford reviews the progress made in dealing with chronic perinatal infections of cytomegalovirus, herpes simplex, *Toxoplasma*, and most recently human immunodeficiency virus, the causative agent of acquired immune deficiency syndrome. The initial difficulty in these cases is in simply making the diagnosis—the infection is often subclinical in both mother and fetus. Thus measures to prevent transmission of maternal infection to the fetus or to treat the infected newborn early in order to minimize sequelae later in life may not be taken. It has been determined that the stage of gestation during which the infection is transmitted influences the relative virulence of the infection, as does the action of various protective factors such as maternal immune response and the placental barrier. Dr. Alford illustrates the issues surrounding chronic perinatal infections using cytomegalovirus as a model of the mechanism of current infection. New methods in molecular biology are revealing information on the replication cycle of these viruses, and thus offering the possibility of controlling infections with drugs tailored to interrupt this cycle.

5 | Prenatal Neurodevelopment
PHILLIP G. NELSON

In discussing prenatal neurodevelopment, it should be noted that there exists now a good general scheme or program that describes the development of the brain and central nervous system. A number of general biological processes have been identified and are under study that, operating together, give a substantial, although certainly partial, picture of how the brain is put together. However, some intrinsic features of this developmental scheme pose very serious problems for analyzing the abnormalities in development that may be involved in mental retardation. Molecular, cellular, and, in particular, developmental neuroscience are very active research areas at present, and a number of probes or tools are becoming available that should give more detail and concreteness to the general aspects of the developmental program. These should be useful in trying to understand abnormalities in that development. In this chapter I discuss some considerations that I think could help in applying these techniques and methods, the tools of developmental neurobiology, to increasing such understanding.

BIOLOGICAL PROCESSES IN EARLY NEURODEVELOPMENT

What are some of the biological processes involved in early neurodevelopment? Several of these are shown in Figure 1 (Moore, 1985) along with some idea of their temporal relationships. There are clearly more processes involved in development of the nervous system than are depicted here; this figure shows only an incomplete version of what is going on during development. The various processes are related in a very strict temporal sequence, and an appropriate and precise interaction between them is required for the normal progression of the entire process.

Furthermore, some of these developmentally important phenomena appear and disappear. An important process may operate during a very restricted period and no longer be observable at a later period, yet a deficit in this process may have a devastating impact on overall

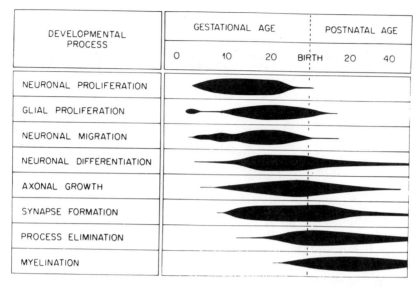

DEVELOPMENTAL PROCESS	GESTATIONAL AGE			POSTNATAL AGE		
	0	10	20	BIRTH	20	40
NEURONAL PROLIFERATION						
GLIAL PROLIFERATION						
NEURONAL MIGRATION						
NEURONAL DIFFERENTIATION						
AXONAL GROWTH						
SYNAPSE FORMATION						
PROCESS ELIMINATION						
MYELINATION						

Figure 1. The timing of major developmental processes in formation of the nervous system is shown as a function of age in weeks. For example, neuronal proliferation begins within first 4 weeks of development and is nearly complete by 24 weeks. In contrast, myelination does not begin until after 20 weeks and continues into childhood. The figure demonstrates the overlap of developmental processes and emphasizes the complexity of interpretation of the effects of insults on the developing nervous system. The timing shown for the developmental processes is an approximation because the timing differs between components of the nervous system and because precise information is not available for all events. (From Moore, R.Y. [1985]. Normal development of the nervous system. In J.M. Freeman (Ed.), *Prenatal and perinatal factors associated with brain disorders*. NIH publication 85-1149. Washington, DC: U.S. Public Health Service; reprinted by permission.)

brain development. Therefore, at the time that one may study a damaged organism, the ability to study directly the pathogenetic process may no longer be available.

Some of the processes important during prenatal development may go on for extended periods. Peter Huttenlocher's work (Huttenlocher, de Courten, Garey, & Van Der Loos, 1982) (Figure 2) showed that a decrease in the density of synapses in the cerebral cortex of humans (also see Rakic, Bougeois, Eckenhoff, Zecevic, & Goldman-Rakic, 1986), corresponding to the process of synapse elimination, actually goes on for months and even years after birth. This process of synapse elimination leads to a reduction in the absolute numbers of synapses, but an increase in the number of appropriately connected

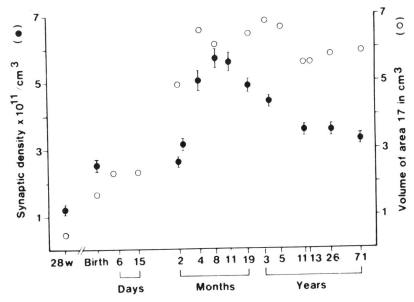

Figure 2. Synapse elimination in the human cerebral cortex. Mean synaptic density values for all layers of area 17 are indicated by closed circles (left-hand scale). Each point represents the mean of several thousand counts. Vertical bars represent the standard error of the mean of six separate synapse counts in the same brain in strips of cortex 3 μm in width. The open circles are the values for the volume of area 17 (right-hand scale). Age is plotted on a logarithmic scale. (From Huttenlocher, P.R., de Courten, C., Garey, L.S., & Van Der Loos, H. [1982]. Synaptogenesis in human visual cortex—evidence for synapse elimination during normal development. *Neuroscience Letters*, *33*, 247–252; reprinted by permission.)

synapses. This process, which may be abnormal in some forms of mental retardation (Cragg, 1975) and which has been investigated in a number of experimental situations, is in fact dependent on input from the environment, which may mean that it is malleable to some degree. This is an issue of particular interest and is dealt with below.

RESEARCH FINDINGS IN DEVELOPMENTAL NEUROSCIENCE

What kind of information is becoming available from the research in developmental neuroscience? One area that is very active in development generally is an increasing interest and experimental capability in studying *differential gene expression* during the process of development. Sargent and Dawid and colleagues in the Intramural Program of the National Institute for Child Health and Human Development are doing some very elegant work on developmentally regulated expression of genes (Sargent, Jamrich, & Dawid, 1986). One of their observations is that many genes are turned on for a very restricted period of time. The expression of a given gene comes on at a particular developmental stage and then is turned off; succeeding waves of transient genetic expression characterize the progression of development. Those genes that are turned on only transiently may well play a very critical role in development, but not be available for study at a later time in development when the eventual effects of their expression may be manifested.

The number of genes expressed in the nervous system is substantially greater than the number of genes expressed in any other tissue. There are a large number of nervous system–specific genes and there is intense research interest in this area (Hahn, Van Ness, & Chaudhari, 1982). A complete picture is not yet available, but the notion that there may be something rather special about the genes specifically expressed in the nervous system is an attractive one.

Apart from that general approach to gene expression in the nervous system, an increasing number of *specific gene products* are becoming analyzed and understood in great detail. A number of membrane proteins, specifically receptor molecules and either the ionic channels that they represent or the ionic channels associated with them, are, in a sense, the elements that determine nervous system function. These are among the molecules responsible for neuronal function, and the knowledge and analysis of these membrane proteins has progressed to a very high level. The full amino acid sequence is now available for such molecules as the acetylcholine receptor and voltage-sensitive sodium channels; domains within these molecules are recognized and their function has been closely related to their structure. There is no question that this approach to understanding cellular function in terms of the specific structure and function of individual molecules will continue to expand (see the *Cold Spring Harbor Symposium on Quantitative Biology*, volume 47, 1983, for reviews).

Rapid progress is similarly being made in understanding the *coupling of various receptors* to cell-biological phenomena, such as the transduction between these receptors and intracellular metabolic and regulatory processes. Particularly important is the regulation of various ion channels (Kaczmarek, 1986; Kandel et al., 1983).

A number of workers, including Edelman, Rutishauser, and Shachner, have been working on a class of molecules responsible for adhesion between cells (Crossin, Chuong, & Edelman, 1985). These molecules are presumably involved in cell recognition or cell-cell association. In a system such as the brain, where cellular interactions are so precise and critical, this class of molecules is clearly of great importance.

Furthermore, Edelman in particular has articulated some rather general schemes of development such that a restricted number of cell adhesion molecules could, when expressed in a proper sequential temporal and spatial order, generate a high degree of structural specificity (Edelman, 1984).

Another very active area of study has to do with a variety of growth factors and soluble material concerned with *regulation of phenotypic expression*. The discovery and analysis of nerve growth factor (Levi-Montalcini, 1976), for which Levi-Montalcini and Cohen received the Nobel Prize in Medicine and Physiology, exemplifies the sort of work in progress on a number of other regulatory molecules that are becoming implicated in the regulation of the functional development of the nervous system.

NEURONAL ELECTRICAL ACTIVITY
AND NERVOUS SYSTEM DEVELOPMENT

As mentioned above, reduction in the number of neurons and synapses is an important feature of nervous system development. An initial redundancy in brain structure is reduced in a functionally effective manner; this reductional selection is influenced strongly by the patterns of neural activity imposed on the nervous system during development by input from the environment. My colleagues and I have been interested in this question of neuronal survival as affected by neuronal electrical activity.

The preparation we have used is the dissociated cell culture system from the fetal mouse spinal cord (Figures 3 and 4). We dissociate this tissue into a suspension of single cells. This initial preparation of individual, small, round cells goes through a rather elaborate developmental process such that highly differentiated neurons growing on a background of nonneuronal, mostly glial, cells establish highly effective synaptic networks with one another.

We have sought to investigate the mechanisms regulating this development. One major question we asked is, how important is electrical activity in this regard? Experiential inputs to the nervous system are mediated by electrical activity in neurons, and we wanted to determine how important that was for development.

Neurons and glia can be specifically identified by immunocytochemical and other stains (Figures 3 and 4). Inhibitory neurons utilizing the transmitter γ-aminobutyric acid (GABA) or cholinergic neurons can be demonstrated. A variety of peptidergic neurons can

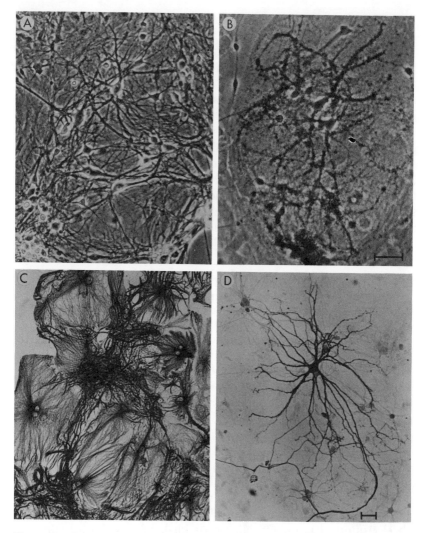

Figure 3.   Dissociated cell cultures from fetal mouse spinal cord and dorsal root ganglion. *A*, Living culture viewed with phase-contrast optics. *B*, Culture in which neurons are labeled by [125]-I-labeled tetanus toxin radioautography. *C*, Culture in which astrocytes are stained by immunohistochemistry for glial fibrillary acidic protein (antibody generously supplied by Dr. Doris Dahl). *D*, Culture in which a large spinal cord neuron is injected with horseradish peroxidase. *A–C*, ×230; bar in *B* = 50 μm. *D*, ×120; bar = 50 μm. *A–C* are from cultures 3 weeks after plating; *D*, more than 6 weeks after plating. (Courtesy of Dr. Elaine Neale.)

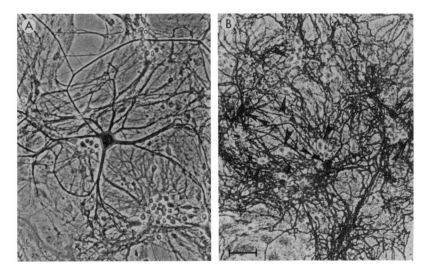

Figure 4. Spinal cord cultures in which cholinergic (A) and GABAergic (B) neurons were identified. A, The large, multipolar spinal cord neuron was among the neurons that stained after immunohistochemistry using an antibody (generously provided by Drs. Bruce Gordon and Louis Hersh) against choline acetyltransferase. The axon of this cell could be followed for long distances; its branches ultimately terminated in swelling that contacted other neurons. A larger percentage of neurons in these cultures appear to be GABAergic, as demonstrated in B by radioautography following high-affinity accumulation of [^{3}H]GABA. Silver grains are seen over cell bodies and neurites of the GABA uptake neurons. Five labeled cell bodies are indicated by double arrowheads; several of the nonlabeled somata are marked by large single arrowheads. Both cultures were photographed using phase-contrast optics. A was 6 weeks in culture, B was 3 weeks. Magnification in both is ×230; bar = 50 μm. (Courtesy of Dr. Elaine Neale.)

be selectively stained with appropriate antibodies. Such methods allow us to look for cell-specific developmental effects of various experimental manipulations. Other techniques allow us to measure various biochemical indicators of neuronal development, as shown in Figure 5.

What happens to neuronal development in this system if we block all electrical activity with an agent such as tetrodotoxin (TTX), the specific blocker of the voltage-sensitive sodium channel? The results of such an experiment are shown in Figure 6. Total numbers of neurons, and particularly numbers of cholinergic neurons, are greatly reduced but inhibitory GABAergic neurons are not affected. The effects of electrical activity blockade are strongly dependent on the age of the preparation, with a window of maximum vulnerability from

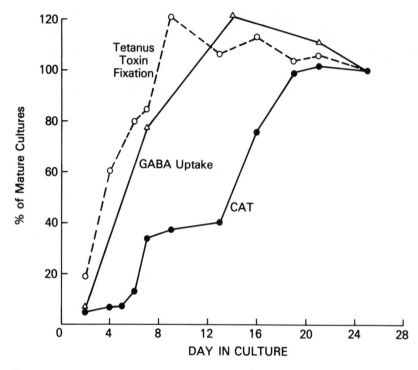

Figure 5. Development of choline acetyltransferase (CAT) activity, high-affinity GABA uptake, and ^{125}-I-labeled tetanus toxin fixation in spinal cord cultures. High-affinity uptake of GABA was measured on intact cultures with 10^{-7} M [^{3}H]GABA for 10 min. Neuronal GABA uptake was taken to be the difference in uptake in the presence and absence of 1 mM diaminobutyric acid. CAT activity was measured in cells that were disrupted in the culture well for 30 min with the following buffer: 50 mM KPO$_4$ (pH 6.8), 1 mM K-EDTA, 0.25% Triton X-100, and 0.2 M NaCl. The CAT reaction mixture contained 0.1 μCi [1-^{14}C]acetyl coenzyme A, 0.2 mM acetyl coenzyme A, 4 mM choline chloride, and 0.1 mM neostigmine bromide. Product was isolated by anion-exchange chromatography. Specificity of the reaction was estimated as the difference between the activity in the presence of 60 μM of the CAT inhibitor N-hydroxyethyl-4-(1-naphthylvinyl)pyridinium bromide. Tetanus toxin fixation was measured during 60-min incubations at 30°C with ^{125}I-labeled toxin (2 × 10^{-10} M; 100,000 counts/minute). Nonspecific fixation was determined by a 1-hour preincubation with 2 × 10^{-8} M unlabeled toxin in a parallel series of cultures. (From Brenneman, D.E., & Nelson, P.G. [1985]. Neuronal development in culture:1 Role of electrical activity. In J.E. Bottenstein & G. Sato (Eds.), *Cell culture in the neurosciences* [pp. 289–316]. New York: Plenum Publishing Corp.; reprinted by permission.)

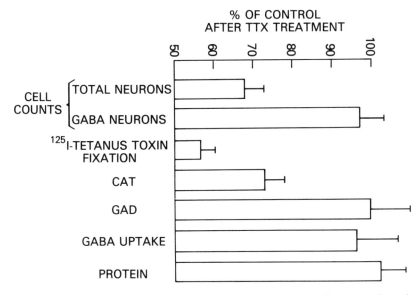

Figure 6. Comparison of various culture parameters after tetrodotoxin (TTX) treatment between days 7 and 14 in culture. ^{125}I-labeled tetanus toxin fixation, choline acetyltransferase (CAT), and [3H]GABA uptake were assayed as described for Figure 5. Neuronal cell counts were made directly on the stage of an inverted phase-contrast microscope at a magnification of 160×. Labeled ([3H]GABA autoradiography) and nonlabeled neurons were counted in 130 regularly spaced fields (each 0.12 mm^2) at predetermined locations on the culture dish. Glutamic acid decarboxylase (GAD) was measured in the culture well after disruption of the cells with the following buffer: 0.25% Triton X-100, 50 mM KH_2PO_4, 0.5 mM 2-amino-ethylisothiouronium bromide hydrobromide, and 0.1 mM pyridoxal phosphate. The reaction was initiated by the addition of 8 mM [3H]glutamate. Product was isolated by ion-exchange chromatography. GAD activity was determined by subtracting the activity measured in the presence of 2 mM amino-oxyacetic acid from the total activity. Error bars are standard error of the mean. (Data from Brenneman et al., 1983.)

about day 5 to day 21 in culture. Thus there is specificity in the deleterious effects of activity blockade with regard to both cell type and developmental stage.

Brenneman and colleagues (Brenneman & Eiden, 1986; Brenneman, Neale, Foster, d'Autremont, & Westbrook, 1987; Brenneman, Neale, Habig, Bowers, & Nelson, 1983; Brenneman & Nelson, 1985, 1987) have utilized this culture system to show that electrical activity causes the release of a soluble material into the culture medium that mediates the survival-promoting activity associated with the electrical activity. Medium taken from electrically active cultures (conditioned medium) prevents neuronal death when applied to electrically inactive cultures. (This is done by adding TTX to the conditioned medium and treating test cultures with it.) Furthermore, Brenneman and Eiden (1986) have shown that these effects can be attributed to the action of a specific peptide, vasoactive intestinal peptide (VIP) (Figure 7). Further experiments demonstrate that VIP is released by neurons in an activity-dependent manner and that it activates glial cells to, in turn, release a macromolecular neuronotrophic material. The evidence for this can be summarized as follows:

1. VIP can be measured by radioimmunoassay in the culture medium bathing electrically active neuronal cultures.
2. The amount of VIP in the culture medium is drastically reduced if the cultures are rendered electrically silent with TTX.

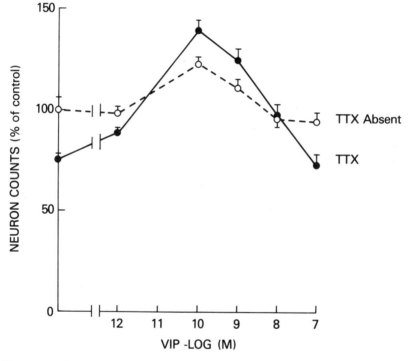

Figure 7. Concentration-effect study of VIP on neuronal cell counts in spinal cord cultures. VIP was added on day 9 to either electrically active (TTX absent) or TTX-treated cultures. After 5 days, the cultures were fixed and counted. Each point is the mean of six to eight determinations from two experiments. (From Brenneman, D.E., & Eiden, L.E. [1986]. Vasoactive intestinal peptide and electrical activity influence neuronal survival. *Proceedings of the National Academy of Science (USA)*, *83*, 1159–1162; reprinted by permission.)

3. VIP, when added to cultures containing only non-neuronal, primarily glial cells, produces a striking enhancement of the neuron survival-promoting activity of medium conditioned by such cells, when the medium is assayed on electrically silent, neuron-enriched test cultures. These cultures do not respond to VIP alone. The activity of VIP is highly specific; closely related peptides do not have similar actions.

CONCLUSIONS

The point to be made from the kind of experiment discussed in the previous section and from related experiments done in other laboratories is that molecular entities crucial for normal nervous system development are being isolated and analyzed in terms of their mechanism of action. In the case presented, we can say that VIP is important, so one would want to look for the gene for VIP, which also has other peptides coded in it; at the control elements for those peptide-related genes; and at the VIP receptors on glial cells and the timing of their development. The release of the trophic material is of importance and we would like to understand the mechanism by which the glia-derived neurotrophic material acts to support neuronal survival.

One could give a similar scenario for other probes that are available for assaying various aspects of neurodifferentiation that have been identified in a model system, but that should be applied to the study of development of the intact nervous system.

Applying the techniques and tools of developmental neuroscience in an attempt to understand clinical problems such as mental retardation involves at least two strategies. One is to utilize various models of human pathology, such as the mouse TS16 analogue of Down syndrome. The other would be to establish chromosomal, genetic, or somatic markers of various retardation syndromes that could be used to identify early abortuses as pathological. The molecular basis for the pathogenetic process might well be more evident in such early developmental stages. Probes that are available now, such as neural cell adhesion molecule antibodies, peptide immunocytochemistry, or receptor markers, might then be productively applied to such material.

REFERENCES

Brenneman, D.E., & Eiden, L.E. (1986). Vasoactive intestinal peptide and electrical activity influence neuronal survival. *Proceedings of the National Academy of Science (USA)*, *83*, 1159–1162.

Brenneman, D.E., Neale, E.A., Foster, G.A., d'Autremont, S.W., & West-brook, G.L. (1987). Non-neuronal cells mediate neurotrophic action of VIP. *Journal of Cell Biology, 104*, 1603–1610.

Brenneman, D.E., Neale, E.A., Habig, W.H., Bowers, L.A., & Nelson, P.G. (1983). Developmental and neurochemical specificity of neuronal deficits produced by electrical impulse blockade in dissociated spinal cord cultures. *Developmental Brain Research, 9*, 13–27.

Brenneman, D.E., & Nelson, P.G. (1985). Neuronal development in culture. Role of electrical activity. In J.E. Bottenstein & G. Sato (Eds.), *Cell culture in the neurosciences* (pp. 289–316). New York: Plenum Publishing Corp.

Brenneman, D.E., & Nelson, P.G. (1987). Peptide modulation of neuronal differentiation in culture. In A. Vernadakis (Ed.), *Model systems of development and aging in the nervous system* (pp. 257–276). Boston: Martinus Nijhoff.

Cragg, B.G. (1975). The density of synapses and neurons in normal, mentally defective and aging human brains. *Brain, 98*, 81–90.

Crossin, K.L., Chuong, C-M., & Edelman, G.M. (1985). Expression sequences of cell adhesion molecules. *Proceedings of the National Academy of Sciences (USA), 82*, 6942–6946.

Edelman, G.M. (1984). Cell adhesion and morphogenesis: The regulator hypothesis. *Proceedings of the National Academy of Sciences (USA), 81*, 1460–1464.

Hahn, W.E., Van Ness, J., & Chaudhari, N. (1982). Overview of the molecular genetics of mouse brain. In F.O. Schmitt, S.J. Bird, and F.E. Bloom (Eds.), *Molecular Genetic Neuroscience* (pp. 323–334). New York: Raven Press.

Huttenlocher, P.R., de Courten, C., Garey, L.S., & Van Der Loos, H. (1982). Synaptogenesis in human visual cortex—evidence for synapse elimination during normal development. *Neuroscience Letters, 33*, 247–252.

Kaczmarek, L.K. (1986). Phorbol esters, protein phosphorylation and the regulation of neuronal ion channels. *Journal of Experimental Biology, 124*, 375–392.

Kandel, E.R., Abrams, T., Bernier, L., Carew, T.J., Hawkins, R.D., & Schwartz, J.H. (1983). Classical conditioning and sensitization share aspects of the same molecular cascade in Aplysia. *Cold Spring Harbor Symposium on Quantitative Biology, 48*, 821–830.

Levi-Montalcini, R. (1976). The nerve growth factor: Its role in growth, differentiation and function of the sympathetic adrenergic neuron. *Progress in Brain Research, 45*, 235–258.

Moore, R.Y. (1985). Normal development of the nervous system. In J.M. Freeman (Ed.); *Prenatal and perinatal factors associated with brain disorders.* NIH publication 85-1149. Washington, DC: U.S. Public Health Service.

Rakic, P., Bougeois, J-P., Eckenhoff, M.F., Zecevic, N., & Goldman-Rakic, P.S. (1986). Concurrent overproduction of synapses in diverse regions of the primate cerebral cortex. *Science, 232*, 232–235.

Sargent, T.D., Jamrich, M., & Dawid, I.B. (1986). Cell interactions and the control of gene activity during early development of *Xenopus laevis*. *Developmental Biology, 114*, 238–246.

6 | Prenatal Diagnosis and Treatment

MITCHELL S. GOLBUS

The field of prenatal diagnosis and therapy is even younger than the National Institute of Child Health and Human Development (NICHD). The mainstay of efforts in this field has been amniocentesis, the ability to draw amniotic fluid from the pregnant uterus. Within that fluid will be living cells that can be grown in tissue culture media and thus yield information about the chromosomal and biochemical nature of the fetus.

PRENATAL DIAGNOSIS

Indications

The most common indication for prenatal diagnosis is maternal age. Although not a reproductive cutoff, in the United States 35 is generally used as the age at which prenatal diagnosis is discussed with the mother and offered to the couple. Couples who have had a previous child with trisomy or who are carriers of a translocation fall into the chromosomal risk group, another indication for prenatal diagnosis. Pregnancies in which the fetus is at risk for an X-linked disease or a biochemical defect, usually an autosomal recessive defect such as Tay-Sachs disease, represent most of the remainder of indications for prenatal diagnosis.

It is important to remember that in the advanced maternal age group, which is where most of the prenatal diagnosis is done, over 97% of the pregnancies are found to be normal. It has been my experience that there are a great number of pregnancies that are conceived and come to term that would never have been conceived without the availability of prenatal diagnosis.

α-Fetoprotein Testing

Diagnostic testing for neural tube defects was pioneered by the British. The test was based on α-fetoprotein (AFP), which is made first in the yolk sac and then in the fetal liver. In conditions in which capillaries are exposed to the amniotic fluid, such as a myelomeningocele or anencephaly, AFP is found in the amniotic fluid in abnormally high amounts. In the early 1970s this test was added to the prenatal diagnosis armamentarium and became a standard across the world. In the United States, the risk of having another child with a neural tube defect after having one such child is 2–3%. Therefore, the test was first offered to couples who had prior offspring with a neural tube defect; later it became common to perform the test on all amniotic fluids, such as those drawn for chromosomal studies because of advanced maternal age.

The success of the AFP test for amniotic fluid led to the search for a similar test to use for maternal serum AFP. A simpler, less invasive test was needed in order to identify fetuses with neural tube defects in the general population, rather than screening only those women who were at high risk. If only women who had already had a child with a neural tube defect were tested, the disease incidence could be reduced by only 10% (the number of neural tube lesions that were recurrent). The 90% of lesions that were first occurrences in a family would be unnoticed until delivery, a delivery that might occur in a small hospital without a pediatric neurosurgeon, without neonatologists, without all of the armamentarium necessary to have the best outcome for that neonate.

There have been a number of pilot studies both in Britain and in the United States and there are now large state-wide programs such as that exemplified by the California state program offering maternal serum AFP screening. The California program is only 6 months old and already two thirds of pregnant women are asking for the serum AFP screening. I believe there will be very high compliance and utilization rate of this particular test.

One serendipitous outcome of the AFP programs is related to low AFP values. In both amniotic fluid and maternal serum, there is a very good correlation between low AFP levels and trisomy 21 in the fetus. A number of programs are contacting patients who have a low serum AFP level and offering them amniocentesis for karyotyping of the fetus. A method has been worked out taking into account the woman's age, race, and weight, which also influence AFP levels, in order to arrive at a relative risk of trisomy in comparison to that of a 35-year-old woman. The younger the woman the lower her AFP level must be to raise her risk to the same level as that of a 35-year-old, which would qualify her for amniocentesis. Most programs are using this approach to AFP testing, and it may turn out that for a population such as that in the United States, where the neural tube defect incidence is not as high as it is in Britain, for example, aneupliody detection will be the major usage of serum AFP programs.

The Fetoscope

The fetoscope is a small fiberoptic scope that is actually a modification of an arthroscope. It has a power source and a teaching head so that two people may use it at the same time. The original use of a fetoscope was in order to visualize the pregnancy in a search for neural tube defects. Following the development of the AFP test, the British began to use the fetoscope to identify cases of spina bifida with myelomeningocele during pregnancy.

There are some intrinsic physical problems with a small fiberoptic scope. For example, scope of vision can be improved by backing away from the object(s) being viewed—more can be seen from a distance (although in less detail). However, in fetoscopy one can withdraw only so far before the fetoscope passes out of the uterus; therefore diagnosis is often compromised by poor visual angle. Another unfortunate physical problem is that when a lens is placed in an aqueous medium such as amniotic fluid, the angle of vision narrows considerably from what it is in air. Although these scopes allowed a certain amount of visualization, they have been completely surpassed by ultrasonography. Currently, there is little use for fetoscopy as a visualization instrument.

Fetal Blood Sampling

The vessels on the inside of the surface of the placenta carry fetal blood, which can be used to make prenatal diagnoses that could not be made with amniocytes or amniotic fluid constituents. The use of the fetoscope to obtain fetal blood samples worked reasonably well, but there was one significant problem. The scope itself is monocular, which means that the operator does not have good depth vision. In attempting to obtain a sample from the fetal blood vessel, the operator may misjudge the depth of the target vessel and pass through it into the placenta, thus contaminating the sample with maternal blood. Therefore, fetoscopy-directed fetal blood sampling has been replaced by sonography-directed umbilical cord blood samplings.

Fetal blood sampling has been found to have many applications. All of the constituents of fetal blood are available for use in diagnosing a number of entities, both genetic and physiological. Fetal blood sampling has frequently been used in Rh typing, but the major use today is for rapid karyotyping when the fetus is found to have anatomical abnormalities by sonography. Outside of the United States the largest use of fetal blood sampling is in the prenatal diagnosis of hemoglobinopathies, because few other countries have the DNA technology now used to make the diagnoses.

Fetal Tissue Biopsy

Following the development of fetal blood sampling, the ability to biopsy other fetal tissues—primarily skin and liver—began to be exploited. A technique was developed for performing fetal liver biopsies in utero. There are a number of significant genetic disorders in which an enzyme is only expressed in fetal liver cells, and therefore a deficiency in that enzyme can only be identified by obtaining a fetal liver sample. Prenatal diagnoses of a few of these disorders have now been made using an intrauterine fetal liver biopsy technique.

The newest of the diagnostic techniques is chorionic villus sampling. The operator places a catheter transcervically near the chorionic villi that will form the placenta; with aspiration at the tip of the catheter a few of those villi can be drawn out. The villi are genetically fetal material and can show the chromosomal and biochemical nature of the fetus and if one is searching for particular defects, whether those defects are or are not present in a given pregnancy.

There have been somewhat over 25,000 chorionic villus samplings performed around the world. There is currently an ongoing investigation of the procedure's efficacy under the auspices of NICHD, very similar to the collaborative study for amniocentesis that took place in the early and mid-1970s.

Future Directions

Looking ahead, one of the important areas of research in prenatal diagnosis is maternal bloodstream sampling, which would be somewhat less invasive than other prenatal diagnostic techniques. The interest in the maternal bloodstream is fostered by attempts to obtain fetal cells that are circulating in it. The greatest use of prenatal diagnosis is for chromosomal abnormalities; thus if even a small number of fetal cells could be obtained from the maternal bloodstream in order to determine the chromosomal nature of the fetus, a more invasive procedure for prenatal diagnosis would be unnecessary. A number of attempts to obtain fetal cells have been made, but the technique is in a preliminary state at present.

PRENATAL TREATMENT

The current techniques and ongoing research in prenatal diagnosis also focus interest on its complement, prenatal treatment. Although most treatment of prenatal conditions will occur after delivery, the import of prenatal diagnosis is not necessarily lessened. A fetus found to have a defect may need to be delivered by a different method (i.e., cesarean rather than vaginally) or to be delivered in a tertiary center where neonatologists and a pediatric surgeon or a pediatric neurosurgeon are available for immediate repair of the lesion. In the case of conditions that can be treated in utero, there are two categories of therapy—medical and surgical.

Medical Therapy

The most common model of a medical approach is that in which a substance is administered to the mother that will cross the placenta and affect the well-being of the fetus. There are a number of examples of this treatment model. In one group of vitamin-dependent enzyme deficiencies the enzymes are actually intact, but cannot work because the vitamin coenzymes either are not absorbed or do not attach well to the enzymes. These conditions are normally treated postnatally by giving large doses of the vitamin coenzymes to the child. However, there have been a number of in utero diagnoses of such conditions, and large doses of the vitamin coenzymes were given to the mother. These very small molecules are able to cross the placenta well to the fetus, and the child is then born heavily dosed with this vitamin coenzyme and does not suffer any of the ill effects of the enzyme deficiency.

Another example of medical therapy is the use of cardiotropic drugs in fetuses that have a tachycardia. Their heart rates are so fast that they develop heart failure. It is now possible to treat the fetus by giving the mother cardiotropic drugs that reduce the tachycardia to a normal sinus rhythm, allowing the fetus to recover from its heart failure. There will be further applications of this type of medical therapy to treat the fetus with a particular condition so that it can remain in utero, but in better physiological shape.

Surgical Treatment

The counterpart to medical therapy is surgical therapy. The idea of performing surgery on a fetus prompts an immediate question as to what type of situation would demand so extreme a response. The criterion for surgical intervention is the presence of an ongoing worsening condition such that, without intervention, the fetus will not be able to survive as a neonate.

Surgical therapy can be divided into closed and open procedures. Closed procedures include intrauterine transfusion and placement of a catheter into a closed space in the fetus. Catheter placement has been used to resolve obstruction of the urethra so that the urine could pass from the bladder to the amniotic space. Urethral blockage in the fetus has two adverse outcomes. First, because of the high backpressure the fetus develops hydronephrosis and renal dysplasia. Second, because the urine is not passing into the amniotic space, the lack of amniotic fluid leads to lung hypoplasia. In such a situation, without some type of intervention there is little likelihood of fetal survival. The simple solution to urethral obstruction is to place a catheter from the fetal bladder to the amniotic space so that the urine can pass through the catheter into the amniotic space.

The other category of surgical therapy is open surgery. Such a procedure consists of entering the uterus through an abdominal incision, removing the fetus, performing the surgical repair on the fetus, returning the fetus to the uterus, closing the incision, and then allowing the pregnancy to continue to term. There are a number of advances that have made this type of surgery possible. One has been ultrasonography, which enables better diagnoses. Another advance has been better fetal monitoring mechanisms.

Several anatomical abnormalities have been suggested as possibilities for an intrauterine surgical approach, including hydrocephalus and diaphragmatic hernia. The proposed treatment for hydrocephalus is to place a shunt, very much as was done with the obstructed urethra, from the ventricles to the amniotic sac to allow the high pressure in the ventricles to be vented. The problems with this suggestion is that hydrocephalus, as opposed to bladder obstruction, is not a solitary defect. Very often there are other unassociated or associated abnormalities. Also, what is seen in utero may not be the same as what is seen in the neonatal period. A common neurosurgical criterion for placement of a shunt in a neonate is progressive enlargement of the ventricles. However, in utero ventriculomegalies do not seem to progress. In the first 60 such patients my colleagues and I observed, only 2 were seen to have progression of their ventriculomegaly. Clearly, more research is needed before in utero shunt placement can be considered an appropriate therapeutic response to fetal hydrocephalus.

A survey of some 94 in utero–diagnosed diaphragmatic hernias in the United States and Canada found that the mortality rate was over 80%. Experimentally created diaphragmatic hernias in sheep and monkey fetuses resulted in death of the newborns from lung hypoplasia. This ensues following intestinal herniation into the chest, preventing full development of the lung. Surgical creation and repair of a fetal diaphragmatic hernia has been accomplished in animal models. Lamb and monkey fetal lungs were found to experience sufficient catch-up growth after surgical repair to sustain the fetus as a neonate.

The next step is to attempt to correct a small series of human diaphragmatic hernias found in utero to see if the results of the animal experiments can be duplicated.

In summary, although the surgical approach attracts a great deal of attention, there are many problems it will not solve. This approach will never save large numbers of fetuses; it is attention to the therapy of the single gene defect that will make a greater difference.

7 | Assessment of Fetal Well-Being

JOHN C. HOBBINS

PARAMETER OF FETAL DEVELOPMENT AND CONDITION

Today it is possible to weigh the fetus in utero using a formula based on various fetal measurements. For example, putting together a head measurement (the biparietal diameter, or BPD) and abdominal circumference, one encounters a standard error of the method of 100 g/kg. To put this into clinical perspective, using this formula one is within 10% of the actual fetal weight about 80% of the time and within 5% of the fetal weight about 50% of the time.

This takes on importance when assessing how big certain babies are compared with what they should be at different times in gestation. For instance, if a fetus is supposed to be 2500 g at 35 weeks of gestation, and the fetus in fact is 1000 g, the deficit can be quantified; this fetus is, in fact, 1500 g lighter than it should be, and a careful clinical watch should be instituted. However, if despite clinical concern a particular fetus is found to be no more than 200–300 g lighter than it should be, the surveillance can be diminished a bit.

The use of this fetal measurements formula has been found to be the most precise way to diagnose intrauterine growth retardation (IUGR). For good or bad, IUGR is still based on a definition of mean weight for gestational age. Using this formula can perhaps enable the clinician to more correctly pick out the fetus that is small for dates.

Next, the reason the fetus is small for dates must be determined. Small-for-dates babies fall into three groups:

1. Fetuses that are "small for dates" because the mother's menstrual dates are off (this occurs about 30% of the time).
2. Constitutionally small fetuses.
3. Fetuses that are truly small for dates and have suffered intrauterine deprivation.

Fetuses in the first two groups are unlikely to suffer complications, such as the increased rates of mental retardation seen in truly deprived IUGR infants. Fetuses in the third group require further assessment,

99

usually using the techniques of magnetic resonance imaging and ultrasound.

Magnetic Resonance Imaging

Magnetic resonance imaging (MRI) has emerged as the tool of the
future. However, it is also a very expensive and lengthy procedure.
Theoretically MRI should be safe for the fetus, but this must be
comprehensively investigated before it can be used routinely. With
current technology, there is a lag time between the buildup of the
image and the point at which it can ultimately be interpreted, and
any type of movement during the examination will affect the image.
Presently, the only way to keep a fetus still is to give an intrafetal
injection of curare, a practice sometimes used during intrauterine
transfusions.

Nevertheless, with NMR it will be possible to see how thin the
fetal limbs are and how big the liver actually is, and, even better, to
determine the amount of fat that is deposited in the subcutaneous
tissue. A normal fetus will deposit about 9 g of brown fat in its subcutaneous tissue per day, exclusively for thermal stability. A growth-
retarded baby has very little in the way of fat stores (which explains
the extensive wrinkling of his or her skin). NMR should definitely be
able to show the amount of deposited subcutaneous fat.

Ultrasound

In the case of a small-for-dates fetus, ultrasound assessment of amniotic volume is diagnostically important. In the face of severe intrauterine deprivation, there is oligohydramnios in almost all cases. It is
also possible to determine the size of the fetus using ultrasound. An
electronic digitizer can be used to trace the perimeter of the thigh on
a transverse scan at the midshaft of the femur in order to obtain a
thigh circumference. Using nomograms for thigh circumference, the
status of fetal nutrition can be indirectly determined.

Pulsed Doppler ultrasound analysis of various fetal and maternal
vessels also has good potential for use to determine fetal condition.
With the pulsed Doppler technique sound is emitted in small pulses
that can be beamed in almost any direction. For instance, if the beam
encounters fetal blood flowing through the aorta, these pulses will
bounce off the aorta and off individual blood particles within the
vessel. The pulsed ultrasound will be reflected back to be received by
the same transducer that sent it out. The transducer perceives any
change in frequency of the sound based on the velocity of the objects
that these sound waves are striking. The resulting jumble of delta

frequencies is then processed by the Doppler machine and cosmetically converted through spectral analysis into a waveform that schematically represents systole and diastole.

In normal pregnancies, at about 18–22 weeks of gestation the arteries that send blood into the intravillous space actually become invaded by the trophoblast. This normal phenomenon produces low peripheral resistance in the placental circulation. Because of this low resistance there is a great deal of diastolic runoff. Therefore, in a low peripheral resistance circuit one encounters a low systolic-to-diastolic (S/D) ratio. In IUGR and toxemia of pregnancy, this invasion by the trophoblast does not occur. Therefore, there is very high resistance in the placental circulation, and the S/D ratio is higher than usually seen.

The same phenomenon also causes a decrease in resistance on the fetal side of the placenta. The umbilical arteries therefore display higher S/D ratios in toxemia and, most often, in IUGR. Occasionally, there is even reverse flow noted in the umbilical artery (in other words, the diastolic trough is below the zero point). In the five cases I have seen, this has represented an ominous sign: the fetus was in acute distress.

It is hoped that Doppler ultrasound will provide a good amount of information about fetal condition, and allow the differentiation of the deprived fetus that is growth retarded from the one that is constitutionally small.

FETAL HEART RATE MONITORING

In the late 1950s, Dr. Edward Hon developed a way to continuously monitor fetal heart rate. His initial goal was to detect fetal hypoxia in a laboring woman, and he identified three pathological patterns. The one that seemed to correlate with a low pH at the time of birth, low Apgar scores, and a low oxygen content in the fetal blood was the pattern of late deceleration (a deceleration that occurred after contractions). This revolutionized the surveillance of the fetus during labor.

Recently, the method has been challenged. One of the reasons it has come under fire is that there is not always a correlation between the predicted and the actual outcome. Rather recently, a task force was convened by the National Institutes of Health that was charged with determining factors that were associated with neurological sequelae in infants. The conclusion of the task force was that events in labor were less well associated with outcome than events occurring before labor. In other words, the writing was on the wall in many cases of brain damage and labor represented simply another adjunctive insult to an already severely compromised infant.

However, one can determine whether or not there are any difficulties before the patient goes into labor by monitoring the fetal heart rate. A normal fetus will accelerate its heart rate at least twice in a 20-min period. This "reactive" heart rate is a rather typical sign of fetal well-being. Consequently, a baby with this type of finding is unlikely to be hypoxic. This reassuring observation now has been used extensively in assessing the antepartum fetus.

Also, there seems to be a very delicate balance between the sympathetic and the parasympathetic system. this push-pull phenomenon results in discernible beat-to-beat variability.

Smooth heart rates are found in fetuses that are in quiet sleep or, frequently, in fetuses that are hypoxic. The combination of decreased beat-to-beat variability and the lack of acceleration of fetal movement is a worrisome sign. Again, although not invariably predictive of fetal ill-being, this combination is very strongly suggestive of it. The additional finding of repetitive late decelerations with spontaneous contractions is even more powerful evidence of a fetus that is in trouble.

STUDY OF FETAL BEHAVIOR

In an effort to diminish the amount of false-positives with antepartum fetal heart rate monitoring, some investigators have attempted to actually observe fetal behavior with ultrasound. A pediatrician can tell when a fetus is in bad condition simply by observing its movement and breathing. A nonhypoxic fetus will spend about 30% of its time making breathing motions, whereas a hypoxic fetus will hardly ever breathe. Therefore, the presence of fetal respirations is a very reassuring sign.

The group at the University of Southern California designed a set of parameters that correlated in their original investigation with fetal outcome. This "biophysical profile" consists of a nonstress test and an assessment of breathing, fetal movement, fetal tone, and fluid volume. Each element of the profile is given an arbitrary score of 0 to 2, and a total perfect score is 10. This has been a useful adjunct in assessing fetal condition. The combination of biophysical profile and antepartum fetal heart rate monitoring has been extremely useful in identifying the baby that is potentially hypoxic.

FUTURE TESTING

It is now possible simply with ultrasound visualization to advance a tiny needle into the umbilical cord of the fetus and draw a sample of blood. This has enabled intrauterine transfusions and many prenatal diagnostic studies that cannot be performed without the use of fetal blood, and, recently, has also opened up the possibility of finding out more about the third trimester fetus that is potentially hypoxic.

By drawing fetal blood and subjecting it to various types of analyses, it is possible to determine the degree of hypoxia. For example, one can make determinations of PO_2, pH, and base deficit. Lately, my colleagues and I have been looking at some liver enzymes that seem to be liberated in chronic hypoxia (γ-glutamytransferase, which reflects the amount of primordial erythroblasts in fetal blood). Obviously, there are other markers of chronic hypoxia that can be identified simply by acquisition of fetal blood. Thus, fetal blood represents a new diagnostic tool that will be very useful in the future.

I have given a brief overview of what perinatologists can tell about the fetus in utero, and these techniques represent only the tip of the iceberg. In the next few years it should be possible not only to be able to tell more about the fetal condition, but also to reverse some of the problems that have occurred as a result of fetal hypoxia.

8 | Modification of Maternal Behavior in Efforts to Reduce Infant Mortality and Childhood Morbidity Associated with Low Birth Weight

DEBORAH L. COATES

This review presents what is currently known about modifying maternal behavior in attempting to reduce risk factors that have been clearly associated with infant mortality and childhood morbidity outcomes in pregnancy. Low birth weight is a major factor contributing to infant mortality and childhood morbidity and may be significantly preventable. Several maternal behaviors, which can be characterized as preventive health behaviors, have been associated with reduced risk of infant mortality and childhood morbidity. These behaviors were identified in a recent Institute of Medicine (1985) report on low birth weight and include:

1. Timely and appropriate use of prenatal care resources.
2. Adequate nutrition and weight gain.
3. Knowledge of the causes and symptoms of preterm labor and use of that knowledge to manage early labor.
4. Avoidance of smoking.
5. Avoidance of alcohol and other inappropriate drugs.

This paper is based on an invited address presented at the National Institute of Child Health and Human Development conference *Mental Retardation: Research Accomplishments and New Frontiers*, November 17–18, 1986. Dr. Coates is Project Director of the Better Babies Project and Associate Professor of Psychology at the Catholic University of America, Washington, DC. The author appreciates comments by Joan Maxwell, Heinz Berendes, and Mary Overpeck, and by Peter Vietze on an earlier draft of this manuscript.

THE PROBLEM OF LOW BIRTH WEIGHT

Low birth weight is a major factor contributing to the United States' relatively high rate of infant mortality and to childhood morbidity. It may be significantly reduced through changed maternal behavior.

The problem of low birth weight and its consequences have been well documented and will not be reviewed here. Excellent reviews of the problem have been presented by the National Center for Health Statistics (1985) and several others (Brent & Harris, 1976; Falkner, 1984; Institute of Medicine, 1985; McCormick, 1985; McManus, 1985; Office of Technology Assessment, 1981; Shapiro, Mccormick, Starfield, Krischer, & Bross, 1980; World Health Organization, 1961).

Less than 7% of all U.S. births in 1981 were infants of low birth weight (National Center for Health Statistics, 1985). About 1% of all infants were very low birth weight, weighing less than 1,500 g (3 1/4 pounds). The differences among black and white rates of low birth weight and very low birth weight dramatically highlight racial disparities in risk for infant mortality. The black low birth weight rate during the same time period was 12.5% versus 5.7% for whites. The black very low birth weight rate shows similar differences: 2.5% versus 0.9% for whites. Using combined 1977–1979 national data, the Institute of Medicine (IOM) found that although blacks made up only 16.4% of all live births, they represented 30% of all low birth weight births, and 27% of infant deaths. The mortality and some of the morbidity consequences of low birth weight are well documented (see, e.g., Hack, Caron, Fanaroff, Klaus, Mendalawitz, & Merkatz, 1983; McCormick, 1985; McCormick, Shapiro, & Starfield, 1981; Ramey, Stedman, Borders-Patterson, & Mengel, 1978; van den Berg & Yerushalmy, 1966; Westwood, Kramer, Numz, Lovett, & Watters, 1983).

The remainder of this chapter presents:

1. Research that describes which maternal characteristics—both behavioral and demographic—are associated with low birth weight.
2. Research that describes behavioral interventions designed to reduce the behavioral risks associated with low birth weight.
3. A discussion of critical methodological issues and unexplored questions in the area of low birth weight intervention.

SPECIFIC MATERNAL BEHAVIOR, PREGNANCY, AND CHILDHOOD MORBIDITY

The outcome variable in most studies of preventable maternal health risk behavior has been low birth weight and the associated outcomes of infant mortality and morbidity. The clinical and epidemiological research on low birth weight and premature birth has focused on the identification of broad demographic risk factors, medical risks, and health care risks (e.g., risks such as accidental prematurity from cesarean section delivery or accidental induction of labor prior to term). Behavioral risks, prenatal care use, and environmental conditions such as stress have also been identified as risks. This discussion will consider only those interventions designed to address risks that are directly under some aspect of maternal control or that influence maternal motivation or control. A brief review[1] of the nature of these risks will provide some context for the consideration of promising maternal behavior interventions designed to reduce them.

Prenatal Care

Premature deliveries have consistently been found to be related to fewer prenatal care visits (IOM, 1985). Kessner's (1973) landmark study of New York City births in 1968 found a significant relationship between adequate prenatal care, based on number of prenatal care visits adjusted for duration of pregnancy and other relevant factors, and percentage of low birth weight infants. The clearest risks were experienced by women with low socioeconomic status and medical risks.

Gortmaker (1979) has reanalyzed the same data and confirmed these results. Data from a California study found adequate prenatal care to be associated with an increase of 197 g in the average birth weight for 1978 births (Showstack, Budetti, & Minkler, 1984). In a Massachusetts study Harris (1982) found that early initiation of prenatal care for black women was associated with an increased average birth weight and gestation term for 1975 and 1976 births. Several similar studies found an association between late or no prenatal care, particularly for low-income and black women, and the risk of low birth weight in Los Angeles, Detroit, Texas, Washington state, and the health maintenance organization system in New York state (Fisher, LoGerfo, & Daling, 1985; Leveno, Cunningham, Roark, Nelson, & Williams, 1985; Moore, Origel, Key, & Resnick, 1986; M. Poland, personal communication, 1986; Quick, Greenlick, & Roghamm, 1981). There is no examination in most of these studies of the content or quality of prenatal care. This fact severely limits the interpretability of these findings.

---

[1] This review and a review of demographic risk factors that follows is based in part on a literature review by M. McManus that was commissioned by the Better Babies Project.

Nutrition Intake and Weight Gain

Anderson (1979) reviewed studies that show that maternal nutrition behavior is related to pregnancy outcomes. Maternal weight gain during pregnancy has consistently been related to infant birth weight. In the Montreal Diet Dispensary Study, as pregravid weight and prenatal weight gain increased so did birth weight (Higgins, 1976). Results from the Collaborative Perinatal Study of the National Institute of Neurological and Communicative Disorders and Stroke (Hardy, Drage, & Jackson, 1979; Niswander & Gordon, 1972) show that, for a sample of 10,500 infants at 8 months of age, the incidence of abnormalities in motor functioning was 11.3% in infants born to women who had gained less than 15 pounds during pregnancy as compared to 5.2% in infants whose mothers had gained 36 pounds or more during pregnancy (Singer, Westphal, & Niswander, 1968). This study also reports that women who gained less than 14 pounds were four times as likely to have a low birth weight infant as compared to those gaining between 30 and 35 pounds. This has special implications for black women and for teenage mothers because they are more likely to gain less weight in pregnancy. The 1980 National Natality and Fetal Mortality Survey (Kessel & Kleinman, 1984) reported that black women are twice as likely as white women to gain less than 16 pounds during pregnancy (see also Snowman, 1979).

The timing of weight gain and the relationship of nutritional status to weight gain and birth weight have also been considered [see Corbett & Burst, (1983) and H. Jacobson (1981) for brief reviews]. Metcoff and colleagues (1985) reviewed international studies that indicate the relationship between nutritional supplement interventions at mid- and third trimester of pregnancy and fetal weight increase. They also presented results from an evaluation of the U.S. Department of Agriculture (USDA) Women, Infants, and Children (WIC) Supplemental Food Program that indicate that leukocyte protein synthesis and mean birth weight were significantly greater for supplemented mothers in a prospective, randomized, controlled study. Weight gain is often affected by other behaviors such as smoking and stress reactions (Papoz, Eschwege, Pequignot, Barrat, & Schwartz, 1982; Picone, Allen, Olsen, & Ferris, 1982; Picone, Allen, Schramm, & Olen, 1982). Obesity has been thought to be related to several pregnancy outcomes, but this relationship is not clear in a study reported by Calandra, Abell, and Beischer (1981).

Preterm Labor

Analyses of the causes of low birth weight should distinguish between those related to premature birth and those related to intrauterine growth retardation (IUGR). Separating the contributing influence of these two factors is complex because IUGR and prematurity occur together in a substantial number of low birth weight cases (IOM, 1985). Physiological and biochemical events as well as environmental conditions that might initiate and maintain normal human labor are not well understood. It is assumed by some low birth weight intervention experts, however, that education of pregnant women about the warning signals of early labor and the need to seek prompt prenatal health care assistance if these signals are detected may provide the possibility of containing this labor and thus preventing a preterm delivery.

Smoking

The Surgeon General in 1979 reported that smoking may be a major contributing factor in 20–40% of all low birth weight infants (National Center for Health Statistics, 1980). Over the past 20 years, epidemiological research has consistently found a strong relationship between smoking and birth weight (Oster, Delea, & Golditz, 1986; Ounsted & Scott, 1982; Rantakallio & Hartikainen-Sorri, 1981; Rush et al., 1986; Shiono, Klebanoff & Rhoads, 1986) and recently between smoking and long-term childhood morbidity (Stjernfeldt, Berglund, Lindsten, & Ludvigsson, 1986).

Stein and Kline (1983) found that smoking during pregnancy has been associated with a reduction in an infant's birth weight of 150–250 g. The National Center for Health Statistics also reports that the prevalence of smoking is higher among mothers experiencing stillbirths than among mothers of live-born infants (Graves et al., 1983).

Alcohol and Other Drug Abuse

The link between alcohol use and lowered birth weight is not as clear as that between smoking and lowered birth weight. However, maternal alcohol consumption has been associated with negative outcomes such as IUGR, low birth weight, and fetal alcohol syndrome (Mills, Graubard, Harley, Rhoads, & Berendes, 1984; Ouellette, Rosett, Rosman, & Weiner, 1977; Stein & Kline, 1983; Streissguth, Barr, & Martin, 1982; Wright et al., 1983). Graves et al. (1983), in an analysis of the 1980 National Natality and Fetal Mortality Survey, found that drinking even small amounts (one drink or more per day) significantly increased the risk of low birth weight.

In contrast to the literature available on smoking and alcohol use, there is little information available on the consequences of other substance abuse during pregnancy. Sample sizes are comparatively small because of the relatively lower incidence of drug use and difficulty in collecting these sensitive data. Before 1961 most studies of the effects of pharmacological agents on the fetus were concerned with the effects of narcotics and analgesics on the fetus at the time of delivery. The thalidomide tragedy focused attention on the effects of legal drugs.

More recently the concern is with illegal or "street" drugs. The use of these drugs has increased dramatically in the general population. Chambers and Hunt (1977) reported on a cross-sectional, cross-ethnic survey of over 30,000 women of childbearing age conducted in 1974–1975. Of this group 34 were identified as addicted to heroin or other illicit drugs. Using this sample the authors projected that about 1.7 million women of childbearing age used prescription narcotics or minor tranquilizers, about half a million were users of barbiturates, half a million used marijuana, and almost 100,000 used cocaine. Fried and colleagues presented data on the changing patterns of soft drug use before and during pregnancy (Fried, Innes, & Barnes, 1984; Fried, Watkinson, Grant, & Knights, 1980). They reported that except for heavy social drinking, soft drug habits (e.g., use of marijuana) remained essentially unchanged after the first trimester of pregnancy. Finnegan (1976) reported on the effects of maternal drug use on 303 newborns. Low birth weight was common among infants of drug-dependent mothers, and maternal narcotic withdrawal was associated with stillbirth. The rate of neonatal death was three times that of a non-drug-using control group. Neonatal morbidity was observed in 75% of all infants born to drug-using mothers, requiring an average hospital stay of between 17 to 26 days. Depressed sucking rates were also characteristic of these infants when compared to high-risk infants of mothers who had been treated for toxemia. Other studies document the negative consequences of drug use on the fetus and the newborn (Kandall et al., 1977; Perlin & Simon, 1978; Strauss, Andresko, Stryker, & Wardell, 1976).

Fried, Watkinson, and Willan (1984) provided the only major study that examines the effect of marijuana use during pregnancy on duration of gestation. They reported that in a prospective study of 583 moderately high-income women delivering single live infants, 84 used marijuana to varying degrees during pregnancy. Compared to nonusers, an average use of marijuana of 6 times or more per week resulted in a statistically significant reduction of 8 weeks in the length of gestation but no increase in low birth weight. Gestational age reduction was greatest for heavy users. Hingson and colleagues (1982) reported reduced birth weight but not gestational length for a Boston City Hospital sample. Marijuana use may have interacted with other risk factors in the Boston study to produce the results reported. Barry

Lester and Cynthia Garcia-Coll are collecting data on pregnancy outcomes for Jamaican women who use marijuana frequently in the practice of their religion. A.W. Brown (1979), in a discussion of drug use in the context of providing clinical prenatal care, indicated that drug use may also affect the fetus because it "compromises the physical and psychological well-being of the woman." This limits her ability to protect and promote the health of the fetus through positive health behavior.

Multiple Risk Factor Risk Identification

Few studies have examined the contribution of multiple risk factors to pregnancy outcomes. These factors are sociological, behavioral, and medical. Miller, Hassanein, and Hensleigh (1981) reported that low socioeconomic status was related to increased incidence of behavioral risk but not to medical risk complications during pregnancy. There was a high incidence of low birth weight among the lowest socioeconomic status groups for both black and white mothers. Scott, Moar, and Ounsted (1981) also examined the relative contribution of behavioral and medical risks to prediction of the incidence of low birth weight. They found that the medical risk of having had a previous low birth weight infant was the best predictor of low birth weight, followed by smoking, presence of hypertension, and preeclampsia.

Stress: Environmental Mediator of Maternal Behavior

Both physical and psychological stress have been related to prematurity, perinatal death, dysmaturity, and congenital anomalies. The Collaborative Perinatal Study and research done in France by Mamelle, Lauman, and Lazar (1984) found a relationship between prematurity and 10 occupational requirements for physical exertion. Papiernik and Kaminski (1974) also reported a relationship between IUGR, prematurity, and activities involving lengthy periods of standing or other work requiring significant physical stress.

Several studies have associated perinatal death and congenital anomalies with psychological stress (e.g., Crandon, 1979; Gorsuch & Key, 1970; McDonald 1968; Norbeck & Tilden, 1983). M.A. Brown (1986) found the presence of stress related to health expectations of both expectant mothers and fathers. The way in which stress probably directly affects outcomes is through a mother's stress reaction, which typically may be characterized as anxiety. This reaction is sensitive to the type of social support available and the timing of such support (D.E. Jacobson, 1986). Numerous studies from 1956 to 1980 link anxiety with pregnancy complications and poor outcomes such as low birth weight, fetal distress, and asphyxsia (see Wolkind & Zajicek, 1981, for a review). Boone (1985) presented anecdotal/interview results, using a sample of 8 black, low-income women whose infants died within the first year, suggesting that lack of social support, psychological distress, and alienation were key characteristics of this group. The physiological mechanism directly responsible for some of these outcomes has not been identified; anxiety may also affect the fetus indirectly by causing a woman to neglect her diet, to smoke, to abuse alcohol or other drugs, to require or use medications, and otherwise to engage in negative health behaviors (Barnett & Parker, 1986). Wolkind and Zajicek (1981) reviewed pioneering studies from the years 1941–1966 indicating a relationship between fetal movement and extreme emotional upset. Where stress interferes with mothering after pregnancy, long-term morbidity may result. It is important to note that the effects of stress are mediated by a number of factors, including nutritional status and weight gain (Kinsley & Svare, 1986).

MODERATORS OF MATERNAL HEALTH BEHAVIOR

In considering the relationship between maternal behavior and pregnancy outcome there are several sets of variables that have a moderating effect on maternal behavior. The presence of some amount of these variables may cause the influence of the maternal behavior or the efficacy of a maternal behavior intervention to vary across women. Three classes of moderate variables are outlined here:

1. *Environmental conditions*   Broad sociological conditions such as poverty and/or certain life events such as immediate circumstances or tense personal relations may result in psychological stress, which in turn can influence the next moderator variable class.

2. *Psychological state of the mother*   The woman's attitude toward the fetus and the pregnancy and her level of anxiety may influence her ability to modify health behavior (e.g., discussion by Laukaran & van den Berg, 1980).

3. *Shared genetic background of mother and child*   Shared genetic background may be especially important in the consideration of maternal behavioral influences on child outcomes that are genetically linked to the maternal behavior in question. Wolkind and Zajicek (1981) discussed this when presenting results on the relationship between maternal stress, maternal anxiety, and irritability in offspring. The influence of shared genetic background may be less likely in the case of stress, but still merits consideration as an influence on morbidity outcomes that is independent, in any conceptual or statistical model, from maternal behavior.

BEHAVIORAL INTERVENTIONS DESIGNED
TO REDUCE INFANT AND CHILDHOOD MORBIDITY

Most interventions designed to reduce the incidence of low birth weight have focused on reducing the impact of a single risk factor. However, those interventions that have been most effective in reducing low birth weight have used a combination of strategies or a multidisciplinary approach. Although it is extensive, the value of this intervention literature is limited, particularly for interventions focusing on minorities. Many program evaluations fail to look separately at race and risk factors. Not surprisingly, they are often unable to detect changes in risk factors or outcomes (Peoples & Siegel, 1983). Another drawback of the intervention literature is that it tends to focus on risk assessment, failing to provide sufficient descriptive and analytic details of interventions that appear to reduce the risk factors (McManus, 1985).

The use of professionals versus paraprofessionals to provide low birth weight interventions has been a subject of considerable debate (Kent & Smith, 1967; Wise, Torrey, McDade, Perry, & Bograd, 1968). The discussion has centered around cost, compliance of target populations, and effectiveness associated with various levels of professional expertise and of paraprofessional counseling. The use of nurse-midwives has been associated with improvements in pregnancy outcomes. To what extent this is due to their risk assessment and referral of high-risk women and/or their extensive counseling is unclear. Nurse-midwives and obstetrical nurse-practitioners appear to be particularly effective with pregnant women at high risk because of social and economic factors (Piechnik & Corbett, in press). Certified nurse-midwives (CNMs) and nurse-practitioners approach these pregnant women in nonauthoritarian ways and focus on extensive education and support as well as patient satisfaction. A 1981 study of CNMs found that they spent an average of 24 minutes during their prenatal care visits compared to about 10 minutes spent by office-based obstetricians (Lehrman, 1981). The literature on effectiveness of nurse-midwives also shows improved compliance rates (Slome et al., 1976).

Single-Factor Interventions

Single-factor behavior intervention approaches include increasing use of prenatal care, nutrition intervention, early labor management, programs to reduce smoking and substance abuse, and stress reduction techniques.

Increasing Use of Prenatal Care   The effectiveness of enrolling women in prenatal care early and maintaining that care has been examined in the California Obstetrical Access Project. This project used aggressive outreach and treatment within existing community and university hospital clinics to increase access to prenatal services (Korenbrot, 1984). Gregory (1984) reported that more women initiated care in the first trimester, and the study group that remained in care throughout pregnancy had half the incidence of low birth weight that a comparison group had. The interpretability of this study, however, is limited since persons who dropped out of the project before delivery were not included in final analyses. One study has used access to Medicaid as an intervention in Missouri to improve access to prenatal care and reports that adequate prenatal care was associated with improved pregnancy outcomes (Schramm & Land, 1984).

Strobino and colleagues (1986) reported on the impact of the Mississippi Improved Child Health Project. Two versions of an intervention were offered in 1978 and 1979. The intervention, as best as can be determined from published reports, involved using extra funds to enhance existing services and community advisory groups. The intervention was evaluated using a quasi-experimental nonequivalent control group design. For the first year the percentage of women with adequate prenatal care rose in the study as compared to the control counties, but the reverse was true in the second year. For neither project was an impact on low birth weight detected. Selection bias and other issues related to internal validity and appropriate comparison groups make it difficult to determine how effective these interventions have been. The following results are reported in studies that have addressed the issue of prenatal care access:

1. Women are more satisfied with care provided consistently by one prenatal care provider rather than care provided by a host of providers, and this is especially true of young mothers (M. Poland, personal communication, 1986; Wilner, Schoenbaum, Monson, & Winickoff, 1981).
2. There are major differences between the perceptions of older patients and teenaged prenatal patients with respect to prenatal information needs (Levenson, Smith, & Morrow, 1986).
3. Despite receiving comprehensive prenatal care through a large teaching hospital, adolescent mothers were still at greater risk for low birth weight and for preterm infants than older mothers (ages 20 to 36) (Leppert, Namerow, & Barker, 1986).
4. Some surveys of women of childbearing age in large urban areas have identified what they view as incentives to encourage prenatal care, such as coupons for services on goods, transportation vouchers, and baby showers (Juarez & Associates, Inc., 1982; Robitaille & Kramer, 1985; WRC Report, 1986).

5. The cutback in the use of outreach workers to enroll pregnant women in prenatal care was significantly associated with declines in the average number of prenatal care visits in public clinics (Feldman & Mosher, 1984).

6. Knowledge is limited about what types of specific aggressive outreach efforts improve use of prenatal care in terms of initiating and maintaining prenatal care.

Nutrition Intake and Weight Gain   Evaluations of nutritional supplemental programs and nutrition interventions have included examination of women in the WIC Supplemental Food Program and interventions in private care in both this and other countries (e.g., Kotelchuck, Schwartz, AnDerka, & Finison, 1984; Sweeney et al., 1985). These studies have not used rigorous experimental designs to assess the efficacy, if any, of these food entitlements in improving birth outcomes. Despite these design limitations, these evaluations report some promising trends:

1.   Program evaluations of WIC by the General Accounting Office for the USDA indicate that despite the fact that many of these evaluations lack appropriate control groups, WIC participation was associated with increases in birth weight of as much as 20%. Also, WIC participation between pregnancies was associated with increases in birth weight in subsequent pregnancies (Kotelchuck, et al., 1984; Schramm, 1983).

2.   Dietetic students and home visitors have been used to provide patient education programs in physician offices with high physician and patient satisfaction and limited and fairly undocumented nutrition intake results (Morales & Cheung, 1980; Snowman & Dibble, 1979).

3.   A modification of the Higgins nutritional intervention used in the Montreal Diet Dispensary Study was successful in reducing the incidence of low birth weight and infant mortality for teenage mothers. Especially dramatic are the comparisons between the rates for mothers less than 15 years of age and mothers of average childbearing age. The success of this program depended on encouragement and social support through establishing a nonthreatening relationship, education of significant others in nutrition intake and enlistment of their social support, reliance on milk as a major source of protein, treatment of the women's dietary habits with respect, and understanding their emotional and cultural attachment to diet (Corbett & Burst, 1983).

Identification and Management of Early Labor Prevention of preterm labor has been attempted in several perinatal health education efforts. Papiernik and colleagues (1985) reported a 31% decrease in the incidence of premature births in France from 1971 through 1982 for 16,000 live births. This program uses a risk assessment scale, education of the pregnant woman to understand the clinical signs of early labor, aggressive case management by prenatal care providers, and use of early and long-term tocolysis. Papiernik et al. suggested that the reported success of this behavioral intervention is the result of its focus not only on affecting the women's diagnostic and reporting behavior but also on affecting the behavior of her obstetrical and immediate community. This study has been replicated in California by Creasy and is being tested in other places with March of Dimes funding. It is known that:

1. There are available some fairly good instruments to predict preterm labor that include consideration of both behavioral and medical risk factors (Gonik & Creasy, 1986).
2. It is possible to improve women's knowledge of these risk factors and the frequency with which they report this labor to their health care providers (Herron, Katz, & Creasy, 1982).
3. Use of ambulatory tocodynamometers to record prelabor uterine activity indicates that the frequency of preterm contractions is indeed significantly greater in women who develop early labor as compared with women who labor at term, thus indicating the possibility of detecting early labor (Katz, Newman, & Gill, 1986).
4. An important element of successful preterm birth prevention efforts is the education of obstetrical staff in the proper management of reported preterm labor symptoms (Herron et al., 1982).

Smoking Cessation A growing body of literature suggests that pregnancy is a strong motivator for women to stop smoking, both spontaneously and with assistance [see reviews by Wilner, Schoenbaum, Palmer, and Fountain (1983) and Barnes, Vulcano, & Greaves (1985)]. Several interventions with pregnant women have been evaluated. Randomized, prospective and controlled studies have shown that it is possible to reduce smoking significantly in pregnant women. Examples come from Sexton and colleagues (Sexton & Hebel, 1984; Sexton, Nowicki, & Andebel, 1986), Bailey (1981), and Windsor and colleagues (1985). Also:

1. The successful elements of these programs include one-on-one counseling, use of self-help guide materials, use of counseling and involvement of significant others and social support, and use of

group counseling primarily as reinforcement in addition to one-on-one counseling.

2. Reinforcement of cessation behavior is especially important to maintain the cessation behavior.

Sexton and Hebel (1984) reported a reduction in low birth weight in a randomized intervention for 935 pregnant smokers. Treatment group mothers significantly reduced their smoking by 8 months' gestational age and their infants' birth weight average was 92 g heavier than the nontreated control group. Hebel, Nowicki, and Sexton (1985) reported that the positive effect of the intervention on smoking cessation was greatest for women who experienced medical problems early in pregnancy. They also suggested that the beneficial effect on low birth weight was greater for women who had experienced previous fetal loss and who had shorter smoking histories.

Windsor and colleagues (1985) reported a 14% quit rate compared to a 27% quit rate reported by Sexton and Hebel (1984). The differences may be attributable to differences in the maternal and score characteristics of the women and in the intervention used. The Sexton-Hebel sample was better educated, and a larger percentage were in private care and had higher incomes. Windsor et al. used a self-help guide, and the limited contact with health educators, clinic personnel, and others was focused on providing support. The Sexton-Hebel intervention used extensive counseling, phone and mail contact, structured group contacts, and monetary rewards.

The results of the Windsor et al. and the Sexton and Hebel interventions (as described by Nowicki et al., 1984) raise some important unexplored methodological questions: Does a combined self-help guide/intense social support and contact model increase the effect of the intervention on smoking and on the low birth weight outcome? How durable are the effects of the smoking cessation intervention after delivery? Is the effect of the smoking intervention on low birth weight outcome enhanced for women participating in a comprehensive multifactor intervention?

Reduction of Alcohol and Drug Use Much of the literature on substance abuse examines different screening tests and medical questionnaires to assess the quantity and frequency of alcohol or other drug use. Very little has been written that describes specific intervention strategies for pregnant women. Three major interventions have been described:

1. Streissguth et al. (1982), using a community education program and the motivation of having a healthy baby, have been able to encourage more women to participate in outpatient counseling.

2. Dr. Henry Rosett of Boston City Hospital has integrated therapy for heavy drinkers into routine prenatal care at the hospital and found a reduction in alcohol consumption before the last trimester in 33 of 49 problem drinkers who participated in at least three counseling sessions (Rosett, Ouellette, Weiner, & Owens, 1978; Rosett, Weiner, & Edelin, 1983). In this case also, the desire to have a healthy baby was a strong motivating force. Supportive counseling was focused on reduction of alcohol consumption and potential benefit to the fetus. Referrals were made when women did not respond within the first 2 weeks. Examinations of two cohorts of newborns previously demonstrated benefits to offspring when drinking ceased before the third trimester.

3. Larson (1983), in Sweden, has devised an assessment scale for identifying and classifying alcohol users. Heavy users were provided with various kinds of support—more frequent visits to the clinic and access to counseling by a social worker or psychiatrist to improve domestic or interpersonal situations. The majority of women reduced their drinking or stopped drinking after receiving information about alcohol's effects on the fetus. It is not clear how this was measured. Other literature on alcohol abuse summarizes theoretical perspectives or treatment considerations (see Bry, 1984; Finney & Moos, 1984; Nichols, 1985).

As in the case of alcohol, the literature on drug abuse interventions is sparse. Some papers present global therapeutic recommendations (Davis, 1978; Einstein, 1985; Finnegan, 1979; Lawson & Wilson, 1979; Nichols, 1985). Some of the literature describes the less acute effects on the drug-abusing mother's offspring of methadone maintenance (A.W. Brown, 1979; Stimmel & Adamsons, 1976). These methadone studies may be irrelevant because they do not address the issue of behavioral change directly.

One tool that may be indirectly useful for studying the effects of drug abuse interventions on behavior during pregnancy is reported by Chappel, Veach, and Krug (1985). Chappel and colleagues have developed a substance abuse attitude survey for use by physicians and other professionals working with substance-abusing pregnant women or other groups. This could be useful in determining what aspects of an intervention have a specific effect on outcomes since the attitudes of the professionals offering the helping intervention may be tempered by their attitudes toward substance abuse.

Psychosocial Stress Interventions Although there is some evidence to indicate that stress and resulting anxiety may be implicated in poor pregnancy outcome, there are almost no available studies that review stress reduction interventions with pregnant women. Nuckolls,

Cassel, and Kaplan (1972) reported that the use of social support to reduce psychosocial stress during pregnancy resulted in decreases in pregnancy complications, although it is not clear how this was determined.

Papiernick et al. (1985) in France and Jeffrey, Bowes, and Delaney in a 1974 paper discussed the benefit of physical stress reduction through problem-solving counseling, social support, and education. This major study, which has explored the efficacy of social support as a low birth weight intervention, has several methodological limitations. There have been no careful randomized clinical trials examining the effects of high levels of programmatic or intervention-arranged social support as compared with no such services. In addition, the level of social support available to individual women before pregnancy and during pregnancy has not been assessed in any quantifiable manner. This makes it difficult to isolate any specific effects associated with social support in current work. Several such projects are currently in progress including the Better Babies Project (Washington, DC), the Healthy Baby Program (Boston), the Maternity and Infant Outreach Project (Hartford, CT), and work done by Anne Oakley in England.

Multifactor Interventions

Few multifactor interventions aimed at reducing low birth weight have been attempted. Olds, Henderson, Tatelbaum, and Chamberlin (1986) reported that infants born to young adolescents in their treatment group were on an average almost 400 g heavier and that treatment group smokers showed a 75% reduction in the incidence of preterm delivery in a randomized trial of nurse home visitation. While indicating treatment effects, this study does not focus on reduction of the incidence of low birth weight in the population.

Olds et al.'s (1986) nurse visitation intervention included a focus on prenatal education and reduction of risks associated with low birth weight, enhancement of social support, and linkage to existing social and health services. They compared low birth weight outcomes for a no-treatment control group to outcomes for women exposed to one of three different interventions: transportation assistance for regular prenatal care and well-baby visits: prenatal home visiting, and prenatal and continued visits until the child was 2 years of age. Overall treatment effects were not reported. This study is the first to suggest that a comprehensive prenatal services model can improve birth weight outcome for a sample of women most of whom were from semi-skilled and unskilled occupational classifications.

Another notable project has focused on the reduction of infant mortality rather than low birth weight. The Rural Infant Care Program, initiated in 1979, was designed to improve perinatal care services in 10 rural sites with a history of high infant mortality rates. Gortmaker and his colleagues (Gortmaker, Clark, Graven, Sobol, & Geronimus, 1985; Gortmaker, Sobol, Clark, Walker, & Geronimus, 1985) reported that significant declines in neonatal mortality were found following the intervention. The intervention, which varied considerably across sites, primarily improved clinic care, including access to prenatal care and increased monitoring of high-risk pregnancies. It is difficult to determine exactly what treatment characteristics were common across all sites and which treatment characteristics were unique to each site. Thus it is difficult to determine which treatment characteristics contributed to the effects found when the 10 sites were compared to three comparison sites. Results of an interrupted time-series regression model analysis, using vital records data and adjusting for preintervention linear trends in mortality rates, indicate that treatment effects were pronounced and effective in reducing mortality for black infants.

KEY METHODOLOGICAL ISSUES
IN LOW BIRTH WEIGHT INTERVENTIONS

Several methodological issues arise from an evaluation of existing low birth weight interventions. Some of these factors are related to several of the single-factor approaches and include the consideration of generalizability or validity, quantification of the treatment, psychometric measurement of other independent variables, and selection of a research design. Another important consideration is understanding the importance of critical periods and the timing of intervention approaches. Finally, the influence of demographic characteristics, previously associated with low birth weight, must be considered.

"Internal" and "External" Validity
in Applied Social Science Evaluation

A critical issue in the evaluation of the quality of intervention research has been the feasibility and strength of an experimental versus a quasi-experimental design. The difficulties associated with treatment and comparison group equivalence, isolation and control of the experimental situation, and random assignment to treatment effects and comparison groups have been discussed. Campbell (1986; personal communication, 1986) has suggested that this distinction is not useful for evaluating the quality of most research questions in the applied social sciences. He refers particularly to the assessment of the scientific merit of intervention designs.

Campbell suggested that in examining programmatic effects a different conceptualization of validity might apply. He labels this type of validity "*local molar casual validity*" and argues that the crucial issue is to answer the question: "Did this complex treatment package make a real difference in this unique application at this particular place and time?" His molar characterization indicates a recognition that the treatment is often a complex combination of expert clinical judgment and other types of service delivery behaviors. *Molar* also connotes an interest in evaluating the complex treatment first rather than trying to detect the effects of its components. This conceptualization assumes that we have some epidemiological evidence that certain treatments are worth testing as a molar package. If this package shows an effect then it may be worth examining the package further to determine which components are responsible for which effects.

Campbell suggests that the local delineation connotes the special importance of understanding if a treatment is effective in a given setting. Because a treatment must often be tailored to fit the special circumstances of a community or local setting, it is essential to determine if it works in that setting first before exploring the boundaries of effects in other settings and with specialized populations. This is not to suggest that generalization is not possible. This exaggerated conclusion is an important reminder that very frequently in the physical sciences, as Campbell describes, dependable but misunderstood causal models are the basis for new and productive theorizing. Several single-factor interventions have reported trends toward reduced low birth weight incidence but have not yet examined the overall effect of an intervention that combines in one comprehensive treatment all of the successful intervention components. In the Better Babies Project intervention, for example, it is not possible either practically or morally to isolate the component interventions. The impossibility of disentangling the singular effects of each intervention component does not eliminate the necessity of testing its overall effect.

Quantifying Treatment Effects

It is extremely difficult to isolate and quantify treatment interventions. In the written descriptions of the low birth weight interventions described in the sections above it is often difficult to ascertain precisely what the intervention consists of, and in almost every case there is little quantification of the intervention. Some reports indicate an average amount of time spent with each woman on a given task or on the intervention as a whole, but no individual quantity of treatment measures is reported or examined in final analyses. This makes it difficult to isolate component treatment effects or to examine the cost-benefit ratio of various exposures to treatment.

Psychometric Measurement of Other Independent Variables

Most low birth weight interventions use an outcome measure that is assumed to be extremely reliable and have high validity because it is easily quantifiable and is collected in a relatively uniform way. Measures of maternal characteristics, social support, low birth weight risk, level of participation in the intervention, and attitudes toward pregnancy are not used consistently across interventions nor are the validity and reliability of these measures reported. Because of the unique nature of most interventions attempted, however, it is difficult to argue for uniformity in measurement of the intervention or other independent variables. This will remain a problem in interpreting results until some studies can be replicated and/or measures of these variables developed adequately.

Selecting a Research Design

The ideal test of an intervention is a clinical trial. Some health scientists would consider the "true" experimental design using randomization or an A-versus-B intervention design to be the design of choice (Campbell & Stanley, 1966). However, it is not always possible to isolate and control the experimental condition in situations involving human participants and most especially in situations involving major community or public health problems. The negative political consequences of denying a treatment with any degree of benefit, regardless of how speculative, are great and potentially could destroy the usefulness of any randomized trial because of contamination and the difficulty of gaining the cooperation of community leaders in supporting such an activity, which they perceive as discriminatory (Lilienfeld & Lilienfeld, 1980). An alternative approach is to employ a comprehensive services model that incorporates aggressive outreach, home visiting, and drop-in center services with a multiple risk factor linkage and direct services approach. It is important to determine if this approach is effective before attempting to explore the benefit of various other approaches to the problem or isolating various components of the intervention (D.T. Campbell, personal communication, 1986).

We have employed the comprehensive services model in the design of the Better Babies Project. A unique aspect of this intervention is that it is free standing and community based. A randomized clinical trial would offer a powerful analytical test of the effectiveness of this intervention. However, such a trial was not possible, given the need to explore the intervention in a community setting. Early in the development of the project it was determined that it would be impossible to offer what would be perceived as valuable, free, and beneficial services to some women and not others with no rationale offered other than the abstractions of scientific method.

If randomization is not possible a suitable substitute design may be an interrupted time series with a nonequivalent no-treatment control group time series (Cook & Campbell, 1979). Others have referred to this design as a nonequivalent comparison group design with multiple data points. The multiple data point characteristic of this time series design makes it a considerably stronger test than a simple pre-posttest intervention design. In the Better Babies Project study low birth weight incidence data for 10 years prior to the initiation of the intervention will be examined and compared before and during the intervention.

This particular design can also be characterized as a "human community trial" in the sense that a community is being saturated with information about a particular intervention and sensitized to the importance of prenatal care and of doing other things to reduce the incidence of low birth weight. Lilienfeld and Lilienfeld (1980) described this design as necessary when a "particular circumstance requires that a community as a whole serve as the experimental unit with regard to testing a specific etiological hypothesis or preventive procedure." These authors suggested that this necessity does not usually allow the use of randomization.

Critical Periods

A comprehensive intervention model should consider the timing of maternal behavior and the occurrence in the child's lifespan of the morbidity outcome of concern. In other words, it is important to know whether a behavioral risk factor has a critical influence on outcomes relative to the stage—pregnancy, prenatal, or postnatal–in which it occurs. Thus in designing an intervention it is important to focus the intervention on the particular pregnancy period that is important for the outcome of interest.

The importance of considering the timing of maternal behavior in explaining risk factors and in exploring how interventions can be designed to influence maternal behavior is illustrated by work done in the area of nutrition behavior. Some studies have shown that the pregnant mother's maternal grandparents' socioeconomic status is the best predictor of pregnancy outcome. Social class status of the maternal grandparent can be indicative of nutritional resources, behavior, and the prepregnancy pubertal development status of the woman's reproductive system. This behavior as linked to socioeconomic status, as well as the mother's behavior immediately prior to and during pregnancy and her postnatal behavior, may all have different effects on child outcomes.

It is also important that an intervention or risk assessment model identify whether the morbidity outcomes are short term or long term. Low birth weight and infant mortality rates are examples of short-term outcomes, whereas childhood developmental status (e.g., intellectual functioning) is an example of a long-term morbidity outcome.

A review of maternal risk indices developed to identify risk factors during pregnancy has recently been completed by a multidisciplinary team of researchers collaborating in the Infant Health and Development Project. It indicates that most pregnancy risk indices are focused on short-term and not long-term outcomes (Benasich, Brooks-Gunn, & McCormick, 1986). A study by Littman and Parmelee (1978) represents an example of risk scales with a long-term morbidity focus.

Demographic Risks Associated with Low Birth Weight

The nutrition example cited above illustrates the importance of timing in examining maternal behavior modification and is illustrative of the importance of demographic characteristics or history in examining maternal behavior intervention approaches. Several broad demographic characteristics have been associated with childhood morbidity. Much of what is known about maternal risk factors in pregnancy, from the Collaborative Perinatal Project of the National Institute of Neurological and Communicative Disorders and Stroke and other sources, indicates that several broad maternal demographic characteristics are clearly associated with poor pregnancy outcomes. These characteristics include:

1. *Race* A 2:1 black-to-white ratio of low birth weight infants is a confirmed finding. What is not confirmed are the reasons for this increased risk (IOM, 1985).

2. *Age* Being an adolescent is not an independent risk factor for having a low birth weight infant. However, the rate of births of such infants to both blacks and whites is highest under age 20 and again after age 35. Adolescents under the age of 15 who are having a second or subsequent birth have a 30% chance of producing a low birth weight infant. Black women are more likely than white women to be teenagers when they have their children. In Washington, DC, for example, more than 37% of all black births in 1984 were to teenagers as compared to 7% of white births. When age is held constant, however, blacks are still at greater risk of having low birth weight

infants than whites at any age. The interaction of age, low socioeconomic status, late prenatal care, and poor nutritional status affects the likelihood of having a low birth weigh infant (Horon, Strobino, & MacDonald, 1983).

3. *Education* For both races, women with less than 12 years of education have higher rates of low birth weight pregnancies. Black women are more likely to be less educated than white women, with 35% of black women delivering live births not having completed high school as compared to 20% of whites (Kessell & Kleinman, 1984). Still, educational differences do not account for the racial differences after matching for age and education.

4. *Socioeconomic status* The literature on the association of socioeconomic status to low birth weight is limited because of the variety of measurements used to define socioeconomic status: income, education, occupation, residence, social class, and marital status, to mention a few. Studies have consistently shown, however, that women of lower socioeconomic status have a greater risk of delivering a low birth weight infant (Berkowitz, 1981). In Gortmaker's (1979) study of poverty and infant mortality, poverty was associated with a relative risk of infant mortality that was 1.5 times greater than that of infants of nonpoor mothers, independent of several maternal and familial characteristics and birth weight. Gortmaker concluded that "increasing access to health services and increased help to families through income supports and employment programs are indicated as possible policy actions to reduce these differentials" (p. 280).

5. *Marital status* Using 1980 data, the low birth weight infant rate for unmarried women was twice as high as it was for married women (National Center for Health Statistics, 1980). Although this risk varies by age and race, it is a critical issue since the rate of birth to unmarried adolescents and women has increased in the last decade.

Research on demographic risk factors is limited since most risk factors are examined as independent contributors to birth outcome, rather than as they interact (e.g., age and race, or race and socioeconomic status). Several conceptual and methodological limitations in demographic factor risk research have been described by Showstack et al. (1984). In reviewing these studies and considering how their results can be incorporated into intervention research it is important to bear in mind that the demographic characteristics themselves are not useful for designing interventions beyond identifying populations or samples on which to base an intervention. Even when controlling for age, residency, and use of prenatal care, Geronimus (1985) found in a population-based study of over 300,000 births that racial disparities in low birth weight incidence exist. These results indicate that something other than simple demographics is operating. These demographic characteristics may represent, in some cases, physiological processes or intergenerational effects.

In order to fully understand how these data can be useful to an intervention approach one must consider what behaviors, social experiences, or psychological processes these broad demographic characteristics may represent. These processes may represent an individual's life-style. Life-style may be a developing concept of risk in health prevention efforts.

DIRECTIONS FOR FUTURE RESEARCH

Several issues and questions need further exploration if efforts to modify maternal behavior in the interest of achieving positive pregnancy outcomes are to be attempted. Prenatal care seems to be important for positive outcomes, yet women who are most at risk for negative outcomes do not take advantage of prenatal care systems and providers. It is not yet fully understood what barriers operate to demotivate women from seeking prenatal care.

Although some of these barriers have been identified, incentives to seek care sufficiently powerful to overcome the negative effects of the barriers have not, nor is it understood which outreach techniques are most successful with which kinds of women to recruit women into care. Further studies are needed in order to understand women's perceptions of the usefulness and quality of prenatal care. This information could be useful in applying behavioral incentives designed to influence care-seeking behavior.

There is very little information on the knowledge, beliefs, and attitudes toward pregnancy of high-risk women in this country. These attitudes are powerful mediators of behavior and as such need to be understood. If interventions are to be successful, they should not work in unwitting conflict with attitudes and beliefs but in concordance with them and at times in spite of them. They must be understood for this to be possible.

Women's ability to improve their own health care through self-monitoring of such things as nutritional intake, health behavior, and clinical symptoms should be explored. M. Poland (personal communication, 1986) has found in Detroit that women who discovered later in their pregnancies that they were pregnant were less likely to enroll in care and had poorer pregnancy outcomes. Self-monitoring could offer a meaningful and necessary precursor to positive health behavior. If in fact women differ in their ability to monitor their own bodies this could provide an intervention opportunity.

Less traditional forms of health education delivery must be fully explored. In the 1950s and 1960s literature on home visitor programs using both professionals and paraprofessionals indicated moderate success with home visiting as a way of influencing maternal behavior. However, this approach fell into disuse as a result of financial constraints and a rise in professionalism in the field of social work. The use of the home visit and of paraprofessionals to influence maternal behaviors most clearly associated with birth and childhood risks should be explored for groups of women who persistently remain outside the traditional prenatal care provider settings.

There are virtually no extensive, multisite, high-risk population–based interventions in place for substance-abusing pregnant women. Since the etiology of these health behavior problems is probably wide ranging and extensive, an intervention that is not comprehensive and multidisciplinary will probably not be successful.

In general, the problems with most maternal behavior interventions is that they do not address the problem of pregnancy risk in a comprehensive fashion. Only a very limited number of interventions could be characterized as using a more comprehensive approach than the single risk factor focus described in most of the interventions reviewed. The Rural Infant Care Project supported by the Robert Wood Johnson Foundation and described by Gortmaker offers an unusual example of a multisite project with an intervention designed to focus on a wide range of perinatal needs.

SUMMARY

This chapter has presented a review of what is known about reducing the behavioral risks associated with low birth weight and its morbidity consequences. Most of this research is based on interventions conducted with pregnant women. Although considerable evidence is available to establish which risk behaviors are associated with poor pregnancy outcomes, there is considerably less evidence about how to influence these behaviors so as to change these negative outcomes to positive ones for pregnant women.

Most of the intervention work that has been conducted has focused on single-factor approaches, and few multifactor or comprehensive services interventions have been conducted. The single-factor intervention approaches, such as smoking cessation, increasing the use of prenatal care, and reducing the use of alcohol and other drugs, have been largely effective despite some methodological shortcomings and the fact that few intervention studies have been replicated or conducted with large samples of women.

Several methodological considerations, if explored fully, would considerably enhance the potential of research intervention efforts to document their effectiveness in reducing behavioral risks during pregnancy. These have been reviewed and include selection of an appropriate research design, a focus on molar rather than single-factor validity, development of psychometrically appropriate measures of the intervention and independent variables, and consideration of critical periods during the prepregnancy, pregnancy, and postpregnancy periods.

Future intervention efforts need to explore how to encourage women to enter prenatal care early and to maintain this care. This care should focus on educating women about how to detect and manage early labor. These efforts should also focus on the moderating effects on maternal health behavior of such maternal psychological characteristics as self-monitoring, beliefs, attitudes, management of stress, and modification of smoking, drug use, and poor nutritional intake behavior. On the whole it appears that interventions that provide for a comprehensive consideration of these factors will be more successful in reducing the morbidity outcomes associated with maternal health risk behavior.

REFERENCES

Anderson, G.D. (1979). Nutrition in pregnancy—1978. *Southern Medical Journal, 72*, 1304–1314.

Bailey, W. (1981). Malnutrition among babies born to adolescent mothers. *West Indies Medical Journal, 30*, 72–76.

Barnes, G.E., Vulcano, B.A., & Greaves, B.A. (1985). Characteristics affecting successful outcome in the cessation of smoking. *The International Journal of the Addictions, 20*, 1429–1434.

Barnett, B., & Parker, G. (1986). Possible determinants, correlates and consequences of high levels of anxiety in primiparious mothers. *Psychological Medicine, 16*, 177–185.

Benasich, A.A., Brooks-Gunn, J., & McCormick, M. (1986). Summary scales: obstetric and neonatal status. Unpublished manuscript, Princeton, NJ.

Berkowitz, G.S. (1981). An epidemiological study of preterm delivery. *American Journal of Epidemiology, 113*, 81–92.

Boone, M.S. (1985). Social and cultural factors in the etiology of low birth-weight among disadvantaged blacks. *Science of Medicine, 20*, 1001–1011.

Brent, R.L., & Harris, M.I. (Eds.). (1976). *Prevention of embryonic, fetal, and perinatal disease* (Vol. 3). Washington, DC: U.S. Government Printing Office.

Brown, A.W. (Ed.). (1979). *Psychological care during pregnancy and the postpartum period*. New York: Raven Press.

Brown, M.A. (1986). Social support, stress, and health: A comparison of expectant mothers and fathers. *Nursing Research, 35*, 72–76.

Bry, B.H. (1984). Substance abuse in women. *Issues in Mental Health Nursing, 5*, 253–272.

Calandra, C., Abell, D.C., & Beischer, N.A. (1981). Maternal obesity in pregnancy. *Obstetrics and Gynecology, 57*, 8–12.

Campbell, D.T. (1986). Relabeling "internal" and "external" validity for applied social scientists. In M.K. Trochim (Ed.), *Advances in quasi-experimental design and analysis (New Directions in Program Evaluation*, Vol. 31, pp. 67–77). San Francisco: Jossey-Bass.

Campbell, D.T., & Stanley, J. (1966). *Experimental and quasi-experimental designs for research*. Chicago: Rand McNally.

Chambers, C.D., & Hunt, L.G. (1977). Drug use patterns in pregnant women. In J.L. Rementeria (Ed.), *Drug abuse in pregnancy and neonatal effects* (pp. 73–81). St. Louis: Mosby.

Chappel, J.N., Veach, T.L., & Krug, R.S. (1985). The substance abuse attitudes. *Journal of the Study of Alcoholism, 46*, 48–52.

Cook, T.D., & Campbell, D.T. (1979). *Quasi-experimentation: Design & analysis issues for field settings*. Chicago: Rand McNally.

Corbett, M., & Burst, H.V. (1983). Nutritional intervention in pregnancy. *Journal of Nurse-Midwifery, 28*, 23–29.

Crandon, A.J. (1979). Maternal anxiety and obstetric complications. *Journal of Psychosomatic Research, 23*, 109–111.

Davis, R.C. (1978). Psychosocial care of the pregnant narcotic addict. *The Journal of Reproductive Medicine, 20*, 316–322.

Einstein, S. (1985). Drug use intervention with and for special populations. *The International Journal of the Addictions, 20*, 1–12.

Falkner, F. (Ed.). (1969). *Key issues in infant mortality*. Washington, DC: U.S. Government Printing Office

Falkner, F. (Vol. Ed.). (1984). *Prevention of perinatal mortality and morbidity* (Vols. 3 and 4). Basel: S. Karger.

Feldman, P.H., & Mosher, B.A. (1984). *Preserving essential services: Effects of the MCH Block Grant on five inner city Boston neighborhood health centers. Executive Summary*. Boston: Harvard School of Public Health.

Finnegan, L.P. (1976). Clinical effects of pharmacologic agents on pregnancy, the fetus and the neonate. *Annals of the New York Academy of Sciences, 281*, 74–89.

Finnegan, L.P. (Ed.). (1978). *Drug dependency in pregnancy: Clinical management of mother and child*. Services Research Monograph Series. Rockville, MD: National Institute on Drug Abuse.

Finnegan, L.P. (1979). Women in treatment. In R.L. DuPont, A. Goldstein, & J. O'Donnell (Eds.), *Handbook on drug abuse*, National Institute on Drug Abuse (pp. 121–131). Washington, DC: U.S. Government Printing Office.

Finney, J.W., & Moos, R.H. (1984). Environmental assessment and evaluation research: Examples from mental health and substance abuse programs. *Evaluation and Program Planning, 7*, 151–167.

Fisher, E.S., LoGerfo, J.P., & Daling, J.R. (1985). Prenatal care and pregnancy outcomes during the recession: The Washington State experience. *American Journal of Public Health, 75*, 866–869.

Fitzhardinge, P.M., & Steven, E.M. (1972). The small-for-date infant. II. Neurologic and intellectual sequelae. *Pediatrics, 50*, 50–57.

Fried, P.A., Innes, K.S., & Barnes, G.E. (1984). Soft drug use prior to and during pregnancy: A comparison of samples over a four-year period. *Drug and Alcohol Dependence, 13*, 161–176.

Fried, P.A., Watkinson, B., Grant, A., & Knights, R.M. (1980). Changing patterns of soft drug use prior to and during pregnancy. *Drug and Alcohol Dependency, 6* 323.

Fried, P.A., Watkinson, B., & Willan, A. (1984). Marijuana use during pregnancy and decreased length of gestation. *American Journal of Obstetrics and Gynecology, 150,* 23–27.

Geronimus, A.T. (1985). *The effects of race, residence, and prenatal care on the relationship of maternal age to neonatal mortality.* Cambridge, MA: Harvard University Center for Population Studies.

Gonik, B., & Creasy, R.K. (1986). Preterm labor: Its diagnosis and management. *American Journal of Obstetrics and Gynecology, 154,* 3–8.

Gorsuch, R.L., & Key, M.A. (1970). *Abnormalities of pregnancy as a function of anxiety and life stress.* Nashville, TN: John F. Kennedy Center for Research on Education and Human Development. George Peabody College for Teachers.

Gortmaker, S.L. (1979). Poverty and infant mortality in the United States. *American Sociological Review, 44,* 280–297.

Gortmaker, S.L., Clark, C.J.G., Graven, S.N., Sobol, A.M., & Geronimus, A. (1985). *Reducing infant mortality in rural America: Evaluation of the Rural Infant Care Program.* Unpublished manuscript, Harvard School of Public Health.

Gortmaker, S., Sobol, A., Clark, C., Walker, D.K., & Geronimus, A.B. (1985). *Survival of very low-birth-weight infants by level of hospital birth: A population study of perinatal systems in four states.* Unpublished manuscript, Harvard School of Public Health.

Graves, C., Malen, H., & Placek, P. (April, 1983). *The effect of maternal alcohol and cigarette use on infant birthweight.* Unpublished manuscript. Available from P. Placek, National Center for Health Statistics, Hyattsville, MD.

Gregory, M. (1984, December). *Final evaluation of the obstetrical Access Pilot Project: July 1979–June 1982.* Final report submitted to Health Care Financing Administration.

Hack, M., Caron, B., Rivers, A., & Fanaroff, A.A. (1983). The very low birth-weight infant: The broader spectrum of morbidity during infancy and early childhood. *Journal of Behavioral and Developmental Pediatrics, 4,* 243–249.

Hardy, J.B., Drage, J.S., & Jackson, E.C. (Eds.). (1979). *The first year of life. The collaborative Perinatal Project of the National Institute of Neurological and Communicative Disorders and Stroke.* Baltimore: Johns Hopkins University Press.

Harris, J.E. (1982). Prenatal medical care and infant mortality. In V.R. Fuchs (Ed.), (pp. 15–52). *Economic Aspects of Health.* Chicago: University of Chicago Press.

Hebel, J.R., Nowicki, P., & Sexton M. (1985). The effect of antismoking intervention during pregnancy: An assessment of interactions with maternal characteristics. *American Journal of Epidemiology, 122,* 135–148.

Herron, M.A., Katz, M., & Creasy, R.K. (1982). Evaluation of a preterm birth prevention program: Preliminary report. *Obstetrics and Gynecology, 59,* 452–456.

Higgins, A. (1976). Nutritional status and the outcome of pregnancy. *The Journal of the Canadian Dietetic Association,* 17–35.

Hingson, R., Alpert, J.J., Day, N., Dooling, E., Kayne, H., Morelock, S., Oppenheimer, E., & Zuckerman, B. (1982). Effects of maternal drinking and marijuana use on fetal growth and development. *Pediatrics, 70,* 539.

Horon, I.L., Strobino, D.M., & MacDonald, H.M. (1983). Birthweights among infants born to adolescent and young adult women. *American Journal of Obstetrics and Gynecology, 146*, 444–449.

Institute of Medicine. (1985). *Preventing low birth weight.* Washington, DC: National Academy of Sciences Press.

Jacobson, D.E. (1986). Types and timing of social support. *Journal of Health and Social Behavior, 27*, 250–264.

Jacobson, H.N. (1981). Nutritional risks of pregnancy during adolescence. In E.R. McAnarney & G. Stickle (Eds.), Pregnancy and childbearing during adolescence. Research priorities for the 1980s. *Birth Defects: Original Article Series, 17*(3), 69–83.

Jeffrey, R.L., Bowes, W.A., Jr., & Delaney, J.J. (1974). Role of bed rest in twin gestation. *Obstetrics and Gynecology, 43*, 822–826.

Juarez & Associates, Inc. (1982). Reaching Mexican-American and black women with health information. Report in Contract No. 282-81-0082, DHS, DHHS. Washington, DC: Author.

Kandall, S.R., Albin, S., Gartner, L.M., Lee, K.S., Eidelman, R., & Lowinson, J. (1977). The narcotic-dependent mother: Fetal and neonatal consequences. *Early Human Development, 1*(2), 159–169.

Katz, M., Newman, R.B., & Gill, P.J. (1986). Assessment of uterine activity in ambulatory patients at high risk of preterm labor and delivery. *American Journal of Epidemiology, 121*, 843–855.

Kent, J., & Smith, C. (1967). Involving the urban poor in health services through accommodation—the employment of neighborhood representatives. *American Journal of Public Health, 57*, 997–1003.

Kessell, S.S., & Kleinman, J. (1984). *Preliminary data from the 1980 National Natality and Fetal Mortality Follow-back Survey.* Washington, DC: National Center for Health Statistics.

Kessner, D.M. (Ed.). (1973). *Contrasts in health status, Vol. I.* Washington, DC: National Academy of Sciences.

Kinsley, C., & Svare, B. (1986). Prenatal stress effects: Are they mediated by reductions in maternal food and water intake and body weight gain? *Physiology and Behavior, 37*, 191–193.

Korenbrot, C.C. (1984). Risk reduction in pregnancies of low-income women: Comprehensive prenatal care through the OB Access Project. *Mobius, 4*, 34–43.

Kotelchuck, M., Schwartz, J.B., AnDerka, M.T., & Finison, K.S. (1984). WIC participation and pregnancy outcomes: Massachusetts Statewide Evaluation Project. *American Journal of Public Health, 74*, 1086–1092.

Larson, G. (1983). Prevention of fetal alcohol effects. *Acta Obstretricia et Gynecologica of Scandinavica, 62*, 171–178.

Laukaran, V.H., & van den Berg, B.J. (1980). The relationship of maternal attitude to pregnancy outcomes and obstetric complications. *American Journal of Obstetrics and Gynecology, 136*, 374–379.

Lawson, M.S., & Wilson, G.S. (1979). Addiction and pregnancy: Two lives in crisis. *Social Work in Health Care, 4*(4), 445–457.

Lehrman, E. (1981). Nurse-midwifery practice: A descriptive study of prenatal care. *Journal of Nurse-Midwifery, 26*, 27–41.

Leppert, P.C., Namerow, P.B., & Barker, D. (1986). *Pregnancy outcomes among adolescent and older women receiving comprehensive prenatal care* (Society for Adolescent Medicine). New York: Elsevier.

Leveno, K.J., Cunninghan, F.G., Roark, M.L., Nelson, S.D., & Williams, M.L. (1985). Prenatal care and the low birth weight infant. *Journal of the American College of Obstetricians and Gynecologists, 66,* 599–605.

Levenson, P.M., Smith, P.B., & Morrow, J.R. (1986). A comparison of physician-patient views of teen prenatal information needs. *Journal of Adolescent Health Care, 7,* 6–11.

Lilienfeld, A., & Lilienfeld, D.C. (1980). *Foundations of Epidemiology* (2nd ed.). New York: Oxford University Press.

Littman, B., & Parmelee, A.H., Jr. (1978). Medical correlates of infant development. *Pediatrics, 61,* 470–474.

Lucey, J.F., & Dangman, B. (1984). A re-examination of the role of oxygen in retrolental fibroplasia. *Pediatrics, 73,* 82–96.

Mamelle, N., Lauman, B., & Lazar, P. (1984). Prematurity and occupational activity during pregnancy. *American Journal of Epidemiology, 119,* 309–322.

McCormick, M.C. (1985). The contribution of low birthweight to infant mortality and childhood morbidity. *New England Journal of Medicine, 312,* 82–90.

McCormick, M.C., Shapiro, S., & Starfield, B.H. (1981). Injury and its correlates among 1-year-old children: Study of children with both normal and low birth weights. *American Journal of Diseases of Childhood, 135,* 159–163.

McDonald, R.L. (1968). The role of emotional factors in obstetric complications: A review. *Psychosomatic Medicine, 30,* 222–237.

McManus, M. (1985). Evaluation of interventions to reduce racial disparities in infant mortality. Report to the DHHS Infant Mortality Task Force. Washington, DC: Author.

Metcoff, J., Costiloe, P., Crosby, W.M., Dutta, S., Sandstead, H.H., Milne, D., Bodwell, C.E., & Majors, S.H. (1985). Effect of food supplementation (WIC) during pregnancy on birth weight. *American Journal of Clinical Nutrition, 41,* 933–947.

Miller, H.C., Hassanein, J., & Hensleigh, P.A. (1981). Maternal factors in the incidences of low birth weight infants among black and white mothers. *European Journal of Obstetrics, Gynecology and Reproductive Biology, 2,* 157–166.

Mills, J.L., Graubard, B.I., Harley, E.E., Rhoads, G.G., & Berendes, H.W. (1984). Maternal alcohol consumption and birthweight: How much drinking during pregnancy is safe? *Journal of the American Medical Association, 252,* 1875–1879.

Moore, R.R., Origel, W., Key, T.C., & Resnik, R. (1986). The perinatal and economic impact of prenatal care in a low-socioeconomic population. *American Journal of Obstetrics and Gynecology, 154,* 29–33.

Morales, R., Jr., & Cheung, S.S. (1980). A prenatal nutrition project using dietetic students in physicians' offices. *Journal of the American Dietetic Association, 76,* 593–595.

National Center for Health Statistics. (1980). *National Center for Health Statistics: Vital Statistics of the United States, 1979. Volume 1: Natality.* U.S. Public Health Service. Washington, DC: U.S. Government Printing Office.

National Center for Health Statistics. (1985, September 26). *Annual summary of births, marriages, divorces, and deaths, United States 1984.* Monthly Vital Statistics Report, Vol 33, No. 13. DHHS Pub. No. (PHS)85-1120. Hyattsville, MD: U.S. Public Health Service.

Nichols, M. (1985). Theoretical concerns in the clinical treatment of substance-abusing women: a feminist analysis. *Alcoholism Treatment Quarterly, 2,* 79–90.

Niswander, K.R., & Gordon, M. (Eds.). (1972). *The Collaborative Perinatal Study of the National Institute of Neurological Diseases and Stroke. The women and their pregnancies.* Philadelphia: W.B. Saunders Company.

Norbeck, J.S., & Tilden, V.P. (1983). Life stress, social support and emotional disequilibrium in complications of pregnancy: A prospective study. *Journal of Health and Social Behavior, 24,* 30.

Nowicki, B.A., Gintzid, M.A., Hebel, J.R., Latham, R., Miller, V., & Sexton, M. (1984). Effective smoking intervention during pregnancy. *Birth, 11,* 217–224.

Nuckolls, K.B., Cassel, J.C., & Kaplan, B.H. (1972). Psychosocial assets, life crisis and prognosis of pregnancy. *American Journal of Epidemiology, 95,* 431–441.

Office of Technology Assessment, U.S. Congress. (1981). *The Implications of Cost-Effectiveness Analysis of Medical Technology. Background Paper No. 2: Case Studies of Medical Technologies Case Study No. 10: The costs of effectiveness of neonatal intensive care* (Prepared by P. Budetti, M.A. McManus, N. Barrand, and L.A. Heinen). (GPO Stock No. 052-003-00845-9.) Washington, DC: U.S. Government Printing Office.

Olds, D.C., Henderson, C.R., Jr., Tatelbaum, R., & Chamberlin, R. (1986). Improving the delivery of prenatal care and outcomes of pregnancy: A randomized trial of nurse home visitation. *Pediatrics, 77,* 16–28.

Oster, G., Delea, T.E., & Golditz, G.A. (1986). The effects of cigarette smoking during pregnancy on the incidence of low birth weight and the costs of neonatal care. *Smoking Behavior and Policy: Discussion Paper Series.* Boston: Harvard University, Institute for the Study of Smoking Behavior and Policy, Kennedy School of Government.

Ouellette, E.M., Rosett, H.L., Rosman, N.P., & Weiner, L. (1977). Adverse effects on offspring of maternal alcohol abuse during pregnancy. *New England Journal of Medicine, 297,* 528–530.

Ounsted, M., & Scott, A. (1982). Smoking during pregnancy: Its association with other maternal factors and birthweight. *Acta Obstetrica Gynecologica Scandinavica, 61,* 367–371.

Papiernik, E., Bouyer, J., Dreyfuss, J., Collin, D., Winisdorffer, G., Guegen, S., Lecomte, M., & Lazar, P. (1985). Prevention of preterm births: A perinatal study in Haguennau, France. *Pediatrics, 76,* 2.

Papiernik, E., & Kaminski, M.H. (1974). Multifactorial study of the risk of prematurity at 32 weeks gestation. I. A study of the frequency of predictive characteristics. *Journal of Perinatal Medicine, 2,* 30–36.

Papoz, L., Eschwege, E., Pequignot, G., Barrat, J., & Schwartz D. (1982). Maternal smoking and birth weight in relation to dietary habits. *American Journal of Obstetrics and Gynecology, 142,* 870–876.

Peoples, M.D., & Siegel, E. (1983). Measuring the impact of programs for mothers and infants on prenatal care and low birthweight: The value of refined analyses. *Medical Care, 21,* 586–605.

Perlin, M.J., & Simon, K.J. (1978). The etiology, prevalence and effects of drug use during pregnancy. *Contemporary Drug Problems, 7,* 313–325.

Picone, T.A., Allen, L.H., Olsen, P.N., & Ferris, M.E. (1982). Pregnancy outcome in North American women. II. Effects of diet, cigarette smoking, stress, and weight gain on placentas, and on neonatal physical and behavioral characteristics. *The American Journal of Clinical Nutrition, 36,* 1214–1224.

Picone, T.A., Allen, L.H., Schramm, M.M., & Olen, P.N. (1982). Pregnancy outcome in North American women. I. Effects of diet, cigarette smoking, and psychological stress on maternal weight gain. *The American Journal of Clinical Nutrition, 36,* 1205–1213.

Piechnik, S.L., & Corbett, M.A. (in press). Adolescent pregnancy outcome: An experience with intervention. *Journal of Nurse-Midwifery.*

Quick, J.D., Greenlick, M.R., & Roghmann, K.J. (1981). Prenatal care and pregnancy outcome in an HMO and general population: A multivariate cohort analysis. *American Journal of Public Health, 71,* 381–390.

Ramey, C.T., Stedman, D.J., Borders-Patterson, A., & Mengel, W. (1978). Predicting school-failure from information available at birth. *American Journal of Mental Deficiency, 82,* 525–534.

Rantakallio, P., & Hartikainen-Sorri, A. (1981). The relationship between birth weight, smoking during pregnancy and maternal weight gain. *American Journal of Epidemiology, 113,* 590–595.

Robitaille, Y., & Kramer, M.S. (1985). Does participation in prenatal courses lead to heavier babies? *American Journal of Public Health, 75,* 1186–1189.

Rosett, H.L., Ouellette, E.M., Weiner, L., & Owens, E. (1978). Therapy of heavy drinking during pregnancy. *Journal of Obstetrics and Gynecology, 32,* 41.

Rosett, H.L., Weiner, L., & Edelin, K.C. (1983). Treatment experience with pregnant problem drinkers. *Journal of the American Medical Association, 249,* 2029–2033.

Rush, D., Kristal, A., Blanc, W., Navarro, C., Chauhan, P., Brown, M.C., Rosso, P., Winick, M., Brasel, J., Naeye, R., & Susser, M. (1986). The effects of maternal cigarette smoking on placental morphology, histomorphometry, and biochemistry. *American Journal of Perinatology, 3,* 263–272.

Schramm, W.F. (1983). *An analysis of the effects of WIC.* Jefferson City, MO: Missouri Department of Public Health.

Schramm, W.F., & Land, G. (1984, December). *Prenatal care and its relationship to Medicaid costs.* Final report submitted to the Health Care Financing Administration.

Scott, A., Moar, V., & Ounsted, M. (1981). The relative contributions of different maternal factors in small-for-gestational-age pregnancies. *European Journal of Obstetric and Gynecological Reproductive Biology, 12,* 157–165.

Sexton, M., & Hebel, J.R. (1984). A clinical trial of change in maternal smoking and its effect on birth weight. *Journal of the American Medical Association, 251,* 911–915.

Sexton, M., Nowicki, P., & Andebel, J.R. (1986). Verification of smoking status by thiocyanate in unrefrigerated, mailed saliva samples. *Preventive Medicine, 15,* 28–34.

Shapiro, S., McCormick, M.C., Starfield, B.H., Krischer, J.P., & Bross, D. (1980). Relevance of correlates of infant deaths for significant morbidity at 1 year of age. *American Journal of Obstetrics and Gynecology, 136,* 363–373.

Shiono, P.H., Klebanoff, M.A., & Rhoads, G.G. (1986). Smoking and drinking during pregnancy: Their effects on preterm birth. *Journal of the American Medical Association, 255,* 82–84.

Showstack, J.A., Budetti, P.P., & Minkler, L.D. (1984). Factors associated with birthweight. An exploration of the roles of prenatal care and length of gestation. *American Journal of Public Health, 74,* 1003–1008.

Singer, J.E., Westphal, M., & Niswander, K. (1968). Relationship of weight gain during pregnancy to birthweight and infant growth and development in the first year of life: A report from the Collaborative Study of Cerebral Palsy. *Obstetrics and Gynecology, 31,* 417–423.

Slome, C., Wetherbee, H., Daly, M., Christensen, K., Meglen, M., & Thiede, H. (1976). Effectiveness of CNMs: A prospective evaluation study. *American Journal of Obstetrics and Gynecology, 124,* 177–182.

Snowman, M.K. (1979). Nutrition component in a comprehensive child development program: Nutrient intakes of low-income, pregnant women and the outcome of pregnancy. *Journal of the American Dietetic Association, 74,* 124–129.

Snowman, M.K., & Dibble, M.V. (1979). Nutrition component in a comprehensive child development program: The home visitor's role in the prenatal intervention phase. *Journal of the American Dietetic Association, ;74,* 119–123.

Stein, A., & Kline, J. (1983). Smoking, alcohol and reproduction. *American Journal of Public Health, 73,* 1154–1156.

Stimmel, B., & Adamsons, K. (1976). Narcotic dependency in pregnancy: Methadone maintenance compared to use of street drugs. *Journal of the American Medical Association, 235,* 1121–1124.

Stjernfeldt, J., Berglund, K., Lindsten, J., & Ludvigsson, J. (1986). Maternal smoking during pregnancy and risk of childhood cancer. *Lancet, 1,* 1350–1352.

Strauss, M.E., Andresko, M., Stryker, J.C., & Wardell, J.N. (1976). Relationship of neonatal withdrawal to maternal methadone dose. *The American Journal of Drug and Alcohol Abuse, 3,* 339–345.

Streissguth, A.P., Barr, H.M., & Martin, D.C. (1982). Offspring effects and pregnancy complications related to self-reported maternal alcohol use. *Developmental Pharmacology and Therapeutics, 5,* 21–32.

Strobino, D.M., Chase, G.A., Kim, Y.J., Crawley, B.E., Salim, J.H., & Baruffi, G. (1986). The impact of the Mississippi Improved Child Health Project on prenatal care and low birthweight. *American Journal of Public Health, 76,* 274–278.

Sweeney, C., Smith, H., Foster, J.C., Place, J.C., Specht, J., Kochenour, N.K., & Prater, B.M. (1985). Effects of a nutrition intervention program during pregnancy: Maternal data phases 1 and 2. *Journal of Nurse-Midwifery, 30,* 149–158.

van den Berg, B.J., & Yerushalmy, J. (1966). The relationship of intrauterine growth of infants of low birthweight to mortality, morbidity, and congenital anomalies. *Journal of Pediatrics, 69,* 531–545.

Westwood, M., Kramer, M.S., Numz, D., Lovett, J.M. & Watters, G.V. (1983). Growth and development of full-term nonasphyxiated small-for-gestational-age newborns: Follow-up through adolescence. *Pediatrics, 71,* 376–382.

Wilner, S., Schoenbaum, S.C., Palmer, R.H., & Fountain, R. (1983). Approaches to intervention programs for pregnant women who smoke. In *Proceedings of the Fifth World Conference on Smoking and Health,* Winnepeg, Canada.

Wilner, S., Schoenbaum, S.C., Monson, R.R., & Winickoff, R.N. (1981). A comparison of the quality of maternity care between a health maintenance organization and fee-for-service practices. *New England Journal of Medicine, 304*, 784–787.

Windsor, R.A., Cutter, G., Morris, J., Reese, Y., Manzella, B., Bartlett, E.E., Samuelson, C., & Spanos, D. (1985). The effectiveness of smoking cessation methods for smokers in public health maternity clinics: A randomized trial. *American Journal of Public Health, 75*, 1389–1392.

Wise, H.B., Torrey, E.F., McDade, A., Perry, G., & Bograd, H. (1968). The family health worker. *American Journal of Public Health, 64*, 1056–1061.

Wolkind, S., & Zajicek, E. (Eds.). (1981). *Pregnancy: A psychological and social study.* New York: Grune & Stratton, Inc.

World Health Organization Expert Committee on Maternal and Child Health. (1961). *Public health aspects of low birthweight. Third report of the Expert Committee on Maternal and Child Health.* Technical Report Series, No. 217. Geneva: World Health Organization.

WRC Report. (1986). *Oh, what a beautiful baby prenatal care incentive program patient survey.* A Channel 4 WRC-TV community affairs program in conjunction with the Commission of Public Health, DHHS. Washington, DC: WRC-TV.

Wright, J.T., Barrison, I.G., Lewis, I.G., MacRae, K.D., Waterson, E.J., Toplis, P.J., Gordon, M.G., Morris, N.F., & Murray-Lyon, I.M. (1983). Alcohol consumption, pregnancy, and low birthweight. *Lancet, 2*, 663–665.

9 | Chronic Perinatal Infections and Mental Retardation

CHARLES A. ALFORD

CHRONIC PERINATAL INFECTIONS

Bacterial sepsis and meningitis first come to mind when thinking of infection in relation to mental retardation or other forms of central nervous system damage. Indeed, bacterial infections remain a major problem with respect to mortality and morbidity, particularly among premature infants, in spite of the introduction of many new, more potent antibiotics. A better understanding of pathogenesis is required before further improvement in this area is likely to occur. It is not this group of infections that I intend to address here. Instead, I will focus on a group of infections that not only produce acute disease, as do the bacteria, but have a propensity to cause long-term damage to the brain and perceptual organs. These entities, as a group, have been dubbed chronic perinatal infections, since the causative organisms can remain in the host for prolonged periods of time—years or even for a lifetime. As a result, late sequelae can occur that are particularly troublesome in the central nervous system. Although a number of different microorganisms might qualify as causative agents for chronic congenital and perinatal infections, I will focus on those of greatest current interest and those that have a distinct propensity for injury to the central nervous system and/or perceptual organs.

As noted in Table 1, these agents include: 1) two herpesviruses, cytomegalovirus (CMV) and herpes simplex virus (HSV); 2) rubella virus; 3) *Toxoplasma gondii*; 4) *Treponema pallidum*; and 5) human immunodeficiency virus (HIV), the causative agent of acquired immunodeficiency syndrome (AIDS). All of the agents are distributed worldwide. CMV and HSV can be transmitted by the oral and venereal routes, with the former being the most common but the latter being on the increase as a result of heightened sexual promiscuity. In spite

This work was supported in part by grants from the National Institutes of Health, NICHD (HD10699), General Clinical Research Center (MO1 RR32), and the National Foundation—March of Dimes (6-490).

Table 1. Microbial agents responsible for chronic congenital and/or perinatal infections in relation to whether the infection in the mother and newborn is symptomatic or subclinical

| | Type infection | | | |
| | Maternal | | Newborn | |
Agents	Symptomatic	Subclinical	Symptomatic	Subclinical
Herpesviruses				
CMV	+	+ + + +	+	+ + + +
HSV	+	+ + +	+ + + +	+
Rubella virus	+ +	+ +	+ +	+ + +
Toxoplasma gondii	+	+ + + +	+	+ + + +
Treponema pallidum	+ + +	+	+ +	+ +
HIV (HTLV III–LAV)	+ +	+ +	+	+ + +

of the requirement of intimate contact for transmission, infection by these two agents is very common, with 80–90% of populations infected by late adulthood. Infection by rubella virus, which was exceedingly common in the past, is now well controlled in the United States because of an extensive vaccination program. In other areas of the world epidemics of rubella infection continue to occur as a result of limited use of vaccine. *Toxoplasma* is a natural infection of cats, which transmit it to humans and many other animals. In humans the infection is acquired by exposure to infected cat feces through changing litter, dirt eating, or poor sanitation or by the ingestion of infectious cysts in fresh undercooked meat. Infection by *Toxoplasma gondii* occurs in from 10% to 40% of persons in the United States but is much more common in Europe, because of eating habits, and in underdeveloped areas, probably in part because of poor sanitation.

Treponema pallidum, the causative agent of syphilis, is obviously venereally transmitted. Syphilis is currently reasonably well controlled thanks to public health surveillance and the availability of treatment. HIV infection, by contrast, has reached epidemic proportions since its introduction in the late 1970s into the United States via Africa and the Carribean. This infection is transmitted by exposure to body secretions, especially genital ones, and to blood. Sexual exposure, intravenous (IV) drug abuse, and blood or blood product transfusions are the usual sources for HIV infection, whereas casual contact or nonsexual contact, even in the home, appears to be safe. Male homosexuals are at greatest risk for acquiring HIV infection at present. However, females are at greatest risk through IV drug abuse, prostitution, or repeated exposure to a sexual partner who is infected. There is great concern about the wider heterosexual spread of HIV infection in the United States, a circumstance that would markedly increase the danger for the fetus and young infant. In Africa AIDS is a heterosexual disease, and perinatal infection is more common than in the United States.

DIAGNOSIS

The data in Table 1 indicate the difficulties encountered with the diagnosis of the chronic congenital and perinatal infections. Often the maternal infection is either silent or missed. CMV and *Toxoplasma* almost always produce subclinical infections in the pregnant female. Very rarely they may cause a heterophil-negative mononucleosis syndrome. Even though HSV infection may produce vesicular lesions on the oral or genital areas, more often the infections are silent, but still they may be transmitted to the newborn. In fact, neonatal herpes most often occurs in women with no history of prior herpetic infections, nor is there a history in their sexual partners. The lesions of primary syphilis are often overlooked because of their location or their unusual nature in pregnant women. Even HIV infection is often subclinical. The women are antibody-positive virus shedders but are capable of infecting the fetus and newborn. Therefore there is a need for laboratory screening techniques to recognize these various infections in pregnant women so that appropriate decisions can be made concerning management of the pregnancy.

To further complicate diagnostic problems the infected newborns are more often subclinically infected like their mothers (Table 1). Neonatal herpes is the only one of these infections that is consistently symptomatic during the neonatal period. Congenital infections of both CMV and *Toxoplasmosis* are most commonly subclinical during early infancy. Even congenital rubella may not evidence signs of disease until months after delivery. Likewise, congenital HIV and syphilis infections are often not clinically apparent at birth, only to progress to the point of disease during the first 6–9 months after delivery. Consequently, with respect to diagnosing the infection in the newborn, laboratory screening methods are required in order to recognize subclinically infected infants. This approach is important because the subclinical infections are prone to chronicity or to recurrence and may result in very significant sequelae later in life. The development and employment of diagnostic screening methods for detection of these infections in the mothers and babies should be a major research goal for the future as it has been in the past.

TRANSMISSIBILITY AND STAGE OF GESTATION

It is obvious from the foregoing discussion that there is a spectrum of disease in the infected fetus, neonate, and young infant that varies according to the microorganism involved and, in the case of the congenital infections, the stage of gestation in which the infection is initiated. With regard to the latter, infections in the first half of pregnancy are more virulent for the fetus than those that occur later, probably as a result of immaturity of the developing fetal immune system. Intrauterine transmissibility according to gestational age at the time of infection has a powerful influence on the relative frequency with which these agents cause virulent infections in the fetus. For instance, there is a high rate of intrauterine transmission with primary maternal rubella during early gestation, whereas primary maternal toxoplasmosis is associated with a low rate of fetal infection in this period, because of innate protection against in utero transmission. Consequently, rubella virus causes a greater degree of virulent fetal infections than does *Toxoplasma*.

The microorganisms can be rated as to their ability to produce virulent as opposed to subclinical intrauterine infections, which is in large part a reflection of their capacity to be transmitted during early gestation. Using this rating system, the following agents produce virulent fetal infections in decreasing order of frequency: HSV, *Treponema*, rubella, *Toxoplasma*, and CMV. Intrauterine HSV infection is rare. Instead HSV is usually transmitted to the offspring at or around the time of delivery from virus replicating in the maternal genital tract. Irrespective of when infection is acquired, untreated neonatal herpes is highly virulent, with high frequency of involvement of the central nervous system, as noted in Table 2. With regard to virulence, CMV is on the other end of the spectrum; however, it has the highest incidence, by far, of both intrauterine and perinatally acquired infection of any of the agents under discussion. In virtually all of the perinatally infected infants (who are infected via the maternal genital tract or infected breast milk) the disease is subclinically involved, especially as regards the central nervous system. Indeed, most of those with intrauterine involvement are subclinically infected and remain so in spite of prolonged viral excretion. However, the small percentage of congenitally infected infants with virulent infection represents a relatively large number of sick neonates because of the inordinately high incidence of this congenital infection.

A very high proportion of the infants born with virulent (symptomatic) CMV infection have central nervous system and perceptual organ involvement, as noted in Table 2. Among the larger number of subclinically infected infants a significant proportion will develop varying degrees of hearing impairment as a late sequela, usually within the first 2 years after delivery (Table 2). An as yet unresolved but important issue is whether minimal brain damage with learning and behavioral disorders is a late sequela of subclinical congenital CMV infection. Although less prevalent, congenital toxoplasmosis has many of the features of congenital CMV infection. Central nervous system involvement is a prominent finding with the virulent infections, whereas, in contrast to CMV, recurrent chorioretinitis with varying degrees of blindness is the most prominent late sequela. Chorioretinitis can recur for many years after the birth of the infected infant. Minimal brain damage due to progressive infection may also be a feature of subclinical congenital toxoplasmosis. Chronic encephalitis with extensive brain damage is relatively common in infants born with virulent congenital rubella, as is deafness (Table 2). Deafness can be progressive as a late sequela, and very rarely a subacute form of recurrent brain infection may appear a number of years following the birth of an infant with congenital rubella, even if the original presentation was relatively mild (Table 2).

At this stage there is much to be learned about HIV infections since they are relatively new. Apparently this virus can be transmitted either in utero or in the perinatal period and is potentially fatal for the offspring in all cases. Certainly a devastating form of subacute brain involvement can be a prominent feature of HIV infections in

Table 2. Relative abilities of the chronic congenital and perinatal infections to cause brain and perceptual organ damage when the infection is symptomatic or subclinical during the neonatal period

Agents	Clinically Apparent			Subclinical		
	Brain	Auditory	Visual	Brain	Auditory	Visual
Herpesviruses						
CMV	++++	+++	+	+	++	+
HSV	+++	+	++	+	+	+
Rubella virus	++	+++	++	+	+++	±
Toxoplasma gondii	++++	+	++++	+	±	++++
Treponema pallidum	+++	±	−	+++	±	++
HIV (HTLV III–LAV)	++	±	±	++	±	+

young infants. Whether it will be a late sequela in those infants born with subclinical or mild infections awaits definition, but the chronicity of this infection surely suggests that it may be.

MECHANISM OF RECURRENT INFECTION: CYTOMEGALOVIRUS

In order to focus on some of the newer solutions to the many problems posed by chronic congenital and perinatal infection, those caused by CMV will be discussed in greater detail. CMV infection is the most common intrauterine infection, occurring in 1% of all live births (range 0.2–2.2%) throughout the world. The incidence is highest in developing countries and lower socioeconomic level populations in developed nations. Approximately 36,000 infants are born each year in the United States with congenital CMV infection. All of these infants are chronically infected with virus shedding into the throat or urine for years after delivery. They, along with the even larger number of perinatally infected infants who are also chronic excretors, represent a major source for spread of CMV infection in the general population. Five percent to 10% of the congenitally infected infants (1,800–3,600/year) are born with clinically apparent infection characterized by generalized involvement of the reticuloendothelial system (hepatosplenomegaly with jaundice, thrombocytopenia with or without purpura, bleeding tendency), central nervous system involvement, pneumonia, and less commonly other organ system involvement. About 20% of these infants (350–720/year) may die in the early months as a result of fulminant infection and 90% of the survivors (1,306–2,600/year) are left with severe central nervous system and perceptual organ system damage. It should be emphasized that CMV infection is endemic in the general population and the congenital infection occurs at the 1% level year in and year out. Fortunately, 90% of the congenitally infected infants (32,000/year) are much less severely involved and are born with subclinical infection. Of this group approximately 10% (3,200 infants/year) can develop late sequelae, the most prominent of which is sensorineural hearing loss that may be unilateral or bilateral and may be progressive. Although it has been difficult to define, minimal brain damage with learning and behavioral disorders is believed to be a late feature of subclinical congenital CMV infection. Resolution of this issue is very important given the large number of children who are in jeopardy.

For many years the reason why congenital CMV infection was so much more common than the other congenital infections remained a mystery. Recent large-scale prospective studies in pregnant women revealed the surprising fact that CMV can be transmitted to the fetus not only with primary infection in nonimmune women but with recurrent infection in immune women. It is this feature of the maternal infection that accounts for the high incidence of the congenital CMV infection. Transmission of infection to the fetus or the newborn occurs much more commonly with recurrent maternal CMV infection than with the other infectious agents. In fact, intrauterine CMV infection worldwide is more often associated with recurrent maternal CMV infection than with primary maternal infection.

In recent years the mechanism for these recurrent maternal infections has been examined using molecular virologic techniques. CMV, being a herpesvirus, can become latent in human cells following primary infection and later reactivate in the face of the host's immunity. During these episodes virus can be shed into breast milk, the genital tract, urine, and the throat in decreasing order of frequency. More important from the standpoint of congenital infection, CMV can be reactivated from the latent state internally and be transmitted in utero. The site at which the reactivation occurs is unknown and an important problem to be solved.

CMV, like other of the herpesviruses, has been closely linked to humans over the generations. It is species specific, thus humans are CMV's only reservoir. CMV has apparently mutated over the generations so that thousands of genetic strains are currently in circulation. Since the virus is spread by intimate contact, strains isolated from unrelated individuals or unrelated epidemiological settings are genetically different. This genetic unrelatedness may contribute to the ability of CMV to reinfect individuals who are immune to previously infecting strains. Consequently reinfection is another possible source for recurrent maternal infections with in utero transmission of virus. Since strains of CMV isolated from epidemiologically unrelated individuals differ, it is possible using molecular virologic techniques to more precisely define the complicated epidemiology of CMV. The technique involves comparative restriction enzyme analyses of DNA recovered from the viral isolates. This approach has been used to determine the relative importance of reactivation of latent virus and reinfection as causes for recurrent maternal infections with transmission to the fetus. Examples of the use of this technique are shown in Figure 1 (strain homology) and Figure 2 (strain heterogeneity). As noted in Figure 1, using two enzymes, EcoR I and Bam HI, the DNA recovered from two viral isolates obtained from a mother's urine in 1974 and 1977 had restriction enzyme patterns identical to the DNA recovered from isolates obtained from her congenitally and perinatally infected infants born in 1973 and 1975, respectively. Clearly the

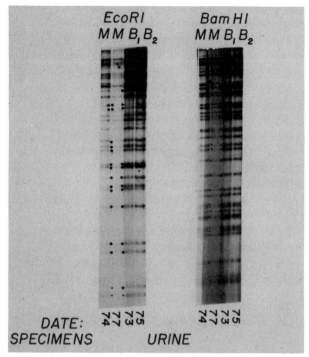

Figure 1. Restriction enzyme analyses of the DNA isolated from CMV strains recovered from a mother on two occasions and from two of her infected offspring, showing a pattern of strain homology. The enzymes included EcoR I and Bam HI. Viruses were isolated from different sites as indicated in the figure. Patterns represent migration of enzyme-digested DNA fragments in gels following electrophoresis. *M*, mother; *B₁*, congenitally infected infant; *B₂*, perinatally infected infant.

recurrent infection in this mother was caused by the same CMV strain, which in turn infected two of her offspring. Reactivation of latent virus is the most likely cause of these results. In most of the cases studied to date reactivation of virus has been responsible for the recurrent maternal infection and subsequent infection of the fetus or young infant. However, as noted from the differing restriction enzyme patterns shown in Figure 2, reinfection remains a cause in some cases. For the patterns shown in Figure 2, CMV isolates recovered from a woman's genital tract on two occasions differed genetically, as did isolates from two mother-baby pairs. Determining the relative importance of reactivation and reinfection as causes for recurrent maternal infection with involvement of the fetus or young infant is certainly in need of more research.

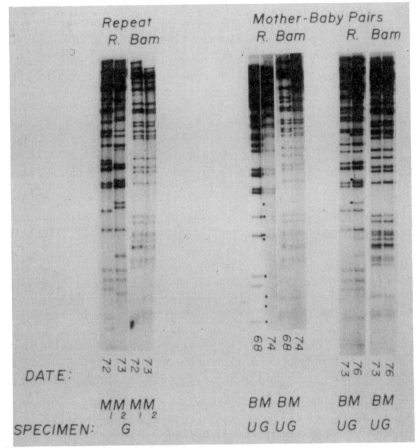

Figure 2. Restriction enzyme analyses of the DNA isolated from CMV strains recovered twice from a female genital tract and from two mother-baby pairs, showing a pattern of strain heterogenity. The enzymes included EcoR I (*R.*) and Bam HI (*Bam*). Viruses were isolated from different sites as indicated in the figure. Patterns represent migration of enzyme-digested DNA fragments in gels following electrophoresis. *M*, mother; *B*, baby; *U*, urine specimen; *G*, genital specimen.

FETAL PROTECTIVE FACTORS

There are other important problems that remain for solution as regards the natural history of chronic perinatal infections in pregnancy. These relate to transmissibility of the infectious agents during pregnancy, during delivery, or in the early postnatal period, and factors that influence the virulence of the infection in the fetus or young infant. Even with primary infection in pregnant females, much less with recurrent infection, infection of the fetus is not inevitable. In fact in most cases, such as with CMV and *Toxoplasma*, the fetus is protected more often than it becomes infected. Exactly what the protective factors are is unknown. Two possible factors, working in concert, that have received inadequate study include the maternal immune response and the role of the placenta as a barrier to transmission of infectious agents. Understanding the factors that influence the expression of infection in the fetus, newborn, or young infant is also important for eventual control, but currently they are poorly delineated. With CMV infection maternal immunity obviously plays a major role in transmission of virus in utero and in the virulence of the fetal infection. CMV is transmitted in utero much more often and the fetal infection is more often virulent following primary maternal CMV infection than with recurrent maternal infection. Certainly the more important elements of the mother's immune response that provide this protection need to be more precisely defined. Gestational age at the time of the fetal infection is also a major factor in the expression of infection in the fetus. With most of the intrauterine infections, involvement in early pregnancy is more dangerous for the fetus than later involvement. In this regard, understanding the fetal immune responses that ameliorate the later gestational infections is also important, as is better defining the placental transfer of antibody. Definition of the host response in terms of important immunogens specified by the infecting agent and in terms of subclass antibody responses is also needed.

CURRENT RESEARCH TECHNIQUES

In recent years knowledge about the molecular aspects of the growth of infectious agents and their physiochemical makeup has been accelerating at a rapid pace. This information is providing new tools and new approaches, both theoretical and real, to unraveling the complex problems posed by the chronic congenital and perinatal infections. Again, I will use CMV by way of example to emphasize how basic knowledge about infectious agents can be used for clinical advantage, as it was with the molecular epidemiological studies previously discussed. Figure 3 illustrates, in a simplified form, the replication cycle of CMV, which is very similar to that of HSV, another important perinatal infectious virus. Following cellular penetration via receptor attachment, the intact virion is rapidly uncoated. Thereafter, a series of events leads to production of new infectious virus and its extrusion from the infected cell. In the course of these events, an interdepen-

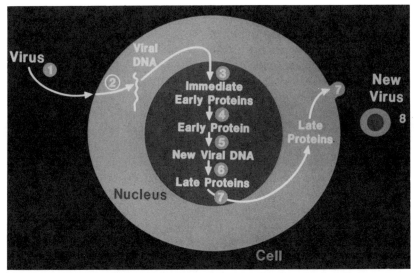

Figure 3. A simplified schematic of the replication cycle of cytomegalovirus.

dent cascade of virus-specified protein production occurs with immediate early, early, and late virus proteins being produced in that order. Since each step is dependent upon the preceding one, any process that interferes in the replication cycle with formation of immediate early or early proteins would block the formation of new virus. The eventual isolation and characterization of the early viral proteins should hasten the development of drugs specific for the treatment of CMV infection without interfering with cellular metabolism. This of course would be a major advance. Acyclovir, the drug currently marketed for the treatment of HSV infection, is an example of a virus-specific chemotherapy. Understanding the structure, function, and immunogenicity of the viral proteins could also lead to the development of safer and perhaps more potent vaccines to provide prophylaxis against CMV and HSV infection. Development of classical live vaccines, such as the one being employed for the successful control of rubella infections, is less likely to be acceptable with the herpesviruses, since they have a DNA genome that is putatively oncogenic. Mapping of the viral genomes and cloning of segments of the genomes in expression vectors (for protein production) are providing new tools to more conveniently study epidemiology of these infections and providing means for rapid and more specific diagnoses.

SUMMARY

In summary, chronic congenital and perinatal infections, in addition to acute perinatal infections, especially the bacterial ones, continue to pose a major public health hazard throughout the world. Together they contribute significantly to the pool of children with brain and perceptual organ damage, plus other crippling forms of morbidity. Because of their nature and complexity, infections in pregnant women and their offspring provide a major challenge for medical, behavioral, and basic scientists. Thanks to the research efforts of the National Institute of Child Health and Human Development, other Institutes of the National Institutes of Health, and many private foundations this challenge is being met, providing new and exciting developments that portend a brighter future for the children of the world.

III | THE NEONATAL PERIOD

Overview
HUGO W. MOSER

Advances pertaining to the newborn child may well represent the most exciting products of mental retardation research during the last 20 years. These past two decades have seen the implementation of mass newborn screening programs that have permitted us to eliminate certain forms of mental retardation that had plagued humanity since antiquity. Phenomenal advances in neonatal care permit premature infants who in the past would have died to survive and in most instances to escape damage. The future promises still more effective and more widely applicable metabolic screening through the application of recombinant DNA technology. The combined use of noninvasive imaging techniques and of refined behavioral observations is expected to lead to exciting new insights into how the brain of the newborn child functions.

Metabolic screening of all newborn children has become such a standard procedure that we tend to forget that it only began during the last 25 years. Before then no one would have predicted that study of a tiny capillary blood sample could provide information that is crucial to the child's lifelong brain function. The major credit here goes to Dr. Robert Guthrie's vision, his ability to devise highly practical and cost-effective filter-paper testing, and his untiring energy that brought about the utilization of newborn screening throughout the world. The screening initially dealt exclusively with phenylketonuria (a 1:11,000 occurrence), but the same screening strategy has been applied to detect hypothyroidism (formerly called cretinism), with its 1:3,500 incidence. Dr. Harvey Levy has been among the key developers of these major public health advances both in Massachusetts and worldwide. In Chapter 10 Dr. Levy updates the technique of newborn screening, both the well-delineated method for phenylketonuria and the newer hypothyroidism and galactosemia tests. Future possibilities for use of the filter-paper specimen technique include DNA analysis of blood to detect inherited disease, blood testing for congenital infections, and urine testing for congenital tumors.

In Chapter 11 Dr. Joseph Volpe deals with an approach that can link biochemistry, anatomy, and physiology with how a child behaves.

The standard neurological examination of the newborn child has many limitations. The newly developed imaging techniques of ultrasound, computed tomography, positron emission tomography, and magnetic resonance imaging permit noninvasive visualization of brain structure with a degree of precision and detail that no one would have thought possible even 5 years ago. Dr. Volpe is a leader in the field of neonatology and has made major contributions to the understanding of the cause and prevention of intracranial hemorrhage, one of the serious complications of prematurity. Neuroimaging techniques have shown that small and previously undetectable hemorrhages occur frequently, and allow us to grade and localize them. These techniques form the cornerstone for the development of preventive measures. The imaging techniques already have proven their capacity to detect major brain structural defects, and future improvements will make it possible to detect structural abnormalities with a resolution of 1 mm^3 or less. In addition, nuclear magnetic resonance spectroscopy will permit detection and treatment of the earliest stages of brain hypoxia and other metabolic abnormalities.

These imaging techniques also provide a linkage to the topic of the next two chapters. It is self-evident that what we do or do not do in the neonatal care unit must eventually be determined by the results of painstaking follow-up of the "graduates" from these units. This is the topic presented by Dr. Mildred Stahlman and her colleagues (Chapter 12). After following several cohorts of over 1,700 newborns at the Vanderbilt University Medical Center Neonatal Intensive Care Unit for as much as 11 years after birth, Dr. Stahlman and colleagues have found encouraging long-term outcome results. Those children classified at birth as very low and low birth weight infants showed statistically significant differences in developmental/intelligence levels from preschool (age 2–3) to school-age (age 5–7) testing. Low birth weight children appear to catch up intellectually to their normal birth weight peers. Improvements in medical care were reflected in a decline in incidence of handicaps from the earlier to the later cohorts—a decline that occurred in the face of dramatic increases in numbers of surviving low birth weight infants. Longitudinal follow-up studies of these infants, many of whom had significant perinatal complications, again indicated attainment of intelligence levels competitive with those of healthy term infants.

The importance of such follow-up studies cannot be overemphasized. At present our prognostic capacity is still limited. Some very sick neonates do very well, whereas others who did not appear as severely involved subsequently show neurological deficits. There is a great need for techniques to assess more accurately the neonates' brain function. More precise assessment is necessary for planning of long-term care and for the design and evaluation of intervention techniques. One current approach to achieving this goal is exemplified by the neuroimaging techniques, which can delineate brain structure as well as its biochemical and physiological function. Such techniques, in combination with behavioral assessment, have been used by Drs. Frank H. Duffy and Heidelise Als to study the differences between healthy preterm and term infants (Chapter 13). Using brain electrical activity mapping (BEAM; a technique for producing computer-generated topographic maps of neurophysiological functioning) and the Assessment of Preterm Infants' Behavior (a test assessing ability to differentiate and modulate behavioral functioning), it was possible to correlate test results with length of gestation, and to show clear differences that persisted to at least age 5. It seems that, like animals, human infants experience a "critical period" of neural development that is triggered by environmental stimuli such as the increased sensorimotor input received by an infant during the perinatal period. In the preterm infant this critical period is triggered before the infant is capable of managing what becomes a sensorimotor "overload," and the neonate may develop internal self-deprivation mechanisms in response. Careful modification of the preterm infant's intensive care environment can result in an improved outcome in childhood.

The second approach to developing assessment techniques for long-term care planning and intervention design and evaluation is exemplified by Drs. Joseph Fagan and Jeanne Montie in Chapter 14. Early detection of cognitive deficits is important for the understanding of mental retardation; infant testing can be used to pinpoint causes of intellectual impairment, and to discover periods in development when specific environmental influences become operable. Early detection also enables early remediation and allows clinicians to allocate resources appropriately. However, the instruments designed to assess infant sensorimotor behavior have not been successful in predicting later cognitive behavior. Drs. Fagan and Montie have applied modern technology to design a screening test to assess the infant's visual information processing, a highly complex cognitive function that is not appraised by more traditional techniques. Using visual recognition tasks, the cognitive abilities of discrimination, recognition memory, and categorization—the processes assessed on intelligence tests later in life—are evaluated in infants. The Fagan Test of Infant Intelligence can be used as a selective screening device for infants suspected of being at risk for later cognitive defects.

In the final chapter in this section (Chapter 15), Dr. Tiffany Field discusses the early interactions of high-risk infants and their parents, a relationship fraught with difficulty from the outset. High-risk infants often respond to parental attention with negative affective displays or with behavioral responses that are unreadable by their parents. Parental attempts to elicit more "appropriate" responses often initiate a cycle of decreased infant responsivity and increasing parental stimulation that becomes stressful to both parties. Many high-risk infants lack the ability to modulate their level of arousal during what is for them excessive stimulation, and they resort to aversive behaviors to terminate the interaction. Coaching parents in interpreting their high-risk infant's behavior correctly and in modifying their own behavior so as to modulate the infant's arousal level has resulted in much more harmonious parent-infant interactions.

In conclusion, this section demonstrates the interaction of a variety of disciplines and techniques, and shows how this interdisciplinary research has improved the understanding of human development. These efforts have already had a very significant impact on the prevention and treatment of mental retardation, and it is anticipated that this success will be amplified in the future.

10 | Newborn Screening
HARVEY L. LEVY

Newborn screening is not usually considered an accomplishment of mental retardation research. I believe that it is. In fact, I believe that it is one of the most important research accomplishments in the prevention of mental retardation in this century.

In the 25 years since newborn screening was developed, it has become a major element in our public health and general medical approach to mental retardation prevention. Less well known is the fact that it arose from research. Dr. Robert Guthrie began his scientific career in basic genetic and cancer research. By 1961 his interests had focused on the bacterial assays, or, as he calls them, the "bug tests," for the identification and the measurement of various amino acids. One of these bug tests was for phenylalanine, and Guthrie learned that this assay might be useful in testing retarded individuals known to have phenylketonuria (PKU), a disorder characterized by increased phenylalanine levels in the blood.

Guthrie knew little about PKU, but he familiarized himself with the literature and learned that if dietary treatment began during early infancy before evidence of mental retardation appeared, the mental retardation could be prevented.

Guthrie realized that his phenylalanine test could lead to dietary treatment in all children born with PKU, not just those few in whom PKU had been suspected because of family history.

Guthrie conceived of a filter paper blood specimen, using only a few drops of blood, that could serve as a practical method of screening all newborn babies. He then adapted his test to the filter paper specimen. It is this simple filter paper specimen that has enabled newborn screening to spread throughout the world; that has accommodated a multiplicity of newborn screening tests; that allows for the identification of many disorders that cause mental retardation, not only PKU; and that has been used in many important research endeavors.

I wish to review the accomplishments of newborn screening for PKU, touch on several areas in which newborn screening has produced new research information, and consider what I believe to be the new frontiers of newborn screening.

ACCOMPLISHMENTS OF NEWBORN SCREENING FOR PKU

During the past two decades, well over 100 million children have received newborn screening. The specimens (sent to laboratories, usually central state laboratories) have identified over 10,000 infants with PKU. Figure 1 shows the filter paper blood specimen from an infant with PKU as discovered by the Guthrie test. The remaining discs on the plate are normal specimens, with a row of control discs in the center. As a result of early dietary treatment, the outcome of PKU has changed dramatically from that of mental retardation to that of normal intelligence.

Importantly, this interest in PKU has led to studies that have greatly increased our knowledge of the biochemical deficiency and the basic genetic defect. The enzyme phenylalanine hydroxylase, which is the defective enzyme in PKU, has been characterized with regard to its subunit structure and its molecular mass. It is a dimer with a mass of about 110,000 daltons. It seems not to have isoenzymes, as

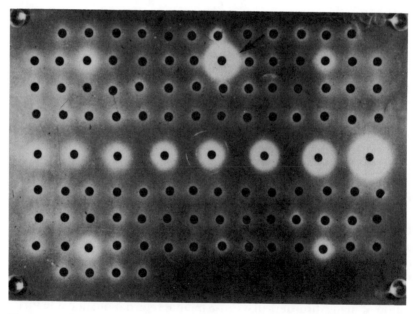

Figure 1. Guthrie bacterial inhibition assay for phenylalanine illustrating the prominent bacterial growth surrounding a filter paper blood specimen from an infant with PKU (*arrow*). The center row consists of control filter paper blood discs with phenylalanine concentrations increasing from 2 mg/dl on the extreme left to 20 mg/dl on the extreme right. Other specimens are from normal newborn infants.

was formerly thought. Its cofactor requirement, tetrahydrobiopterin (BH$_4$), has been identified and its function carefully elucidated. It is now understood that there are defects involving this reduced pterin cofactor that can result in hyperphenylalaninemia, as seen in PKU. However, the increased phenylalanine is only one of several biochemical features of the cofactor defect, and may not be the most damaging of these features.

These pterin defects produce severe mental retardation. Figure 2 indicates the currently known blocks in pterin metabolism that result in BH$_4$ deficiency and that secondarily produce hyperphenylalaninemia. If diagnosed and treated promptly and effectively, the mental retardation from these pterin defects may be preventable.

Interest in PKU has also led to cloning of the phenylalanine hydroxylase gene, and this in turn has allowed for specific molecular characterization of those persons who have PKU, those who carry the

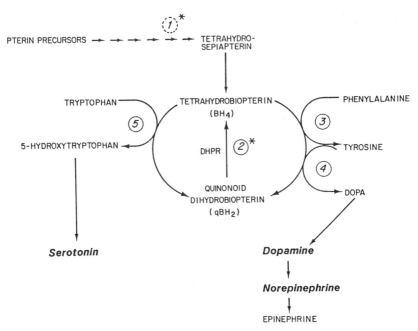

Figure 2.   The pathway of pterin metabolism as it relates to the formation of tetrahydrobiopterin, the cofactor for phenylalanine hydroxylase (3), tyrosine hydroxylase (4), and tryptophan hydroxylase (5). A deficiency of this cofactor leads to reduced hydroxylation activities and deficiencies of the monoamine neurotransmitters dopamine, norepinephrine, and serotonin.

gene for PKU, and those who are normal with respect to the PKU gene.

NEW RESEARCH INFORMATION

A notable achievement in newborn screening was the addition of screening for congenital hypothyroidism. Added to the same filter paper blood specimen that is collected for PKU screening, congenital hypothyroidism screening has led to the early detection of this disease in thousands of infants. Early treatment with thyroid replacement has altered the outcome of this disorder from one of mental retardation to one of normalcy of intelligence.

Screening for galactosemia has led to advances in our knowledge of the enzyme in this disease, so that we now recognize many enzyme types and variants. Infants with galactosemia no longer die or become mentally retarded; with early detection and therapy they may remain normal.

The development of one of the newest additions to newborn screening, that for biotinidase deficiency, is leading to very important information about vitamins and how they function within the cell.

FRONTIERS OF NEWBORN SCREENING

The frontiers of newborn screening seem endless. DNA can be extracted from the filter paper blood specimen, and this can lead to genetic diagnosis of virtually any inherited disease. Already the newborn blood specimen is being used for early postnatal detection of congenital toxoplasmosis and even for congenital acquired immunodeficiency syndrome. Filter paper specimens of urine from infants can be used for the early detection of neuroblastoma and other tumors, so that through early surgery these children can be saved.

In truth, we have only begun to explore the capabilities of newborn screening for an understanding of mental retardation.

11 | Neuroimaging and Intracranial Hemorrhage
JOSEPH J. VOLPE

NEUROIMAGING MODALITIES

There are four major types of imaging modalities that are used currently in neonatal neurology: ultrasonography, computed tomography (CT), magnetic resonance imaging (MRI), and positron emission tomography (PET). *Ultrasonography*, the most widely used of all, is based on ultrasound technology. The technique is safe, noninvasive, portable, and relatively inexpensive, and its application in the neonatal period has resulted in a major advance in our understanding of neonatal brain pathology.

Computed tomography is based on conventional x-ray technology in combination with computerized image reconstruction. The technique is very useful for diagnosis of virtually all intracranial pathology, but its particular disadvantage in the sick newborn is the need to transport the infant to the CT scanner.

Magnetic resonance imaging, or nuclear magnetic resonance (NMR) scanning, is the newest imaging modality on the scene in neurology. The technique is clearly superior in the newborn, I think, only in the diagnosis of posterior fossa lesions. Its particular disadvantages are the need to transport the infant to the scanner and the requirement for relatively long data acquisition times. The latter require that the infant be in the scanner for a considerable period of time.

Positron emission tomography, which is discussed in some detail in this chapter, is a fascinating technique that essentially is a means of biochemical-physiological-type imaging, rather than structural imaging as afforded by the above three techniques. It has provided enormous insight into the pathogenesis and the basic nature of a variety of neonatal hemorrhagic and ischemic disorders.

HEMORRHAGIC INTRACEREBRAL INVOLVEMENT

Perhaps a good way to put PET in perspective is to discuss a lesion of the premature infant that is very important and in which this technique has been very useful. Hemorrhagic intracerebral involvement is considered very important because it is the single most important cause of major neurological sequelae in premature infants. This section addresses three basic questions: What is the appearance of this hemorrhagic intracerebral involvement? How extensive is the lesion? What causes the lesion?

Neuropathology and Structural Brain Imaging

Neuropathology What is the appearance of this lesion both neuropathologically at postmortem examination and in vivo? The gross neuropathology is shown in Figure 1. This is a horizontal section of the brain of a premature infant who died about 3 days after birth. A large lesion is apparent in the left frontal white matter, extending

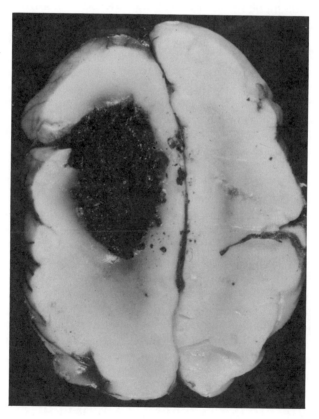

Figure 1. Horizontal section of cerebral hemispheres of premature infant who died at 5 days of age. Note area of hemorrhagic intracerebral involvement in left frontal–anterior parietal white matter.

into parietal white matter. This large area of hemorrhagic necrosis is a typical lesion of hemorrhagic intracerebral involvement.

Cranial Ultrasonography We can identify this lesion in the neonatal period by using the ultrasound sector scan. The ultrasound transducer is placed on the anterior fontanelle, which serves as a kind of bone-free window into the baby's brain. The instrument sweeps through a sector of 90–110°, depending upon the instrument.

Figure 2 illustrates a coronal ultrasound scan, demonstrating bilateral intraventricular hemorrhage and, most importantly, a mushroom-shaped echogenic lesion in the right periventricular white matter. This echogenicity, dorsal and lateral to the external angle of the lateral ventricle (usually unilateral), is characteristic of hemorrhagic intracerebral involvement.

If one turns the ultrasonic transducer on the anterior fontanelle 90° one can obtain a sagittal section through the ventricular system, as illustrated in Figure 3. The hemorrhagic intracerebral involvement appears as a nearly rectangular area of echogenicity superior to the blood-filled lateral ventricle in the frontal white matter.

CT Scan Hemorrhagic intracerebral involvement can also be identified by CT scan, although less conveniently. The CT scan in Figure 4 illustrates bilateral intraventricular hemorrhage but, more importantly, a radiodense lesion in the left frontal white matter, characteristic of hemorrhagic intracerebral involvement.

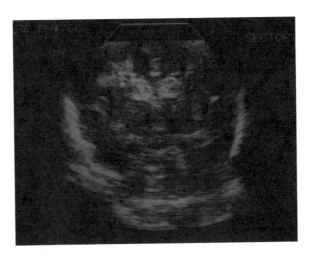

Figure 2. Coronal ultrasound scan of premature infant at 4 days of age. Note bilateral intraventricular hemorrhage and mushroom-shaped echogenicity of hemorrhagic intracerebral involvement in right frontal white matter.

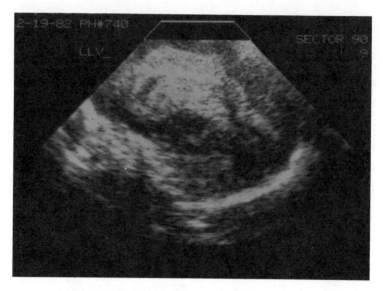

Figure 3. Sagittal ultrasound scan of premature infant at 3 days of age. Lateral ventricle is largely obscured by blood, most apparent anteriorly (reader's left). Superior to the intraventricular blood is a nearly rectangular area of echogenicity in frontal white matter that represents hemorrhagic intracerebral involvement.

Extent of Involvement

How extensive is this hemorrhagic intracerebral lesion? There has been for some time the impression from clinical follow-up of these infants that the lesion is probably more extensive than what is seen during the acute period on either ultrasound or CT scans. The neurological deficits seen on follow-up of these babies are much greater than might be predicted by observation of the lesions on ultrasound or CT scans.

Rationale for Use of PET   We reasoned that a very good way to demonstrate the full extent of the lesion would be to measure cerebral blood flow to various parts of the white matter in these patients, with the hypothesis being that any areas that are injured will show a decrease in cerebral blood flow. Thus decreased cerebral blood flow would be a very sensitive indicator, at least in the acute period, of an area of injury and would give us a better idea of the extent of the lesion.

Until recently it has been really a kind of fantasy to consider measuring regional cerebral blood flow in the human infant. Now,

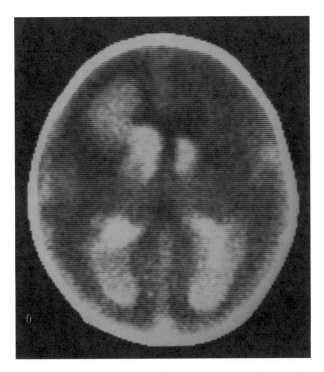

Figure 4. CT scan of premature infant at 6 days of age. Note bilateral intraventricular hemorrhage and hemorrhagic intracerebral involvement in left frontal white matter.

with the advent of PET, it is possible to accomplish such measurements, which task my colleagues and I carried out in a series of these babies.

PET Technique   PET combines a biochemical-physiological-type assessment of pathology with the kind of localization that can be achieved by computerized image reconstruction. The technique utilizes positron-emiting isotopes, such as oxygen-15, nitrogen-13, carbon-11, and fluorine-18, and the relative safety of PET relates at least in part to the short half-life of the isotopes. We have employed oxygen-15, which has a half-life of just 2 minutes, so only a very short time of exposure to the radiation is experienced by the infant.

In our studies we measured regional cerebral blood flow with oxygen-15-labeled water. Water is a very good tracer for measuring regional cerebral blood flow because it is freely diffusible. We inject the compound intravenously and quantitate cerebral blood flow by simultaneous measurements of radioactivity in the brain by PET and in arterial blood by direct sampling.

Figure 5 is a schematic detailing how the technique works. The patient's head is placed within a circular array of detectors. In PET scanning the radiation emanating from within the patient's head is detected by the external detectors, which are linked in coincidence circuits. The linkage in coincidence circuits provides PET's capacity for localization (see legend to Figure 5).

Figure 6 illustrates the actual circular array of detectors in our instrument. The infant's head is on a specially built small platform, and the infant's monitoring equipment can be seen. The infant shown

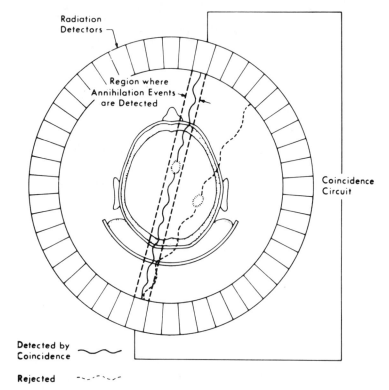

Figure 5. Schematic depiction of patient's head placed within circular array of detectors for PET scanning. Annihilation events caused by collision of positrons emitted from tracer molecules and electrons in brain result in generation of gamma rays that fly off in exactly opposite directions. These high-energy rays are detected by the external detectors, which are linked as pairs in coincidence circuits. Only those gamma rays striking opposing pairs of coincidence circuits are recorded for image formation. This enables the scanner to produce an image in which the radioisotope activity is localized to a particular region of the brain; stray, unmatched rays are not recorded and allowed to distort the image.

is not on a ventilator, but we have studied many babies on ventilators with no problems.

The PET scanner that we used is a sixth-generation scanner at Washington University with an 11-mm resolution, and the total time of the scan, which is a 7-slice scan, is 40 seconds. The radiation exposure that the baby receives with this particular technique is 75 millirads to the brain, in comparison with the typical CT scan, which provides 1,300–1,500 millirads to the central slice of the brain.

Regional Cerebral Blood Flow in Hemorrhagic Intracerebral Involvement Figure 7 shows the PET scans from six different premature infants, each with hemorrhagic intracerebral involvement in the left frontal white matter on ultrasonography. These scans are horizontal sections of brain. The color scale (shown here in black and white) is a linear representation of cerebral blood flow, with highest flows corresponding to white and lowest flows corresponding to black. Corresponding to the region of echogenicity on the ultrasound scan in the left frontal white matter (i.e., the hemorrhagic component of the hemorrhagic intracerebral involvement), there is a region of very low cerebral blood flow. This was an expected finding. However, an unexpected finding was a large area of decreased cerebral blood flow

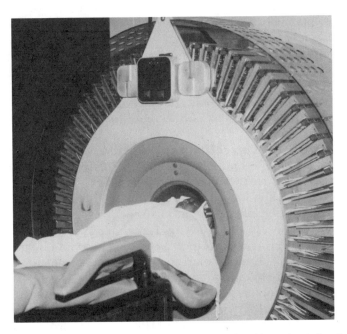

Figure 6. PET scanner at Washington University. Note the infant's head within the circular array of detectors.

that in every case extends posteriorly into parietal and occipital white matter (Figure 7). Thus, a much more extensive area of apparent injury was observed on the PET scans than would have been predicted from the ultrasound scans.

Etiology of the Lesion

What causes this lesion? To approach this question, we reviewed our total experience, with data gathered from the time that we began to do ultrasound scanning in our unit, about 6 years ago. The scans of the 1,100 premature infants who had been studied since that time were the starting sample. Hemorrhagic intracerebral involvement was defined in those 1,100 babies as any intraparenchymal echodensity greater than 1 cm in at least one dimension. We employed that criterion to be sure that we were collecting obvious lesions and not equivocal echodensities, the significance of which is often controversial.

We found, in that starting group of about 1,100 babies, 75 examples of hemorrhagic intracerebral involvement. There are three major points about that population that provide insight into what causes this lesion.

Relation to Large Intraventricular Hemorrhage The first point is that, of those 75 babies, 58 had a hemorrhagic intracerebral lesion in association with grade III intraventricular hemorrhage (IVH), the most severe form of IVH in our grading system (Table 1). Thus, most of the cases of hemorrhagic intracerebral involvement also had an associated large IVH.

Relation to Laterality of Associated Intraventricular Hemorrhage The second point of interest that became apparent as we looked closely at these large IVHs is that they were almost all asymmetric. We also looked at the location of the side of the larger IVH relative to the side of the intraparenchymal echodensity (IPE), which incidentally was also nearly always asymmetric (Guzzetta, Shackelford, Volpe, Perlman, & Volpe, 1986). An IPE on the same side as the larger IVH is termed homolateral, and an IPE on the opposite side from the larger IVH is termed contralateral. As can be seen in Table 2, of those infants who had grade III IVH with the hemorrhagic intracerebral lesion, 47 (*all of them*) had the lesion homolateral to the IPE; none of them had a contralateral IPE. This concordance between side of the IPE and side of a large IVH was not the case with smaller degrees of IVH (Table 2).

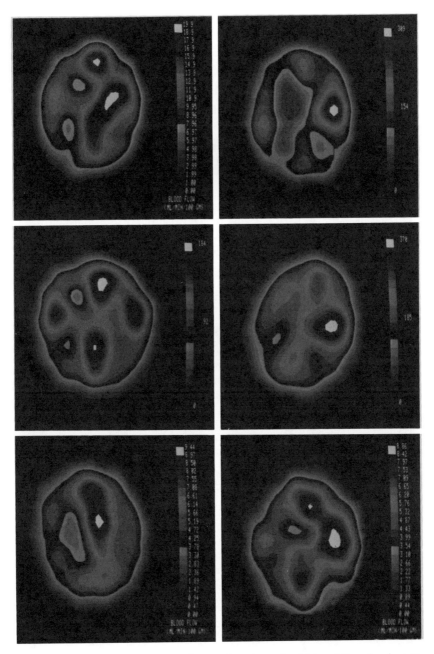

Figure 7. PET scans representing regional cerebral blood flow in six premature infants with hemorrhagic intracerebral involvement in left frontal white matter. Scans are horizontal sections parallel to the orbitomeatal line. Black-white scale shown to the right of each scan is a linear representation of cerebral blood flow. See text for details.

These data prompted us to consider that the IVH, the blood within the ventricle, was doing something to provoke the hemorrhagic intracerebral lesion. In this regard, it should be noted that the timing of the IPE and the IVH indicated that the IPEs were usually occurring 24–48 hours *after* the maximal degree of IVH.

Conclusions We have tentatively concluded that the hemorrhagic intracerebral involvement is in large part caused by the large asymmetric IVH. How could that happen? The pathological specimen illustrated in Figure 8 may provide an important clue. In this coronal section of the brain from a baby who died 4 or 5 days after birth, an asymmetric IVH with a very large amount of blood in the left lateral ventricle is apparent. In the left periventricular white matter can be seen a very striking amount of venous congestion (the darkened area). This tissue was not yet infarcted, but I think that if this congestion had persisted for another 12–24 hours the periventricular region in question would have exhibited hemorrhagic intracerebral necrosis. I suspect that the mass of blood is having some effect, whether it be because of periventricular venous pressure from the distending clot, or vasospasm caused by K^+ released from lysed red blood cells, or direct injury caused by lactic acid associated with the metabolizing red blood cells. I favor the first of these mechanisms: impaired venous flow leading to a venous infarction. It is, of course, well known that venous infarctions are hemorrhagic. We suspect that the intraventricular hemorrhage is in some way impairing flow in the cerebral white matter and causing the periventricular infarction.

SPECULATION

These considerations lead to a speculation that if the large IVH can be prevented (which can be done by muscle paralysis), perhaps hem-

Table 1. Association of IVH and IPE[a]

Severity of IVH	No. with IPE
Grade III	58
Grades I and II	13
No IVH	4

[a]IVH, intraventricular hemorrhage; IPE, intraparenchymal echodensity.

Table 2. Relation of side of IPE with side of asymmetric IVH

Severity of IVH	No. of patients with	
	IPE homolateral	IPE contralateral
Grade III	47	0
Grades I and II	5	4

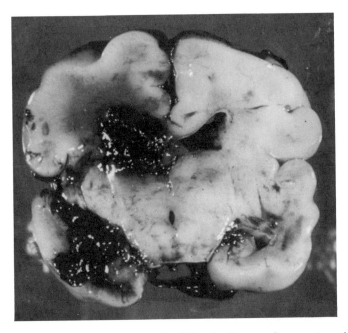

Figure 8. Coronal section of cerebral hemispheres of premature infant who died at 3 days of age. Note large, asymmetric intraventricular hemorrhage distending right lateral ventricle and large darkened area of venous congestion in right periventricular white matter.

orrhagic intracerebral involvement can also be prevented. Further research will be needed to prove this speculation, but I think that with the combination of PET and ultrasound technology we have been able to at least move in the right direction.

REFERENCES

Guzzetta, F., Shackelford, G.D., Volpe, S., Perlman, J.M., & Volpe, J.J. (1986). Periventricular intraparenchymal echodensities in the premature newborn. *Pediatrics, 78*, 995–1006.

Volpe, J.J. (1987). *Neurology of the Newborn* (pp. 311–361). Philadelphia: W.B. Saunders.

12 | Neonatal Intensive Care and Developmental Outcome

MILDRED T. STAHLMAN,
JENS GROGAARD,
DANIEL P. LINDSTROM,
NANCY HAYWOOD, and
BARBARA CULLEY

Neonatal intensive care as we know it now began 25 years ago. Since that time neonatal mortality rates have changed dramatically in the United States for a variety of reasons, including better obstetrical practices and technological and informational advances in neonatal care. Also, the importance of the regionalization of perinatal and neonatal high-risk care nationwide cannot be overemphasized.

The authors of this chapter have been evaluating babies since neonatal intensive care was begun at Vanderbilt University Medical Center in October of 1961. The first population studied longitudinally was born during the time period October 1961–June 1971. Babies who had hyaline membrane disease were the major focus of interest during that time, and these infants were followed up to 11 years of age. The next group of infants studied was born in the 5-year period July 1971–June 1976. Since 1976 there has been a dramatic increase in the survival of babies weighing less than 1,500 g (3.25 lb) at birth, so more recent cohorts have included these babies as well as those with hyaline membrane disease. The evaluation of these infants has included both medical and psychological testing. For the purposes of this paper we will use the definitions of terminology outlined in Table 1.

This work was sponsored by two NIH grants: Newborn Lung Center SCOR #14214 and General Clinical Research Center #RR 00095.

Table 1. Definitions of birth weight terminology

Terminology	Birth weight
Premature infants	≤ 2,500 g
Low birth weight (LBW) infants	1,501–2,500 g
Very low birth weight (VLBW) infants	≤ 1,500 g
Extremely immature infants	≤ 1,000 g

VERY LOW AND LOW BIRTH WEIGHT AND INTELLIGENCE

Of the babies in the 1962–1971 cohort who had hyaline membrane disease, particular interest was focused on longitudinal studies of 174 babies who had been followed up at 2 or 3 years of age and again at 5, 6, or 7 years (Mayes et al., 1985). The mean birth weight of this group was rather high (2,133 g), and they had a mean gestation of 34.6 weeks, reflecting the fact that many babies with severe hyaline membrane disease who were born prematurely and with low birth weight did not survive during that time period (Stahlman, Hedvall, Lindstrom, & Snell, 1982).

When one looks at those babies who were longitudinally studied it is interesting to note that the preschoolers (the 2–3-year age group) had mean developmental quotient (DQ) scores of 91, whereas the school-age group (5–7 years of age) had IQ scores of 101.4. Table 2 shows the developmental tests used to measure DQ and IQ in the different time periods studied. Thirty preschoolers had a DQ of less than 80, but when tested again at the age of 5–7 years only 18 of these children had an IQ of less than 80. At preschool age, only 13

Table 2. Developmental tests used in the different cohorts studied from 1961 to 1985

	Age group (years)	Years of test use
Gesell Developmental Schedules	1–3	1961–1976
Leiter International Performance Scale	3	1961–1971
Peabody Picture Vocabulary Test	3	1961–1971
McCarthy Scales of Children's Abilities	3	1971–1976
Wechsler Preschool and Primary Scale of Intelligence	5	1961–1971
Stanford-Binet Intelligence Scale	3–7	1976–1985
Bayley Scales of Infant Development	1–3	1976–1985
Wechsler Intelligence Scale for Children	5–7	1961–1985

children had a DQ ≥ 111, whereas 50 school-age children showed an IQ ≥ 111 (Mayes et al., 1985).

In the July 1971–June 1976 cohort there were 144 longitudinally studied children with hyaline membrane disease; by this time increasing numbers of babies of less than 1,500 g birth weight had begun to survive. The mean birth weight (1,960 g) was somewhat less than that of the earlier cohort and their mean gestational age was 33.0 weeks. These children showed the same interesting pattern of test score increase between preschool and school age. The mean DQ score measured in the preschoolers was 92.4, versus a mean IQ score of 99.4 at school age. The number of preschoolers with low DQs decreased by the time they reached school age and the number of children with high DQs (≥111) increased from 15 to 39. It seems that most babies of greater than 1,500 g birth weight (all but 25 of this cohort were over 1,500 g and only two were less than 1,000 g) do well at long-term developmental evaluation.

In examining the survival of babies weighing 1,001–1,500 g who were admitted to the neonatal intensive care unit (NICU) between 1962 and 1985, one can see that in 1962 not many very low birth weight babies survived neonatal intensive care (Figure 1). Few extremely immature babies (500–1,000 g) were transferred to Vanderbilt because survival was not considered likely. Between 1974 and 1977 significant numbers of very low birth weight babies began to be admitted (inborn and outborn) with a substantial increase in survival; since that time both number of admissions and percentage of survivors have continued to increase. In the babies weighing between 500 and 1,000 g, the same pattern holds, with almost no survival until the years 1974 to 1977, when there were an increasing number of admissions and increasing percentages of survivors (Figure 2). In 1986 these increases continued, even in the lowest birth weight groups.

The outcomes of 108 very low birth weight babies born between 1976 and 1980 who have reached the age of at least 5 years have been studied longitudinally. These children were tested at 2–3 years and again at 5–7 years, and the pattern described above for children in the 1961–1971 and 1971–1976 cohorts was seen. Their developmental/intelligence levels have increased by about 10 points and are highly statistically significantly different at the two periods studied. Figure 3 shows the distribution of DQ/IQ outcomes for these 108 very low birth weight babies. Most were found to have increased scores on IQ tests compared to their DQ test scores: the number of these babies with a DQ of less than 80 decreased from 34 to 21, and the number with an IQ ≥ 111 increased from 2 to 15; 60 children's developmental/intelligence scores remained in the same range.

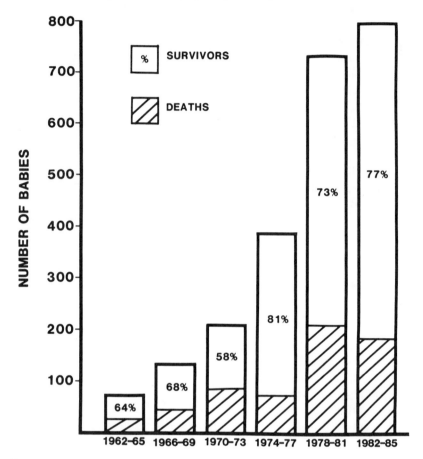

Figure 1.   Number of babies and survival percentages of babies with birth weights of 1,001–1,500 g admitted to Vanderbilt University Medical Center NICU, 1962–1985.

VERY LOW BIRTH WEIGHT
AND INCIDENCE OF HANDICAP

There were 1,904 babies weighing less than 1,500 g at birth admitted to the Vanderbilt University Medical Center NICU between 1976 and 1985, and of these 1,402 survived (Grogaard, Culley, Lindstrom, Haywood, & Stahlman, 1987). There is a high attrition rate for follow-up in the Middle Tennessee area and only 530 of these babies (38%) have been followed for 1 year or more. It was therefore important to establish baseline data on all of the infants admitted in order to allow predictive comparison between the infants who were followed and those who were not. Some of the population characteristics mea-

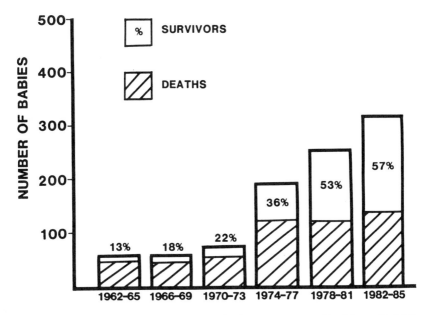

Figure 2. Number of babies and survival percentages of babies with birth weights of ≤ 1,000 g admitted to Vanderbilt University Medical Center NICU, 1962–1985.

surements (e.g., whether the infant was born at Vanderbilt (inborn) or elsewhere (outborn); Apgar scores; incidence of bronchopulmonary dysplasia, intracranial hemorrhage, hydrocephalus) were not statistically different between these two groups, although the follow-up group tended to contain somewhat sicker infants (Table 3). However, there were other comparability parameters (e.g., gestational age; birth weight; incidence of cesarean section; and incidence of such conditions as hyaline membrane disease, air leak, symptomatic patent ductus arteriosus, and recurrent apnea of prematurity) that were statistically significantly different, and had greater occurrence in the follow-up babies. Since the follow-up infants were somewhat more immature, with slightly lower birth weights and slightly lower gestational ages in addition to a higher incidence of perinatal complications, it seems that, if anything, one might expect a worse outcome for the babies who were followed up than for the babies who were not followed.

Of this group of 530 babies who were followed up, 96 (18%) were identified as having handicaps. Of these, 43 (8%) had cerebral palsy. Six percent had IQs of less than 70, which is a very low incidence for this high-risk group of babies. Seven percent had retinopathy of prematurity (ROP); this included cicatricial disease or blindness, so these

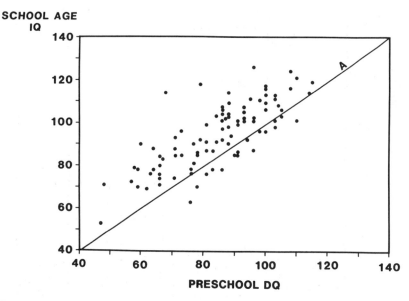

Figure 3. Scatterplot comparison of preschool DQ and school-age IQ for each of 108 very low birth weight infants born between 1976 and 1980, longitudinally tested at 2–3 years (preschool DQ) and at 5–7 years (school-age IQ). *A* = the line of identity. Each dot may represent more than one infant.

cases represent the most severe variety of ROP. Two percent had sensorineural hearing loss, and 4% had hydrocephalus with a shunt in place. (These percentages add to more than 18 because some of these infants have multiple handicaps, the most common combination being cerebral palsy and mental retardation.)

Upon examining these babies by 250-g intervals of birth weight at two different time periods (1976–1980 and 1981–1985), the numbers of survivors in each 250-g birth weight interval increased dramatically. It was predicted that, with increasingly lower birth weight survival, the percentages of morbidity rates and sequelae would also increase, and that outcome data would reflect increasing percentages of handicapped infants. However, the percentage of handicapped babies had not increased, but had actually declined during these two 5-year periods. Among the babies weighing 500–1,500 g followed during this 10-year span, there were 30 babies of less than 750 g with a 37% incidence of handicap. This incidence rate fell progressively with increasing birth weight to 12% in babies weighing 1,250–1,500 g.

Table 3. Comparability of follow-up infants versus those not followed[a]

Characteristic[b]	Follow-up	Not followed	p
n	530	853	
Gestational age (wks)	30 ± 2.2[c]	30.5 ± 2.2[c]	ns
Birth weight (g)	1156 ± 234[c]	1189 ± 232[c]	ns
Inborn/outborn	309/221	517/337	ns
Apgar 1 min	4.7 ± 2.4[c]	4.6 ± 2.5[c]	ns
Apgar 5 min	6.7 ± 1.9[c]	6.8 ± 1.9[c]	ns
C-section	41%	35%	<0.02
HMD	45%	30%	<0.001
Air leaks	22%	14%	<0.02
sPDA	53%	36%	<0.001
Recurrent apnea	19%	14%	<0.01
BPD	17%	13%	ns
ICH	9%	5%	ns
Hydrocephalus and shunt	4%	2%	ns

[a]Infants were born from 1976 to 1985, and all weighed <1,500 g.

[b]HMD = hyaline membrane disease, sPDA = symptomatic patent ductus arteriosus, BPD = bronchopulmonary dysplasia, and ICH = intracranial hemorrhage grade III–IV.

[c]Mean ± SD

SUMMARY

There has been an enormous increase in survival of very low birth weight babies (less than 1,500 g) over the past 10 years in this country. This is a national phenomenon, and this increased survival rate has occurred essentially without increasing the percentage of handicaps in these low birth weight infants. Longitudinal follow-up in several cohorts has shown an increase in developmental/intelligence levels from preschool age (2–3 years) to school age (5–7 years) that is statistically significant. The reason for this increase may be partially related to the extremes of prematurity from which these babies have had to catch up developmentally, and may be partially related to the fact that different kinds of test instruments are used at these two age periods so that different types of information processing are being tested. We conclude that most infants of very low birth weight who survive newborn intensive care are competitive intellectually. One-fifth still have significant handicaps, but even the lowest birth weight category cannot be abandoned as having a hopeless outcome.

ACKNOWLEDGMENTS

The authors thank the neonatal fellows in the Vanderbilt Medical Center for their help in evaluating the medical outcome of these infants.

REFERENCES

Grogaard, J.B., Culley, B.S., Lindstrom, D.P., Haywood, N., & Stahlman, M.T. (1987). Increased survival in VLBW infants (<1500 g) is not associated with increased handicap rate. *Pediatric Research, 21*, 396A.

Mayes, L.C., Kirk, V., Haywood, N., Buchanan, D., Hedvall, G., & Stahlman, M.T. (1985). Changing cognitive outcome in preterm infants with hyaline membrane disease. *American Journal of Diseases of Children, 139*, 20–24.

Stahlman, M.T., Hedvall, G., Lindstrom, D., & Snell, J. (1982). Role of hyaline membrane disease in production of later childhood lung abnormalities. *Pediatrics, 69*, 572–576.

13 | Neural Plasticity and the Effect of a Supportive Hospital Environment on Premature Newborns

FRANK H. DUFFY and HEIDELISE ALS

It is well known that continuing advances in medical technology have resulted in greater survival and functional viability of premature human infants. It is not uncommon for premature babies less than a kilogram (2.2 lb) in weight at birth to survive. It is nonetheless true that these premature infants are not as likely as full-term infants to grow into well balanced, capably functioning children and adults. As they grow older, premature infants are overrepresented in the population of children with learning dysfunction, behavior problems, and mental retardation. Drillien, Thomson, and Bargoyne (1980) noted that up to 50% of small-for-gestational-age (SGA) premature babies are later found to have some degree of learning disability. The questions the authors of this chapter have asked in their research are: Why are prematurely born infants at greater risk for subsequent problems? Are the majority of premature infants destined to experience functional neurological disabilities in later life by the fact of their premature birth, or are there ways in which neurological development in premature newborns can be directly and positively influenced such that some percentage of these infants will demonstrate greater mental viability in their childhood years?

Underlying these questions is the academic issue of nature versus nurture. Although the issue is of theoretical interest, it is clear that "nurture," or the environment, is most under direct control and most modifiable. Neonatal research conducted by the authors of this chapter has led to the belief that the aversive environment that most premature newborns experience in the first few weeks of extrauterine life can be modified in such a way as to enhance later life functioning. The premature newborn is thrust unexpectedly and, in a state of biological unpreparedness, into an aversive milieu. Furthermore, the very medical strategies that are required to maintain the biological systemic functioning of very premature newborns introduce additional pain and stress-producing stimuli (e.g., Als, 1982). This chapter presents the findings on the strategies developed in the Neonatal Intensive Care Unit at Children's Hospital in Boston to counteract these aversive environmental factors. Initial findings are presented on research examining two comparable groups of premature newborns, one of which received nurturing environmental support at birth, the other of which received current traditional hospital care at birth. However, the basic theoretical premise of the influence of the environment on animal and human development is addressed first. Also, the new and/or refined assessment methods that have necessarily been developed so as to reliably demonstrate the effects of environment on neurological development are discussed.

NEURAL PLASTICITY—THE ANIMAL MODEL

One of the animal models best demonstrating environmental impact on development was the pioneering work of Wiesel and Hubel (1963a, 1963b, 1965) in their research on "critical period monocular deprivation amblyopia." Briefly stated, they raised kittens through the first 16 weeks of life with one eyelid sutured shut, and observed resulting behavioral and electrophysiological alterations. They discovered that the kittens were essentially blind in the monocularly deprived (MD) eye whereas visual behavior was normal when the nondeprived eye was used. Furthermore, neurophysiological studies indicated that the neuronal cells at the visual cortex could not be activated in response to visual stimulation of the deprived eye. This visual deficiency is referred to as *amblyopia*. Once established, it is relatively permanent. Only slight behavioral and little or no electrophysiological amelioration is possible in response to subsequent visual experience.

In contrast to the profound visual disturbances produced by even short periods of MD in kittens, prolonged MD in the adult cat is without significant effect. Wiesel and Hubel were the first to thus demonstrate a developmental "critical period" during which manipulations of the environment could profoundly affect neural development (e.g., 4–16 weeks of age for the feline visual system). Environmental manipulations outside of this period produce little or no effect.

The authors and their colleagues decided to extend this visual research on kittens in an attempt to determine whether the critical period is genetically determined or whether it is somehow environmentally triggered at birth. To investigate, a series of experiments was designed to determine whether one could delay onset of the critical period by preventing visual experience (Mower, Berry, Burchfiel, & Duffy, 1981). Initially, binocular lid suture (BS) was performed on kittens near the time of spontaneous eye opening. At the end of the classic critical period (16 weeks), one eyelid was opened and the animal was given several months of MD experience. The thought was that, if the critical period had already ended, the animals would show the classic binocular deprivation neurophysiological pattern; however, if the critical period had been postponed, the MD paradigm should have a significant effect. The BS-to-MD preparation did not produce the classic behavioral or physiological effects of MD amblyopia. These animals were "blind" bilaterally and showed the neurophysiological pattern associated with binocular deprivation. However, another set of kittens was reared in total darkness (DR) until 16 weeks and then brought into a normal environment after having one lit sutured shut. These two groups (BD and DR) permitted a comparison between the effects of diffuse light (BS) and complete light deprivation (DR), since the sutured lids do not eliminate light stimulation but merely attenuate it. After a period of MD experience this DR-to-MD preparation did reproduce the classic cortical effects of MD despite the fact that the environmental manipulation occurred beyond the end of the classic critical period.

In the binocularly sutured kittens, the diffuse light through closed eyelids was enough to trigger onset of the critical period. In the kittens initially raised in total darkness, the critical period was delayed until first exposure to light at 16 weeks. Thus the timing of the critical period is not controlled entirely by genetics; it requires environmental stimulation for initiation. Furthermore, one might logically ask if the critical period can be delayed by withholding exposure to light, can it be prematurely initiated by early exposure to light? These findings seem to hold significance for the premature infant. Is it possible that premature exposure to complex environmental stimuli trigger critical periods in many or even all sensory and motor systems in humans before they are biologically capable of integrating them?

BRAIN ELECTRICAL ACTIVITY MAPPING

A standard tool in the neurological assessment of the newborn is electroencephalography. Figure 1 provides a page of standard electroencephalogram (EEG) tracings. The electroencephalographer is confronted with the complex task of evaluating the neurological status of a patient by interpreting as many as a hundred pages of these tracings in a brief diagnostic session. First, the EEG record is examined

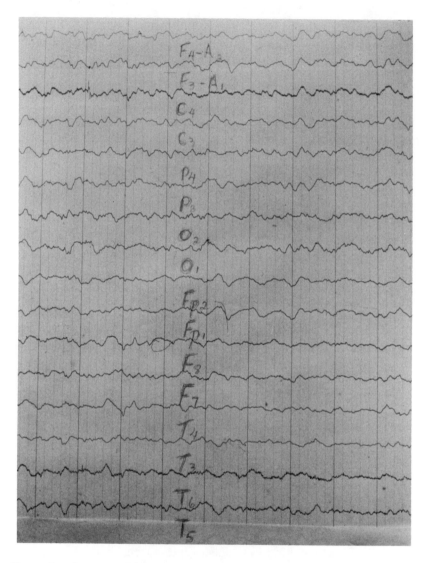

Figure 1. One page (10 sec) of standard EEG tracings. Letter designations with numeric subscripts indicate location of the electrodes on the scalp, based on the international standard 10–20 placement system. Each vertical line represents passage of 1 sec. This tracing was read as normal for age (neonate).

for obvious paroxysmal activity, such as spike or spike-and-wave readings, which are probabilistically indicative of underlying seizure disorder. The EEG reader must be careful to distinguish these readings from artifact such as eye blink, muscular movement, or equipment-related false indicators. Once these readily identifiable signals are detected, the task becomes much more nuanced. Electroencephalograms contain an immense amount of information that must be analyzed in four general dimensions: 1) spatial (physical extent and movement); 2) spectral (amplitude of electrical charge within the frequency band); 3) temporal (duration of each given electrical event); and 4) statistical (comparison of a given individual's brain electrical activity with that of normal subjects).

The diagnostic limitations of electroencephalography and evoked potential (EP) analysis are not due to too little information in the recordings, but rather to their wealth of information and their complexity. This complexity can create problems in reliability of interpretation between different readings, and between different readers of the same electroencephalographic data. The solution developed by the authors for the extraction of further information from EEG and EP data is called brain electrical activity mapping (BEAM), or topographic mapping. This technique uses recently evolved computer imaging techniques, as well as relatively sophisticated statistical paradigms, to provide the clinician with an evaluation of neurophysiological functioning. In the case of EEG, data are typically collected from 20 electrodes and an interpolation algorithm is used to generate intermediate values between electrodes. A grid composed of pixels (picture elements) is formed by assigning numeric values to frequency bands. These are translated into scale values of white-gray-black or color (rainbow scale). The result is a graphic representation of brain electrical activity at a point in time. Topographic images of EPs can be generated at millisecond intervals over a period of seconds and then viewed, in cartoon fashion, as the computer displays a series of images evidencing spatial intensity and trajectory of brain electrical activity over time.

When interpreting a traditional EEG, the neurophysiologist may take advantage of these imaging techniques to enhance their diagnostic capability. An example from clinical practice is provided in Figure 2. These topographic maps are based on EEG and EP data from an 8-year-old who has suffered a left-hemisphere stroke. In the top portion of the figure, one sees that EEG spectral activity is diminished or absent over the left hemisphere. EP mapping (bottom) again depicts the virtual absence of normal brain response in the left hemisphere to auditory stimuli.

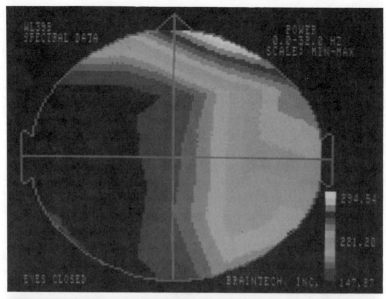

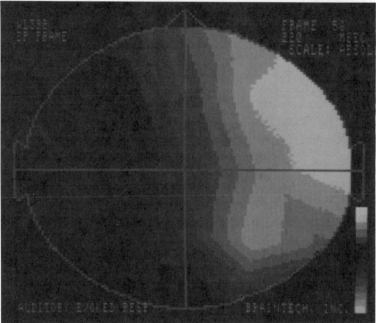

Figure 2. Brain electrical activity mapping (BEAM). *Top:* The image is shown in vertex view, nose toward top of page, left to viewer's left. This map is developed from EEG recordings, taken with eyes closed, of an 8-year-old girl who has suffered a left-hemisphere stroke. *Bottom:* A top-ographic map based on auditory-evoked potentials data from the same 8-year-old. Note the lack of left hemisphere electrical activity evidenced in both mappings.

The application of topographic mapping to assessment of such gross neurophysiological insults as brain tumor or epilepsy is relatively straightforward. However, it became clear that normal subjects often demonstrate a degree of asymmetry or focality of brain wave activity. Frequently it became necessary to assess whether seeming neurological abnormalities could be explained by normal variation, or whether actual clinically abnormal readings were evidenced. In 1981, in conjunction with Dr. Peter Bartels from the University of Arizona, the authors developed a technique known as significance probability mapping (SPM) (Duffy, Bartels, & Burchfiel, 1981).

In SPM, the topographic image of EEG or EP data of an individual can be compared to that of a control group data set. The image that is generated is that of the degree of difference between the individual and the group, statistically quantified using the z transform, essentially displaying an image of standard deviation from the norm. This imaging process fulfilled the final complicated step in clinical evaluation of EEG and EP data, that is, the delineation of that which is abnormal. This technique has proven singularly valuable in a substantial number and range of clinical applications. In addition, SPM is not limited to diagnosing the difference between individuals and a normative group. Significance probability mapping images can also be utilized to identify between-group differences, generating images based on the Student's t statistic. This mapping strategy has been utilized in research applications such as the comparison of brain electrical activity in children with dyslexia and in normal children (Duffy, Denckla, Bartels, & Sandini, 1980; Duffy, Denckla, Bartels, Sandini, & Kiessling, 1980). Figure 3 provides an example of both a z transform SPM (z-SPM) delineating individual versus normative group differences, and a t statistic SPM (t-SPM) comparing two groups. Figure 3A provides a computed tomography (CT) scan of a 59-year-old male with a brain tumor in the right parietal–posterotemporal region, and Figure 3B shows the z-SPM of this man. The t-SPMs (Figs. 3C–F) compare alpha activity in other individuals during restful alertness with no auditory stimulus to that when listening to speech (e.g., a poem) and to music (e.g., the Nutcracker Suite). Figures 3C and 3D are SPMs of normal boys and 3E and 3F are those of dyslexic boys, ages 9–13. Note that although the dyslexics show well-localized alpha differences during speech and music, the locations of these differences are quite distinct from those of the control subjects.

Figure 4 provides a direct comparison of the two groups. This figure is a composite t-SPM summarizing in one image all regions of between-group difference using a criterion t level of $p<.02$ or better, based on EEG recordings. The figure indicates group divergence in

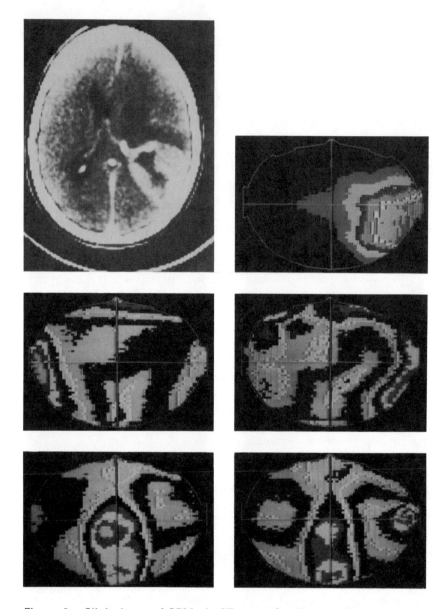

Figure 3.   Clinical use of SPM. *A:* CT scan of a 59-year-old male with a confirmed glioblastoma multiforme of the right parietal–posterotemporal region (*lower right*). There is considerable edema surrounding the tumor. *B: z* Transform SPM of same patient. The temporal regions appear exaggerated because of the method of projection, which is designed to give equal representation to all scalp regions. The SPM represents the sustained deviation from normal of the visual-evoked potential (VEP) over the

latency interval 290–366 msec. Each shade of the display represents a particular value of z, from 1 to 7. Note how the SPM highlights the VEP abnormality, and the close agreement between the region of maximum z and the location of the tumor on CT scan. Note also that the physiologically derived SPM identified a more extensive area of abnormality surrounding the tumor; this probably represents functional deficits due to edema. C and D: t Statistic SPMs showing differences in alpha activity (8– 12 Hz) within a group of normal subjects depending upon whether they are listening to speech (C) or music (D). In each case the t statistic is derived in comparison to alpha activity recorded during the state of restful alertness, eyes closed with no auditory stimulation. In these and subsequent plots, different shades represent different values of t. Note that listening to speech significantly alters alpha activity over the left temporal region (C) whereas listening to music affects right temporal alpha (D). E and F: t statistic SPMs showing differences in alpha activity in a group of dyslexic boys listening to speech (E) or music (F). This is the same paradigm as shown in C and D for normal controls. Note that although the dyslexic subjects show well-localized alpha differences during speech and music, the locations of the differences are distinct from those shown by the control subjects. (From Duffy, F.H., Bartels, P.H., & Burchfiel, J.L. [1981]. Significance probability mapping: An aid in the topographic analysis of brain electrical activity. *Electroencephalography and Clinical Neurophysiology, 51*, 455–462; reprinted by permission.)

---

the classic left posterior quadrant associated with speech. This would concur with the conceptualization of reading disability primarily as a language disorder. However, note that there are also significant differences imaged in the medial frontal region. This unusual finding was surprising at first, but subsequent studies in Scandanavia of regional cerebral blood flow and brain function in language (Larsen, Skinhoj, & Lassen, 1978; Lassen, Ingvar, & Skinhoj, 1978) have reinforced these findings and have led to the conclusion that, in dyslexia, there is electrophysiological dysfunction in the entire complex and bihemispheric cortex involved in language. Postmortem anatomical studies of brain structure by Dr. Albert Galaburda of Beth Israel Hospital (Galaburda & Kemper, 1979) further support this interpretation.

The use of BEAM and SPM have also been applied to clinical and research studies of autism, Alzheimer disease, and schizophrenia. Current research attempts to expand the areas of brain function whose understanding may be bettered by these analytic techniques. A final clinical example may prove of particular interest to those concerned with neonatal applications of topographic mapping techniques.

An infant born about 1 week early was brought to the authors' attention because of neonatal seizures and signs of blood in his spinal

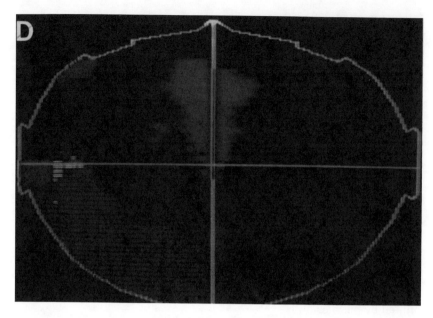

Figure 4. Composite *t*-SPM summarizing in one image all regions of between-group difference between dyslexic and nondyslexic 10–12-year-old boys. Mapping convention is as described in legend to Figure 2. Imaged are regions of difference at *t* levels corresponding to *p*<.02, two-tailed. In addition to the expected regional difference in the classic speech regions of the left hemisphere, there are bihemispheric and medial frontal regional differences (see text).

fluid. His initial CT scan and EEG were read as entirely normal and the baby was so improved after 2 weeks that he was thought well enough to go home. The attending nurse intervened at this time and stated that the baby was not ready to go home; she had noticed a deficiency in the baby's hearing. Dr. Als then examined the child and confirmed a distinct defect evinced by inability to attend to or locate auditory stimuli in the left hemispace. The subsequent BEAM demonstrated findings that concurred with the perceptions of the nurse and the behavioral evaluation findings: when Dr. Als brought the baby to focused processing, his theta distribution (the infant analog of alpha) was missing on the right side (Figure 5, top). This reading was corroborated by the visual-EP which showed a deficiency in the right posterior quadrant (Figure 5, bottom). Parenthetically, the recordings shown in Figure 1 are those of this child's EEG. The careful reading of this EEG by the child's neurologist had failed to diagnose the right posterior dysfunction. On the basis of these findings, the

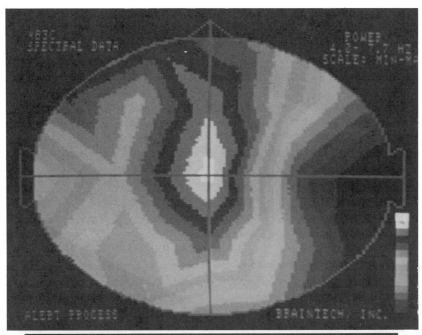

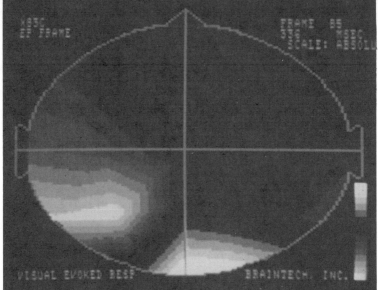

Figure 5. *Top:* Topographic distribution of theta (4–8 Hz) activity in a newborn infant with a large infarction in the right posterior quadrant. Note the diminishment of electrical activity in this region. *Bottom:* The distribution of electrical activity during a visual-evoked response is shown in the same infant. There is, again, a striking asymmetry with activity diminished over the site of the lesion in the right posterior quadrant.

baby received a second CT scan and was found to have a large infarction in this region, an infarction that had apparently not shown up on the initial CT scan. This diagnosis is of value to neurologists in being one of the very first cases of documented left hemiauditory agnosia in a newborn resultant from an anatomical lesion. Equally important, however, is the fact that input from an observant, attentive nurse and the application of new technologies resulted in detection and documentation of an abnormality that otherwise would have gone unnoticed until some point well into the future. The application of BEAM is a valuable addition to the assessment technologies and strategies available to neurologists.

ASSESSMENT OF PRETERM AND
FULL-TERM INFANT BEHAVIORS: THE APIB

Topographic mapping provides a tool for the assessment of neurophysiological development in newborns. The authors have simultaneously sought to develop reliable neuropsychological measures of behavioral development. The Assessment of Preterm Infants' Behavior (APIB) (Als, Lester, Tronick, & Brazelton, 1982) is appropriate as well for full-term and at-risk infants. The APIB is designed to systematically assess the newborn infant's ability to differentiate and modulate behavioral functioning in five mutually interactive and supportive subsystems: the autonomic system, the motor system, the state organizational system, the attention/interaction system, and the self-regulatory, balancing system. The APIB also evaluates the level of examiner facilitation that is required by the newborn in order to attain smooth modulation. The concept underlying the APIB assessment is that stimulation, if inappropriate in its timing, intensity, or quality, will cause the infant to defend himself or herself against it; if properly timed and appropriate in intensity and quality, stimulation will cause the infant to respond positively, actively seeking for it and interacting with it while maintaining a systemic balance.

This formulation of a newborn assessment system juxtaposing stress avoidance with modulation and integrative behaviors can provide caregivers with the means of identifying the infant's current thresholds of balanced, well-modulated functioning and can, in turn, facilitate the individualization of caregiving and interaction with the infant. Figure 6 contrasts two infants engaged in social interaction at 2 days after birth. The left-hand photo shows a withdrawn, poorly integrated full-term newborn (Als, Tronick, Adamson, & Brazelton, 1976); the right-hand photo, in contrast, shows a well-integrated, animated, and robust infant of the same age (Als, 1983). The difference between these infants is quite apparent. The APIB is designed to quantify the areas of qualitative behavioral difference between infants along a scale between these two extremes. The APIB yields 30 mutually exclusive summary scores, quantifying not only the skill repertoire of the newborn, but the infants' reactivity and threshold of stress and disorganization in response to environmental input.

Recently 98 newborns were studied with this assessment (Als, Duffy, McAnulty, & Badian, in press). They were selected on the criteria of: 1) no known neurological impairment, 2) no major medical problems in infant and mother, and 3) no severe social hardships evident in the family history. The infants were selected to represent a full range of preterm to full-term births:

1. Thirty-three infants born at less than 33 weeks' gestational age, referred to as PPTs or pre-preterm infants.
2. Thirty-one infants born at 32–36 weeks' gestational age, referred to as PTs (middle preterms).
3. Thirty-four infants born at 37–41 weeks' gestational age and referred to as FTs (full-terms).

All infants were healthy and living at home at 42 weeks after conception. They were examined with the APIB at this time to see whether the APIB results would allow the infants to be sorted into behaviorally defined, functionally distinct subgroups, independent of gestational age. Cluster analysis was employed (Anderberg, 1973; Bartels, 1980; Bartels & Wied, 1973; Beale, 1969) to establish whether three naturally occurring behavioral clusters that would have meaning could be defined. The 98-subject group was randomly split into equal halves, one being the group used to develop a set of behavioral classification rules (training set); the other being the group upon which the rules would be tested (test set). The results of the split-half analysis were extremely robust, providing for selection of six behavioral variables that consistently differentiated the total group of newborns and established three distinct groupings (clusters or "nimbuloids") of behavioral functioning. A more complete discussion of this analytic method is given in Als et al. (in press). Figure 7 provides graphic representation of the groupings that emerged when these APIB behavioral measures were analyzed for all 98 subjects. Nimbuloid I shows well-modulated, overall stable infants and, as one would anticipate, was predominantly made up of full-term infants. Note, however, that three extremely preterm infants were included in this group. Nimbuloid III shows infants who were greatly disorganized in terms of

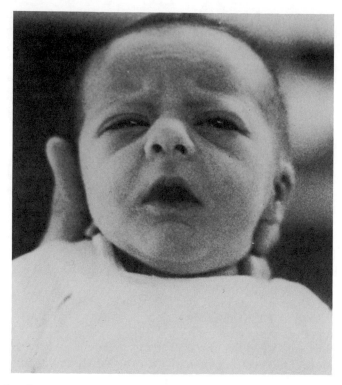

Figure 6.   Comparison of poorly integrated and well-integrated newborns. *Left:* Poorly integrated, drawn, full-term newborn at 2 days after birth. The infant is having difficulty in alerting, as evidenced by the strained expression. (From Als, H., Tronick, E., Adamson, L., & Brazelton, T.B. [1976]. The behavior of the full-term but underweight infant. *Developmental Medicine*

(continued)

autonomic and motor behaviors and ability to self-regulate. The expected predominance by the very preterm infant is evidenced here (20 PPTs), but this least well-functioning group did include three full-term infants.

The APIB provided us with the desired subject grouping based upon behavioral functioning without regard to gestational age. Given the stability of the behavioral clusters, it was then asked whether these group configurations could be validated by electrophysiological (EEG and/or EP) evidence (Als et al., in press). This was investigated using the previously described BEAM topographic mapping methodology.

To locate regional differences among the three APIB nimbuloids, group means and standard deviations were found separately for each cluster in each brain activation state while maintaining topographic

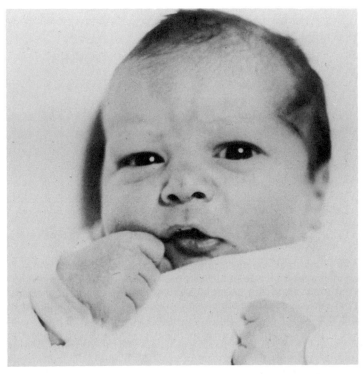

and Child Neurology, 18, 590–602.) *Right:* An infant of the same age who, by comparison, is well integrated, animated in social interaction, and robust. (From Als, H. [1983]. Infant individuality: Assessing patterns of very early development. In F. Call, E. Galensen, & R.L. Tyson [Eds.], *Frontiers in infant psychiatry* [p. 368–378]. New York: Basic Books; reprinted by permission.)

specificity. Using the SPM technique (Duffy et al., 1981), the results of a one-way analysis of variance were imaged as F statistic SPMs (F = SPMs), the summary SPM being provided in Figure 8. These F-SPMs were used to form templates that were, in turn, used to generate numerical BEAM descriptors of features. BEAM feature mean values for the APIB nimbuloids and univariate t-test comparisons between all pairs of clusters were developed. We then asked whether the BEAM features would rank the APIB nimbuloids in the same order as did the APIB variables. A simplistic approach was taken, identifying the "better" feature values by their means for the FT group. It was pleasing that the APIB nimbuloids were ranked in the same order whether BEAM features or APIB variables were used.

It can be concluded that the APIB-generated clusters of infants show large, identifiable electrophysiological differences. Moreover,

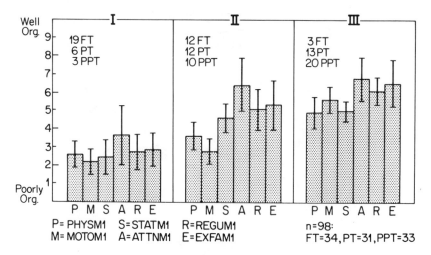

Figure 7.   Results of cluster analysis performed on 98 healthy newborns, ranging in gestational age at birth from pre-preterm to full-term (see text). Three naturally occurring behavioral clusters were defined based on APIB system sheet scores. For each cluster, the mean centroid value for the six APIB system scores is depicted, with values of 1 indicating well-organized behaviors and higher values indicating increasing levels of poorly integrated behavior. P= autonomic system, M= motor system, S= state organizational system, A= attention/interaction system, R= self-regulatory system, E= degree of examiner facilitation required by the newborn. (From Als, H., Duffy, F.H., McAnulty, G., & Badian, N. [in press]. Assessment of neurobehavioral functioning in preterm and fullterm newborns and the question of predictability of later development. In N. Krasnegor & M. Bornstein [Eds.], *Continuity in development*. New York: Plenum; reprinted by permission.)

cluster ranking by BEAM features coincides with the ranking by APIB variables. Electrophysiological differences represent decreased voltages for both EEG and EP data for the lower ranked clusters. This is most prominent over the right hemisphere, especially during sleep (Baby Tracé Alternant, or BTA) and in the visual EP (Baby Visual Evoked Response, or BVR), and involves secondarily the frontal lobes and to a lesser degree the left hemisphere. Whether such prominent right hemispheric and frontal findings have any relationship to later spatial and attentional problems is, of course, still speculation at this point, yet it is a tempting notion to entertain.

Twenty-eight infants, 14 full-term and 14 preterms (<34 weeks' gestation), from a previous cohort of 20 preterm and 20 full-term infants who were assessed with the APIB at 42 weeks, were recently reevaluated at the age of 5 years after estimated date of mother's

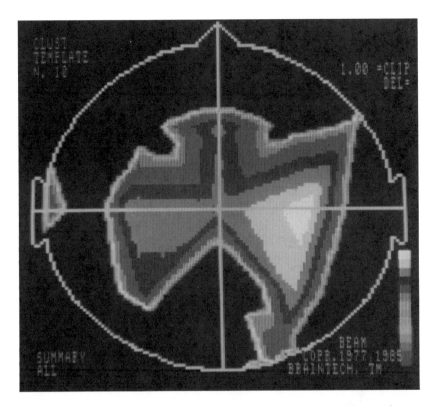

Figure 8. F-statistic SPM topographic image depicting regions of neurophysiological difference among the three behaviorally defined APIB nimbuloids. Differences were most prominent in the right hemisphere and frontal regions (see text). (From Als, H., Duffy, F.H., McAnulty, G., & Badian, N. [in press]. Assessment of neurobehavioral functioning in preterm and fullterm newborns and the question of predictability of later development. In N. Krasnegor & M. Bornstein [Eds.], *Continuity in development*. New York: Plenum; reprinted by permission.)

confinement (EDC) (Als et al., in press). This study was concerned with whether or not the initial behavioral and functional groupings based on the APIB and neurophysiological testings at birth would maintain their integrity when the infants were reassessed via comparable instruments at age 5 years.

In addition to a standard battery of neuropsychological assessments, the children were examined in a paradigm called the Kangaroo Box, or K-Box, which has been designed to evaluate the same behavioral functions as does the APIB. The emphasis again is not only on specific functional capabilities, but on the integration of the various subsystems of functioning. In the 5-year-old version of the K-Box, the assessment paradigm utilizes a large three-tiered transparent Plex-iglas box in an otherwise empty playroom. As shown in Figure 9, in the top and bottom levels of the Plexiglas box sit wind-up kangaroos. Accessories available to the child include manipulating tools, a key, and a footstool. There is no right or wrong way to play with the K-Box apparatus. The child and his or her parent are asked to play in

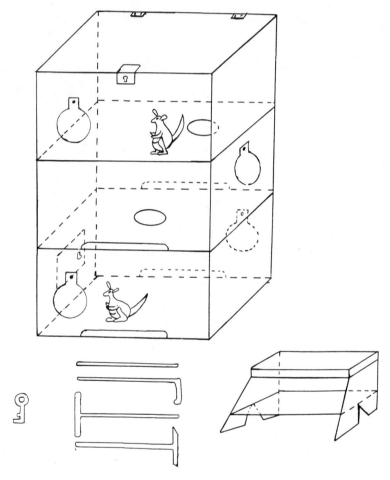

Figure 9. Schematic of multileveled Kangaroo Box (K-Box) apparatus for preschool children. Paradigm is described in some detail in the text. (From Als, H., Duffy, F.H., McAnulty, G., & Badian, N. [in press]. Assessment of neurobehavioral functioning in preterm and fullterm newborns and the question of predictability of later development. In N. Krasnegor & M. Born-stein [Eds.], *Continuity in development*. New York: Plenum; reprinted by permission.)

whatever manner they find most enjoyable. Their "play episode" is videotaped for a period of 6 minutes. The parent is then instructed to withdraw from the play and to sit noninteractively, with a still face, at the edge of the room. The child is then videotaped on his or her own for 6 additional minutes, during the "still face episode." The videotapes are scored across a range of 1 to 5 on a number of behavioral parameters for each of the two episodes. (Videotape analysis often provides the opportunity for greater detail in assessing a child's behaviors. Figure 10 shows a child overreaching with splayed hand, a behavior not readily obvious from live observation.) The parameters examine autonomic, gross and fine motor, attentional, spatial, affective, and social interactive dimensions. The raters are blind to the gestational age of the child and to the child's previous test performance and the rating process has been standardized to ensure interrater reliability. The lack of structure, the predesigned sequence of behaviors inherent in the paradigm, and the need to integrate motor

Figure 10. Preschool child at play with Kangaroo Box apparatus, as extracted from stop frame of videotape. Unlike live observation, such filmed analysis allows for detailed assessment of fine and gross motor skills, autonomic functioning, affective behavior, and social interactions. Note the overreaching posture with splayed hands, a motoric overflow seen in the mild motor system dysfunction of premature children.

planning with social planning appear to make this paradigm a test of right hemisphere and frontal brain functioning.

The K-box results for these children indicated a distinct superiority of function in the full-term infant subgroup (Als et al., in press). As with the APIB results of the newborns, the data were subjected to cluster analysis. Figure 11 provides a bar graph depiction of the two nimbuloids that resulted from the analysis. The parameters defining the strongest group differentiations were gross and fine motor modulation, motoric overflow, and tempo of motoric action. Nimbuloid I children are well modulated in these parameters; Nimbuloid II children are very poorly modulated. Note the predominance of full-term infants in the well-modulated group.

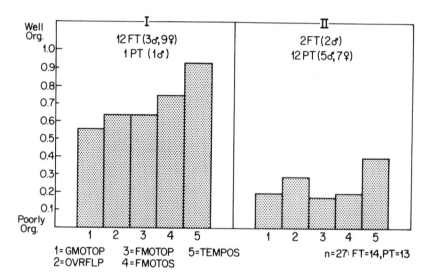

Figure 11. Results of cluster analysis performed on Kangaroo Box assessments of 27 study children originally tested with APIB who were reevaluated at 5 years after EDC. Analysis included 14 full-term children and 13 preterm children. For each cluster, the mean centroid value for five Kangaroo Box parameters is depicted, with values near 1.0 indicating well-organized behaviors and lower values indicating increasingly poorly organized behaviors. *1*=gross motor organization, *2*=motoric overflow, *3*=fine motor organization while at play, *4*= fine motor organization in "stillface episode," *5*=tempo of motoric action. See text. (From Als, H., Duffy, F.H., McAnulty, G., & Badian, N. [in press]. Assessment of neurobehavioral functioning in preterm and fullterm newborns and the question of predictability of later development. In N. Krasnegor & M. Bornstein [Eds.], *Continuity in development.* New York: Plenum; reprinted by permission.)

The K-Box cluster membership based on the testing at 5 years of age was then compared with the APIB cluster membership in the newborn period for these infants. Figure 12 shows the cluster membership concordance between test periods. These ratings show a remarkable continuity, with a Kendall statistical test (T) of .83, significant at $p<.0003$.

The 28 infants were also reevaluated using BEAM, and the EEG and EP results were compared to the nimbuloids created on the basis of the K-Box results. The BEAM data showed consistent, highly significant correlations to the K-Box data (Als et al., in press). Furthermore, when a summary map was developed comparing the brain

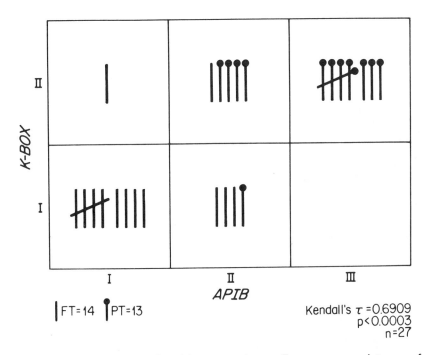

Figure 12. Cluster membership concordance. To assess consistency of neurobehavioral assessment and predictability, cluster membership based on the K-Box results of the 27 follow-up children (14 full-term and 13 preterm) shown in Figure 11 is compared with original cluster membership when tested on the APIB as newborns. A statistical comparison using Kendall's T yields a statistically significant concordance between test periods ($p<.0003$). (From Als, H., Duffy, F.H., McAnulty, G., & Badian, N. [in press]. Assessment of neurobehavioral functioning in preterm and fullterm newborns and the question of predictability of later development. In N. Krasnegor & M. Bornstein [Eds.], *Continuity in development*. New York: Plenum; reprinted by permission.)

electrical activity of the two nimbuloids, there were again significant differences in the right hemisphere and frontal lobe regions of the brain, corroborating the assessments by neuropsychological and behavioral paradigms. Figure 13 provides the topographic map depicting these electrophysiological differences. From a clinical point of view, the measurement of right hemisphere and frontal behaviors is more difficult; it is the left hemisphere that controls speech and language and, thus, is more accessible to differentiated assessment. Nonetheless, right hemispheric function is critical to ultimate performance.

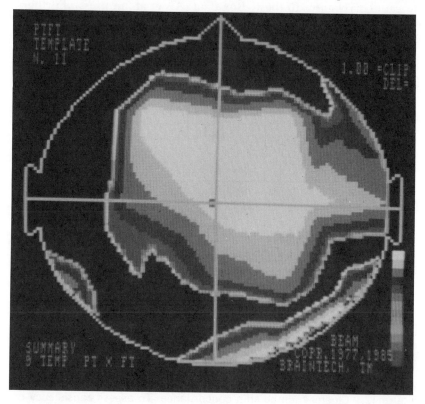

Figure 13. Summary *t*-SPM topographic map delineating regions of neurophysiological differences between the two behavioral groups (nimbuloids) based on 5-year-old Kangaroo Box variables. Note significant differences in the right hemispheric and bilateral anterior regions, corroborating neuropsychological assessments and consistent with the earlier APIB findings (see Figure 8). (From Als, H., Duffy, F.H., McAnulty, G., & Badian, N. [in press]. Assessment of neurobehavioral functioning in preterm and full-term newborns and the question of predictability of later development. In N. Krasnegor & M. Bornstein [Eds.], *Continuity in development*. New York: Plenum; reprinted by permission.)

IMPACT OF ENVIRONMENTAL CARE
OF PRETERM INFANTS ON LATER FUNCTION

If the premature infant is not equipped to interact appropriately with his or her environment and, in fact, expends much energy shutting out the environment, one might logically predict that such infants develop internal mechanisms of sensoral self-deprivation during this prematurely induced developmental period (Als, 1982; Duffy, Mower, Jensen, & Als, 1984). This led to the hypothesis that the respiratory and functional states of the very low birth weight infant with bronchopulmonary dysplasia could be improved in the neonatal intensive care unit (NICU) by individualized behavioral care designed to minimize adverse responses to necessary invasive sensory input. It was furthermore believed that the amelioration of the stressful environment of premature newborns could have a long-term positive effect on mental functioning as a result of the child being less reliant on the "shutting out" of sensory phenomena at this early age.

Preterm infants with bronchopulmonary dysplasia spend inordinate time and energy responding to intensive medical treatment; they are exceptionally sensitive to external stimuli. A strategem for the reduction of stress and an increase in the infant's self-regulatory behaviors was developed (Als et al., 1986). Three major areas of care were emphasized: 1) the physical environment of the infant in the NICU, 2) direct caregiving behaviors in interacting with the infant, and 3) enhancement of discharge planning such that the child received structured support toward increasingly autonomous functioning from early on. Figure 14 shows an infant placed in flexor posture to avoid overreaction to necessary manipulations. This is an example of a mother surrogate helping to avoid extreme extensor spasm and overreaction.

An analysis (Als et al., 1986) of the developmental effects of these nurturing strategies was designed by carefully selecting eight control and eight study infants, comparable in all relevant variables: birth weight, gestational age, severity of respiratory status, incidence of intraventricular hemorrhage and patent ductus arteriosus, medical treatment variables (respirator time and FiO_2 levels), and socioeconomic status. Both the medical and the developmental effects of the nurturing program on the treatment group were dramatic. The study infants spent significantly fewer days on the respirator and fewer days in increased oxygen. Their feeding behaviors normalized significantly sooner than the comparison group. On the behavioral regulation assessment instrument, the APIB (Als et al., 1982), the treatment infants scored significantly higher. The long-term beneficial effects of the

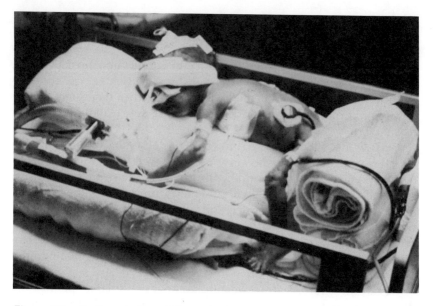

Figure 14. Preterm infant with severe chronic lung disease placed supine on mother surrogate, a maneuver that obviates obligatory extensor posture, allowing for relaxed flexor positioning by infant.

treatment were underscored over the next several months. The treatment group measured significantly better in Mental and Psychomotor Development than the control group on the Bayley Scales of Infant Development at all ages tested (3, 6, and 9 months after EDC) (see Figure 15) (Als et al., 1986, in press). Although the intervention had its biggest impact on the mental development of these infants, it also had significant impact on the motor development. The K-Box paradigm analysis of variance at 9 months (Als et al., in press) shows that the intervention children performed significantly better than the control infants (15 of the 20 play episode parameters and 11 of the 19 still face episode parameters). Again, the initial advantage of the intervention children is well maintained, whereas the control children deteriorate over time on many of the parameters. All parent-child interaction parameters favor the intervention children significantly (Als et al., in press).

The authors have followed these children recently to age 18 months and 3 years and preliminary analyses show that the intervention effect holds up strongly over time. The authors have also very recently undertaken to replicate these results on a larger sample of infants. It thus appears that preterm infants whose environment provides sup-

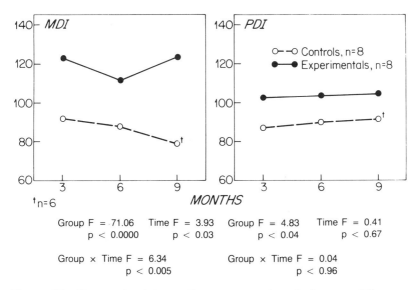

Group F = 71.06   Time F = 3.93   Group F = 4.83   Time F = 0.41
    p < 0.0000   p < 0.03   p < 0.04   p < 0.67

Group × Time F = 6.34   Group × Time F = 0.04
    p < 0.005   p < 0.96

Figure 15.   Supportive intervention group and control group differences on the Mental Development Index (MDI) and Psychomotor Development Index (PDI) from the Bayley Scales of Infant Development. Infants were tested at 3, 6, and 9 months after EDC. The treatment group measured significantly better on both indices across ages. On the MDI the intervention group maintained or improved its initial advantage over time.

port in modulation of their behavior exhibit beneficial long-term effects, at least to age 3 years.

SUMMARY COMMENTS

Behavioral and neurophysiological evaluations with APIB and BEAM have demonstrated that medically healthy preterm infants are clearly different from infants born at term, and evidence from the authors' laboratory and others suggest that these differences persist to at least 5 years of age. Reports in the animal literature strongly support the formative role of the environment in "critical periods." Indeed, evidence from the authors' animal laboratory indicates that the critical period may be triggered by initial sensory stimulation and ultimate outcome shaped by the quality of the sensory milieu during that subsequent critical period. It was hypothesized that at least one cause of the cognitive, behavioral, and neurophysiological differences between premature and full-term infants lies in the striking dissimilarities between the intra- and extrauterine environment experienced by the infants during the final weeks and months of the gestation. Although theoretically possible, it is medically impractical to attempt to recreate the womb environment for the premature infant given the many necessary life-sustaining interventions these children require. As a result of these necessary manipulations, these infants experience prominant visual, auditory and somatosensory stimulations many of which, by their very nature, are stressful to the immature nervous system. On the basis of animal experiments it seems reasonable to assume that critical periods in humans may be triggered by abrupt increase in background levels of sensory and motor stimulation. It is probable that the critical period for the prematurely born infant is initiated at the time of his or her premature birth rather than at the gestationally appropriate time period (40 weeks after conception). Furthermore, it was hypothesized that the sensory input necessary and appropriate for the healthy full-term infant may be more inappropriate for the prematurely born infant and more than he or she can tolerate. Clinical evidence suggests that the preterm infant manages this gestational age–inappropriate sensory overload by a series of strategies that effectively "shut out" such stimulation or "shut off" receptivity. On the basis of work performed in the Children's Hospital (Boston) NICU the authors suggest that the premature infant exhibits improved medical, behavioral, psychomotor, and developmental cognitive skills if caregiving is modified to provide a more soothing, less sensorially demanding environment. Such modification includes both the physical environment (e.g., shielding from bright overhead lighting and from noise) and the caregiving practices by nurses and other professionals (e.g., provision of prone or side-lying flexor position with bunting supports, protection of sleep state regulation). The goal is to reduce sensory overload. The relative advantage for infants receiving such "intervention" has been demonstrated in testing from very early childhood and continues through at least the age of 3 years. It is the authors' belief, on both theoretical and practical grounds, that the intervention of a carefully structured and supportive environment at the point of birth will reap lifelong benefits for infants born prematurely.

REFERENCES

Als, H. (1982). Towards a synactive theory of development: Promise for the assessment of infant individuality. *Infant Mental Health Journal, 3*, 229–243.
Als, H. (1983). Infant individuality: Assessing patterns of very early development. In F. Call, E. Galensen, & R.L. Tyson (Eds.), *Frontiers in infant psychiatry* (pp. 368–378). New York: Basic Books.

Als, H. (in press). Self regulation and motor development in preterm infants. In J. Lockman (Ed.), *Action in social context*. New York: Plenum Press.

Als, H., Duffy, F.H., McAnulty, G., & Badian, N. (in press). Assessment of neurobehavioral functioning in preterm and fullterm newborns and the question of predictability of later development. In N. Krasnegor & M. Bornstein (Eds.), *Continuity in development*. New York: Plenum Press.

Als, H., Lawhon, G., Brown, E., Gibes, R., Duffy, F.H., McAnulty, G., & Blickman, J.G. (1986). Individualized behavioral and environmental care for the very low weight preterm infant at high risk for bronchopulmonary dysplasia: Neonatal intensive care unit and developmental outcome. *Pediatrics, 78*, 1123–1132.

Als, H., Lester, B.M., Tronick, E.C., & Brazelton, T.B. (1982). Manual for the assessment of preterm infants behavior (APIB). In H.E. Fitzgerald, B.M. Lester, & M.W. Yogman (Eds.), *Theory and research in behavioral pediatrics, Vol. I.* (pp. 65–132). New York: Plenum Press.

Als, H., Tronick, E., Adamson, L., & Brazelton, T.B. (1976). The behavior of the full term but underweight infant. *Developmental Medicine and Child Neurology, 18*, 590–602.

Anderberg, M.R. (1973). *Cluster analysis for applications*. New York: Academic.

Bartels, P.H. (1980). Numerical evaluation of cytologic data VI. Multivariate distributions and matrix notation. *Analytical and Quantitative Cytology, 2*, 155–160.

Bartels, P.H., & Wied, G.L. (1973). Extraction and evaluation of information from cell images. In *Proceedings of the first annual life sciences symposium: Mammalian cells, probes, and problems*. Los Angeles: University of California Press.

Beale, E.M.L. (1969). Euclidean cluster analysis. *Bulletin of the I.S.I., 43*(2), 92–94.

Drillien, C.M., Thomson, A.J.M., & Bargoyne, K. (1980). Low birthweight children at early school-age: A longitudinal study. *Developmental Medicine and Child Neurology, 22*, 26–47.

Duffy, F.H., Bartels, P.H., & Burchfiel, J.L. (1981). Significance probability mapping: An aid in the topographic analysis of brain electrical activity. *Electroencephalography and Clinical Neurophysiology, 51*, 455–462.

Duffy, F.H., Denckla, M.B., Bartels, P., & Sandini, G. (1980). Dyslexia: Regional differences in brain electrical activity by topographic mapping. *Annals of Neurology, 7*, 412–420.

Duffy, F.H., Denckla, M.B., Bartels, P., Sandini, G., & Kiessling, L.S. (1980). Automated diagnosis by computerized classification of brain electrical activity. *Annals of Neurology, 7*, 421–428.

Duffy, F.H., Mower, G.D., Jensen, F., & Als, H. (1984). Neural plasticity: A new frontier for infant development. In H.E. Fitzgerald, B.M. Lester, & M.W. Yogman (Eds.), *Theory and research in behavioral pediatrics, Vol. II*. New York: Plenum Press.

Galaburda, A.M., & Kemper, T.L. (1979). Cytoarchitectonic abnormalities in developmental dyslexia: A case study. *Annals of Neurology, 6*, 94–100.

Larsen, B., Skinhoj, E., & Lassen, N.A. (1978). Variations in regional cortical blood flow in the right and left hemispheres during automatic speech. *Brain, 101*, 193–210.

Lassen, N.A., Ingvar, D.H., & Skinhoj, E. (1978). Brain function and blood flow. *Scientific American, 239*, 62–71.

Mower, G.D., Berry, D., Burchfiel, J., & Duffy, F.H. (1981). Comparison of the effects of dark rearing and binocular suture on development and plasticity of cat visual cortex. *Brain Research, 220,* 255–267.

Wiesel, T.N., & Hubel, D.H. (1963a). Receptive fields of cells in striate cortex of very young visually inexperienced kittens. *Journal of Neurophysiology, 26,* 994–1002.

Wiesel, T.N., & Hubel, D.H. (1963b). Simple cell response in striate cortex of kittens deprived of vision in one eye. *Journal of Neurophysiology, 26,* 1003–1017.

Wiesel, T.N., & Hubel, D.H. (1965). Comparison of the effects of unilateral and bilateral eye closure on cortical unit responses in kittens. *Journal of Neurophysiology, 28,* 1029–1040.

14 | Behavioral Assessment of Cognitive Well-Being in the Infant

JOSEPH F. FAGAN, III and
JEANNE E. MONTIE

The purpose of the present chapter is to review historical trends in the assessment of the infant's cognitive well-being. Specifically, the chapter focuses on behavioral measures of cognitive well-being administered during the first year of life.

The history of the assessment of infant cognition contains two separate trends: the assessment of sensorimotor behavior and the assessment of visual information processing. The first trend began in the 1930s with the study of the normal time sequence for development of sensorimotor behaviors. Norms were established for such behaviors as visual tracking, rolling over, sitting, and walking. As an outgrowth of the normative studies, instruments for the purpose of assessing sensorimotor behavior were published. Probably the best standardized and most widely used of the sensorimotor measures is the Bayley Scales of Infant Development (Bayley, 1969). As we shall see, the assessment of sensorimotor behavior in the infant has not been very successful in predicting later cognitive behavior. The second trend, the study of information processing in the infant, has a briefer history. It became possible to study visual information processing in the infant with the development of the visual interest test by Fantz in 1956. In particular, the infant's visual attention to novel targets has been used extensively since about 1970 to study the early development of perception, memory, and cognition. Unlike the work on sensorimotor behavior, the assessment of information processing in the infant *has* been successful in predicting later cognitive behavior. This chapter will look at both trends in more detail.

The preparation of this chapter was supported, in part, by a Perinatal Emphasis Research Center Grant (HD-11089) and by a Mental Retardation Research Training Grant (HD-07176), both from the National Institute of Child Health and Human Development.

ASSESSMENT OF SENSORIMOTOR BEHAVIOR

Instruments used to assess infant sensorimotor behavior grew primarily out of Gesell's work, which focused on gathering extensive normative data describing behavioral development and its relationship to neurological functioning. Gesell's seminal work provided the basis for a variety of assessment instruments including the Gesell Developmental Schedules (Gesell & Amatruda, 1954), the Cattell Infant Intelligence Scale (Cattell, 1960), the Griffiths Scale of Mental Development (Griffiths, 1954), and the Bayley Scales of Infant Development (Bayley, 1969). Although the prediction or determination of an infant's intelligence was not necessarily the primary purpose for which these tests were developed, many of the instruments have been employed and are being employed today for just that purpose. The rationale for the prediction of intelligence from such tests, although largely unstated, seems to be that infants who are faster in achieving developmental milestones such as head control, hand-eye coordination, rolling over, and sitting independently will be quicker and better later on at such tasks as naming, remembering, categorizing, and counting. However, as early as 1955, it was recognized that the attempt to predict later intellectual outcome from individual differences in sensorimotor behavior in infancy was not going to be successful (Bayley, 1955). In the ensuing years a variety of investigators (Fagan & Singer, 1983; Gorski, Lewkowicz, & Huntington, 1987; Kopp & McCall, 1980; Lewis, 1973; McCall, Hogarty, & Hurlburt, 1972) have noted the fact that instruments designed to measure infant sensorimotor function are poor predictors of later intelligence. For example, Fagan and Singer (1983) reviewed a series of studies using sensorimotor tests in the first year of life to predict intellectual function from 3 to 6 years in both normal and abnormal populations. In a total of 50 studies employing normal samples, reviewed by the authors, the mean correlation between infant test scores and later IQ is .14. For 51 samples employing high-risk infants, although the authors found results of the individual studies to be more variable depending on the risk condition, the mean correlation between infant test scores and later IQ is only .21. In spite of the failure to predict, infant sensorimotor tests continue to be widely used in clinical and research settings. The rationale behind the current use seems to be that the tests give a picture of the current functioning of the infant compared to others the same age.

In any case, ample evidence exists that demonstrates that infant sensorimotor tests administered in the first year of life are poor predictors of intelligence later in life. A variety of factors have been proposed to account for the poor predictive validity of infant tests, among them: poor test construction, cultural differences, environmental influences, and difficulty in eliciting cooperation from infants. Some theorists, including Honzik (1976), Lewis (1973), and Kopp and McCall (1980), have argued that the fault lies not in the tests themselves, but in the belief in a general intelligence ("g") that is genetically fixed, incremental, and unaffected by environmental influences. The predictive shortcomings of infant tests are thought to reflect a fundamental change in the nature of intelligent behavior with growth. In other words, the growth of intelligence may be a "discontinuous" process, and no measurable corollary of later intelligent activity exists in infancy. The fact that McCall et al. (1972) found greater instability among test scores at ages corresponding to Piagetian stages lent support to the Piagetian view of intelligence as progression through a series of hierarchical stages, each characterized by its own unique type of intelligent behavior.

A major weakness in the view that intelligence is discontinuous over age lies in the fact that the argument relies on negative evidence, that is, the failure of infant tests to predict intelligence later in life. There is an alternative explanation for the lack of a strong positive correlation between performance on infant sensorimotor tests and later intelligence test scores. As noted above, standard infant tests tap the infant's developing sensorimotor skills, skills that later in life are not related to differences in intelligence and, thus, would not be expected to be early indicators of intelligence. On later intelligence tests children are asked to discriminate among stimuli, to retain new information, to categorize stimuli, and to retrieve useful information. However, progress in the study of infant visual information processing over the past 30 years has made it possible to ask an infant to exhibit discrimination, retention, categorization, and retrieval (see Fagan, 1984a; Fagan & McGrath, 1981; Fagan & Singer, 1983).

ASSESSMENT OF VISUAL INFORMATION PROCESSING

Historically, the study of infant visual perception began with the visual interest or preferential looking test originated by Fantz (1956). The basic assumption of the test is that if an infant looks more at one stimulus than at another when the two are paired simultaneously, he or she must be able to differentiate between the two stimuli. A detailed description of the procedure used to measure infants' visual fixations can be found in Fagan (1970). Basically, the infant is held in front of a "stage" to which the visual targets are fixed. An observer, positioned behind the stage, is able to observe the corneal reflection of the targets over the pupils of the infant's eyes through a peephole centered in the stage. The length of fixation paid to each stimulus is recorded. Interobserver agreement as to length of fixation is quite high ($r > .95$) even for tests made during the first days of life (Miranda, 1970). Differential fixation, operationally defined, is when one of a pair of targets elicits significantly more than 50% of the infant's total fixation time.

It is a well-documented finding that, after exposure to only one of a pair of targets, infants prefer to look at the previously unseen, or novel, target if the pair are presented simultaneously (Fagan, 1970). Preference for a novel over a previously viewed target shows that the infant finds the two targets discriminable, and also indicates that the infant can recognize one of the targets as familiar. Thus, it is possible, through the use of the visual interest test, to tap the processes of discrimination and recognition memory. In addition, by controlling the manner in which novel and previously exposed targets vary, investigators have explored, for example, the development of the infant's ability to discriminate among and remember colors, shapes, orientations, and faces (for reviews see Banks & Salapatek, 1983; Fagan, 1982; Olson & Sherman, 1983).

Infants, from birth, are able to recognize a previously seen target (Werner & Siqueland, 1978). In general, the recognition memory of infants, like that of adults, varies with length of study time and the nature of the distinctions to be made between novel and previously exposed targets; also, memory, when evidenced, is usually long lasting and is not easily disrupted (Bornstein, 1976; Cohen, Deloache, & Pearl, 1977; Cornell, 1979; Fagan 1973, 1977; Martin, 1975; McCall, Kennedy, & Dodds, 1977; Topinka & Steinberg, 1978).

Categorization has been operationally defined as treating two or more discriminable objects as equivalent in some manner (Mervis & Rosch, 1981). A number of studies of visual novelty preference have demonstrated that the ability to detect similarities or invariances among otherwise diverse stimuli is present in infancy. McGurk (1972), Cornell (1975), and Fagan (1979) found that infants between 4 and 6 months of age recognize a pattern even though its orientation has changed. Studies by Fagan (1976), Cohen and Strauss (1979), Nelson, Morse, and Leavitt (1979), and Strauss (1979) indicate that infants from 7 months of age recognize invariant aspects of faces. In addition, Strauss (1979), Younger (1985), and Sherman (1985) have demonstrated that infants in the latter half of the first year of life are able to form prototypes and perceive correlations among attributes, both processes used by adults to categorize information.

The foregoing brief discussion of research employing variations of visual recognition tests presents a sampling of the evidence that demonstrates that visual recognition tests tap an infant's ability to discriminate, remember, and categorize. Each of these—discrimination, recognition memory, and categorization—represents a process tapped on intelligence tests given later in life. Thus, it seems reasonable to suppose that since the infant's ability to recognize a previously seen target may reflect some of the processes tapped on later intelligence tests, individual differences in scores on recognition memory tests administered early in life may be related to individual differences on intelligence tests administered later in life.

Research has confirmed that variations in novelty preference during infancy are related to later intelligence. Concurrent validity for the extent of an infant's visual preference for a novel stimulus as a measure of intelligence is provided by the results of a number of studies in which groups of infants expected to differ in intelligence later in life have also differed in their ability to recognize a previously seen stimulus (e.g., Caron & Caron, 1981; Cohen, 1981; Fantz & Nevis, 1967; Miranda & Fantz, 1974). For example, studies by Cohen (1981) and Miranda and Fantz (1974) comparing samples of normal infants and infants with Down syndrome found that normal infants were able to recognize and discriminate between abstract patterns at an earlier age than were the infants with Down syndrome.

In addition to research providing concurrent validity, studies by Yarrow, Klein, Lomonaco, and Morgan (1975), Fagan (1981, 1984b), Fagan and McGrath (1981), Lewis and Brooks-Gunn (1981), Fagan and Singer (1983), Caron, Caron, and Glass (1983), and Rose and Wallace (1985, in press) present initial evidence for the predictive validity of infant visual recognition memory tests for later intelligence. These tests of predictive validity are based on data from 15 samples of infants drawn from essentially normal populations (i.e., infants not at risk for later cognitive deficit). For each of 15 samples of children significant positive correlations were reported between performance on visual recognition memory tests administered during infancy and scores on intelligence tests administered between 2 and 7 years of age. Preferences for visual novelty during infancy yielded moderate predictive validity coefficients ranging from .33 to .66 across the 15 samples, with a mean of .42. The general finding that early novelty preferences are related to later intelligence appears to be quite robust. The associations between early novelty preferences and later IQ hold for blacks as well as whites and males as well as females. Procedural variations across the 15 samples, different paradigms for measuring recognition memory, and different stimuli make little difference as to outcome.

When the mean correlation of .42 between measures of infant visual recognition memory and later IQ is compared with the mean correlation of .14 noted earlier between measures of infant sensorimotor behavior and later IQ, it is readily apparent that measures of visual information processing in infancy hold greater promise than do tests of sensorimotor functioning for the prediction of intelligence later in life.

The Fagan Test of Infant Intelligence

As a practical matter, it would be highly desirable to be able to differentiate normal from cognitively deficient infants within groups of high-risk infants. Given that need, and given that early novelty preferences are linked to later intelligence, the overall objective of the authors' work for the past 10 years has been to develop a valid test of infant intelligence based on the infant's ability to recognize visual stimuli. To that end, the Fagan Test of Infant Intelligence (FTII) has been constructed to be used as a screening device to differentiate potentially normal from potentially deficient infants within groups of infants suspected to be at risk for later intellectual deficit as a result of various prenatal or postnatal conditions.

The basic component of the FTII is a "novelty problem." Each novelty problem consists of a pairing of two stimuli immediately following a standard period of study of one of the two stimuli. One estimate of the predictive validity for the FTII comes from a recent study of 128 high-risk infants originally tested at 3–7 months and then followed to 3 years of age. The infants in the sample were suspected to be at risk for later mental retardation as a result of prematurity (birth weight <1,500 g [3.25 lb]), intrauterine growth retardation, treated hypothyroidism, a diagnosis of failure to thrive, or a history of maternal diabetes. Our intention was simply to draw infants from populations where the incidence of IQ scores <70 at 3 years of age was expected to be greater than 2%. All infants were tested at home by means of a portable apparatus.

The screening device administered to each infant was composed of a maximum of 15 novelty problems, three of which were administered at 52, two at 56, four at 62, and six at 69 weeks of conceptional age (i.e., for term infants, at 12, 16, 22, and 29 weeks of postnatal age). Every attempt was made to test each infant at each of the four ages, but more infants were seen at 22 or 29 weeks than were seen at 12 or 16 weeks because of late referrals. In the final analysis, infants were only included in the sample if they had been tested on at least seven of the novelty problems. Such a restriction ensured that an infant was seen at least twice with at least one test given at 22 or 29 weeks. The score assigned to each infant on the FTII was a mean novelty preference score over problems.

Intellectual outcome at 3 years was assessed by administering the Stanford-Binet Intelligence Scale (Terman & Merrill, 1973) and the Peabody Picture Vocabulary Test (Form L) (Dunn & Dunn, 1981) and giving the child a mean IQ score for the two tests. If necessary, the Bayley Scales of Mental Development (Bayley, 1969) were given and an IQ score was estimated by dividing the age attained on the test by the child's chronological age. The technicians who administered the intelligence tests at 3 years were unaware of how the child had performed as an infant.

The mean IQ at 3 years for the sample of 128 children was 98.3 (SD 18.6). The mean novelty preference score over problems from 3 to 7 months was 58.8% (SD 6.5). The correlation between early novelty preferences and later IQ was high and significant at .49 (df 127, $p<.0001$). Of the 128 children, 15 had IQs ≤ 70 at 3 years and 113 had IQs > 70. The FTII was highly sensitive to retardation, with a mean novelty preference score over problems of ≤ 53% in correctly identifying 12 out of 15 (80%) of the children with mental retardation. The test was also highly specific in identifying 89% (101 out of 113) of the children with normal intelligence. The overall validity of the screening device for predicting retardation was 50%, since 12 out of 24 infants predicted at 7 months to be at risk were indeed retarded at 3 years. Validity for the prediction of normality was 97%, that is, 101 out of 104 children predicted to be normal were later found to be normal.

The 128 infants actually represent infants in two separate samples used for cross-validation. The first sample (Fagan, Singer, Montie, & Shepherd, 1986) was comprised of 62 infants tested with an early version of the FTII that included a maximum of 12 novelty problems (3 at 52, 2 at 56, 4 at 62, and 3 at 69 weeks' postconceptional age). It was this original sample that was used to establish a cutoff score of ≤53% fixation to novelty as the score that maximized the sensitivity and specificity of the screening device. The sample yielded a group mean novelty preference score of 59.9% (SD 8.1), and a mean IQ at 3 years of 96.3 (SD 23.1, range 25–135). Novelty preference scores of ≤53% correctly identified 6 out of 8 of the children with mental retardation for a sensitivity of the 75% and 49 out of the 54 children with normal intelligence for a specificity of 91%. The second sample (Fagan & Montie, 1986) included 66 infants tested with a maximum of 15 novelty problems at ages of between 3 and 7 months. In the cross-validation sample novelty preference scores of ≤53% correctly identified 6 out of 7 children as delayed, for a sensitivity of 86%, and 52 out of 59 as having normal intelligence, for a specificity of 88%. The two samples taken together demonstrate that a cutoff score of ≤53% on the FTII yields essentially the same sensitivity and specificity values from one sample to another, as long as the two samples have a similar prevalence of later cognitive delay.

In an earlier study (Fagan, Singer, & Montie, 1985), a preliminary version of the FTII consisting of only four novelty problems was administered between 5 and 7 months of age to a group of 20 infants diagnosed as having failure to thrive. The prevalence of retardation at 3 years was 40% (8 out of 20 had IQs ≤70). Novelty preference scores correctly identified 7 out of 8 of the children with IQs ≤70, for a sensitivity of 88%, and 10 out of 12 of the children with normal IQs for a specificity of 83%. The validity for predicting retardation was 78% (7 out of 9 children predicted to be at risk for retardation were later found to be retarded). The validity for the prediction of normal intelligence was 91% (10 out of 11 correct predictions).

Two important questions regarding the worth of the FTII for the prediction of intelligence may be answered by combining the data yielded by the 128 children from various risk groups and the 20 children with failure to thrive discussed by Fagan, Singer, and Montie (1985). The first question is whether the FTII is as predictive for children with mild and moderate retardation (IQs of 50–70) as it is for children afflicted with severe or profound retardation (IQs <50). Of the 23 children from both studies found to be retarded at 3 years, 5 had IQs <50, and 18 had IQs between 50 and 70. The visual novelty test correctly predicted retardation for 4 out of 5 of the children with IQs <50 (80%) and correctly identified as retarded 15 of the 18 (83%) children with IQs from 50 to 70. In effect, detection of retardation from early tests of visual novelty preferences is as accurate for children who will later be moderately or mildly retarded as it is for those who will later be severely or profoundly retarded.

A second question concerning the value of visual novelty tests for the prediction of mental retardation is whether conventional senso-rimotor tests of infant "intelligence" might not have done just as good a job of prediction in these samples. In fact, 27 of the 148 children in the combined samples had also been assessed with the Bayley Scales during infancy, allowing a direct comparison of the predictive power of novelty preference tests with that of a conventional test of senso-rimotor development. The 27 children given both types of assessment had a mean IQ of 74.4 (SD 20.2, range 25–115). Prediction from the FTII for this subsample of 27 children was highly sensitive, with 91%

(10 out of 11) of the children correctly identified as retarded, and was specific in identifying 81% (13 out of 16) as being of normal intelligence at 3 years. Predictive validity estimates for retardation and for normal intelligence on the FTII were high at 77% and 93%, respectively. In contrast, the Bayley Scales administered at about 6–8 months were low in sensitivity, with Mental Development Index (MDI) scores ≤80 correctly identifying only 45% (5 out of 11) of the delayed children. The scales were also low in specificity since they correctly identified only 38% (6 out of 16) of the children with normal intelligence. The validity of the 8-month Bayley scores for the prediction of retardation or normal intelligence was correspondingly low at 33% and 50%, respectively. In fact, for the samples just discussed, the use of the Bayley Scales resulted in the misclassification of individuals more often than their correct classification.

Summary

Tests of infant visual information processing appear to represent a valid means of assessing infant cognitive function and, furthermore, are predictive of later intellectual function. In addition, the use of visual novelty preference for the detection of cognitive deficit in high-risk populations appears to be as valid for infants who will later be mildly retarded as for those who will be severely retarded. Such results stand in contrast to those obtained with conventional tests of sensorimotor development.

BENEFITS OF EARLY DETECTION OF COGNITIVE DEFICIT

There are a number of reasons why the early detection of cognitive deficit is important for the understanding of mental retardation. Recent medical technological and management advances have resulted in large numbers of survivors of extreme prematurity and perinatal traumas with questionable developmental outcome (Hunt, 1981; Robertson, 1979). Happily, the majority of such infants will be intellectually normal (e.g., see Stewart, Reynolds, & Lipscomb, 1981). However, early detection of the small number who will suffer from cognitive deficit will allow clinicians to concentrate scarce resources on infants and parents in need of intervention services, while the majority of families can be reassured that their baby's development will be normal. A second benefit of the early detection of cognitive deficit is that it cuts the lead time on evaluating outcome in prospective research studies. At present investigators studying pre- or perinatal causes of intellectual impairment or investigators concerned with the effects of intervention programs for at-risk infants must wait 2–3 years to obtain a valid estimate of intellectual function. The use of a standardized test based on infant visual information processing makes it possible to evaluate cognitive outcome within the first year of life. In addition, if early screening allows certain risk conditions to be ruled out as causes of intellectual deficit, investigators can allocate research time and money to the study of a smaller number of known handicapping conditions.

In other words, tests of infant intelligence based on recognition memory should allow us to discover periods in development when specific environmental effects on intelligence become operable. For example, specific medical problems in the neonatal period such as asphyxia, anoxia, hypoxia, respiratory distress syndrome, hyperbilirubinemia, neonatal seizures, intracranial hemorrhage, profound acidosis, hypoglycemia, hyponatremia, and hypocalcemia can be evaluated for their influence on infant intelligence. Demographic factors of race, sex, birth order, and socioeconomic status can also be assessed for their influence on early and later intelligence.

To date, a variety of empirical studies have employed early versions of the FTII to investigate potential causes of intellectual impairment. Two studies investigating potential teratogens have been published. One study looked at the relationship between maternal exposure to polychlorinated biphenyls (PCBs) and infant outcome. Jacobson, Fein, Jacobson, Schwartz, and Dowler (1985) were able to plot a dose-response curve describing the relationship between maternal cord blood level of PCBs and infant recognition memory scores. Their results indicated that infant novelty scores were depressed as a function of increasing levels of maternal PCBs.

Another study, employing an animal model, investigated the effect of low-level prenatal methyl mercury exposure in infant monkeys. Gunderson, Grant, Burbacher, Fagan, and Mottet (1986) reported that infant crab-eating macaques exposed in utero to maternal subclinical levels of methyl mercury devoted less visual attention as infants to novel stimuli than did normal controls. In a related study employing pigtailed macaque infants, visual recognition problems adapted from the FTII were administered to both low- and high-risk monkeys (Gunderson, Grant-Webster, & Fagan, 1987). The low-risk animals were normal, whereas the high-risk animals had a variety of developmental problems (e.g., hypoxia, failure to thrive) that are sometimes correlated with cognitive deficits later in life in humans. Results showed that the low-risk group easily differentiated novel from previously seen targets, whereas no evidence of such recognition was seen in the high-risk sample.

Tests based on visual information processing have also been used to identify infants at risk for mild learning problems. Gotlieb (1986) used the FTII and the Bayley MDI to evaluate a group of 20 intra-uterine growth-retarded (IUGR) infants, whose mean IQ is expected to be 3–10 points below the norm, and their normal birth weight controls. At 7 months of age scores on the FTII (but not the MDI) differentiated the groups, suggesting that the FTII, a test of visual recognition memory, has the potential for identification of infants at risk for mild retardation or learning problems.

Added to the numerous practical benefits that flow from the early detection of intellectual impairment, there are interesting theoretical implications as well. The chief theoretical issue raised by the demonstration of continuity in intelligence from infancy to childhood is the question of the basis for such continuity. It is our assumption that the basis of continuity lies in similarities in the processes underlying early recognition memory tasks and later intelligence (see Fagan, 1984a, for a detailed discussion). The authors believe that there may exist a small set of cognitive processes for knowledge acquisition that provide the basis for continuity in intellectual functioning during development and that underlie "g," the general factor in intelligence.

SUMMARY

The promise of developing a valid means of assessing infant cognitive function through the use of visual recognition memory problems is readily apparent and is, in fact, currently being realized. The present challenge is to continue to develop, refine, and standardize such techniques. In order to accomplish this goal interdisciplinary research is essential. The FTII has been developed, in part, through a Perinatal Emphasis Research Grant allowing psychologists to work in cooperation with obstetricians, neonatologists, and pediatricians. Its development is presently at the state at which the authors think it is beneficial to transfer the technology to the clinician and clinical researcher. To accomplish such transfer, the technology underlying the FTII has been licensed to Infantest Corporation, who have undertaken the task of turning the research version of the FTII into a valuable clinical tool (see Fagan & Shepherd, 1986). In participating in such technology transfer, the authors would emphasize that the FTII, in its current form, should not be used for routine screening with normal populations. It should only be used as a *selective* screening device, that is, one that is applied only after an infant is suspected to be at risk for later cognitive deficit. If used properly, the FTII will relieve the anxieties of many parents, will conserve scarce economic resources, will lead to the identification of some of the causes of mental retardation, and will increase the efficacy of intervention programs.

REFERENCES

Banks, M.S., & Salapatek, P. (1983). Infant visual perception. In P.H. Mussen (Ed.), *Handbook of child psychology, Vol. II: Infancy & developmental psychobiology* (pp. 435–571). New York: John Wiley & Sons.

Bayley, N. (1955). On the growth of intelligence. *American Psychologist, 16*, 805–818.

Bayley, N. (1969). *The Bayley Scales of Infant Development*. New York: Psychological Corporation.

Bornstein, M.H. (1976). Infants' recognition memory for hue. *Developmental Psychology, 12*, 185–191.

Caron, A.J., & Caron, R.F. (1981). Processing of relational information as an index of infant risk. In S.L. Friedman & M. Sigman (Eds.), *Preterm birth and psychological development* (pp. 219–237). New York: Academic Press.

Caron, A.J., Caron, R.F., & Glass, P. (1983). Responsiveness to relational information as a measure of cognitive functioning in nonsuspect infants. In T. Field & A. Sostek (Eds.), *Infants born at risk* (pp. 181–209). New York: Grune & Stratton.

Cattell, P. (1960). *The measurement of intelligence in infants and young children*. New York: Psychological Corporation. (Originally published in 1940 by Science Press, New York.)

Cohen, L.B. (1981). Examination of habituation as a measure of aberrant infant development. In S.L. Friedman & M. Sigman (Eds.) *Preterm birth and psychological development* (pp. 241–253). New York: Academic Press.

Cohen, L.B., Deloache, J.S., & Pearl, R.A. (1977). An examination of interference effects in infants' memory for faces. *Child Development, 48*, 88–96.

Cohen, L.B., & Strauss, M .S. (1979). Concept acquisition in the human infant. *Child Development, 50*, 419–424.

Cornell, E.H. (1975). Infants' visual attention to pattern arrangement and orientation. *Child Development, 46*, 229–232.

Cornell, E.H. (1979). Infants' recognition memory, forgetting, and savings. *Journal of Experimental Child Psychology, 18*, 359–374.

Dunn, L.M., & Dunn, L.M. (1981). *Peabody Picture Vocabulary Test—Revised: Manual for Forms L and M*. Circle Pines, MN: American Guidance Service.

Fagan, J.F. (1970). Memory in the infant. *Journal of Experimental Child Psychology, 9*, 217–226.

Fagan, J.F. (1973). Infants' delayed recognition memory and forgetting. *Journal of Experimental Child Psychology, 16*, 424–450.

Fagan, J.F. (1976). Infants' recognition memory of invariant features of faces. *Child Development, 47*, 627–638.

Fagan, J.F. (1977). Infant recognition memory: Studies in forgetting. *Child Development, 48*, 68–78.

Fagan, J.F. (1979). The origins of facial pattern recognition. In M. Bornstein & W. Kessen (Eds.), *Psychological development from infancy* (pp. 83–111). Hillsdale, NJ: Lawrence Erlbaum Associates.

Fagan, J.F. (1981, April 4). *Infant memory and the prediction of intelligence*. Paper presented at Society for Research in Child Development Meeting, Boston.

Fagan, J.F. (1982). Infant memory. In T. Field, A. Huston, H. Quay, L. Troll, & G. Finely (Eds.), *Review of human development* (pp. 79–92). New York: John Wiley & Sons.

Fagan, J.F. (1984a). The intelligent infant: Theoretical implications. *Intelligence, 8,* 1–9.

Fagan, J.F. (1984b). The relationship of novelty preferences during infancy to later intelligence and recognition memory. *Intelligence, 8,* 339–346.

Fagan, J.F., & McGrath, S.K. (1981). Infant recognition memory and later intelligence. *Intelligence, 5,* 121–130.

Fagan, J.F., & Montie, J.E. (1986). Identifying infants at risk for mental retardation: A cross-validation study. *Journal of Developmental and Behavioral Pediatrics, 7,* 199–200.

Fagan, J.F., & Shepherd, P.A. (1986). *The Fagan test of infant intelligence: Training manual.* Cleveland, OH: Infantest Corporation.

Fagan, J.F., & Singer, L.T. (1983). Infant recognition memory as a measure of intelligence. In L.P. Lipsitt (Ed.), *Advances in infancy research* (Vol. 2, pp. 31–72). Norwood, NJ: Ablex.

Fagan, J.F., Singer, L.T., & Montie, J.E. (1985). An experimental selective screening device for the early detection of intellectual deficit in at-risk infants. In W.K. Frankenburg, R.N. Emde, & J.W. Sullivan (Eds.), *Early identification of children at risk: An international perspective* (pp. 257–266). New York: Plenum Press.

Fagan, J.F., Singer, L.T., Montie, J.E., & Shepherd, P.A. (1986). Selective screening device for the early detection of normal or delayed cognitive development in infants at risk for later mental retardation. *Pediatrics, 78,* 1021–1026.

Fantz, R.L. (1956). A method for studying early visual development. *Perceptual and Motor Skills, 6,* 13–15.

Fantz, R.L., & Nevis, S. (1967). The predictive value of changes in visual preference in early infancy. In J. Hellmuth (Ed.), *The exceptional infant* (Vol. 1, pp. 351–413). Seattle, WA: Special Child Publications.

Gesell, A., & Amatruda, C.S. (1954). *Developmental diagnosis.* New York: Paul B. Holber, Inc.

Gorski, P.A., Lewkowicz, D.J., & Huntington, L. (1987). Advances in neonatal and infant behavioral assessment: Toward a comprehensive evaluation of early patterns of development. *Developmental and Behavioral Pediatrics, 8*(1), 39–50.

Gotlieb, S.J. (1986). *Visual recognition memory: Sensitivity to subtle differences in cognitive potential.* Unpublished Master's thesis, University of Alabama.

Griffiths, R. (1954). *The abilities of babies.* New York: McGraw-Hill.

Gunderson, V.M., Grant, K.S., Burbacher, T.M., Fagan, J.F., & Mottet, U.K. (1986). The effect of low-level prenatal methylmercury exposure on visual recognition memory in infant crab-eating macaques. *Child Development, 57,* 1076–1083.

Gunderson, V.M., Grant-Webster, K.S., & Fagan, J.F. (1987). Visual recognition memory in high and low-risk infant pigtailed macaques. *Developmental Psychology, 23,* 671–675.

Honzik, M. (1976). Values and limitations of infant tests: An overview. In M. Lewis (Ed.), *Origins of intelligence* (pp. 59–95). New York: Plenum.

Humphreys, L.G. (1979). The construct of general intelligence. *Intelligence, 3,* 105–120.

Hunt, J. McV. (1981). Predicting intellectual disorders in childhood for pre-term infants with birthweights below 1501 grams. In S. Friedman & M. Sigman (Eds.), *Preterm birth and psychological development* (pp. 329–351). New York: Academic Press.

Jacobson, S.W., Fein, G.G., Jacobson, J.L., Schwartz, P.M., & Dowler, J.K. (1985). The effect of intrauterine PCB exposure on visual recognition memory. *Child Development, 56*, 853–860.

Kopp, C.B., & McCall, R.B. (1980). Stability and instability in mental per-formance among normal, at-risk, and handicapped infants and children. In P.B. Baltes & O.G. Grim, Jr. (Eds.), *Life-span development and behavior* (Vol. 4, pp. 33–61). New York: Academic Press.

Lewis, M. (1973). Infant intelligence tests: Their use and misuse. *Human Development, 16*, 108–118.

Lewis, M., & Brooks-Gunn, J. (1981). Visual attention at three months as a predictor of cognitive functioning at two years of age. *Intelligence, 5*, 131–140.

Martin, R.M. (1975). Effects of familiar and complex stimuli on infant atten-tion. *Developmental Psychology, 11*, 178–185.

McCall, R.B., Hogarty, P.S., & Hurlburt, N. (1972). Transitions in infant sensori-motor development and the prediction of childhood IQ. *American Psychologist, 27*, 728–748.

McCall, R.B., Kennedy, C.B., & Dodds, C. (1977). The interfering effects of distracting stimuli on the infant's memory. *Child Development, 48*, 79–87.

McGurk, H. (1972). Infant discrimination of orientation. *Journal of Experi-mental Child Psychology, 14*, 151–164.

Mervis, C.B., & Rosch, E. (1981). Categorization of natural objects. In *Annual Review of Psychology, 32*, 89–115.

Miranda, S.B. (1970). Response to novel visual stimuli by Down syndrome and normal infants. *Proceedings of the 78th Annual Convention of the American Psychological Association, 4*, 275–276.

Miranda, S.B., & Fantz, R.L. (1974). Recognition memory in Down's syn-drome and normal infants. *Child Development, 45*, 651–660.

Nelson, C.A., Morse, P.A., & Leavitt, L.A. (1979). Recognition of facial expres-sions by seven-month-old infants. *Child Development, 50*, 1239–1242.

Olson, G.M., & Sherman, T. (1983). Attention, learning, and memory in infants. In P.H. Mussen (Ed.), *Handbook of child psychology, Vol. II: Infancy & developmental psychobiology* (pp.1001–1080). New York: John Wiley & Sons.

Robertson, E. (1979). Prenatal factors contributing to high-risk offspring. In T. Field (Ed.), *Infants born at risk: Behavior and development*. New York: Spectrum Publication.

Rose, S.A., & Wallace, I.F. (1985). Visual recognition memory: A predictor of later cognitive functioning in preterms. *Child Development, 56*, 843–852.

Rose, S.A., & Wallace, I.F. (in press). Cross-modal and intra-modal transfer as predictors of mental development in fullterm and preterm infants. *De-velopmental Psychology*.

Sherman, T. (1985). Categorization skills in infants. *Child Development, 56*, 1561–1573.

Stewart, A.L., Reynolds, E.O.R., & Lipscomb, A.P. (1981). Outcome for in-fants of very low birthweight: Survey of world literature. *Lancet, 0*, 1038–1041.

Strauss, M.S. (1979). Abstraction of prototypical information by adults and 10-month-old infants. *Journal of Experimental Psychology: Human Language and Memory, 5*, 618–632.

Terman, L.M., & Merrill, M.A. (1973). *Stanford-Binet Intelligence Scale: 1973 Norms Edition.* Boston: Houghton-Mifflin.

Topinka, C.V., & Steinberg, B. (1978, March). *Visual recognition memory in 3½ and 7½ month-old infants.* Paper presented at the International Conference on Infant Studies, Providence, RI.

Werner, J.S., & Siqueland, E.R. (1978). Visual recognition memory in the preterm infant. *Infant Behavior and Development, 1*, 79–94.

Yarrow, L.J., Klein, R.P., Lomonaco, S., & Morgan, G.A. (1975). Cognitive and motivational development in early childhood. In B.X. Friedlander, G.M. Sterritt, & G.E. Kirk (Eds.), *Exceptional Infant* (Vol. 3, pp. 491–502). New York: Brunner/Mazel.

Younger, B.A. (1985). The segregation of items into categories by ten-month-old infants. *Child Development, 56*, 1574–1583.

15 | High-Risk Infant-Parent Interactions
TIFFANY FIELD

SOURCES OF INTERACTIONAL ASYNCHRONY

Infant Response to Parents

A series of studies have demonstrated the disturbances that occur during early interactions when parents are unable to read their infant's signals (Goldberg, 1979) and provide optimal stimulation and arousal modulation (Field, 1982). Interactions with high-risk infants provide a particularly challenging task for the parent. High-risk infants such as those who are preterm or have Down syndrome or cerebral palsy spend less time looking at their parents and appear to enjoy interactions with their parents less than normal infants. Their smiles and vocalizations are less frequent, and their frowns and cries more frequent than those of normal infants. The greater incidence of negative affective displays among these infants together with their elevated heart rate suggests that interactions may be stressful for high-risk infants and their parents. In addition, parental stimulation, infant gaze aversion, negative affect, and heart rate appear to be related. Elevated heart rate, gazing away, and negative affect of the infants may relate to an information overload and elevated arousal level deriving from excessive stimulation. In their natural attempts to elicit positive affect, parents of high-risk infants appear to provide excessive stimulation and fail to modulate arousal as their infants become distressed.

Some investigators have suggested that asynchrony in the interactions of high-risk infants and their parents is related to the limited responsivity of these infants and the overstimulation by their parents (Crnic, Ragozin, Greenberg, Robinson, & Barham, 1983; Field, 1977; Goldberg, Brachfield, & DiVitto, 1980). Relationships between their

I would like to thank the infants and parents who participated in these studies and the researchers who collaborated with me in conducting these studies. This research was supported in part by a Research Scientist Development Award #1K02MH00331-01 from The National Institute of Mental Health.

behavior as neonates and their later interactive behavior suggest some continuity of the limited responsivity of high-risk infants (Field, 1979; Greene, Fox, & Lewis, 1983). Goldberg (1979) has maintained that the basic problem is the unreadability of the high-risk infants' signals. McGehee and Eckerman (1983) similarly suggest that the high-risk infant is responsive but unreadable. In their study on the behavioral responses of preterm and term infants at the neonatal stage they noted that the two groups did not differ in their ability to orient visually and sustain *en face* gaze, but the preterm infants were unable to control erratic body movements and vocalizations and showed more frequent shifts in state. Friedman, Jacobs, and Werthmann (1982) have also reported that preterm infants as neonates fuss and cry more, are more difficult to soothe, and change state more frequently than full-term newborns. They continue to be fussier than full-term infants at 4 months (Field, 1979) and 8 months (Goldberg, 1979), and during later interactions the most frequently reported behaviors for these infants are withdrawal behaviors such as gaze aversion, squirming, and fussing, as if the infants are highly aroused, have difficulty modulating their own arousal, and are trying to terminate the interaction. These behaviors have been noted to persist across the first year of life (Crnic et al., 1983).

Gianino and Tronick (1988) have developed an interesting model describing these averting behaviors as the infants' coping strategy for regulating the amount of stimulation they receive. Indeed, they would appear to be effective coping behaviors because they typically signal the parent to modify his or her stimulation or terminate the interaction. However, if the high-risk infant's signals are more difficult to read (Goldberg, 1979) the parents of those infants may have more difficulty modulating their stimulation.

The picture that emerges from analyses of different types of interactions (feeding, face-to-face, and floor play) at different stages during the first 2 years of life among high-risk infants and their parents is one of a vicious cycle of the infant being relatively inactive and unresponsive, and the parents then trying to engage the infant by being more and more active or stimulating, which in turn leads to more inactivity and unresponsivity on the part of the infant. Although the parents' activity appears to be directed at encouraging more activity or responsivity on the part of the infant, that strategy is counterproductive inasmuch as it leads to less instead of more infant responsivity.

Other groups for which similar phenomena have been observed include the infant with Down syndrome and the child with cerebral palsy. Analyses of interactions between infants with Down syndrome and their mothers suggested that the infants engaged in less eye contact and initiated fewer interactions (Jones, 1980). Their mothers were simultaneously noted to be more active and directive during these play interactions. Similarly, children with cerebral palsy have been noted to exhibit fewer interactive behaviors, and their parents are more active and controlling during interactions (Kogan, 1980).

Parental Response to Infant

Several authors have speculated about the frequently observed hyperactivity of the parents of unresponsive infants labeled "at risk" because of perinatal complications and/or handicapping conditions. The most vague interpretation of this hyperactive behavior suggests that the frustration of receiving minimal responses from the infant leads to a kind of aggressivity on the part of the parents. Another notion is that the parents are more active to compensate for relative inactivity of their infants, perhaps "to keep some semblance of an interaction going." A third interpretation relates to the parents' wanting their child to perform like his or her agemates, and attempting to encourage performance by more frequent modeling of behaviors. Still another interpretation is that the parents view their infants as fragile and delayed and as a result tend to be overprotective. Overprotectiveness in the extreme is construed as overcontrolling behavior.

This last interpretation, that the parents may view their infants as fragile and delayed, such that their preconceived notions about premature babies may affect their behavior, receives some support from the rapidly growing literature on "prematurity stereotyping." Frodi, Lamb, Leavitt, and Donovan (1978), for example, found that parents reacted with a larger electrodermal response (implying greater arousal) and less sympathy to a videotape of a crying infant who was labeled premature than to one labeled full-term. In still another study in which composite drawings were made of full-term and preterm infants' faces (with full-term infants possessing proportionally wider eyes and rounder heads), the composite drawing of the full-term infants evoked more favorable responses from adult judges (Maier, Holmes, Slaymaker & Reich, 1984). Unfortunately, very few studies have been directed to the alternative hypotheses. Nonetheless, interventions have been mounted without understanding the dynamics and underlying mechanisms for these interactive disturbances.

INFANT-PARENT INTERACTION COACHING

That the infant's attentiveness and positive affect can be readily modulated by the behaviors of the parent is demonstrated by interaction coaching studies in which parents have been requested to modify their behaviors (Clark & Seifer, 1983; Field, 1977, 1983). The effect of a manipulation in which mothers were requested to imitate their infants' behaviors (Field, 1977) was that the mothers became less active and more attentive to their infants' cues of being under- or overaroused, and their infants became more attentive and responsive than they had been during spontaneous interactions. Corresponding decreases were noted in tonic heart rate. Clark and Seifer (1983) also reported that maternal imitation of infant behavior was their most effective interaction coaching technique. Conversely, during an attention-getting manipulation in which mothers were asked to keep their infants' attention, mothers became less sensitive to their infants' behavioral cues, and their activity increased, as did infant gaze aversion and heart rate (Field, 1977). This manipulation was apparently aversive for both members of the dyad, as manifested in roughly equivalent, parallel increases in tonic heart rate for both the infants and their mothers. The interpretation made of these data was that high-risk infants may

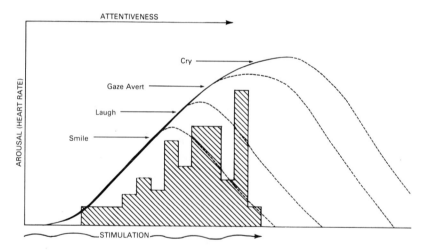

Figure 1.   A schematic illustration of the progression of infant and mother behavior during gameplaying. The x axes depict sustained attention of the infant and variation or modulation of stimulation by the mother. The y axis depicts heart rate. Within the figure the *solid ascending curve* represents increasing heart rate and the *dotted descending curves* represent decreasing heart rate. The *hatched bars* represent variation in the mother's use of stimulus modalities or varying intensity of stimulation. (From Field, T. [1982]. Affective displays of high-risk infants during early interactions. In T. Field & A. Fogel (Eds.), *Emotion and early interaction* (pp. 101–126). Hillsdale, NJ: Lawrence Erlbaum Associates; reprinted by permission.)

have limited information processing and/or arousal modulation abilities, thus requiring more frequent breaks in the conversation to process information and modulate arousal. The parents are "walking a fine line" with these infants in determining the optimal level of stimulation and the points at which arousal modulation is needed. Optimal levels of stimulation may differ for these infants, and they may respond to a narrower range of stimulation, creating the more difficult task for parents of fine-tuning the intensity as well as the amount of stimulation and arousal modulation required by their infants.

A schematic illustration of the progression of behaviors during mother-infant interactions (Figure 1) shows heart rate as progressively increasing prior to smiling, laughing, gaze-averting, and crying behaviors. As these behaviors occur, the level of maternal stimulation decreases, and heart rate peaks and then gradually returns to baseline.

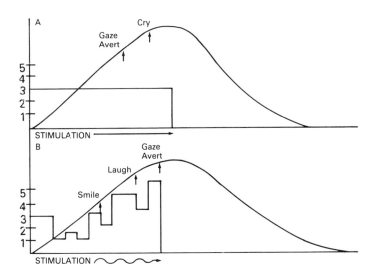

Figure 2. The hypothesized differences between the behavioral curves of normal and high-risk infant-mother dyads. *A:* The hypothetical high-risk dyad, with the mother stimulating her infant at a level sufficient to attain her infant's attention but then sustaining that level rather than modulating stimulation during infant gaze aversion and crying. *B:* The normal infant-mother dyad, showing varied or modulated stimulation by the mother as a function of the infant's affective signals and a cessation of behavior at infant gaze aversion, with the infant returning to a less aroused state. (From Field, T. [1982]. Affective displays of high-risk infants during early interactions. In T. Field & A. Fogel (Eds.), *Emotion and early interaction* (pp. 101–126). Hillsdale, NJ: Lawrence Erlbaum Associates; reprinted by permission.)

Thus, a combination of the infant's affective displays signaling the mother and the mother's diminution of stimulation appears to modulate the arousal level of the infant. If the infant is less able to modulate arousal or the mother does not respond to the affective cues by modulating her stimulation, the infant's aversive threshold may be exceeded and the infant may gaze avert and essentially terminate the interaction. Differences are evident between the behavioral curves of normal and high-risk infant-mother dyads (see Figure 2).

CONCLUSIONS

Determining the nature of optimal stimulation/arousal modulation in complex streams of behavior such as interactions is difficult at best. However, manipulations of interactions, such as asking parents to imitate their infants' behaviors, to become silent during infant gaze aversion, and to simplify their behaviors by repetition, appear to sensitize parents to their infants' gaze and affective signals and thereby seem to diminish infant gaze aversion, heart rate, and crying as well as effect increases in attentiveness and positive affective displays such as smiling and laughing (Clark & Seifer, 1983; Field, 1983). Thus, as the parents and infant become attuned to each other, their interactions become more harmonious. It appears, then, that even with difficult, high-risk infants whose attentiveness occurs less often and whose affective displays are less frequent and more difficult to read, parents can be taught ways of providing optimal stimulation and arousal modulation.

REFERENCES

Clark, G.N., & Seifer, R. (1983). Facilitating mother-infant communication: A treatment model for high-risk and developmentally-delayed infants. *Infant Mental Health Journal, 4*, 67–82.

Crnic, K.A., Ragozin, A.S., Greenberg, M.T., Robinson, N.M., & Barham, R.B. (1983). Social interaction and developmental competence of preterm and full-term infants during the first year of life. *Child Development, 54*, 1199–1210.

Field, T. (1977). Effects of early separation, interactive deficits, and experimental manipulations on infant-mother face-to-face interaction. *Child Development, 48*, 763–771.

Field, T. (1979). Interaction patterns of high-risk and normal infants. In T. Field, A. Sostek, S. Goldberg, & H.H. Shuman (Eds.), *Infants born at risk* (pp. 333–356). New York: Spectrum.

Field, T. (1982). Affective displays of high-risk infants during early interactions. In T. Field & A. Fogel (Eds.), *Emotion and early interaction* (pp. 101–126). Hillsdale, NJ: Lawrence Erlbaum Associates.

Field, T. (1983). Early interactions and interaction coaching of high-risk infants and parents. In M. Perlmutter (Ed.), *Development and policy concerning children with special needs* (The Minnesota Symposia on Child Psychology, pp. 1–34). Hillsdale, NJ: Lawrence Erlbaum Associates.

Friedman, S., Jacobs, B., & Werthmann, M. (1982). Preterms of low medical risk: Spontaneous behaviors and soothability at expected date of birth. *Infant Behavior and Development, 5*, 3–10.

Frodi, A., Lamb, M., Leavitt, L., & Donovan, W. (1978). Fathers' and mothers' responses to infant smiles and cries. *Infant Behavior and Development, 1*, 187–198.

Gianino, A., & Tronick, E. (1988). The mutual regulation model: Infant self and interactive regulation, coping and defense. In T. Field, P. McCabe, & N. Schneiderman (Eds.), *Stress and coping across development* (pp. 47–68). Hillsdale, NJ: Lawrence Erlbaum Associates.

Goldberg, S. (1979). Premature birth: Consequences for the parent-infant relationship. *American Scientist, 67*, 214–220.

Goldberg, S., Brachfeld, S., & DiVitto, B. (1980). Feeding, fussing and playing parent-infant interaction in the first year as a function of prematurity and perinatal problems. In T. Field, S. Goldberg, D. Stern, & A. Sostek (Eds.), *High-risk infants and children: Adult and peer interactions* (pp. 133–154). New York: Academic Press.

Greene, J.G., Fox, N.A., & Lewis, M. (1983). The relationship between neonatal characteristics and three-month mother-infant interaction in high-risk infants. *Child Development, 54*, 1286–1296.

Jones, O. (1980). Mother-child communication in very young Down's syndrome and normal children. In T. Field, S. Goldberg, D. Stern, & A. Sostek (Eds.), *High-risk infants and children: Adult and peer interactions* (pp. 205–226). New York: Academic Press.

Kogan, K.L. (1980). Interaction systems between preschool aged handicapped or developmentally delayed children and their parents. T. Field, S. Goldberg, D. Stern, & A. Sostek (Eds.), *High-risk infants and children: Adult and peer interactions* (pp. 227–250). New York: Academic Press.

Maier, R.A., Holmes, D.L., Slaymaker, F.L., & Reich, J.N. (1984). The perceived attractiveness of preterm infants. *Infant Behavior and Development, 7*, 403–414.

McGehee, I.J., & Eckerman, C.O. (1983). The preterm infant as a social partner: Responsive but unreadable. *Infant Behavior and Development, 6*, 461–470.

IV | CHILDHOOD AND ADOLESCENCE

Overview

H. CARL HAYWOOD

Twenty-five years ago, the framers of the legislation that created the National Institute of Child Health and Human Development, and 23 years ago the framers of Public Law 88-164, the landmark legislation that created the National Mental Retardation Research Centers and the University Affiliated Facilities, had the great wisdom to call for research and research training on mental retardation and related aspects of human development. That great wisdom and foresight has provided some of the most exciting advances in the study of developmental processes in our lifetimes. One of the most important events in the last 25 years has been the emergence of developmental science, not simply multidisciplinary or even interdisciplinary approaches to the study of different problems in development, but recognition that the study of development itself has emerged as a scientific discipline in its own right.

The work is done, of course, from diverse perspectives, recognizing the wide range of influences on development of both commonalities and individual differences in living organisms. Developmental science is based on and has grown from a study of the processes of development—not merely what develops and what fails to develop, but the reasons for both. Studies involving children and adolescents have revealed a broad spectrum of influences on developmental processes, including the adverse mental effects of childhood infections, differential effects of social transactions, and physical and cultural deprivation. This diversity is reflected in the chapters in this section.

Dr. Rachel Schneerson, in Chapter 16, discusses the effects of infectious disease, in particular bacterial meningitis, on cognitive and central nervous system development. Social and scientific improvements over the decades have dramatically reduced the mortality associated with infectious diseases, but in doing so have more clearly revealed the associated morbidity. Analysis of the outcome of bacterial meningitis infections is difficult; incidence data are incomplete and long-term studies of sequelae have used varied data collection and evaluation methods. However, it is clear that the best method of controlling associated morbidity is by preventing infection. Dr. Schneerson details the study of immunity to bacterial meningitis and the efforts to develop a vaccine to use against it.

There are several trends emerging in research on cognition in mentally retarded persons: a lessened emphasis on contrasting retarded and nonretarded performance, the use of single-subject research methodologies for intensive analysis, and the inclusion of studies of high-risk mothers and their infants. These trends are reflected in the discussion of cognitive development presented by Drs. John Borkowski and Lisa Turner in Chapter 17. They stress that current research in mental retardation uses primarily cognitive development theory in preference to a body of theory on intelligence that seems to some researchers impoverished. Much ongoing debate centers on whether mental structures or mental processes define retardation. Drs. Borkowski and Turner argue for an integrated, multicomponent model combining parts of each side of the structure-process debate with motivational and social variables in order to understand memory, cognition, and problem-solving in mentally retarded persons.

Disruptive behavior can interfere with development by adversely affecting learning and performance. In Chapter 18, Dr. Michael Cataldo reviews the implications of behavior analysis research for developmentally disabled persons. A primary use for research results is in treatment of disruptive behavior, especially self-injury. Behavioral treatment has distinct advantages over other possible treatments of self-injurious behavior: it can be targeted to specific behavior, whereas drug treatment affects all behavior; and it lacks the side effects of behavior restriction and loss of function so often associated with mechanical and surgical treatments. Dr. Cataldo's work has employed response classes of behavior, within which modification of one form of behavior has a positive effect on the others, so that a number of forms of behavior can be changed by focusing on one; he has also explored the possibility of a biobehavioral interaction as the cause of self-injurious behavior. That research in mental retardation has become this focused and refined is the result of a concerted effort and significant funding throughout the last three decades. Dr. Cataldo points out that further research gains can be anticipated, but not without a continuation of that intentional effort seen up to now.

Finally, Dr. Craig Ramey and colleagues discuss the history, results, and future applicability of early intervention in Chapter 19. Modifying interventions during the first 5 years of life have become respectable, important components in attempts to overcome developmental deficiencies and disadvantages. However, it was not until the 1950s that a theoretical ground was prepared for early intervention, with the emergence of the early experience paradigm. The "critical periods" postulated to exist for intellectual development became incorporated into educational theories, and programs for enhancing the educational environment of a high-risk child were implemented during the 1960s (e.g., Head Start). The findings of several studies that no permanent benefits of the programs were evident touched off a theoretical argument regarding such types of compensatory education, but contemporary theory largely resolves the issue. Development is now viewed as a continuous, cumulative transactional process, and thus early intervention is still highly significant since in a hierarchical view of development, early gains are multiplied as they are applied in later stages. The question is no longer whether modification of a particular developmental trend is possible, but how to determine which children should receive which kinds of intervention and how to provide it. Dr. Ramey and his colleagues review the research on identification of at-risk children (both physically and environmentally disadvantaged) and present a synthesis of the various programs employed and their results. Several educational approaches are discussed, and guidelines are proposed for program operation.

16 | Vaccines for Prevention of Mental Retardation following Meningitis

RACHEL SCHNEERSON

Social and scientific gains, which have accelerated over the last century, have led to improved nutrition, housing, water and food handling, and reduced attack rates of infectious diseases. The advent of antimicrobials has markedly reduced the lethality of infectious diseases, which in turn has made their morbidity more apparent. Such is the case with bacterial meningitis; antibiotics and supportive therapy have reduced the mortality (from close to 100% to about 5–30%), leaving morbidity, as measured by fixed central nervous system deficits, unacceptably high. The incidence of morbidity that follows "cured" bacterial meningitis is not likely to be reduced.

The extent of mental retardation caused by "cured" bacterial meningitis can be estimated by compounding two rates: 1) the overall incidence of bacterial meningitis, and 2) the incidence of sequelae based upon series of follow-up cases. The incidence of bacterial meningitis can only be estimated because, with the exception of meningococcal and tuberculous meningitis, bacterial meningitis is not a reportable disease. Table 1 reviews several surveys of bacterial meningitis due to *Haemophilus influenzae* type b (Hib) in the United States. Hib is the most common cause of bacterial meningitis in the United States, accounting for about 12,500 cases annually. In an ongoing survey in Mecklenburg county, North Carolina, which includes Charlotte, we showed that about 1 of every 250 newborns contracts Hib meningitis before reaching the age of 5 years. In some communities of Native Americans, the incidence of Hib meningitis is 5 to 8 times higher. Table 2 shows the incidence of Hib and the other most common causes of bacterial meningitis in a Navajo reservation over the past 15 years. Whereas the incidence of tuberculous and meningococcal meningitis declined during this period, the incidence of Hib meningitis remains high and unchanged (Coulehan et al., 1984).

Table 1.   Incidence of *Haemophilus influenzae* type b meningitis in children less than 5 years of age

Population studied	Time	Cases/10⁵ population
Bethel, S.U. Alaska	1972–1976	360
Mecklenburg county, North Carolina	1966–1970	63
Olmstead county, Minnesota	1959–1970	40
Bernalilo county, New Mexico	1964–1971	38
Charleston, North Carolina	1961–1971	38
Vermont	1967–1970	35
Franklin county, Ohio	1960–1968	35
Los Angeles, California	1975	32
Allegheny county, Pennsylvania	1964–1970	32
Tennessee	1963–1971	23

Data from Fraser and Ward, NCDC, personal communication.

Pneumococcal meningitis has the highest mortality rate of all the bacterial meningitides; in developing countries it is about 50%, and in western countries with health care systems, it is about 15–30% (Table 3). The mortality rate of meningitis for the United States is about 28% for pneumococcal, 14.0% for meningococcal, and 7.0% for Hib (Schlech & Broome, 1979).

Estimates of the sequelae of bacterial meningitis are even more difficult to make. Several long-term examinations of patients have been published but it is difficult to compare these data because the methods of collecting and of evaluating sequelae are so different.

Table 2.   Bacterial meningitis among the Navajo indians, 1968–1973 and 1974–1980

Causative organism	No. cases		% total 1974–80	Cases/100,000/ year, ages 0–4	
	Con- firmed	Prob- able		1968–73	1974–80
Haemophilus influenzae	206	10	60.4	152.3	152.5
Streptococcus pneumoniae	77	10	22.6	50.4	45.5
Neisseria meningitidis	7	1	2.0	12.6	0.5
Mycobacterium tuberculosis	17	0	5.0	8.8	2.2
Other	34	22	10.0	15.1	15.6
Total	341	43	100.0	216.3	239.2

Reported central nervous system deficits include hearing loss, mental retardation, seizure disorders, hydrocephalus, paresis, paralysis, cortical blindness, delayed development, language disabilities, and behavior problems. Sell and her collaborators (Sell, Merrill, Doyne, & Zimsky, 1972) followed patients cured of Hib meningitis from their clinic at Vanderbilt University in Tennessee. Of 75 patients, 4 (5%) had severe, 22 (29%) had significant, and 12 (16%) had possible mental deficiency. Similar data have been reported by other investigators (Bohr et al., 1983; Chin & Fitzhardinge, 1985; Claesson, Trollfors, Jodal, & Rosenhall, 1984; Hutchison & Kovacs, 1963; Izuora, 1985; Jadavji, Biggar, Gold, & Prober, 1986; Kaplan, Catlin, Weaver, & Feigin, 1984; Lindbergm, Rosenhall, Nyland, & Ringner, 1977; Taylor, Michaels, Mazur, Baurer, & Liden, 1984; Wald et al., 1986). Since it is not likely that we will have more effective antibiotics or other therapeutic agents for this problem, the best measure to control the morbidity of bacterial meningitis is by prevention; the development of a new generation of polysaccharide vaccines puts this objective within our grasp.

Table 3. Mortality from pneumococcal meningitis in the antibiotic era

Country	Mortality (%)
United Kingdom	13
Denmark	17
United States	
Los Angeles	22
Boston	29
Philadelphia[a]	37
Harlem[a]	47
India	45
Egypt	33
Kenya	24
Malawi	43
Zambia	45
Uganda	51
Nigeria	51
Ghana	55
Upper Volta	60

Data from Baird, D.R., Whittle, H.C., & Greenwood, B.M. (1976). *Lancet, 2,* 1344–1346.
[a]Series containing high proportion of blacks.

PATHOGENESIS OF AND IMMUNITY TO BACTERIAL MENINGITIS

Bacterial meningitis occurs usually in otherwise healthy individuals, mostly infants and children. The primary pathogenic event is invasion of the bacteria from their site on the upper respiratory tract mucosa, where they reside without causing symptoms, into the bloodstream. In the blood the bacteria multiply, and when their concentration reaches a critical level, they may lodge in various tissues and cause localized infections. Of these, meningitis is the most common and represents the most serious health problem. The causative bacteria are gram negative (Hib, meningococci, and *Escherichia coli*) or gram positive (pneumococci and group B streptococci). Common to all these pathogens is the presence of an outer layer consisting of a polysaccharide "capsule" that surrounds each bacterium. These capsules are polymers of one to several sugars in a repeating sequence. By themselves nontoxic, they act to shield the bacteria from the protective actions of complement. Capsular polysaccharides are both obligatory virulence factors and protective antigens.

The first clue to the pathogenesis of and immunity to encapsulated bacteria was provided by Fothergill and Wright in 1933. These workers plotted the age incidence of Hib meningitis against the "bactericidal power" of blood samples (now known to be due to anticapsular polysaccharide antibody) taken from healthy individuals of all ages. Newborns had maternally derived antibodies, the levels of which wane to nondetectable at about 6 months of age. These antibodies start to reappear at about 3–4 years and reach adult levels at 8–12 years. Hib meningitis occurs with high frequency in infants and young children when they have lost their maternally derived antibodies and have not yet started to synthesize their own. These and subsequent observations provide evidence that the age incidence of bacterial meningitis is inversely related to the presence of serum antibodies. This study indicates that, to be effective, vaccine-induced immunity must be in place by age 3–6 months.

DEVELOPMENT OF Hib VACCINE

We worked mostly with Hib because it is the most common cause of bacterial meningitis in the United States as well as the cause of other serious diseases, including epiglottitis, arthritis, and osteomyelitis. The capsular polysaccharides (CPSs) of Hib and of other encapsulated bacterial pathogens can be prepared in a highly pure form and are among the safest vaccines produced to date. These polysaccharides constitute a unique group of antigens conveniently termed "T-cell independent" because they do not induce a "booster" response upon reinjection. Furthermore, most polysaccharides, including Hib, elicit an age-related response. Table 4 shows that when injected into adults, Hib CPS elicited a fourfold or greater rise of Hib CPS antibodies in all 25 subjects; the geometric mean postimmunization level was 14.0 μg of antibody/ml (Robbins, Parke, Schneerson, & Whisnant, 1973). There was no change in the postimmunization level of antibodies 3 years later. A lesser serum antibody response was observed in children ages 2–5 years. In addition, the decline in postimmunization levels was greater in the children than in adults. Infants 2–3 months old failed to respond with protective levels of antibodies when immunized with the Hib CPS. Results of clinical evaluation of the effectiveness of the Hib CPS in preventing meningitis and other invasive diseases caused by Hib paralleled these studies of immunogenicity; children above the age of 18–24 months were protected against Hib meningitis for 1 year. The Hib CPS failed to prevent Hib meningitis in infants and children less than 18 months of age (Parke, Schneerson, Robbins, & Schlesselman, 1977; Peltola, Kayhty, Virtanen, & Makela, 1984).

Based upon these studies, and the fact that a substantial number of Hib meningitis cases occur in 2–5-year-old children, Hib CPS vaccine was licensed by the FDA for this age group. About 5 million doses have been administered without serious toxicity. Since most cases (about 60%) of Hib meningitis occur in the less-than-2-years age group, our laboratory sought methods to develop a more immunogenic Hib CPS for infants and children.

To change the T-cell–independent properties and to increase the immunogenicity of CPS, we utilized the approach of covalently binding CPS to T-cell–dependent immunogenic proteins. The carrier proteins should be medically acceptable and preferably of protective value

Table 4. Age-related serum antibody response elicited by the capsular polysaccharide of *Haemophilus influenzae* type b (μg antibody/ml)

Age group	n	Geometric mean Ab[a]	
		Pre-imm	Post-imm
Adults	25	0.58	13.9
Children (2–5 yrs)	18	0.40	4.2
Infants (2–3 mos)	18	<0.04	0.10

Data from Robbins et al. (1973).
[a]Ab = antibodies.

by themselves, and the bonding should be done in a way acceptable for human use.

In the experiments described below, Hib CPS was activated with cyanogen bromide and a derivative was made with a spacer molecule (adipic acid dihydrazide) and then conjugated to tetanus toxoid (or to other carrier proteins) by a carbodiimide condensation reaction (Schneerson, Barrera, Sutton, & Robbins, 1980). Animal studies of these conjugates in mice, rabbits, and primates have shown: 1) increased immunogenicity and T-cell–dependent properties; 2) booster and carrier effects; and 3) that antibodies induced by both the CPS and protein components of the conjugate had biological functions that correlate with protection (Chu, Schneerson, Robbins, & Rastogi, 1983).

Table 5 shows the Hib CPS antibody responses of seven groups of eight juvenile rhesus monkeys injected subcutaneously three times at 3-week intervals with several vaccine combinations. The components of the conjugates (tetanus toxoid [TT] or Hib CPS) when injected alone in Groups 1 and 2 did not elicit antibodies to the CPS. This lack of responsiveness to bacterial CPS is characteristic of laboratory animals; humans are the best known responders to this type of antigen. In contrast, Hib-TT–induced antibodies were about 10 times higher than the estimated protective level; increases in these levels were also observed after the second injection (booster response). To study compatibility of Hib-TT with diphtheria-tetanus-pertussis (DTP) vaccine, Group 4 was injected Hib-TT plus TT in saline (fluid) and Group 5 with Hib-TT plus DTP. An increase in the levels of Hib CPS antibodies over those elicited by the conjugate injected alone was observed when the two vaccines were injected concurrently at separate sites. Of the two DTP was more effective, possibly because of the presence of the aluminum salts and the pertussis cells, both of which have been shown to exert an adjuvant effect. One group of rhesus monkeys (Group 6) were passively immunized with an adult human dose of tetanus immune globulin (TIG) 24 hours prior to injection with the Hib-TT in order to study the effect of preexisting antibody to the carrier protein, as might exist in human infants. No effect of the passive immunization with the anti-TT antibodies was noted. Another group (Group 7) was injected with a Hib–cholera toxin (CT) conjugate. It is probable that vaccinated individuals will continue to receive TT at intervals. Accordingly, all monkeys were injected with TT 5 weeks after their last injection of the conjugates and the Hib CPS antibodies were measured 3 weeks later. No effect of reinjection of the carrier protein, TT, was noted upon the level of Hib CPS antibodies (Schneerson et al., 1984). Our conclusion drawn from these studies with primates is that Hib-TT is compatible with DTP and their

Table 5. *Haemophilus influenzae* type b capsular polysaccharide (Hib) antibody responses of seven groups of eight juvenile rhesus monkeys[a]

Group	Vaccine[b]	Antibody levels (µg Hib Ab/ml serum; geometric mean)					
		Preimmune	First injection	Second injection	Third injection	TT 7 weeks after third injection	2 weeks after TT
1	Hib (50 µg)	0.06	<0.04	0.05	0.04	0.05	<0.04
2	TT (50 µg)	0.05	0.05	0.06	0.06	0.06	0.06
3	Hib-TT (50 µg)	0.06	1.22	2.15	2.27	2.18	1.80
4	Hib-TT (50 µg) plus TT (50 Lf)[c]	0.10	2.18	4.38	7.29	7.32	5.40
5	Hib-TT (50 µg) plus DTP (0.5 ml)[c]	0.05	4.65	14.61	20.65	13.04	7.25
6	Hib-TT (50 µg) plus TIG[d]	0.08	2.00	2.45	3.78	2.78	1.95
7	Hib-CT (45 µg)[e]	0.06	2.75	6.91	10.35	5.57	4.25

[a]Animals were injected subcutaneously with vaccines in indicated amounts at 3-week intervals, and again with 50 Lf of TT at 7 weeks after the third injection. Hib antibody levels given for each injection were measured from blood samples taken immediately prior to each injection, and from a blood sample taken 2 weeks after TT dose. Hib CPS antibodies were measured by radioimmunoassy.

[b]TT = tetanus toxoid, DTP = diphtheria-tetanus-pertussis toxoid, TIG = tetanus immune globulin, CT = cholera toxin.

[c]Injected concurrently at separate sites.

[d]Injected 24 hours prior to Hib-TT.

[e]Same injection schedule as for the Hib conjugates.

243

Table 6. *Hemophilus influenzae* type b (Hib) serum antibody responses (μg Ab/ml) of young adult volunteers immunized with two doses of conjugates given 3 weeks apart

Group	Vaccine[a]	Geometric mean antibody response (25th/75th percentiles)			
		Preinjection	3 weeks after first injection	2 weeks after second injection	6 months after first injection
1	Hib-TT (50 μg), twice	1.12 (0.55/2.53)	202.2 (95.8/422)	162.0 (71.5/350)	84.2 (48.6/166)
2	Pn6A-TT (50 μg), twice	1.61 (0.59/3.38)	4.3 (1.81/10.2)	5.90 (2.14/11.4)	5.04 (1.57/11.3)
3	Hib-TT + Pn6A (50 μg), then Hib-TT (50 μg)	0.98 (0.32/1.66)	147.7 (96.5/241)	152.3 (97.0/253)	89.4 (56.0/140)
4	Hib-TT + K100-TT (50 μg), then Hib-TT (50 μg)	1.37 (0.70/2.60)	203.8 (156/276)	179.5 (115/264)	109.2 (56.9/187)
5	Hib-TT (100 μg), then Hib-TT (50 μg)	1.18 (0.33/4.52)	235.7 (149/410)	206.8 (131/430)	83.6 (49.6/166)

[a]TT = tetanus toxoid, Pn6A = pneumococcus type 6A, K100 = *Escherichia coli* K100.

244

concurrent injection could enhance the serum Hib CPS antibody response, possibly through a "carrier" effect of the TT component.

Young adult volunteers, five groups of about 20 in each group, were injected with:

1. Hib-TT (50 or 100 µg);
2. Pneumococcus type 6A-TT (Pn6A-TT) (50 µg); (pneumococcus type 6 organisms are a common cause of infection in children and this CPS, which is 23 valent, is the least immunogenic of the types in the pneumococcus vaccine);
3. A combination of these two conjugates; or
4. Hib-TT plus *E. coli* K100-TT conjugate

Table 7. Serum bactericidal activity and radioimmunoassy (RIA) bactericidal titer from volunteers immunized with Hib-TT, Pn6A-TT, and K100-TT conjugates

Volunteer (group[a])	µg Ab/ml	Bactericidal titer
#29 (Group 1)		
Preimmunization	1.18	1:4
After first injection	602.0	>1:4096
After second injection	960.0	>1:4096
#56 (Group 1)		
Preimmunization	0.69	1:16
After first injection	336.0	1:1024
After second injection	120.0	1:512
#40 (Group 2)		
Preimmunization	2.80	1:4
After second injection	44.0	1:16
#105 (Group 2)		
Preimmunization	0.46	1:2
After first injection	5.8	1:8
After second injection	6.1	1:16
#59 (Group 3)		
Preimmunization	0.74	1:2
After first injection	208.0	1:2048
After second injection	336.0	1:1024
#69 (Group 4)		
After second injection	1728.0	>1:4096
#107 (Group 4)		
Preimmunization	0.20	<1:2
5 weeks after first injection[b]	512.0	>1:4096

[a]Group numbers as in Table 6.
[b]Immunized only once. Blood sample taken at 5 weeks after first injection.

Table 8. Antibodies elicited by *Hemophilus influenzae* type b capsular polysaccharide (Hib CPS) and pneumococcus type 6A capsular polysaccharide (Pn6A CPS) alone or as conjugates with tetanus (TT) or diphtheria (DT) toxoids in adults

| | Antibody response (geometric mean) | | |
| | Pre-immunization | Post-immunization | Fold increase |
Vaccine			
Hemophilus[a]			
Hib CPS	1.99	29.5	14.8
Hib CPS	0.56	15.9	28.4
Hib CPS-TT	1.12	202.2	180.5
Hib CPS-DT	3.03	248.0	75.3
Hib CPS-DT	0.56	89.0	158.9
Pneumococcus[b]			
Pn6A CPS	220	686	3.1
Pn6A CPS	117	627	5.3
Pn6A CPS-TT	167	1385	8.2

[a]Micrograms of antibody protein/ml.
[b]Nanograms of antibody nitrogen/ml.

in order to study the possibility that a closely related, but different, CPS (K100) could enhance the Hib CPS response.

All vaccinates injected with Hib-TT, alone or in combination with either Pn6A-TT or *E. coli* K100-TT, responded with an increase of Hib CPS antibodies after one injection (geometric mean increase was about 180-fold) (Table 6). There was no statistical difference between the postimmunization levels among the five groups. No booster response was elicited by a second injection of Hib-TT alone or in combination administered 3 weeks later. There was a decline in Hib CPS antibodies, to about one half of their maximal levels, in blood samples taken 6 months after the first injection. Volunteers injected with Pn6A-TT alone (Group 2) responded with a slight rise of Hib CPS antibodies; 11 of 20 volunteers had a twofold or greater increase. This cross-reaction is consistent with the structural similarities between the two CPSs and reports of the cross-reactivity between typing sera for these two organisms (Neter, 1943). Hib CPS antibodies had biological activities that have been correlated with protection (Table 7). Similarly, increased levels of antibodies to Pn6A and TT were found to correlate with their biological activities (mouse protective activity for Pn6 antibodies and toxin neutralization for the TT antibodies) (Schneerson et al., 1986). A comparison of Hib and Pn6A CPS antibodies elicited alone or as conjugates is shown in Table 8. We are now studying the immunological properties of the Hib-TT conjugates in children. Investigators who have prepared Hib CPS conjugates by other techniques have also reported the increased immunogenicity of the conjugates in children (Anderson et al., 1986; Einhorn, Weinberg, Anderson, Granoff, & Granoff, 1986; Kayhty et al., 1987).

The principles of modifying the immunological properties of CPSs by chemically bonding them to immunogenic carrier proteins has been extended to various CPSs and detoxified lipopolysaccharides (LPSs) of medical interest (Table 9). The techniques required to achieve the synthesis of the conjugate vaccines must be designed to suit the physicochemical properties of the carrier proteins and the structures of the various CPSs. It is possible to prepare conjugates of CPSs to include all the common causes of bacterial meningitis and other invasive diseases caused by encapsulated bacteria. Therefore, prevention of bacterial meningitis and its sequelae is now probable (Gotschlich, 1978).

Table 9. Polysaccharide-protein conjugates under development

Hemophilus influenzae
   CPS-TT
   Oligosaccharide-CRM$_{197}$
   CPS-DT
   CPS-group B meningococcal   OMP = ?
Pneumococcus
   Types 6A and 6B CPS-TT
   Type 6A oligosaccharide-CRM$_{197}$
   Type 3 CPS-TT
   Type 3 hexasaccharide-bovine serum albumin (BSA)
   Phosphocholine-BSA
Meningococci
   Groups A, B, and C oligosaccharide-TT
   Group B *N*-propyloligosaccharide derivative-TT
   Group C CPS-TT
   R-type polysaccharide (LPS) oligosaccharide-TT
Pseudomonas aeruginosa
   LPS immunotype 1-pili
   LPS immunotype 5-exotoxin A
   LPS immunotype 1-BSA
Escherichia coli
   K13 CPS-BSA
Salmonella typhimurium
   LPS disaccharide-BSA
   LPS oligosaccharide-BSA
   LPS oligosaccharide-DT
Klebsiella pneumoniae
   Type 2 oligosaccharide-BSA
   Type 11 oligosaccharide-BSA

REFERENCES

Anderson, P.W., Pichichero, M.E., Insel, R.A., Betts, R., Eby, R., & Smith, D.H. (1986). Vaccines consisting of periodate-cleaved oligosaccharides from the capsule of *Haemophilus influenzae* type b coupled to a protein carrier: Structural and temporal requirements for priming in the human infant. *Journal of Immunology, 137,* 1181–1186.

Bohr, V., Hansen, B., Kjersem, H., Rasmussen, N., Johnsen, N., Kristensen, H.S., & Jessen, O. (1983). Sequelae from bacterial meningitis and their relation to the clinical condition during acute illness, based upon 667 questionnaire returns. [Part II of a three-part series.] *Journal of Infection, 7,* 102–110.

Chin, K.C., & Fitzhardinge, P.M. (1985). Sequelae of early-onset group B hemolytic streptococcal meningitis. *Journal of Pediatrics, 106,* 819–822.

Chu, C.-Y., Schneerson, R., Robbins, J.B., & Rastogi, S.C. (1983). Further studies on the immunogenicity of *Haemophilus influenzae* type b and pneumococcal type 6A polysaccharide-protein conjugates. *Infection and Immunity, 40,* 245–256.

Claesson, B., Trollfors, B., Jodal, U., & Rosenhall, U. (1984). Incidence of prognosis of *Haemophilus influenzae* meningitis in children in a Swedish region. *Pediatric Infectious Disease, 3,* 36–39.

Coulehan, J.L., Michaels, R.H., Hallowell, C., Schults, R., Welty, T.K., & Kuo J.S.C. (1984). Epidemiology of *Haemophilus influenzae* type b disease among Navajo Indians. *Public Health Reports, 99,* 406–409.

Einhorn, M.S., Weinberg, G.A., Anderson, E.L., Granoff, P.D., & Granoff, D.M. (1986). Immunogenicity in infants of *Haemophilus influenzae* type B polysaccharide in a conjugate vaccine with *Neisseria meningitidis* outer-membrane protein. *Lancet, 2,* 299–302.

Fothergill, L.D., & Wright, J. (1933). Influenzal meningitis: Relation of age incidence to the bactericidal power of blood against the causal organism. *Journal of Immunology, 24,* 273–284.

Gotschlich, E.C. (1978). Bacterial meningitis: The beginning of the end. *The American Journal of Medicine, 65,* 719–721.

Hutchison, P.A., & Kovacs, M.C. (1963). The sequelae of acute purulent meningitis in childhood. *Canadian Medical Association Journal, 89,* 158–166.

Izuora, G.I. (1985). Aetiology of mental retardation in Nigerian children around Enugu. *The Central African Journal of Medicine, 31,* 13–16.

Jadavji, T., Biggar, W.D., Gold, R., & Prober, C.G. (1986). Sequelae of acute bacterial meningitis in children treated for seven days. *Pediatrics, 78,* 21–25.

Kaplan, S.L., Catlin, F.I., Weaver, T., & Feigin, R.D. (1984). Onset of hearing loss in children with bacterial meningitis. *Pediatrics, 73,* 575–578.

Kayhty, H., Eskola, J., Peltola, H., Stout, M.G., Samuelson, J.S., & Gordon, L.K. (1987). Immunogenicity in infants of a vaccine composed of *Haemophilus influenzae* type b capsular polysaccharide mixed with DPT or conjugated to diphtheria toxoid. *Journal of Infectious Diseases, 155,* 100–106.

Lindbergm, J., Rosenhall, U., Nylen, O., & Ringner, A. (1977). Long-term outcome of *Haemophilus influenzae* meningitis related to antibiotic treatment. *Pediatrics, 60,* 1–6.

Neter, E. (1943). Antigenic relationship between *H. influenzae* type b and Pneumococcus type VI. *Proceedings of the Society for Experimental Biology and Medicine, 52*, 289–291.

Parke, J.C., Schneerson, R., Robbins, J.B., & Schlesselman, J.J. (1977). Interim report of a controlled field trial of immunization with capsular polysaccharides of *Haemophilus influenzae* type b and group C *Neisseria meningitidis* in Mecklenberg County, North Carolina (March 1974–1976). Symposium on current status and prospects for improved and new bacterial vaccines. *Journal of Infectious Diseases, 136*, S51–S56.

Peltola, H., Kayhty, H., Virtanen, M., & Makela, P.H. (1984). Prevention of *Haemophilus influenzae* type b bacteremic infections with the capsular polysaccharide vaccine. *New England Journal of Medicine, 310*, 1561–1566.

Robbins, J.B., Parke, J.C., Schneerson, R., & Whisnant, J.K. (1973). Quantitative measurement of "natural" and immunization-induced *Haemophilus influenzae* type b capsular polysaccharide antibodies. *Pediatric Research, 7*, 103–110.

Schlech, W.F., & Broome, C.V. (1979, June 22). Bacterial meningitis in the United States, 1978–81 (National Bacterial Meningitis Surveillance Study). *Morbidity and Mortality Weekly Report.*

Schneerson, R., Barrera, O., Sutton, A., & Robbins, J.B. (1980). Preparation, characterization and immunogenicity of *Haemophilus influenzae* type b polysaccharide-protein conjugates. *Journal of Experimental Medicine, 152*, 361–376.

Schneerson, R., Robbins, J.B., Chu, C.-Y., Sutton, A., Vann, W., Vickers, J.C., London, W.T., Curfman, B., Hardegree, M.C., Shiloach, J., & Rastogi, S.C. (1984). Serum antibody responses of juvenile and infant rhesus monkeys injected with *Haemophilus influenzae* type b and pneumococcus type 6A polysaccharide-protein conjugates. *Infection and Immunity, 45*, 582–591.

Schneerson, R., Robbins, J.B., Parke, J.C., Jr., Sutton, A., Wang, Z., Schlesselman, J.J., Schiffman, G., Bell, C., Karpas, A., & Hardegree, M.C. (1986). Quantitative and qualitative analyses of serum *Haemophilus influenzae* type b, pneumococcus type 6A and tetanus toxin antibodies elicited by polysaccharide-protein conjugates in adult volunteers. *Infection and Immunity, 52*, 501–518.

Sell, H.W., Merrill, R.E., Doyne, E.O.L., & Zimsky, E.P. (1972). Long-term sequelae of *Hemophilus influenzae* meningitis. *Pediatrics, 49*, 206–211.

Taylor, H.G., Michaels, R.H., Mazur, P.M., Baurer, R.E., & Liden, C.B. (1984). Intellectual, neuropsychological, and achievement outcomes in children six to eight years after recovery from *Haemophilus influenzae* meningitis. *Pediatrics, 74*, 198–205.

Wald, E.R., Bergman, I., Taylor, H.G., Chiponis, D., Porter, C., & Klark, K. (1986). Long-term outcome of group B streptococcal meningitis. *Pediatrics, 77*, 217–221.

17 | Cognitive Development
JOHN G. BORKOWSKI and
LISA A. TURNER

It is paradoxical that a book on research accomplishments and new frontiers in mental retardation does not contain a single chapter with the word *intelligence* in the title. It might legitimately be asked how a book on mental retardation could fail to focus, with some regularity, on the topic of intelligence. Because our analysis of cognitive development overlaps in thematic context with the field of intelligence, several reasons are offered for what, on the surface, might be seen as a glaring omission in this collection of chapters.

INTELLIGENCE AND RETARDATION: MISSING LINKS

Intelligence tests are as commonplace today in the diagnosis and classification of special children as they were two decades ago. These tests continue to serve as the major index of mental retardation, distinguishing between persons with mental retardation and persons of normal intelligence, and among the various classifications of retardation. In contrast to the 1960s, however, the use of psychometrically defined IQ tests as research instruments has greatly diminished. Consider the chapters in this book that made use of the concept of intelligence or its representations in behavior: Janina Galler, in her chapter on neonatal protein deficiencies, found long-term IQ to be relatively unaffected by early malnutrition, whereas more localized deficits in attentional processes remained pronounced (Chapter 2). In contrast, Mildred Stahlman and colleagues (Chapter 12), Joseph Fagan and Jeanne Montie (Chapter 14), and Frank Duffy and Heidelise Als (Chapter 13) relied on IQ as a major indicant of psychological development. These projects represent examples of predictive or intervention research about the causes of developmental delay, such as very low birth weight. Since IQ was used as a major referent of development rather than as a theoretical framework, these investigators seemed guided more by "classification customs" than by close

The writing of this chapter was supported, in part, by NIH grant HD-21218.

allegiance to intelligence theory. The problem for all who choose to research intelligence, as either cause or consequence, is that the theory lying behind the commonly used IQ tests such as the Binet or Wechsler is impoverished and thus a poor springboard for understanding what Eunice Kennedy Shriver referred to as our chief research agenda—discovering the "inner lives of retarded people."

In contrast to this state of affairs with respect to research on intelligence, contemporary theories of cognition attempt to describe the structures and processes that underlie our mental actions. In a general sense, they provide a more analytic framework about how and why retarded people learn, think, and reason and for determining whether these processes can be accelerated or remediated in inefficient learners. Thus, it is no surprise that the ensuing discussion centers on cognitive rather than intellectual development.

It should be emphasized that "intelligence" will return, in the decades ahead, as a topic in its own right. Recent advances in intelligence theory—by Robert Sternberg, Howard Gardner, and others (see Sternberg & Davidson, 1987)—will be accompanied by new diagnostic instruments useful not only in identifying but also in educating retarded people. If this scenario is correct, we will not only forsake the Binet and Wechsler tests as the diagnostic instruments of choice but our research efforts will, in large part, be derived from these new, more integrative theories of intelligence. The current custom of employing IQ scores to serve as indicants of intervention effectiveness or as correlates of biological substrates of mental retardation will become obsolete. More precise, process-oriented measures of intelligence and cognition will be available, providing more analytical, theoretically rich, and educationally relevant frameworks for research on mental retardation. For the time being, however, conceptual and empirical precision lies more in theories of cognitive development than in intelligence theory.

COGNITIVE-MOTIVATIONAL DEVELOPMENT

The last 25 years have been marked by a heated debate within cognitive psychology about whether structures or processes define mild mental retardation, yet relatively little attention has been given to the development of these structures and processes, and to the importance of their interaction. To complicate matters, the roles of personal, motivational, and familial factors have generally been ignored in the heat of the structure-process debate. In the next sections, two major themes—themes that center on the "inner" mental lives of retarded persons—will be presented:

1. Cognitive activities in retarded persons are extremely complex, multifaceted, and rapidly changing across the life span. Furthermore, it is the interaction of cognitive structures and processes that determines learning ability both in the laboratory and in the classroom.
2. Inner, cognitive lives are inseparably linked to the social events that surround and define outer lives. Hence, the study of social contexts and social interchanges needs to be interrelated with the analysis of cognitive development.

The Structure-Process Debate

Early work on cognition among mentally retarded persons focused on identifying the mental structures that might be causally related to the learning deficiencies experienced by these individuals. In 1963, Ellis proposed that the short-term memory trace, with decreased intensity and duration in mentally retarded people, was a source of their learning and memory deficiencies. That is, information in short-term memory faded more quickly for these individuals, and therefore was less likely to be transferred to a more permanent memory store. Zeaman and House (1979) suggested that retarded individuals attend to fewer dimensions of a stimulus than do nonretarded individuals, and therefore are less likely to focus on the relevant dimensions of a problem, thus decreasing the opportunities for the correct stimulus to be learned. Spitz (1963) proposed that retarded individuals reach a state of cortical satiation more slowly than nonretarded individuals. His data indicated that perceptual aftereffects and illusions take longer to occur and persist longer in mentally retarded individuals.

Although the early structural theories often did not receive adequate empirical evaluation, they led to more recent structural theories that have maintained a consistent theme: Mental structures are often responsible for inefficient learning, memory, and problem-solving in the early stages of information processing. For instance, Sperber and McCauley (1984) found that retarded individuals encode information more slowly than nonretarded individuals. Ellis and Meador (1985) reported that retarded persons show a greater loss of information between a simultaneous and a zero-second delay in a matching paradigm. Spitz and Borys (1984), in their research on problem solving, found that tasks became difficult for retarded persons when they had to plan several moves ahead. In contrast, problems that allowed physical moves (rather than mental moves) were solved equally well by retarded and nonretarded participants. Spitz and Borys (1984) suggested that the working memory capacity is diminished in retarded persons.

Whereas some investigators have attempted to define the structural differences and limitations that lead to learning failures, others have considered the explanatory value of processes and strategies. Belmont and Butterfield (1971) and Brown (1974) established that retarded individuals often do not employ rehearsal strategies to increase recall. Investigators have shown similar strategic "deficits" in paired-associate learning (e.g., Taylor & Turnure, 1979), categorization (e.g., Gerjouy, Winters, Pullen, & Spitz, 1969), and rehearsal and organization (e.g., Spitz & Borys, 1977). Efforts have been extended to the training and generalization of these strategies, with many investigators successful in training retarded individuals to use memory strategies. For instance, Butterfield, Wambold, and Belmont (1973) elevated the performance of retarded individuals up to the level of untrained college students following extensive training of rehearsal and retrieval strategies.

Although retarded individuals have been trained to employ strategies, generalization of these skills has proved to be an illusive phenomena. Research efforts on the generalization problem have centered on understanding the higher-level processes that produce generalization failures. Difficulties in executive function (e.g., Butterfield & Belmont, 1977) and metamemory (e.g., Borkowski, Reid, & Kurtz, 1984) have been posited as potential sources of the problem.

Bad Cognitive Habits   As recently as 1980, the structure-process controversy raged on. In the fall of 1980, Ted Tjossem, Al Baumeister, Carl Haywood, and their staffs convened a conference on "Learning and Cognition in the Mentally Retarded" at the Kennedy Center, Peabody College of Vanderbilt University. The positions on display represented two decades of research on cognitive development in mentally retarded persons, bringing into sharp contrast divergent perspectives on the importance of structures and process for learning in such individuals.

One perspective emphasized the structures of the mind, the other the processes that guide mental activity. Because they are influenced by different assumptions about the fundamental nature of cognition, each camp focused on different research questions, used different methodologies, and invoked different types of explanatory constructs. Investigators of the structural position generally searched for innate, defining features or states in the memory-cognition system and claimed these features to be relatively intractable, whereas those who supported a process position held that mental skills are acquired, relatively easy to modify, and interact with higher or lower order components.

Many who attended the conference were mentally exhausted by the intensity of the debate that framed the formal presentations. It was clear that as late as 1980, cognitive problems in mentally retarded persons were considered to be due to either innate structural deficits or a failure to develop age-appropriate processing skills. Little overlap or compromise of theoretical positions seemed possible.

Those who attended those meetings may recall David Zeaman walking slowly to the podium, pausing longer than usual, then dramatically proclaiming that he had renamed and redirected his planned paper, which was to be on primary and secondary generalization. The new talk—aimed at getting to the heart of the matter—was titled: "Retardation Is More Than Just a Bad Habit."

The authors agree that retardation is more than a bad cognitive habit. In fact, structural deficiencies likely constitute a more basic and fundamental source of cognitive problems for retarded persons than do failures in the development of learning skills and processes. However, while subscribing to this position, the authors must assert with equal vigor: The social side of retardation also breeds many bad cognitive habits.

What is meant by the "habitual" and "nonhabitual" aspects of mental acts requires some clarification. In high functioning, mildly retarded children (the so-called cultural-familial retarded), basic deficits in encoding and decoding processes have consistently been found on tasks such as reaction time (Maisto & Baumeister, 1984), selective attention (Carr, 1984), primary memory (Ellis & Meador, 1985), and retrieval speed (Sperber & McCauley, 1984). The main tenet of the difference or defect position—which is in fact another perspective of the structural position—is that the cognitive development of a retarded person differs from that of a nonretarded person in more ways than mere differences in developmental rates and upper limits. According to the defect position, retarded and nonretarded children, even when equated for level of development, may vary in the cognitive processes they employ because of differences in the operation of essential structures.

Although the structural side of cognition is important, evidence continues to mount suggesting that retardation, at least as it unfolds in our academically oriented society, breeds bad cognitive habits that can lead to negative, self-limiting attributional beliefs about learning potential. In recent research by the authors and their colleagues (Turner, Hale, Wilcox, Borkowski, & Dutka, 1987), it was found that retarded children attribute failure and success to effort less frequently than do nonretarded children. Similarly, parents of retarded children attribute failure and success to effort less than do parents of nonretarded children. Prior research has shown that attributing failure to a lack of effort is positively related to performance on an assembly task

(Zoeller, Mahoney, & Weiner, 1983). These negative beliefs and their relation to performance exemplify "bad cognitive habits."

The process-oriented perspective about cognition finds the developmental theory of Ed Zigler extremely compatible. The developmental position, which applies generally to individuals not suffering from gross organic impairment, holds that retarded and nonretarded people pass through cognitive stages in an identical order, but differ in the rate and upper limit of development. Retarded children are said to traverse the stages more slowly and attain a lower developmental ceiling than nonretarded children. Zigler's position argues that if essential, critical learning opportunities are presented to retarded people, they can and will develop cognitive skills, leading to more efficient learning.

An Integrated Model   Of course, the structural deficit versus the process-developmental positions are not theoretically incompatible. In fact, Doug Detterman (1979) has combined the major constructs reflected in the two positions into a comprehensive model of learning, memory, and cognition. This model, presented in Figure 1, represents an important advance, perhaps signifying the demise of the structure-process controversy. At the left portion of the model are constructs such as selective attention and primary memory that likely represent important sources of structural deficits. They probably account for the major portion of the variance in psychometrically based IQ. At the center and top of the model are process-oriented constructs, such as strategies, executive functioning, and metacognition, that develop across time as children encounter stimulating, challenging learning environments in the home and school.

In many respects, a comprehensive model such as Detterman's can serve as a testable theory, heuristic framework, or, at the very least, cornerstone for a "peace settlement" for those who hold extreme structural or process positions. Simply stated, depending on the task to be learned, the degree of retardation, the type and extent of enriching experiences in the home and school, and the personal-motivational histories of the child and his or her family, either structurally based or process-oriented constructs will prove more useful in explaining cognitive performance. Indeed, with many complex tasks and many mildly retarded children, both types of constructs will be needed for a complete explanation of skilled performance. It is possible that there are two types of mild retardation, with quite different cognitive consequences or correlates: One type is rooted firmly in cultural deprivation, whereas the other is more closely linked to polygenic inheritance. The hypothesis is that process differences characterize the former, whereas structural differences characterize the

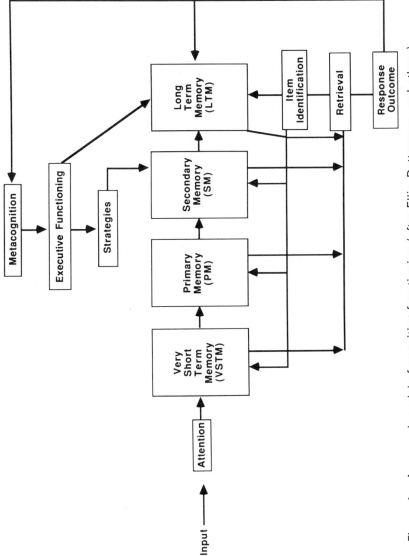

Figure 1. A general model of cognitive functioning (after Ellis, Detterman, and others).

latter. Of course, this hypothesis should be viewed in relative terms with respect to localizing the predominant source of retardation and in assigning major responsibility to underlying mechanisms.

The final epitaph for the structural-process debate about the causes of impaired function might read as follows: Although important insights about cognition in mentally retarded persons have flowed from both the process and structural stances, it now seems clear that neither position can be convincingly demonstrated in isolation. That is, few (if any) important cognitive events can be explained without reliance on a combination of structures and processes that interact bidirectionally over time. Future research will benefit by the adoption of an eclectic stance regarding the fundamental nature of cognition in retarded persons or, perhaps, by abandoning the controversy altogether.

Emphasizing Developmental Patterns

What are the future directions for cognitive research? First of all, it is important to emphasize that retarded individuals almost always have multiple deficiencies that determine cognitive performance—some habitual, some nonhabitual. Researchers are in need of new theoretical perspectives that describe how these deficiencies interact, producing patterns of cognitive performance not predictable from individual factors. What is essential in capturing the nature of these interactions is a greater emphasis on *developmental perspectives*.

The past focus on cognitive deficits and their remediation has sometimes precluded the consideration of development. Researchers have often depended on the theoretical stance that retarded individuals *develop* at a slower rate than nonretarded individuals, yet little *developmental* research has been conducted. In recent cross-sectional studies of cognitive development, improvements in the untrained use of rehearsal strategies have been indicated (Bray, Turner, & Hersh, 1985). However, the factors influencing these changes have yet to be determined. Longitudinal studies are needed to chart the cognitive development of retarded children and the academic and social influences that impact on that development. In addition to the time-honored research question, "What are the relevant processes and structures?," one should ask, "How did these processes arise and how do they change, in combination, across time as the lives of retarded children unfold in a social context?"

The research of Craig Ramey and his colleagues (Ramey, Campbell, & Finkelstein, 1984), using longitudinal designs, has demonstrated the importance of examining intellectual and social abilities that underlie inefficient academic achievement from a developmental perspective. Similarly, cross-sectional research by Earl Butterfield and

John Belmont (1977) on changes in executive functioning during the early and middle school years reveals the power of a developmental perspective on the causes of inefficient cognitive performance.

Motivation and Metacognition

A second change in the cognitive research agenda helps explain the need for a developmental perspective. It is linked to the bad cognitive habits (or processes) that develop because of the fact that retardation occurs in a social context—a context that is often intolerant of failure and generally frightened of human differences. The focus referred to centers on the motivational aspects of cognition. Although Carl Haywood and Ed Zigler have long championed the importance of motivation in explaining performance on cognitive and academic tasks, theories of cognition have all but ignored their pleas. It is clear that the important cognitive acts (such as reading) are bidirectionally linked—in fact, inseparably linked—to motivational states and personal dispositions (such as self-esteem). Furthermore, these interrelationships are all the more important for mentally retarded individuals.

Consider as an illustration the successful emergence of a strategy in a young retarded child. The scenario is drawn from a model of metacognition (see Figure 2) developed several years ago (Pressley, Borkowksi, & O'Sullivan, 1985). The developmental pattern of skilled learning is as follows:

1. The child is taught to use a strategy and, with repetition, comes to learn about the attributes of that strategy (this is called specific strategy knowledge). These attributes include the effectiveness of the strategy, the range of its appropriate applications, and the effort required in using the strategy.
2. Other strategies are learned and repeated (specific strategy knowledge is enlarged and enriched).
3. The child develops the capacity to select strategies appropriate for some tasks (but not others), and to fill in the gaps when essential strategy components have not been adequately taught (metamemory acquisition procedures).
4. The child comes to recognize the general utility of being strategic (general strategy knowledge) and to attribute successful (and unsuccessful) learning outcomes to effort expended in strategy deployment rather than to a lack of ability or intelligence. In this latter sense, the model integrates cognitive acts and their motivational causes and consequences.

The model of metacognition sketched here has implications for both basic and applied research in the linkages it postulates between cognition and motivation. First, it invites analyses of the social context,

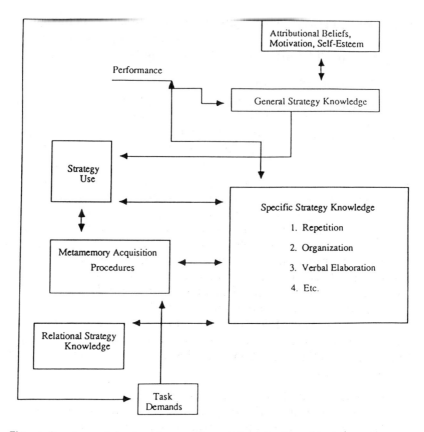

Figure 2. A model of metacognition. (After Borkowski, J.G., Johnston, M.B., & Reid, M.K. [1986]. Metacognition, motivation, and the transfer of control processes. In S.J. Ceci [Ed.], *Handbook of cognitive, social, and neuropsychological aspects of learning disabilities* [pp. 147–174]. Hillsdale, NJ: Lawrence Erlbaum Associates.)

in the home and school, that give rise to the various components of metacognition and how specific human interchange between mother and child, father and child, and teacher and child affects cognition, metacognition, and motivational states. Ann Brown, Joseph Campione, Jeanne Day, Annmarie Palincsar, and others have documented the importance of these social exchanges to their research on reciprocal teaching (see Palincsar, 1986). Their research has demonstrated that reading comprehension and metacognition scores can often be raised 30–40% following repeated training sessions. We have recently found that the teaching of strategies in the home and parents' beliefs about the importance of effort are related to their children's knowledge of strategies and to the acquisition and transfer of new strategies (Kurtz, Borkowski, Carr, Schneider, & Turner, in press).

Thus, general knowledge about the efficacy of learning and memory strategies has motivational properties. High self-esteem, an internal locus of control, and the tendency to attribute success to effort are the consequences of a lengthy history of consistent, relatively successful strategy-governed habits of responding to learning and memory tasks. More specifically, improved learning and academic performance following strategy use strengthens general strategy knowledge, which, in turn, promotes positive self-esteem and attributions of success to effort rather than uncontrollable factors such as luck. Thus, motivational factors play key roles in what sometimes appears as "spontaneous" strategy use by providing incentives necessary for deploying strategies, especially on challenging, difficult tasks.

Based on initial studies about the importance of attributional retraining for cognitive performance, we have derived a set of three principles that should be considered before incorporating attributional statements into strategy training research:

1. Attribution retraining needs to be intensive, prolonged, and consistent in order to combat the debilitating, negative beliefs about self-efficacy. Since these beliefs result from repeated failure experiences that occur over long periods of time, there will be a considerable price to pay—in time and effort—to reshape self-defeating attributions. Thus, not only strategic processes, but also correlated attributional states, form the "habitual" side of cognition in retarded persons.

2. Learning-handicapped students need to become fully aware of the importance of strategy-based effort for successful performance. In order to heighten this awareness, learning tasks should be repeated on numerous occasions, with and without the aid of an appropriate strategy, followed by an explicit comparison of performance under the two conditions. Then an inappropriate strategy might be introduced and the student challenged to explain why it is inappropriate and to identify other tasks for which it would be helpful in improving performance. This series of contrasts sets the stage for increasing the student's awareness about the importance of effort in deploying an appropriate strategy and for enhancing expectations about the control of selected aspects of cognitive and academic performance.

3. Each occasion for strategy instruction is also an opportunity for retraining attributions. Such a perspective enables the instructor to enhance metacognitive and motivational processes simulta-

neously, while concentrating on the implementation of specific strategy instructions.

It is important to note here that this three-pronged approach to strategy training diminishes the existing dichotomy that often separates cognitive functioning and the personality-motivational system. In our view, motivational deficits in mentally retarded people become inevitably linked to poor learning histories, cognitive deficits, and negative attributional states. Both theory and practice will profit from advances in understanding of the complex interplay of attributional beliefs and metacognition, as they determine purposeful, deliberate actions.

CONVERGING RESEARCH TRENDS

The perspectives we have offered are consistent with several trends emerging in the contemporary literature on cognition in mentally retarded persons:

1. The traditional contrast of retarded and nonretarded performance (involving methodologies often fraught with interpretative difficulties) is less frequently used in contemporary research on cognition and should be supplemented with methodologies that examine *development in retarded persons*, per se, with a special focus on the use of longitudinal designs. Given the striking variability in performance among retarded individuals, longitudinal analyses permit a more precise assessment of developmental changes, in both laboratory and naturalistic contexts.
2. Single-subject methodologies need to be borrowed by cognitive psychologists from behavior analysts. As Al Baumeister (1984) has pointed out, these techniques allow for intensive analyses of the emergence of multiple (but related) skills in a few, carefully selected individuals.
3. The study of cognition and retardation will be significantly advanced by research on high-risk infants and high-risk mothers (e.g., teenagers) and the social factors that impede or accelerate the cognitive development of their infants.

These trends lead to the following charge for the next decade of research on cognition in retarded persons: Bidirectional, multisystem perspectives need to be considered in building more comprehensive explanatory frameworks for cognitive development. It seems obvious to state that cognitive acts in retarded individuals need inspiration, often derived from personal beliefs about the sources of control in one's environment (feelings of self-competency); in turn, the outcome of each cognitive act alters beliefs about self-efficacy and self-esteem. Researchers need to understand how these factors influence cognitive processes and, perhaps, cognitive structures.

Despite this intuitively appealing perspective, motivational, social, and cognitive variables have not, to date, been theoretically integrated (within a longitudinal framework) in the analysis of mental functioning. Nor will this be an easy task. The time is ripe, however, for a new approach to theory construction in the area of impaired cognitive functioning because of recent theoretical, methodological, and analytical advances. Researchers need to emphasize the fact that multicomponent theories will be developed and research undertaken, both within and across psychological systems, only when theoreticians become bold enough to include social, familial, and personal constructs—which are so critical to impaired development—in their models of cognition. Only then can the causes and consequences of memory, cognition, and problem-solving in mentally retarded persons be fully understood.

REFERENCES

Baumeister, A.A. (1984). Some methodological and conceptual issues in the study of cognitive processes with retarded people. In P.H. Brooks, R. Sperber, & C. McCauley (Eds.), *Learning and cognition in the mentally retarded* (pp. 1–38). Hillsdale, NJ: Lawrence Erlbaum Associates.

Belmont, J.M., & Butterfield, E.C. (1971). Learning strategies as determinants of memory deficiencies. *Cognitive Psychology, 2,* 411–420.

Belmont, J.M., & Butterfield, E.C. (1977). The instructional approach to developmental cognitive research. In R.V. Kail & J.W. Hagen (Eds.), *Perspectives on the development of memory and cognition.* Hillsdale, NJ: Lawrence Erlbaum Associates.

Borkowski, J.G., Reid, M.B., & Kurtz, B.E. (1984). Metacognition and retardation: Paradigmatic, theoretical, and applied perspectives. In P.N. Brooks, R. Sperber, & C. McCauley (Eds.), *Learning and cognition in the mentally retarded* (pp. 55–76). Hillsdale, NJ: Lawrence Erlbaum Associates.

Bray, N.W., Turner, L.A., & Hersh, R.E. (1985). Developmental progressions and regressions in the selective remembering strategies of educable mentally retarded individuals. *American Journal of Mental Deficiency, 90,* 57–63.

Brown, A.L. (1974). The role of strategic behavior in retardate memory. In N.R. Ellis (Ed.), *International review of research in mental retardation* (Vol. 7, pp. 55–111). New York: Academic Press.

Butterfield, E.C., & Belmont, J.M. (1977). Assessing and improving the executive cognitive functions of mentally retarded people. In I. Bialer & M. Sternlicht (Eds.), *Psychological issues in mental retardation* (pp. 277–318). New York: Psychological Dimensions.

Butterfield, E.C., Wambold, C., & Belmont, J.M. (1973). On the theory and practice of improving short-term memory. *American Journal of Mental Deficiency, 77,* 654–669.

Carr, T.N. (1984). Attention, skill, and intelligence: Some speculations on extreme individual differences in human performance. In P.N. Brooks, R. Sperber, & C. McCauley (Eds.), *Learning and cognition in the mentally retarded* (pp. 189–215). Hillsdale, NJ: Lawrence Erlbaum Associates.

Detterman, D.K. (1979). Memory in the mentally retarded. In N.R. Ellis (Ed.), *Handbook of mental deficiency: Psychological theory and research* (2nd ed., pp. 727–760). Hillsdale, NJ: Lawrence Erlbaum Associates.

Ellis, N.R. (1963). The stimulus trace and behavioral inadequacy. In N.R. Ellis (Ed.), *International review of research in mental retardation* (pp. 134–158). New York: McGraw-Hill.

Ellis, N.R., & Meador, I.M. (1985). Forgetting in retarded and nonretarded persons under conditions of minimal strategy use. *Intelligence, 9,* 87–96.

Flavell, J.H. (1979). Metacognition and cognitive monitoring: A new area of cognitive-developmental inquiry. *American Psychologist, 34,* 906–911.

Gerjouy, I.R., Winters, J.J., Pullen, M.M., & Spitz, H.H. (1969). Subjective organization by retardates and normals during free recall of visual stimuli. *American Journal of Mental Deficiency, 73,* 791–797.

Kurtz, B.E., Borkowksi, J.G., Carr, M., Schneider, W., & Turner, L.A. (in press). Sources of memory and metamemory development: Societal, parental, and educational influences. In M. Gruneberg, P. Morris, & R. Sykes (Eds.), *Practical aspects of memory.* New York: Wiley.

Maisto, A.A., & Baumeister, A.A. (1984). Dissection of component processes in rapid information processing tasks: Comparison of retarded and nonretarded people. In P.H. Brooks, R. Sperber, & C. McCauley (Eds.), *Learning and cognition in the mentally retarded* (pp. 165–188). Hillsdale, NJ: Lawrence Erlbaum Associates.

Palincsar, A.S. (1986). Metacognitive strategy instruction. *Exceptional Children, 53,* 118–124.

Pressley, M., Borkowski, J.G., & O'Sullivan, J.T. (1985). Children's metamemory and the teaching of memory strategies. In D.L. Forrest-Pressley, G.E. MacKinnon, & T.G. Waller (Eds.), *Metacognition, cognition, and human performance* (pp. 111–153). San Diego: Academic Press.

Ramey, C.T., Campbell, F.A., & Finkelstein, N.W. (1984). Course and structure of intellectual development in children at high risk for developmental retardation. In P.N. Brooks, R. Sperber, & C. McCauley (Eds.), *Learning cognition in the mentally retarded* (pp. 419–432). Hillsdale, NJ: Lawrence Erlbaum Associates.

Sperber, R., & McCauley, C. (1984). Semantic processing efficiency in the mentally retarded. In P.N. Brooks, R. Sperber, & C. McCauley (Eds.), *Learning and cognition in the mentally retarded* (pp. 141–164). Hillsdale, NJ: Lawrence Erlbaum Associates.

Spitz, N.N. (1963). Field theory in mental deficiency. In N.R. Ellis (Ed.), *Handbook of mental deficiency: Psychological theory and research* (1st ed.). New York: McGraw-Hill.

Spitz, H.H., & Borys, S.V. (1977). Performance of retarded and nonretarded adolescents on one- and two-bit logical problems. *Journal of Experimental Child Psychology, 23,* 415–429.

Spitz, H.H., & Borys, S.V. (1984). Depth of search: How far can the retarded search through an internally represented problem space? In P.N. Brooks, R. Sperber, & C. McCauley (Eds.), *Learning and cognition in the mentally retarded* (pp. 333–358). Hillsdale, NJ: Lawrence Erlbaum Associates.

Sternberg, R.J., & Davidson, J.E. (1987). *Conceptions of giftedness.* Cambridge, England: Cambridge University Press.

Taylor, A.M., & Turnure, J.E. (1979). Imagery and verbal elaboration with retarded children: Effects on learning and memory. In N.R. Ellis (Ed.), *Handbook of mental deficiency: Psychological theory and research* (2nd ed., pp. 659–697). Hillsdale, NJ: Lawrence Erlbaum Associates.

Turner, L.A., Hale, C., Wilcox, M., Borkowski, J.G., & Dutka, S. (1987, March). *The emergence of strategies in EMR and nonretarded children: Influences from home.* Paper presented at the Conference on Research and Theory on Mental Retardation, Gatlinburg, TN.

Zeaman, D., & House, B.J. (1979). A review of attention theory. In N.R. Ellis (Ed.), *Handbook of mental deficiency: Psychological theory and research* (2nd ed., pp. 63–120). Hillsdale, NJ: Lawrence Erlbaum Associates.

Zoeller, C., Mahoney, G., & Weiner, B. (1983). Effects of attribution training in the assembly task performance of MR adults. *American Journal of Mental Deficiency, 88,* 109–112.

18 | Analysis and Modification of Disruptive Behavior
MICHAEL F. CATALDO

BEHAVIOR ANALYSIS

The significance of the scientific study of learning processes is that it has led to a knowledge base and subsequent technology with immediate application to the unique problems of each individual. That is, regardless of the genetic, biological, and physiological competence of an individual, the processes of learning from the environment are the same *and* are able to be subjected to study using the scientific method, *and* thus are able to be replicated, modified, and maintained. Differences across individuals are therefore the result not only of the degree of individual competence, but also of the degree to which the environment has facilitated learning. For example, research has shown that performance and skill competence both are a function of and may be improved by the differential manner with which the environment responds to these behaviors.

This area of scientific study did not develop by chance but rather by design. The design was to understand behavior by the use of the scientific method in a manner not previously permitted by psychoanalytical approaches. Since science requires attention to observable events that can be quantified, this "new" area focused attention on observable behavior and thus has been characterized, and referred to, as *behavior analysis*, in contrast to psychoanalysis.

Implications for Developmentally Disabled Persons

For developmentally disabled individuals the implications of behavior analysis research have been profound. The most important and consistent finding has been that very significant improvements in learning and performance can be achieved with even the most profoundly retarded individuals. Three decades of scientific research demonstrating that retarded individuals are capable of learning, and the extensions of this finding across a wide range of populations and behaviors, have had a major impact on the provision of service to retarded people on a national level. Legal mandates, fiscal appropriations, and programs for mentally handicapped persons have undergone a dramatic shift in the past three decades.

The numerous demonstrations that these individuals can achieve improved vocational, educational, self-help, social, and communication skills, and often integration into society, have been critical factors in obtaining improvements in educational and community living programs. For example, studies reported in but one of the field's journals, the *Journal of Applied Behavior Analysis* (Bailey, Shook, Iwata, Reid, & Repp, 1986), demonstrate methods for training:

Independent toileting	Clothing selection	Mealtime behaviors
Pedestrian skills	Oral hygiene	Eating in public
Menstrual care	Job interview skills	Social skills
Janitorial skills	Sign language	Job independence
Object identification	Leisure behavior	

Most important has been the fact that these programmatic advances have ultimately resulted in changes in public attitudes about developmentally disabled persons.

Thus, behavioral research has provided important implications both about the ontogeny of developmental disability as it relates to the environment and about the intervention strategies that may be employed to otherwise alter these disabilities. In this sense, the behavioral status of retarded individuals is in part the direct result of how the environment responds to their behavior. Treatment research in behavior analysis emphasizes only those environmental events that can be manipulated and can serve as antecedents or consequences for behavior, because such manipulations are often the only means for modifying performance deficits and excesses of developmentally disabled persons. This approach is to be contrasted with research that identifies other causal independent variables for developmental delay that cannot presently be altered, such as genetic anomalies, pre- and postnatal trauma, and permanent neurological pathology.

Behavior analysis has continued to address the problems of retarded persons not by chance but by design. The results have been scientific productivity and extremely successful programs.

Disruptive Behavior

The problem of disruptive behavior has become an important priority for behavioral research, primarily because of the restrictive consequences for retarded persons when such behavior occurs in its most severe forms. Many among the mentally retarded/developmentally disabled population, and especially severely and profoundly retarded persons, exhibit a high degree of noncompliance, aggression, and sometimes severe self-injury. In addition to the harmful physical effects, such behavior often prevents individuals from participation in the habilitative programs that have been so long in development.

One of the most problematic types of disruptive behavior is self-injury. Especially when severe, self-injury is particularly restrictive in its consequences, and in many ways is baffling; it is the subject of major investigative efforts. In retarded persons, self-injurious behavior (SIB) is that behavior that produces physical injury to the individual's own body. Self-injurious behavior here does not imply an attempt to "destroy," nor does it suggest "aggression" or imply suicidal behavior (see Tate & Baroff, 1966). The most frequently observed behaviors are biting, eye gouging, head banging, hitting, ruminative vomiting, and scratching. The severity of this problem is manifest along a number of dimensions, including intensity, frequency, duration, and time to onset of each episode.

Treatment approaches to date include the use of drugs, mechanical and surgical procedures, and behavioral treatment. Drug treatment approaches are not well documented in the research literature and, where reported, results are equivocal across studies. The use of stimulants and depressants demonstrates a general suppression of behavior, but is not specific to SIB. Thus, the result is one that reduces both disruptive and appropriate, desirable behavior. Mechanical procedures, such as restraint and protective equipment, and surgical interventions, such as the removal of teeth in the case of the severe self-biting of Lesch-Nyhan patients, can be effective but have the obvious side effects of restriction of both desired and undesired behavior and occasional loss of function. Behavioral treatment is presently supported by the best data base and can be sufficiently targeted on discrete behaviors so that disruptive behavior is reduced and desired behavior strengthened (Favell et al., 1982).

The behavioral research over the past three decades indicates that SIB is readily altered by its consequences. This reliable finding has suggested that several aspects of self-injury in retarded persons are developed and maintained as learned behaviors. It is from this finding that current treatment approaches proceed.

Under the leadership of Hugo Moser, a Center for the Study and Treatment of Self Injury in the Retarded has been developed at the Kennedy Institute (Iwata, Pace, Cataldo, Kalsher, & Edwards, 1984). For the past 4 years, behavioral research at the Center, supported by the National Institute of Child Health and Human Development (NICHD) and carried out by Brian Iwata, Gary Pace, the author, and a number of others, has focused on the possible adaptive functions SIB could have for an individual. That is, SIB may provide one or more sources of reinforcement, both positive and negative. The consequences of self-injury could, in this analysis, lead to social attention or self-stimulation, an important event for a retarded person in an unstimulating residential environment, or for an individual who has very limited communication. Another consequence could be to escape or avoid unpleasant or undesired activities, a motivation shared by us all but exercised with a much different behavioral repertoire. Finally, the behavior could occur to attenuate pain or discomfort, as has been shown in animal studies with surgically induced paresthesia (see Cataldo & Harris, 1982).

The analysis and treatment strategies from this approach have been described in a number of papers. In general, the analysis is based upon data obtained during a repeated series of conditions that isolate each possible functional explanation for the SIB (Iwata, Dorsey, Slifer, Bauman, & Richman, 1982; Iwata et al., 1984). Patients demonstrating significant SIB in any particular condition can then be differentially treated with procedures based on the presumed function. For example, some patients show high SIB in conditions that result in social attention, and sometimes also when they are alone, both indicating that the behavior may be motivated by social reinforcement. For other individuals SIB is high only when they are alone, suggesting the behavior is self-stimulatory. A third circumstance is high incidence of self-injury when requests are made to engage in self-care, classroom, and other daily tasks, suggesting an escape or avoidance function. Finally, patients who exhibit high levels of SIB in more than one condition can be considered to have learned SIB repertoires that serve multiple functions or, alternatively, to be responding for entirely different and unknown reasons. Treatment results to date show that most patients' SIB can be rapidly reduced with behavioral treatment procedures based on such a functional analysis approach (Iwata, Pace, Willis, Gamache, & Hyman, 1986; Pace, Iwata, Edwards, & McCosh, 1986; Parrish, Iwata, Dorsey, Bunck, & Slifer, 1985; Slifer, Iwata, & Dorsey, 1984).

The functional relationship between behavior and environmental consequences also allows for the study of how behaviors come to be related as groups, which are called response classes. The notion here is that groups of behaviors can become related to each other by their learning history (Baer, 1982). The treatment implications are exemplified by one child's data from a clinical analogue study (Russo, Cataldo, & Cushing, 1981). As shown in Figure 1, in the condition labeled baseline, the child's behavior initially was characterized by a low amount of compliance to adult requests, and a considerable amount of aggression, crying, and SIB. With the initiation of a behavioral treatment program (labeled Reinf Comp), the situation rapidly changed: com-

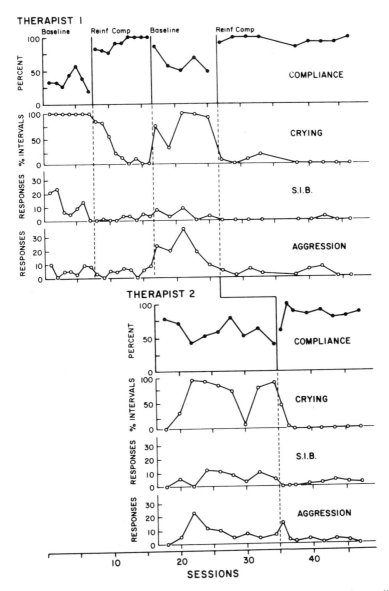

Figure 1. Percentage of compliance and the three untreated corollary behaviors—crying, self-injurious behavior, and aggression—for one patient across experimental conditions and therapists.

pliance increased, and the problem behaviors decreased to zero or near zero. This treatment approach, however, had only procedures to train compliance to the adult's requests, not to reduce the problem behaviors. Nevertheless, all behaviors improved. The improvement was the result of the behavioral intervention as demonstrated by the reversal in the behaviors when the condition was withdrawn and then reinstituted (Therapist 1), and was replicated across therapists.

The results from this child, and *all* others studied in this manner, show that the modification of a target behavior such as compliance affects other problem behaviors, including self-injury, in an inverse manner (Cataldo, Ward, Russo, Riordan, & Bennett, 1986; Neef, Shafer, Egel, Cataldo, & Parrish, 1983; Parrish, Cataldo, Kolko, Neef, & Egel, 1986). This approach to the problem of disruptive behavior, replicated across a series of studies with various populations and problems, may offer a particularly effective and economical approach to intervention in that it can change a number of behaviors by focusing on but one; and when a positive procedure can be employed to increase an important behavior such as following instructions, the ethical and abuse liabilities of punishment paradigms can be avoided.

Biobehavioral Research

The most fascinating aspect of SIB is that it exists at all. Although aspects of its frequency, intensity, and certainly maintenance are very likely the result of learning processes, the self-injury prevalence in severely retarded persons and the injury patterns in classified disorders, such as Lesch-Nyhan syndrome, strongly implicate biological causes as well.

Two current theories implicate dopamine and endogenous opiates (Cataldo & Harris, 1982). The latter is a fascinating consideration, and one truly representative of a biobehavioral interaction. A pain insensitivity would allow the aversive aspect of SIB to be attenuated, thus permitting the functional aspects of the behavior in controlling the environment to be maximized. Also, self-injurious individuals could be engaging in a form of self-administration of endogenous opiates once the correct intensity and frequencies were achieved, with the secondary gain of environmental control. Although a few preliminary intervention studies have been reported and tend to support the opiate theory, study design has been poor and mechanisms were not explored. Technologies for studying brain structure and function can be critical here. The future of research on self-injury will now quite rapidly be characterized by studies employing multiple types of data, and data from a number of scientific disciplines.

The Center at the Kennedy Institute has afforded the opportunity to conduct studies on these possible biobehavioral interactions. The Center's medical director, Susan Hyman, has, for example, initiated studies of endogenous opiates in the cerebrospinal fluid of SIB patients. The Johns Hopkins Hospital's positron emission tomography (PET) scanner affords another opportunity for research. The techniques of opiate scans have been reported by Henry Wagner and others (Wong, Gjedde, & Wagner, 1986; Wong, Gjedde, Wagner, Dannals, et al., 1986a). Furthermore, most recently two PET scans have been completed for assessment of dopamine receptor density in a child with severe SIB secondary to Lesch-Nyhan syndrome (Wong, Gjedde, Wagner, Dannals, et al., 1986a, 1986b).

The emphasis and approaches in the study of SIB are not by chance but by design. The problem is an important priority and the research has generality to other areas of behavioral and biological science.

THE FUTURE?

The more important speculation regarding the future may concern a larger view than the specific area of behavior analysis, although behavior analysis is a relevant set of glasses through which to view the future. In the past, progress has been facilitated by national commitment to retarded persons and impeded by lack of knowledge and lack of cooperation across disciplines and programs. However, the progress of the last three decades has largely eliminated the impediments of the past. How has this occurred and what are our opportunities and barriers for the future?

The development of the scientific study of retardation and developmental disability is not a static process. Like individual development, it too can be understood by the processes that have contributed to its success in competing with and adapting to other areas in science. The behavior of scientists, and thus science, is influenced by the same variables we have just discussed. Scientists attend to the history of findings because these show where successful versus unsuccessful work has occurred. Furthermore, scientists are responsive to the contingencies and priorities of society. Scientists study phenomena of considerable generality; how and with what subject populations such studies occur can sometimes be influenced without compromising and often benefiting both science and those studied.

The functional link between society's priorities and research is arranged not by chance but by design. The rapid series of advances

In behavioral science in general and behavioral research on retardation in particular was influenced by the support of NICHD during a period of unprecedented grant funding on this topic in the 1960s and 1970s. Certainly, behavioral scientists would have investigated the phenomena their findings led them toward, but to do so with retarded populations was not by chance but by the design of the NICHD.

Another example is the activities of Robert Cooke and President Kennedy in creating the University Affiliated Facility (UAF) legislation that provided funds for buildings, support staff, and faculty specifically for the purpose of studying the problems of retarded persons and *training* other professionals about this area. The benefits have been many. For example, the self-injury center is at the Kennedy Institute, the first UAF. Thousands of professionals have received specialized training and many of these have gone on to careers in child development and retardation, including the Director of the NICHD. Certainly, universities would have garnered support for buildings and staff and faculty, but to do so for the specific purpose of the problems of retarded individuals was not by chance but by design.

But what of the future? The best predictor of the future is the past. So, scientists will continue to study that which is dictated by their findings. Behavioral scientists will continue to employ scientific method to verify and extend behavioral analytical techniques. Increasingly, complex human behavior will be studied, understood, and developed into therapies, which will then be studied as to their functional, necessary components, then cost-analyzed and compared to the previously investigated, now traditional therapeutic approaches in an attempt to document and change practice patterns. Behavioral scientists will continue to study interesting leads such as response classes, and in so doing will better understand the relationships between behaviors and develop more effective and economical interventions. Ethical problems of treatment will be considered, debated, and resolved. Similar activities will proceed in the areas of the biological sciences, only focusing on different variables.

Those of us interested in biobehavioral relationships will do double duty, attempting to work in both science bases and, harder yet, attempting to work with each other. We will develop even more elegant methods for quantifying behavior and comparing these data to anatomical data from magnetic resonance imaging, drug level data from bioassays, and drug action data from PET scans. All of this will be done not by chance but by design. But which design? Research priorities in the future, as in the past, will continue to be influenced by the problems in society. These problems include the changing nature of the nation's health problems that compete for health care dollars.

The nation's primary health problems are related to substance abuse, injury, cardiovascular disease, and cancer, not retardation. The post–World War II baby boom will create a demand for health care and then programs for the elderly as we enter and move through the 21st century. By the second and third decades of the 21st century 25% of the population will be over 65 years of age and 20% will be under 18 years of age. For the first time in our history we will be faced with close to half of our population attempting to support the other half. Nor will we be likely to buy our way out of the problems of the future. The cumulative federal deficit is now over $1.5 trillion, an amount almost incomprehensible. So great is this deficit that if we stopped overspending today and began paying back the debt at the rate of $1 million per day, the debt would not be paid until the year 6096.

Faced with such an array of competing priorities how will research on retardation adapt? Without a very specific effort to continue an emphasis on retardation, one can envision that we may have experienced the Golden Age of research on retardation in the 1950s through the 1970s. Thus, the potential areas for the future of research are exciting and many. Nonetheless, in the face of present and predicted priorities for our scientific interests, what would be the consequences without the processes that have influenced retardation research as exemplified by the history of NICHD? Such research on retardation would continue, but by chance.

REFERENCES

Baer, D.M. (1982). The imposition of structure on behavior and the demolition of behavioral structures. In D.J. Bernstein (Ed.), *Response structure and organization* (1981 Nebraska Symposium on Motivation, pp. 217–254). Lincoln: University of Nebraska Press.

Bailey, J.S., Shook, G.L., Iwata, B.A., Reid, D.H., & Repp, A.C. (1986). Behavior analysis in developmental disabilities 1968–1985. *Journal of Applied Behavior Reprint Series* [Monograph], *1*.

Cataldo, M.F., & Harris, J. (1982). The biological basis for self-injury in the mentally retarded. *Analysis and Intervention in Developmental Disabilities, 2,* 21–39.

Cataldo, M.F., Ward, E.M., Russo, D.C., Riordan, M.M., & Bennett, D. (1986). Compliance and correlated problem behavior in children: Effects of contingent and noncontingent reinforcement. *Analysis and Intervention in Developmental Disabilities, 6,* 265–282.

Favell, J.E., Azrin, N.H., Baumeister, A.A., Carr, E.G., Dorsey, M.F., Forehand, R., Foxx, R.M., Lovaas, O.I., Rincover, A., Risley, T.R., Romanczyk,

R.G., Russo, D.C., Schroeder, S.R., & Solnick, J.F. (1982). Treatment of self-injurious behavior. *Behavior Therapy, 13,* 529–554.

Iwata, B.A., Dorsey, M.F., Slifer, K.J., Bauman, K.E., & Richman, G.S. (1982). Toward a functional analysis of self-injury. *Analysis and Intervention in Developmental Disabilities, 2,* 3–20.

Iwata, B.A., Pace, G.M., Cataldo, M.F., Kalsher, M.J., & Edwards, G.L. (1984). A center for the study and treatment of self-injury. In J.C. Griffin (Ed.), *Proceedings of the Laity Symposium on self-injurious behavior* (pp. 27–39). Richmond, TX: Texas Department of Mental Health and Mental Retardation.

Iwata, B.A., Pace, G.M., Willis, K.D., Gamache, T.B., & Hyman, S.L. (1986). Operant studies of self-injurious handbiting in the Rett syndrome. *American Journal of Medical Genetics, 24,* 157–166.

Neef, N.A., Shafer, M.S., Egel, A.L., Cataldo, M.F., & Parrish, J.M. (1983). The class specific effects of compliance training with "do" and "don't" requests. *Journal of Applied Behavior Analysis, 16,* 81–99.

Pace, G.M., Iwata, B.A., Edwards, G.L., & McCosh, K.C. (1986). Stimulus fading and transfer in the treatment of self-restraint and self-injurious behavior. *Journal of Applied Behavior Analysis, 19,* 381–389.

Parrish, J.M., Cataldo, M.F., Kolko, D.J., Neef, N.A., & Egel, A.L. (1986). Experimental analysis of response covariation among compliant and inappropriate behaviors. *Journal of Applied Behavior Analysis, 19,* 241–254.

Parrish, J.M., Iwata, B.A., Dorsey, M.F., Bunck, T.J., & Slifer, K.J. (1985). Behavior analysis, program development, and transfer of control in the treatment of self-injury. *Journal of Behavior Therapy and Experimental Psychiatry, 16,* 159–168.

Russo, D.C., Cataldo, M.F., & Cushing, P.J. (1981). Compliance training and behavioral covariation in the treatment of multiple behavior problems. *Journal of Applied Behavior Analysis, 14,* 209–222.

Slifer, K.J., Iwata, B.A., & Dorsey, M.F. (1984). Reduction of eye gouging using a response interruption procedure. *Journal of Behavior Therapy and Experimental Psychiatry, 15,* 369–375.

Tate, B.G., & Baroff, G.S. (1966). Aversive control of self-injurious behavior in a psychotic boy. *Behavior Research and Therapy, 1,* 281–287.

Wong, D.F., Gjedde, A., & Wagner, H.N., Jr. (1986). Quantification of neuroreceptors in the living human brain: I. Irreversible binding of ligands. *Journal of Cerebral Blood Flow and Metabolism, 6,* 137–146.

Wong, D.F., Gjedde, A., Wagner, H.N., Jr. Dannals, R.F., Douglass, K.H., Links, J.M., & Kuhar, M.J. (1986a). Quantification of neuroreceptors in the living human brain: II. Inhibition studies of receptor density and affinity. *Journal of Cerebral Blood Flow and Metabolism, 6,* 147–153.

Wong, D.F., Gjedde, A., Wagner, H.N., Jr., Dannals, R.F., Douglass, K.H., Links, J.M., & Kuhar, M.J. (1986b). Assessment of D1 and D2 dopamine receptors in Lesch-Nyhan syndrome by positron tomography. *Journal of Nuclear Medicine, 27,* 1027 (abstract).

19 | Early Intervention

Why, for Whom, How, at What Cost?

CRAIG T. RAMEY, DONNA M. BRYANT, and TANYA M. SUAREZ

When the concept of intervention is applied to human development the goal is usually to enhance functioning or to prevent some unwanted condition. During the past 20 years the United States has committed itself to an early intervention position regarding young children who are socioeconomically, educationally, or physically disadvantaged. Federal legislation such as the Economic Opportunity Act of 1964, which contained Head Start, and the Education for All Handicapped Children Act of 1975, which included the Handicapped Children's Early Education Program, made provisions for a variety of developmentally supportive services with early education construed as the core of the effort. A great deal of scientific knowledge and practical experience has been accumulated since these legislative commitments to high-risk children. The purpose of this paper is to summarize the knowledge base concerning early educational intervention and to recommend future actions concerning public policy and associated research.

WHY INTERVENE EARLY?

The idea that an individual's early experience is of consequence for later development is an old one, yet the importance of early experience has been advanced only intermittently in the history of Western thought. Concepts other than early experience have more frequently been regarded as central to the process of development.

In the 19th century, *predeterminism* was advanced by Galton and other proponents of the *primacy of heredity* in development. Predeterminism, unlike the earlier notion of preformationism, acknowledged maturational changes in structure as well as size, but held that these

277

changes were relatively encapsulated and consequently unaffected by early experience (Gottlieb, 1971).

In the 1950s the early experience paradigm became the chief competitor of the predeterministic view of development. Evidence from three major streams of investigation flowed together to establish the premise of the primacy of early experience. First, Freud's (e.g., 1910) theory of psychosexual development focused attention on childhood experiences and contributed significantly to the popular acceptance of the idea that early experience is a major determinant of adult behavior. Second, ethological concepts and especially the phenomenon of imprinting (Lorenz, 1937), were interpreted as representing a unique predisposition for learning, present for only a brief *critical period*. The third scientific stream flowed from the early experience research of Hebb (1949). He provided a neuropsychological theory for the existence of critical periods in intellectual as well as social development with this emphasis on neuropsychological phase sequences and cell assemblies as a function of experience. Subsequent investigations with animals revealed that variations in early experiences affected both the *organization* and the *biological bases* of behavior (Kretch, Rosenweig, & Bennett, 1960; Thompson & Heron, 1954.

As the early experience paradigm flowered, its roots branched from the Freudian idea that early experience is important for later social and sexual behavior to the belief that it is also critical for human intellectual competencies. The conceptualization of the impact of early experience was broadened and deepened. Initially, early experience was seen to *predispose* an individual toward a certain personality structure and a consequent propensity to respond to situations in predictable ways. Later, the extension of the concept of critical periods to humans from phylogenetically lower animals conceptualized early experience as imparting *stable and irreversible neurological consequences* that could set a ceiling for later problem-solving behavior (e.g., Harlow, 1958). Although the empirical support for this notion was scant and limited to investigations with laboratory animals, this interpretation of the effects of early experience formed the theoretical basis for much of the work done in the area of human intellectual development in the past two decades.

The implications of critical period research were assimilated in the influential *educational* theories of J. McVicker Hunt (1961) and Benjamin Bloom (1964). Hunt's concept of the "match" put forth in *Intelligence and Experience* was an application of Piaget's dialectical stage model of intellectual development, and assigned a greater role to the characteristics of the environment than to the hereditary makeup of the individual. Developmental advances were seen as the result of a child's successful interaction with increasingly complex stimuli. Hence, adequate intellectual development depended upon the child's receiving specific stimulation at appropriate points in development. Although Hunt's general thesis did not postulate critical periods in development, it implied that early experiences were particularly important.

In *Stability and Change in Human Characteristics*, Bloom (1964) made two major points that provided a critical period focal point for *preschool* intervention. First, he argued that intellectual growth occurred most rapidly in the first 3 years of life and tapered off by the time the child entered grade school. Second, Bloom specifically argued that the first 5 years of life were a critical period for intellectual development. Intellectual development was, in his opinion, characterized by plasticity only during the early years of life. Consequently, the first few years provided the major and perhaps *only* opportunity for facilitating intellectual development by enriching the child's environment.

The early experience paradigm purported to identify the causes of retarded development and to specify the means by which it could be eradicated. According to the early experience paradigm, intellectual deficiencies arose from the inadequacies of the high-risk child's environment. These deficiencies, it was postulated, could be eradicated by providing the high-risk child with compensatory education during the preschool years, the paradigm-specified critical period for intellectual development.

Operating within the early experience paradigm, a body of literature documenting widely held beliefs and substantiating generally accepted theories was compiled through the 1960s. Yet, in spite of the selective attention and self-perpetuating characteristic of scientific paradigms (Kuhn, 1962), an anomaly appeared and persisted: Compensatory education was judged not to have kept its central promise. A nationwide evaluation of Project Head Start concluded that no *permanent benefits* with regard to intelligence could be found. The initial positive effects of Head Start attendance, moreover, were judged to be moderate in magnitude (Cicirelli, 1969). A similar pattern of results was discerned from an influential secondary analysis of the results of other early intervention programs reported by Bronfenbrenner (1974).

The resulting attack on compensatory education indirectly became a battle concerning the early experience paradigm. Jensen (1969) argued that compensatory education "has been tried but it apparently has failed." He moreover attributed depressed intellectual development in socially disadvantaged and black children to genetic inferiority rather than to environmental insufficiencies—a retreat to a predeterministic point of view. In Jensen's view, if the early environment could no longer be considered the prime determinant of intellectual development, then the genetic makeup of the individual must be the critical factor and early educational intervention was therefore doomed to ineffectiveness.

Only a rigid adherence to the early experience paradigm, however, necessitates the conclusion that early experience is *unimportant* for later performance. More recently, development has been conceptualized as a continuous process, a cumulative series of transactions between individuals and their environments (e.g., Ramey, Trohanis, & Hostler, 1982). This cumulative and transactional nature of development, rather than a critical period perspective, still renders the early years of human life highly significant for later development for two main reasons. First, the natural ecologies of home environments tend to remain stable over time in the absence of systematic intervention (Gottfried, 1984). Thus, poor environments will tend to remain poor. Second, capitalizing on potential plasticity in later development may be practically lessened by society's tendency to associate particular experiences, such as schooling, with specific and limited age spans. Thus, in reality there is a lowering of the probability that certain developmental tasks *will* be accomplished after a specific time period even if it is theoretically possible.

Several recent experimental findings buttress the case for a cumulative transactional model of development. First, individual differences in home environments are characterized by stability during the preschool years in disadvantaged homes (Yeates, MacPhee, Campbell, & Ramey, 1983), in advantaged homes (Gottfried & Gottfried, 1984), and in socioeconomically mixed samples (Elardo, Bradley, & Campbell, 1985). Thus, stable individual differences in quality of home environments are not merely artifacts of a family's socioeconomic status.

Second, in natural home ecologies (i.e., those uninfluenced by systematic interventions) individual differences in quality of home environments are additive over the preschool years in accounting for increasing percentages of variation in IQ scores until age 4, whereas maternal IQ accounts for a relatively constant percentage of variation in IQ scores (Ramey, Yeates, & Short, 1984). Thus, environments appear to be cumulative in their influence on intellectual development.

Third, experimental evidence, as well as natural history research, indicates that children's characteristics contribute to the creation of the home environments that they occupy (Breitmayer, & Ramey, & Goldman, 1984; Zeskind & Ramey, 1978, 1981), thus supporting Sameroff and Chandler's (1975) hypothesis that the child's biological and behavioral characteristics and the quality of the home environment interact to codetermine developmental outcomes.

EARLY INTERVENTION: FOR WHOM?

If *early* intervention is theoretically justified for high-risk children, the next major issue is determining who is at high risk for developmental retardation. Unfortunately, estimates of the incidence and prevalence of mental retardation and associated developmental disabilities during the first 3 years of life are, at present, imprecise. There is an urgent need for high-quality epidemiological studies. At present, estimates of mental retardation and cognitively involved developmental disabilities range from about 0.5% to about 3% of the population under 3 years of age (Hayden & Beck, 1982). Whatever the exact figure of occurrence is, however, there are at least three types of young children likely to need access to special early intervention: 1) children at risk for developmental retardation because of medical conditions such as genetic damage or low birth weight, 2) children at high risk for developmental retardation because of poor home environments, and 3) children at risk because of parental neglect or abuse.

It has been hypothesized for some time that children with biological damage detectable at birth, whether from genetic causes or from environmental teratogens such as lead or other toxins, have a spectrum of developmental outcomes that can be influenced by the quality of the environment to which those children are exposed (Sameroff & Chandler, 1975). Thus, biological damage is a risk factor with respect to developmental outcomes. It does not necessarily express itself as clinical pathology, however, unless the damage is of such a severe nature as to seriously impair the young child or if the slight impairment is exposed to an environment that does not compensate for that damage through various self-righting mechanisms.

It is also known that children who are biologically healthy at birth, if exposed to inadequate or inappropriate stimulation, will begin to evidence developmental delays during the preschool years (Ramey, MacPhee, & Yeates, 1982). This delay is found almost exclusively among economically and educationally disadvantaged families. It is also more frequently found among blacks than whites (Finkelstein & Ramey, 1980). Thus, clearly there is inequality in the incidence and prevalence of retarded development. Information has been gathered that will help in the selection of children in most need of early intervention (Ramey & MacPhee, 1985), but young children at risk must continue to be monitored and further research must be conducted in order to better identify the children who would benefit from early educational intervention.

HOW TO INTERVENE

One of the best kept secrets in psychology and education is that early intervention works! Recent reviews of the early intervention literature have revealed at least 19 studies that the authors describe as employing random assignment to educationally treated or control groups (Bryant & Ramey, 1985; Ramey, Bryant, Sparling, & Wasik, 1982; Ramey, Bryant, & Suarez, in press). These reviews have included some of the experimental studies that were part of the Consortium on Longitudinal Studies (Lazar, Darlington, Murray, Royce, & Snipper, 1982), which are the first-generation intervention projects that were begun in the late 1950s and early 1960s, as well as second-generation projects such as the Milwaukee Project (Garber & Heber, 1981), the Carolina Abecedarian Project (Ramey & Campbell, 1979), and the Consortium known as the Parent-Child Development Centers (Andrews et al., 1982). The reviews also included a third-generation project known as the Carolina Approach to Responsive Education or Project CARE (Ramey, Bryant, Sparling, & Wasik, 1984).

In aggregate these diverse projects have presented evidence for the following conclusions:

1. Early intervention can reduce grade retention and special class placement during public school, but it has not resulted in *permanent changes* in IQ. However, significant elevations exist, typically for several years after early intervention is terminated (Darlington, Royce, Snipper, Murray, & Lazar, 1980).
2. More educationally intense programs produce larger and longer lasting developmental changes than less intense programs (Ramey & Bryant, 1982).
3. Structured intervention programs lead to better cognitive outcomes than unstructured programs (Karnes & Teska, 1975).

These conclusions provide clues about how to intervene with the child and family. The developing child and the child's family are elements of a larger developmental system including the household, neighborhood, and society. The experiences that the child has in the presence of adult caregivers provide him with what Feuerstein (1977) has called mediated learning experiences, which form the young child's *primary knowledge acquisition device*. The interchanges that young children have with adults, with all of the variations in quality and sensitivity that we know to exist in those interactions, become, functionally, the child's culture and class. Therefore, in accordance with this principle, early childhood educators concerned with enhancing the development of high-risk children or with preventing retarded development among mildly damaged or environmentally high-risk children have focused on the child, the parent, or the parent-child relationship as the target for developmental change. Researchers and educators have tended to do this either within children's own homes or within educational or developmental centers. In addition to these forms of intervention, programs have varied considerably in the extent to which they explicitly treated the family as a system embedded within a larger network.

Four major approaches can be distinguished on a continuum of educational practice. The first approach could be called a *critical event* or *critical attribute approach*. Programs following this approach focus either upon providing services for young children during a specific critical period or upon encouraging the development of an alleged critical attribute that will, if successfully encouraged, influence positively other attributes, ultimately resulting in the child's normal development.

A second type of approach is what can be called the *enrichment technique*. The basic idea behind such an approach is that some children, particularly those from very poor families, are exposed to fewer developmentally enhancing experiences than are more advantaged children. Therefore, using this approach, the basic task of the early childhood educator is to ensure a richer exposure of experiences to children in much the same way that a nutritionist might advocate taking more vitamins and minerals as a way to ensure nutritionally based health.

A third approach can be labeled *compensatory education*. Compensatory education is designed to reach the same goals that regular education strives to attain but does it by capitalizing on alternate pathways. For example, for biologically handicapped children, such as a child with a severe speech impairment, language might be taught using a communication board or some other prosthetic device. Unlike the enrichment approach, the task of the early educator is not to provide more of what is allegedly missing, but to seek out alternative pathways to ensure adequate development.

The fourth major approach that can be distinguished is what the authors call a *systems integrative approach*. This approach specifically recognizes that the child is the product of multiple forces—genetic, psychological, sociological, and economic. The child's development is affected by the stresses and strains that operate at various levels within a dynamic and developing system. The task of those who seek to ensure normal development using this approach is to analyze those diverse forces and to create interventions timed and placed so as to have multiple and synergistic effects on the child and his or her environment.

INTERVENTION—AT WHAT COST?

Effective early interventions are expensive. There is no quick cure for delayed development. Early intervention is a field that has existed only for the past 20 years. The pioneers in this field are, largely, self-taught. There is a need both to celebrate the accomplishments that have been made so far and to find systematic avenues to recruit sophisticated new professionals. It should not be assumed that the knowledge is at hand to educate effective psychologists, teachers, social workers, or pediatricians. The discipline is also badly in need of technical assistance activities that will provide in-service training to existing early interventionists. At the same time, colleges of education, psychology, social work, and medicine need to produce the next generation of individuals who will be able to see more clearly what needs to be done in research and clinical service and to act in an even more comprehensive and coordinated fashion.

Although efforts are underway to develop cost-effective models of early intervention, there is a major cost-saving step that can be taken now to reduce the overall costs of early intervention. That step is to make better use of early intervention sites as multipurpose family centers in which to integrate the delivery of health, education, and social services to families. Through the better coordination of such efforts and the elimination of redundancy in administration, a greater percentage of the total early intervention dollar can go directly for services to children and families.

SUMMARY AND IMPLICATIONS FOR PUBLIC POLICIES

Based on the authors' understanding of the early intervention literature and their experiences conducting two longitudinal programs, five guidelines concerning the operation of early intervention programs are recommended:

First, practitioners should assume that detrimental conditions will not change spontaneously and therefore high-risk children should be placed in systematic educational programs as soon as that risk status can be verified.

Second, special emphasis should be placed on risk indicators in the child's natural ecology rather than solely on the child's own cognitive or social performance.

Third, high-risk children should remain in systematic educational programs at least until there is evidence that there has been a positive change in risk indicators.

Fourth, educators should try to involve parents meaningfully in the child's educational program.

Fifth, systematic variations in educational curricula, format, and timing should be tried with the aim of increasing both program effectiveness and client satisfaction.

Whichever intervention approach is adopted by a particular program or agency, there are at least four major criteria that we suggest by which the success of the programs should be evaluated.

First, are they *enjoyable?* The concern here is whether programs are enjoyable to the children and the family members who participate in them as well as to the professional staff who help to conduct them. Well-intentioned but grim programs will not attract and hold those who are most needy.

Second, are the programs *flexible?* That is, do they allow the needs of the individual families to be taken into account in the design of a particular set of services? Rigid and joyless programs are not likely to be effective.

Third, are the programs *comprehensive?* This criterion concerns issues such as whether an adequate range of disciplines is represented in the planning and conducting of an intervention program. If an agency seeks to serve a diverse clientele with a mixture of biological and environmental handicaps, then clearly the knowledge base from nutritionists, health professionals, social workers, psychologists, occupational therapists, and physical therapists, to mention just a few, must be taken into accounts.

Fourth, are the programs *effective* in positively modifying the growth and development of the child and his or her family? Well-intentioned but ineffective programs do not deserve the public's support. Scientists must be available to help inform debates about public policy alternatives. It must also be realized that the formulations of public policy and of good science almost always proceed by fundamentally different rules. Therefore, every opportunity must be taken both to understand the policy concerns and constraints of elected officials and to inform them of what science can and cannot legitimately do. There is, however, no inherent contradiction between excellent science and excellent participation in the policy arena.

REFERENCES

Andrews, S.R., Blumental, J.B., Johnson, D.L., Kahn, A.J., Ferguson, C.J., Lasater, T.M., Malone, P.E., & Wallace, D.B. (1982). The skills of mothering: A study of Parent Child Development Centers. *Monographs of the Society for Research in Child Development, 47*(6, Serial No. 198).

Bloom, B. (1964). *Stability and change in human characteristics.* New York: John Wiley & Sons.

Breitmayer, B., Ramey, C.T., & Goldman, B. (1984). Learning and cognition during infancy. In M. Hansen (Ed.), *Atypical infant development* (pp. 237—279). Baltimore: University Park Press.

Bronfenbrenner, U. (1975). Is early intervention effective? In M. Guttentag & E.L. Struening (Eds.), *Handbook of evaluation research* (Vol. 2, pp. 279—303). Beverly Hills, CA: Sage Publications.

Bryant, D.M., & Ramey, C.T. (1985). Prevention-oriented infant education programs. *Journal of Children in Contemporary Society, 7*(1), 17–35.

Cicirelli, V. (June, 1969). *The impact of Head Start: An evaluation of the effects of Head Start on children's cognitive and affective development.* Athens, OH: Westinghouse Learning Corporation.

Clarke, A.M., & Clarke, A.D.B. (1976). *Early experience: Myth and evidence.* New York: Free Press.

Darlington, R.B., Royce, J.M., Snipper, A.S., Murray, H.W., & Lazar, I. (1980). Preschool programs and later school competence of children from low-income families. *Science, 208,* 202–204.

Elardo, R., Bradley, R.H., & Caldwell, B.M. (1975). The relation of infants' home environments to mental test performance from six to thirty-six months: A longitudinal analysis. *Child Development, 46,* 71–76.

Feuerstein, R. (1977). Mediated learning experience: A theoretical basis for cognitive human modifiability during adolescence. In P. Mittler (Ed.), *Research to practice in mental retardation* (Vol. 2). Baltimore: University Park Press.

Finkelstein, N.W., & Ramey, C.T. (1980). Information from birth certificates as a risk index for educational handicap. *American Journal of Mental Deficiency, 84,* 546–552.

Freud, S. (1905). *Drei abhandlungen zur sexual theorie.* Vienna: Deuicke.

Garber, H., & Heber, R. (1981). The efficacy of early intervention with family rehabilitation. In M. Begab, H.C. Haywood, & H.L. Garber (Eds.), *Psychosocial influences in retarded performance* (pp. 71–87). Baltimore: University Park Press.

Gottfried, A.W. (Ed.). (1984). *Home environment and early mental development.* New York: Academic Press.

Gottfried, A.W., & Gottfried, A.E. (1984). Home environment and mental development in young middle-class families. In A.W. Gottfried (Ed.). *Home environment and early mental development.* New York: Academic Press.

Gottlieb, G. (1971). *Development of species identification in birds.* Chicago: University of Chicago Press.

Harlow, H.F. (1958). The nature of love. *American Psychologist, 13,* 673–685.

Hayden, A.H., & Beck, G.R. (1982). The epidemiology of high-risk and handicapped infants. In C.T. Ramey & P.L. Trohanis (Eds.), *Finding and educating high-risk and handicapped infants* (pp. 19–52). Baltimore: University Park Press.

Hebb, D.O. (1949). *The organization of behavior.* New York: John Wiley & Sons.

Hunt, J.McV. (1961). *Intelligence and experience.* New York: Ronald Press.
Hunt, J.McV. (1979). Psychological development: Early experience. *Annual Review of Psychology, 30,* 103–143.
Jensen, A.R. (1969). How much can we boost IQ and scholastic achievement? *Harvard Educational Review, 39,* 1–123.
Karnes, M., & Teska, J. (1975). Children's response to intervention programs. In J.J. Gallagher (Ed.), *The application of child development research to exceptional children.* Reston, VA: The Council for Exceptional Children.
Krech, D., Rosenwig, M.R.,& Bennett, E.L. (1960). Effects of early environmental complexity and training on brain chemistry. *Journal of Comparative and Physiological Psychology, 53,* 509–519.
Kuhn, T. (1962). *The structure of scientific revolutions.* Chicago: University of Chicago Press.
Lazar, I., Darlington, R., Murray, H., Royce, J., & Snipper, A. (1982). Lasting effects of early education: A report from the consortium for Longitudinal Studies. *Monographs of the Society for Research in Child Development, 47*(2–3, Serial No. 195).
Lorenz, K. (1937). Companion in the bird's world. *Auk, 54,* 245–273.
Ramey, C.T., & Baker-Ward, L. (1983). Early stimulation and mental retardation. In B. Wolman (Ed.), *International encyclopedia of neurology, psychiatry, psychoanalysis, and psychology.* New York: VanNostrand Reinhold.
Ramey, C.T., & Bryant, D.M. (1982). Evidence for primary prevention of developmental retardation. *Journal of the Division of Early Childhood, 5,* 73–78.
Ramey, C.T. & Bryant, D.M. (in press). Prevention-oriented infant education programs. *Journal of Children in Contemporary Society.*
Ramey, C.T., Bryant, D.M., Sparling, J.J., & Wasik, B. (1982). Primary prevention of developmental retardation during infancy. *Journal of Prevention in Human Services, 1,* 61–83.
Ramey, C.T., Bryant, D.M., Sparling, J.J., & Wasik, B. (1984). A biosocial systems perspective on environmental interventions for low birthweight infants. *Clinical Obstetrics and Gynecology, 27* (3), 672–692.
Ramey, C.T., Bryant, D.M., & Suarez, T.M. (in press). Preschool compensatory education and the modifiability of intelligence: A critical review. In X. Detterman (Ed.), *Current topics in human intelligence* (pp. 247–296). Norwood, NJ: Ablex Publishing Corporation.
Ramey, C.T., & Campbell, F.A. (1979). Compensatory education for disadvantaged children. *School Review, 87,* 171–189.
Ramey, C.T., & MacPhee, D. (1985). Developmental retardation among the poor: A systems theory perspective on risk and prevention. In D.C. Farran & J.D. McKinney (Eds.), *Risk in intellectual and psychosocial development* (pp. 61–81). New York: Academic Press.
Ramey, C.T., MacPhee, D., & Yeates, K.O. (1982). Preventing developmental retardation: A general systems model. In J.M. Joffee & L.A. Bond (Eds.), *Facilitating infant and early childhood development* (pp. 343–401). Hanover, NH: University Press of New England.
Ramey, C.T., Trohanis, P.L., & Hostler, S.L. (1982). An introduction. In C.T. Ramey & P.L. Trohanis (Eds.), *Finding and educating high-risk and handicapped infants* (pp. 1–18). Baltimore: University Park Press.

Ramey, C.T., Yeates, K.O., & Short, E.J. (1984). The plasticity of intellectual development: Insights from preventive intervention. *Child Development, 55,* 1913–1925.

Sameroff, A.J., & Chandler, M.J. (1975) Reproductive risk and the continuum of caretaking casualty. In F.D. Horowitz (ed.), *Review of child development research* (Vol. 4, pp. 187–244). Chicago: University of Chicago Press.

Thompson, W.R., & Heron, W. (1954). The effects of early restriction on activity in dogs. *Journal of Comparative and Physiological Psychology, 47,* 77–82.

Yeates, K.O., MacPhee, D., Campbell, F.A., & Ramey, C.T. (1983). Maternal IQ and home environment as determinants of early childhood intellectual competence; A developmental analysis. *Developmental Psychology, 19,* 731–739.

Zeskind, P.S., & Ramey, C.T. (1978). Fetal malnutrition: An experimental study of its consequences on infant development in two caregiving environments. *Child Development, 49,* 1155–1162.

Zeskind, P.S., & Ramey, C.T. (1981). Preventing intellectual and interactional sequelae of fetal malnutrition: A longitudinal, transactional, and synergistic approach to development. *Child Development, 52,* 213–218.

Zigler, E., & Anderson, K. (1979). An idea whose time has come. In E. Zigler & J. Valentine (Eds.), *Project Head Start.* New York: Free Press.

V | ADULTHOOD AND OLD AGE

Overview

ROBERT E. COOKE

Dr. Richard Masland once said that the problems of mental retardation will be solved not by one single scientific achievement, as with the prevention of poliomyelitis, but by many small steps. What has been presented thus far in this volume are many giant steps all leading toward the goal of prevention of mental retardation, or, if not prevention, a better life for mentally retarded persons and their families. In this section the youngest challenge in mental retardation, the study of adult and elderly mentally retarded persons, is examined.

The "graying" of the mentally retarded and developmentally disabled population has finally been appreciated by professionals, many years after the same phenomenon had been observed in the general population. Yet, the magnitude of this "graying" is relatively greater by virtue of the application of major advances in the medical sciences, particularly in the treatment of bacterial infections such as pneumonia with antibiotics. Indeed, survival in cases of Down syndrome, as an example, has increased severalfold as a consequence of improved surgery and antibiotic therapy.

A public policy decision that was initiated in the Kennedy administration—the allocation of federal funds to improve the care of mentally retarded individuals in institutions—certainly affected longevity. Furthermore, the use of Medicaid funds for the care and treatment of mentally retarded persons has unquestionably increased their life span, as well as improved their quality of life.

Recent studies have shown two distinct aging populations in institutions for mentally retarded persons. The non–Down syndrome residents were shown, in a pilot study financed by the Kennedy Foundation, to be as fit physically or even more so than their nonretarded peers of the same age. These people were still interested in learning, recreation, and traveling—comparable to other senior citizens. By contrast, persons with Down syndrome have been known to exhibit many signs of premature aging.

Of greatest interest in relation to the premature aging of individuals with Down syndrome is the presence of extensive neuropathological changes consistent with Alzheimer disease, first noted in this country by George Jervis some 40 years ago in an autopsy series of persons with Down syndrome dying in their 20s, 30s, and 40s. The studies of Wisniewski and others confirm these findings but also demonstrate that mental deterioration may (but not invariably) accompany the pathological changes. The intensive study of older persons with Down syndrome is therefore of importance in its own right, but is also important for the general population since the triplicated segment of chromosome 21 may hold the answer to presenile dementia.

Less well appreciated is the observation made a few years ago by Murdoch in Scotland that Down syndrome may represent "an atheroma-free model." The absence of obvious arteriosclerotic coronary artery disease and aortic atheroma even in elderly persons with Down syndrome, despite many other manifestations of premature aging, suggests that there may be some protective effect from triplication of this same segment of chromosome 21. Of the several enzymes identified on the 21q22 segment, superoxide dismutase (SOD-1) may theoretically have a protective action by reducing the concentration of free oxygen radicals. SOD-1 is present at levels approximately 150% of normal in all tissues of persons with Down syndrome so far studied. SOD-1 function, as part of the free radical scavenging systems of the body and free radical buildup, has been postulated as a cause of lipoperoxidation and possibly vascular damage or as a protector against vascular damage.

Thus, the intensive study of the biochemical and enzymatic processes of aging persons with Down syndrome may shed light on two of the medical scourges of the general population—Alzheimer disease and arteriosclerosis and coronary heart disease. In this regard, mentally retarded persons are not to be seen as experimental subjects for our well-being, but as persons with severe problems that deserve study in their own right. To make any progress, ethical guidelines for research with mentally retarded persons are desperately needed, a situation still extant some 8 years after the National Commission for the Protection of Human Subjects in Biochemical and Behavioral Research submitted its report on the subject to the Department of Health and Human Services.

Over the past 25 years, the major sociological development has been the application of the normalization principle. Over the past several decades the changes in demographics and character seen in the general population—improvements in economic well-being, health status, level of education, and longevity—have occurred in the mentally retarded population as well. As detailed by Dr. Matthew Janicki in Chapter 20, these changes are reflected in three significant areas. First, there has been a shift in the locus of services to mentally retarded persons from that of the institution to predominantly at-home or alternative care community settings. This shift has left a much reduced population of very disabled, elderly, or difficult-to-manage persons in the institutions. Second, a shift has occurred in the composition of the population of mentally retarded persons as a result of a change in taxonomy. Contemporary health practices and social conditions have enabled the survival of even severely disabled infants, thus raising the numbers of more impaired retarded persons. A change in definitions and attribution of percentages for estimating prevalence of persons with mental retardation has also affected the nature of the population, as has the use of early intervention education and remediation services. Finally, various programs, such as early intervention and prenatal diagnosis, have altered the age distribution of the population itself: there are now more severely impaired younger individuals and a larger number of elderly mentally retarded persons, fewer persons born with genetic conditions associated with retardation and more persons living long enough to experience aging-related conditions new to this population. These are trends that Dr. Janicki sees continuing into the future.

With this massive conceptual change, the need for community services has increased as massively. It is widely accepted that most mentally retarded adults and older persons are able to adapt well to life in community settings and that many can achieve levels of adaptation similar to those of their non-retarded peers. However, Dr. Robert Edgerton points out that this consensus may be illusory (Chapter 21), because little is known about the "hidden majority" of retarded persons—those diagnosed as retarded who lost contact with the service system, and the even larger group who were never identified as mentally retarded. In order to obtain reliable data on community adaptation among retarded persons, both short- and long-term research must be undertaken. In the short term, the "hidden majority" must be identified and their adaptive success documented. Also, studies comparing the retarded population with illiterate non-retarded persons, more complete life span studies, and closer analysis of setting-specific competence would be valuable research goals. In the longer term, probably the most important research need is for the exploration of the association between mental retardation and poverty. Dr. Edgerton notes that barriers exist to accomplishing these tasks: lack of recognition that social competence can change markedly in adulthood, lack of resources and personnel, and reluctance to finance the costly retardation-poverty research. However, these barriers must be overcome, especially in the latter case, because the situation continues to worsen.

Because the life span of retarded persons has increased, the need for comprehensive, continuing, and innovative systems for community health care for middle and older age mentally retarded individuals is critical. The integration of behavioral, sociological, and biological, as well as computer, technology will be essential to fill this need. Such a goal represents a challenge to all researchers and practitioners in health care delivery. It is hoped that the University Affiliated Facilities and the Mental Retardation Research Centers will continue to provide leadership in this area as well. The authors of the remaining chapters in this section present a wide-ranging examination of some of these issues.

One issue that continues to be significant in the lives of mentally retarded adults and older persons is behavior; mental retardation places individuals at heightened risk for behavioral and emotional disturbances. Some of these behavioral disorders represent manifestations of an underlying neurophysiological dysfunction and others may represent responses to situational factors that may precipitate an emotional disturbance in an individual regardless of cognitive competence. During the past decade increasing attention has been paid to individuals with both retardation and serious psychiatric disorders. There is a paucity of clinical research on psychiatric problems of retarded individuals that is especially acute in relation to the treatment of older retarded individuals and the long-term results of treatment. Although the manifestations of psychiatric disorders are affected by a person's level of cognitive competence, retarded individuals are vulnerable to the entire gamut of psychiatric disturbance seen in nonretarded persons. In Chapter 22, Drs. Donald Cohen and Joel Bregman present a convincing argument for the use of pharmacological intervention in such cases. Such intervention is only one aspect of treatment, and usually neither the first nor the primary mode. Based on careful assessment, drug therapy is indicated for specific target symptoms or for amelioration of a specifically defined disorder. When used appropriately, pharmacological treatment may be an important part of an optimal treatment plan.

Dr. Marty Wyngaarden Krauss reviews the various issues involved in long-term care for mentally retarded persons in Chapter 23. Over the last decade there has been a notable increase in research on aging retarded persons and the services available to meet their needs. A diversity of program models exists, but there is no consensus regarding the most effective means for ensuring a high quality of life for these persons. Innovations in services for the nonretarded elderly population have rarely influenced the design of service models for elderly mentally retarded persons. Dr. Krauss identifies three research questions that must be addressed with regard to the elderly retarded population: How large is the population, what are the functional characteristics of these individuals, and what is known about current service delivery mechanisms for these persons? The existing service strategies—the age-integrated option, the generic services option, and the specialized service option—may not be sufficient to meet the needs of the growing population of elderly retarded persons, especially when those individuals not presently known to the service network and those persons now living with their natural families present themselves for services. Two recently developed programs that may help to fill this growing service need are social/health maintenance organizations and continuing care retirement communities.

How do the results of research such as that described in the previous chapters affect active service providers? In Chapter 24, Dr. Mary Howell describes the impact of these research results in a health professionals training program. For example, research has indicated the primacy of problems of family relationships, particularly planning for long-term care of a retarded family member. Many family issues are involved here—coping with behavioral changes in adult retarded family members in the face of sparse or conflicting information on the topic; dealing with the physical and medical consequences of aging in a retarded person, again with little applicable information or guidelines; and resolution of individual and family beliefs and attitudes about death and dying. Health care professionals must often deal with these problems on a practical, rather than research-oriented, basis. Of necessity, these professionals design programs and interventions to resolve these and other problems, including deterioration of client behavior, translocation trauma, maintenance of function, and learned helplessness. The information gleaned from their relative success and failure points up avenues for research that may be important in providing underlying skills and support for elderly mentally retarded people that will transfer across many of these problem areas.

20 | The Changing Nature of the Population of Individuals with Mental Retardation

Historical Artifacts and Future Trends

MATTHEW P. JANICKI

Over the past years, we have observed major shifts in the demographics and character of the population of the United States. These shifts have also had an effect on the character of the nation's population of persons with mental retardation. Since the early 1900s the population of the United States has increased 315% from 76 million to over 240 million. During this period, per capital income rose, availability of health care increased, educational levels improved, and life expectancy advanced. Such changes are also mirrored by improvements in the economic well-being, health status, level of education, and longevity of the nation's population of individuals with mental retardation and other lifelong disabling conditions. These changes, a function of shifts in social conditions, public policies, public health practices, and vagaries of the political process, can be viewed in terms of three significant indicators: locus of services, population taxonomies, and the effects of programs.

SHIFTS IN THE LOCUS OF SERVICES

Workers in the early part of this century noted the character and condition of persons with mental retardation and the means with which they were served. For example, in the early part of this century, Fernald (1917) reported on the nature of the known mentally retarded population. For the most part, specialized services, although found in almost every state, were confined to residential and training institutions. At that time only a handful of states or localities offered remedial public school education.

The early part of this century was also a time when the population was experiencing change. Fernald noted that there was a 750% increase in both severely/profoundly and mildly/moderately mentally retarded residents of public facilities over the 25-year period from 1890 to 1916. This resulted in an increase in the number of residents from 4,000 in the late 1800s to 34,000 in the early 1900s. These institutions were originally designed to be training centers. Many provided housing to persons who were functionally retarded and needed education and supervision, but who for the most part were not grossly physically and mentally impaired. Although the original purpose of these facilities was to provide safe housing and special training, they soon became overcrowded and understaffed. Many of their residents were not capable of leaving and living on their own or were unwanted by parents, relatives, and communities as they grew into adulthood.

For some, however, transition was possible and did occur. Consequently, although there was a continued need for what today is called "long-term care" facilities, there was also a need for services in the community. The overall resident population of these facilities was, in many ways, dissimilar from that of the population that occupies today's facilities. Communities often used these public facilities as a place to send individuals considered to be deviants and those with marginal capabilities, so that many of the residents were individuals who were young and relatively capable, and who often made up the bulk of a facility's unpaid workers.

Health conditions and birthing practices at the turn of the century contributed to a high early mortality among infants born with birth defects, and those who survived were predominantly the least impaired. These survivors formed yet another group who were often admitted to public institutions. Furthermore, because of conditions at many of these institutions, limited numbers of individuals lived to or past middle age. Those who did were usually individuals who were only marginally or minimally impaired. Individuals who during that period were classified as "severely retarded" were in many aspects quite different from those individuals today who are considered to be severely retarded.

Contemporary workers (Hauber et al., 1984; Lakin, Krantz, Bruininks, Clumpner, & Hill, 1982) have noted that institutional services peaked in the late 1960s (Figure 1). By 1967 some 195,000 persons were residing in the nation's public mental retardation institutional facilities. Current census figures reveal that this institutional population is now at 60% of that amount, some 115,000 persons. Also, the emphasis in public policy regarding the housing of the mentally retarded population has shifted from institutional services to models

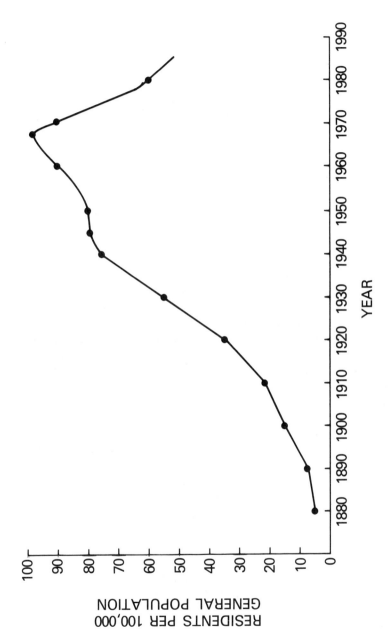

Figure 1. Proportion of retarded persons who resided in institutions, 1880–1985. (From Lakin, K.C., Krantz, G.C., Bruininks, R.H., Clumpner, J.L., & Hill, B.K. [1982]. One hundred years of data of populations of public residential facilities for mentally retarded people. *American Journal of Mental Deficiency, 87,* 1–8.)

that stress services provided at home or in alternative care community programs (Janicki, Castellani, & Norris, 1983). These shifts in population care practices, in large part the result of changing social conditions, more available health care, and enlightened public policies, have resulted in a redistribution of persons with mental retardation through a variety of community care settings, leaving largely those individuals who are very disabled or aged or who pose management challenges as the residual institutional population (Best-Sigford, Bruininks, Lakin, & Hill, 1982; Bruininks, Hauber, & Kudla, 1980).

The distribution of the population remaining in the nation's institutions reflects an increasingly older resident population, with generally few new admissions of young persons (Best-Sigford et al., 1982; Bruininks et al., 1980). Indeed some have projected that within 10 years many of the nation's public mental retardation institutions will become geriatric care facilities (Janicki, 1985) as states continue to deinstitutionalize the remaining "work-age" (i.e., 21–65 years) adult population.

Although in one sense one could argue that what is characterized by mental retardation has remained unchanged, the character of the population of persons with mental retardation has changed, with notable shifts in age, disability, and loci of services. By the mid-1950s special education programs began to serve more mentally retarded students than there were total residents in institutions for mentally retarded people (Lakin, Krantz, Bruininks, Clumpner, & Hill, 1982). The subsequent drop in the number of school-age children in the general population as well as the effects of concerted deinstitutionalization efforts and public policy shifts supporting the social integration of handicapped individuals has led to a decrease of the numbers of persons in institutions (Lakin, Krantz, Bruininks, Clumpner, & Hill, 1982). Markedly fewer children are now being admitted (Best-Sigford et al., 1982) and first admissions are mostly comprised of increasingly older (albeit not aging) individuals (Lakin, Hill, Hauber, & Bruininks, 1982). Indeed, even the sex ratio has shifted: males now represent 57% of the institutional population, 3% more than in the 1970s (Scheerenberger, 1982). Furthermore, numerous agencies are demonstrating that severely and multiply handicapped individuals can be served in community care settings (Keith & Ferdinand, 1984).

Consequently, one determinant of population characteristics has changed markedly—the number of mentally retarded people in institutions. Furthermore, in terms of population characteristics, it has also been demonstrated that institutional populations are not necessarily reflective of the overall population of mentally retarded people (e.g., Janicki, 1986a; Krauss & Seltzer, 1986). This means that much of what has been written about mentally retarded people has often been drawn from biased sources.

THE EFFECTS OF TAXONOMIES

Population taxonomies, or the terminology for and categorization of those who are described as being mentally retarded, have also affected the composition of the population (Patrick & Reschly, 1982). Workers in the early part of this century worked within the framework of a different classification system for defining persons with mental retardation and the nature of how they were to be served (Fernald, 1917). With increasing emphasis on school-based services, identification of children by level of retardation became more prominent. Those who could benefit from classroom education were admitted to schools, and education classifications of "educable" or "trainable" determined the type of educational services they received. "Custodial" category children, or those most impaired, were deemed inappropriate for schools and relegated to institutions.

Furthermore, the individuals who were available for inclusion affected the composition of the population. For example, the characteristics of "severity" as a taxonomic category in 1917 are far from those comprising "severity" today. It is evident from epidemiological studies that one of the most problematic aspects of conducting such studies is how to define who is to be included (Lubin & Kiely, 1985).

How mental retardation is conceptualized is a significant issue, because the decision on what constitutes mental retardation has an impact upon the number of people considered to be mentally retarded. The current conceptualization of mental retardation is much more limited (albeit more complex) than it was a number of years ago. Up to about 20 years ago anyone with an IQ of 85 or less was considered mentally retarded, or "borderline" at least, and within the framework of the expected normal distribution of intelligence this was a significant number of people. A much smaller segment of the population is today considered mentally retarded because the definition is qualified to include variables other than intellectual functioning. One effect that this realignment of definition has had is to create a shift in the character of the in-service population. For example, although the actual number of persons with severe-profound mental retardation is relatively low, this group represents a high proportion of persons currently receiving more comprehensive services.

Mental retardation terminology, definitions, and classification elements vary widely across states, affecting the manner in which persons with mental retardation are identified and counted. A case in point is the educational system, where variations in these factors are most noted and seriously affect the determination of prevalence of school-age mentally retarded children (Patrick & Reschly, 1982). Indeed, it would appear that although such school situation–bound variables as adaptive behavior measurement, mental retardation definition, and IQ scores are a means of gathering prevalence data, they are largely unrelated to school system prevalence. Patrick and Reschly (1982) found that population demographics such as per capita income, educational level, and illiteracy rate were much more powerful in assessing school-age prevalence in the mild-moderate levels of mental retardation.

Another case in point is population surveys of childhood disability. Newacheck, Budetti, and McManus (1984) have noted that such recent national surveys have revealed trends that point to a doubling of the population of children with limitations of activity due to chronic illness over the past 10 years. They explored several possible explanations for these trends, including changes in survey design and procedures, changes in awareness of conditions on the part of informants, and changes in the number of handicapped children remaining in the community. Their comments as to which of these factors had more of an effect on the data are less important than the point that many factors can influence the manner in which persons with disabilities are identified and counted.

A number of factors, including unsafe birthing practices, lack of availability of physicians and other health services, poor sanitation, poor nutrition, and substandard general living conditions historically have contributed to a high infant mortality rate (Lesser, 1985), thus limiting the number of infants surviving with severe forms of mental retardation. The result had been an overall population composed of less impaired individuals. Contemporary health practices and social conditions have changed this so that in most instances even the most disabled infant has a reasonable chance of survival. Indeed, many multiply disabled infants are now living longer and are comprising a new wave of severely disabled children.

Consequently, a shift in definitions and attribution of percentages for estimating prevalence of persons with mental retardation also has affected the nature of the population. For example, by not including a large group previously classified as "borderline," and redefining mental retardation in terms of both IQ and adaptive behavior, the determination of the prevalence of mental retardation has been affected.

THE EFFECTS OF PROGRAMS

The changes in emphasis to prevention and early identification of disabilities has also affected the character and composition of the mentally retarded population. The institution of early childhood and school-age education and remediation services (the result of PL 94-142—the Education for All Handicapped Children Act), designed to minimize the nature of the effects of childhood mental retardation and delayed development, is expected to have a marked effect upon the definition and composition of the population (Lakin, Krantz, Bruininks, Clumpner, & Hill, 1982). The expectation is that with intensified remediation and both physical and social integration the next generations of handicapped youngsters will be a better prepared population. It will also undoubtedly be a larger and broader population, as more parents seek special assistance for their children with developmental delays or learning difficulties. These outcomes are only beginning to be felt, and it will be a number of years before marked population differences will become fully evident.

The results of increased birth weight, lowered infant mortality rates, effective nutritional and early intervention practices, health maintenance, and community care for all age groups (Shonkoff, 1984; Wilton & Irvine, 1983), and notable increases in longevity among older adults (Richards & Siddiqui, 1980; Thase, 1982), are contributing to a change within the distribution of the mentally retarded population. Furthermore, the increased rate of survival of severely and profoundly retarded infants into childhood and even adolescence has shifted the distribution of the population to include a greater percentage of younger, yet more organically impaired individuals.

In contrast to these trends, however, are the reports that many mentally retarded youngsters are not getting adequate and appropriate health care (Larson & LaPointe, 1986). Handicapped adolescents in particular, who demonstrate a high prevalence of physical, emotional, and socialization problems, have difficulties that are compounded by inadequate primary medical care and surveillance (Larson & LaPointe, 1986). Furthermore, among those individuals who are institutionalized, the number and degree of serious, chronic health problems may now be increasing as many more of these persons are sustained though improvements in medical knowledge and health care practices (Lakin, Krantz, Bruininks, Clumpner, & Hill, 1982).

Indeed, studies have noted an increased mortality rate among persons recently admitted to institutions, among whom are those with the most serious health problems or complicated physical and mental deficiencies (Eyman, Chaney, Givens, Lopez, & Lee, 1986).

Changes in prenatal procedures (e.g., the use of amniocentesis) have resulted in a drop in the number of live births of persons with certain genetic conditions associated with mental retardation (e.g., Down syndrome). In fact, some have noted that if there is no increase in the use of prenatal diagnosis and consequent reduction of genetic conditions such as Down syndrome among newborns, then a relatively stable birth rate of infants with genetic conditions may be expected over the next 20 years (Huether, 1983). Indeed, studies have shown that, using a broader definition of genetic causation, genetic disease can account for approximately 40% of the basis for mental retardation (Thoene, Higgins, Krieger, Schmickel, & Weiss, 1980). This in itself will have an effect upon the population.

Decreased mortality (Lakin, Krantz, Bruininks, Clumpner, & Hill, 1982) and increased longevity among adults overall has contributed to a greater survivor rate among older persons with mental retardation, drawing out the age distribution within the older end of the population. The life expectancy of mentally retarded people, including those individuals with Down syndrome, has increased considerably over recent years (Dupont, Vaeth, & Videbech, 1986; Fryers, 1986; Thase, 1982). Although still relatively infrequent, it is no longer rare to find centenarians among a state's older mentally retarded service population.

Greater longevity has also introduced new concerns over conditions not previously experienced, such as Alzheimer's disease. Indeed, reports show a higher rate of occurrence of Alzheimer's disease among older persons with Down syndrome than in the general population (Wisniewski & Merz, 1985). As persons with other mental retardation etiologies continue to live to old age, what other currently unanticipated effects will become evident (Janicki, 1986b)?

It is clear from a number of demographic studies that the overall population of persons with mental retardation is changing in accordance with changes in the general population. As shown in Figure 2, the population bulge represented by the "baby boom" group (those persons now approximately 20–35 years of age) contains a large number of mentally retarded persons. This bulge is steadily growing older, progressively shifting the age distribution of the population and consequently affecting its composition (Janicki & Jacobson, 1982). Whereas many earlier studies focusing on epidemiological considerations of mentally retarded persons were conducted on samples drawn

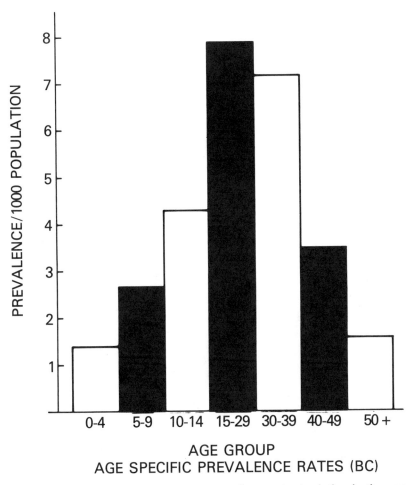

Figure 2. Age-specific prevalence rates of mental retardation in the general population. (From Baird, P.A., & Sadovnick, A.D. [1985]. Mental retardation in over half-a-million consecutive lifebirths: An epidemiological study. *American Journal of Mental Deficiency, 89*, 323–330.)

from school-age populations, recent population-based and registry reports (Cocks & Ng, 1983; Janicki & Jacobson, 1982; Janicki & MacEachron, 1984; Sutton, 1983) are beginning to show that the bulk of the known population is made up of adults and that the mean age of this adult population is steadily shifting upward toward late middle age. (This is shown by Figure 3; here the distribution of a mentally

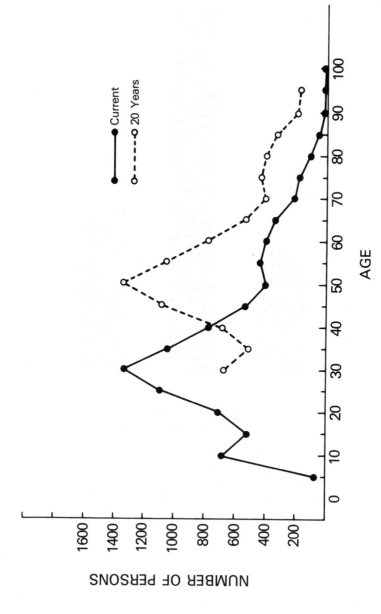

Figure 3. Distribution of mentally retarded population by age: current and 20-year projection.

retarded population was shifted 20 years to show the effects of aging on the overall population.)

The implications of these changes are profound. Whereas some 4–6% of an area's population may be elderly today, this percentage will grow considerably over the next 10–20 years. Greater overall numbers resulting from the demographic "baby-boom" effect, increased longevity, improved medical care, and a greater proportion of individuals in community living will mean that the overall mentally retarded population, too, is "graying" and that significant shifts in programs and resources and a redirection of research efforts will need to be made over the next several years.

Probably most problematic is that virtually no research effort has been devoted to studying the older adult who is mentally retarded or the aging process as it applies to individuals with a life-long handicapping condition. What little is known of the aging process and its effects has come from either anecdotal reports, rudimentary population assessments, or studies examining dementia in persons with Down syndrome.

Studies are beginning to reveal that both medical and behavioral interventions have an effect upon the character of the mentally retarded population. In addition, the population is experiencing an overall greater longevity, and decreased morbidity and mortality. Improvements in functional abilities have been noted that can be attributed to increased applications of interventions and prophylactic attention. Also, some natural demographic shifts in the population are occurring that reflect the American population in general. Most importantly, however, a seasoning of the field of mental retardation can be observed, as both services and research reflect a life span approach.

COMMENTARY

What is in store? As the level of sophistication in identifying the causes of mental retardation and other disabling conditions rises, the population falling under the definition of mental retardation will only increase. As technology continues to become more complex the number of potential causes of mental retardation and birth defects will increase. As society becomes more commercially complex and demanding of intellectually based skills, the frustrations of those who already only marginally compete will be compounded.

It seems that when one problem is overcome, another is introduced. Remedial programs should have a profound effect upon those children now enrolled in them—again changing the character of successive generations of persons with mental retardation. Unfortunately, although progress is being made in educational services directed toward preschoolers and school-age youngsters, programs directed toward at-risk families and newborns, such as nutrition services, income supports, and readily available health care, are being withdrawn (due to purely political considerations), which compounds the problems already facing at-risk infants and toddlers.

Improved community integration of capable work-age mentally retarded adults has provided them with new experiences that enhance learning and competence building. Yet, in some areas, as adults become more capable they are in jeopardy of loosing the very supports that underpin their independence. With regard to older adults, the nation has not yet responded by adapting programs to an aging population. Yet, the pressures of an increasing population demand are building to help disabled seniors begin to explore new experiences as they retire.

The eventual impact of these countervailing forces is unclear; however, it would appear that these changes in the composition of the population have and will continue to have profound implications for services, research, and public policies, as well as in the political arena. What will it be like tomorrow? One can only speculate; much of the speculation is dependent upon the future direction of public policies. Fiscal conservatism tends to be associated with decreased resources and diminished programs to help at-risk and needy populations. The continued future availability and enhancement of programs directed toward prevention, early identification and intervention programs for preschoolers, remediation and special services for adolescents and young adults, work and skill-building programs for adults, and range of challenging opportunities for elderly persons will be the telling points in terms of defining the composition of tomorrow's population of mentally retarded persons.

REFERENCES

Best-Sigford, B., Bruininks, R.H., Lakin, K.C., & Hill, B.K. (1982). Resident release patterns in a national sample of public residential facilities. *American Journal of Mental Deficiency, 87,* 130–140.
Bruininks, R.H., Hauber, F.A., & Kudla, M.J. (1980). National survey of community residential facilities: A profile of facilities and residents in 1977. *American Journal of Mental Deficiency, 84,* 470–478.
Cocks, E., & Ng, C.P. (1983). Characteristics of those persons registered with the Mental Retardation Division. *Australian and New Zealand Journal of Developmental Disabilities, 9,* 117–127.

Dupont, A., Vaeth, M., & Videbech, P. (1986). Mortality and life expectancy of Down's syndrome in Denmark. *Journal of Mental Deficiency Research, 30*, 111–120.

Eyman, R.K., Chaney, R.H., Givens, C.A., Lopez, E.G., & Lee, C.K.E. (1986). Medical conditions underlying increasing mortality of institutionalized persons with mental retardation. *Mental Retardation, 24*, 301–306.

Fernald, W.E. (1917). The growth of provision for the feebleminded in the United States. *Mental Hygiene, 1*, 34–59.

Fryers, T. (1986). Survival in Down's syndrome. *Journal of Mental Deficiency Research, 30*, 101–110.

Hauber, F.A., Bruininks, R.H., Hill, B.K., Lakin, K.C., Scheerenberger, R.C., & White, C.C. (1984). National census of residential facilities: A 1982 profile of facilities and residents. *American Journal of Mental Deficiency, 89*, 236–245.

Huether, C.A. (1983). Projection of Down's syndrome births in the United States 1979–2000, and the potential effects of prenatal diagnosis. *American Journal of Public Health, 73*, 1186–1189.

Janicki, M.P. (1985). *The aging population in state developmental centers.* Paper presentation at 1985 annual meeting of the New York State Association of Retarded Citizens, Albany, NY.

Janicki, M.P. (1986a). Older mentally handicapped persons residing at home and in institutions. *British Journal of Mental Subnormality, 32*, 30–36.

Janicki, M.P. (1986b). Some comments on aging and a need for research. In H.M. Wisniewski & D.A. Snider (Eds.), *Mental retardation: Research, education, and technology transfer* (pp. 261–264). New York: New York Academy of Sciences.

Janicki, M.P., Castellani, P.J., & Norris, R.N. (1983). Organization and administration of service delivery systems. In J.L. Matson & J.A. Mulick (Eds.), *Handbook of mental retardation* (pp. 3–23). New York: Pergamon Press.

Janicki, M.P., & Jacobson, J.W. (1982). The character of developmental disabilities in New York state: Preliminary observations. *International Journal of Rehabilitation Research, 5*, 191–202.

Janicki, M.P., & MacEachron, A.E. (1984). Residential, health and social service needs of elderly developmentally disabled persons. *The Gerontologist, 24*, 128–137.

Keith, D.K., & Ferdinand, L.R. (1984). Changes in levels of mental retardation: A comparison of institutional and community populations. *TASH Journal, 9*, 26–30.

Krauss, M.W., & Seltzer, M.M. (1986). Comparison of elderly and adult mentally retarded persons in community and institutional settings. *American Journal of Mental Deficiency, 91*, 237–243.

Lakin, K.C., Hill, B.K., Hauber, F.A., & Bruininks, R.H. (1982). Changes in age at first admission to residential care for mentally retarded people. *Mental Retardation, 20*, 216–219.

Lakin, K.C., Krantz, G.C., Bruininks, R.H., Clumpner, J.L., & Hill, B.K. (1982). One hundred years of data on populations of public residential facilities for mentally retarded people. *American Journal of Mental Deficiency, 87*, 1–8.

Larson, C.P., & LaPointe, Y. (1986). The health status of mild to moderate intellectually handicapped adolescents. *Journal of Mental Deficiency Research, 30*, 121–128.

Lesser, A.J. (1985). The origin and development of maternal and child health programs in the United States. *American Journal of Public Health, 75*, 590–598.

Lubin, R.A., & Kiely, M. (1985). Epidemiology of aging in developmental disabilities. In M.P. Janicki & H.M. Wisniewski (Eds.), *Aging and developmental disabilities: Issues and approaches* (pp. 95–114). Baltimore: Paul H. Brookes Publishing Co.

Newacheck, P.W., Budetti, P.P., & Halfon, N. (1986). Trends in activity-limiting chronic conditions among children. *American Journal of Public Health, 76*, 178–184.

Newacheck, P.W., Budetti, P.P., & MacManus, P. (1984). Trends in childhood disability. *American Journal of Public Health, 74*, 232–236.

Patrick, J.L., & Reschly, D.J. (1982). Relationship of state educational criteria and demographic variables to school-system prevalence of mental retardation. *American Journal of Mental Deficiency, 86*, 351–360.

Richards, B.W., & Siddiqui, A.D. (1980). Age and mortality trends in residents of an institution for the mentally handicapped. *Journal of Mental Deficiency Research, 24*, 99–105.

Scheerenberger, R.C. (1982). Public residential services, 1981: Status and trends. *Mental Retardation, 20*, 210–215.

Shonkoff, J.P. (1984). Social support and the development of vulnerable children. *American Journal of Public Health, 74*, 310–312.

Sutton, M. (August, 1983). *Treatment issues and the elderly institutionalized developmentally disabled individual.* Paper presented at the 91st annual meeting of the American Psychological Association, Anaheim, CA.

Thase, M.E. (1982). Longevity and mortality in Down's syndrome. *Journal of Mental Deficiency Research, 26*, 177–192.

Thoene, J., Higgins, J., Krieger, I., Schmickel, R., & Weiss, L. (1980). Genetic screening for mental retardation in Michigan. *American Journal of Mental Deficiency, 85*, 335–340.

Wilton, K.M., & Irvine, J. (1983). Nutritional intakes of socioculturally mentally retarded children vs. children of low and average socioeconomic status. *American Journal of Mental Deficiency, 88*, 79–85.

Wisniewski, H.M., & Merz, G. (1985). Aging, Alzheimer's disease, and developmental disabilities. In M.P. Janicki & H.M. Wisniewski (Eds.), *Aging and developmental disabilities: Issues and approaches* (pp. 177–184). Baltimore: Paul H. Brookes Publishing Co.

21 | Community Adaptation of Persons with Mental Retardation
ROBERT B. EDGERTON

The past two decades of intensive research on the deinstitutionalization of persons with mental retardation have added rich detail to the previous corpus of knowledge. Although it is clear that there is considerable variation from one part of the country to another, from one ethnic group to another, and even within seemingly homogeneous populations, it is nevertheless widely accepted that some basic generalizations about community adaptation can be made. Surprisingly, many of these generalizations are the same as those made by investigators at the time of World War I. It can be said now, as then, that although relatively few persons with mental retardation become fully self-reliant, *most* people with mild mental retardation, and a sizeable percentage of those with more moderate degrees of handicap, can achieve a semi-independent adjustment to life in community settings *if* 1) they are given enough time to learn coping skills, *and* 2) they have the support of other persons (Bruininks, Meyers, Sigford, & Lakin, 1981; Cobb, 1972).

This central finding does much to support the philosophy of normalization, but these two conditions are not always met and the realities of community adaptation are sometimes unfortunate. For example, not everyone is able to gain or maintain reliable support by others; these persons usually have adaptive problems. The most reliable social support is usually provided by parents or other close kinsfolk (Kernan & Koegel, 1984), but these persons, although well-intentioned, often socialize persons with mental retardation to become more dependent and socially incompetent than need be (Edgerton, 1986b; Kaufman, 1980). So it is with much of the mental retardation service delivery system (Bercovici, 1983). This system is far better than anything available to deinstitutionized mentally ill persons, and it often delivers essential services, yet in most parts of the country its most essential service—the provision of appropriate residential alternatives—is limited by the lack of more normalized alternatives in appropriate geographic locations, and geographic location is strongly associated with successful adaptation (Landesman-Dwyer, 1981).

This leads to the second point. Some agency personnel, like some parents, do not allow persons with mental retardation the time that is required for them to develop the skills and attitudes necessary for successful adaptation to life in community settings (Bruininks et al., 1981). Unlike nonretarded persons, who may fail at many of life's challenges yet be allowed a second and third chance, persons with mental retardation are often removed from more normalized settings and placed in more restrictive environments in which there is little opportunity for a second chance. The intent is usually good—the safety and well-being of the persons involved—but the result is needlessly restricted lives. The economic marketplace also serves to deny these people the time they need to improve their work skills and their overall adaptation. Relatively few persons with mental retardation are able to find and hold competitive jobs (Greenspan & Shoultz, 1981), and the Supplemental Security Income (SSI) regulations pose powerful disincentives even to seek work. Finally, many residential neighborhoods are intolerant of mentally retarded persons; lower socioeconomic status (SES) areas may be more accepting, but they may also be unsafe (Halpern, Close, & Nelson 1986).

This is not to suggest that most persons with mental retardation are offensive or dangerous in public. Although it cannot be denied that a minority of such persons do commit deviant or criminal acts, the majority do not (Edgerton, 1981). For example, they seldom abuse or even use alcohol or drugs (Edgerton, 1986a). In fact, mentally retarded persons are much less often a threat to nonhandicapped persons than they are exploited or victimized by them. Similarly, the great majority of persons with mental retardation dress and behave appropriately in public places, including on public transportation. Most maintain appropriate standards of personal hygiene. The most problematic aspect of their community adaptation is not their negative impact on community life, it is their isolation from it. Deinstitutionalization has allowed persons with mental retardation to live in community settings, but it has not integrated them into community life.

Few mentally retarded persons have social relationships with nonhandicapped persons. Instead, their relationships are typically with other mentally retarded persons in sheltered workshops, social clubs, or residential facilities. Many of these persons have difficulty making or maintaining friendships despite their almost desperate longing for friends and intimate relationships (Landesman-Dwyer & Berkson, 1984). Without friends and isolated from ordinary community activities, many of these people combat their loneliness by absorbing themselves in passive recreational activities such as watching television or listening to music (this is perhaps little different from what many people do, but is perceived to be so by them), and a significant number develop rich fantasy lives that allow them to find imaginary friends and vicarious excitement (Graffam & Turner, 1984; Turner, 1983). Not all persons with mental retardation live such isolated lives. A sizeable minority do find close friends and rewarding social relationships, and a growing number of these establish intimate relationships, including marriage. Although many have difficulty with sexual intimacy (Craft & Craft, 1979), some do become parents. Most have significant difficulty parenting their children but some parent quite well and many others can be helped by training (Johnson & Tucker, in press).

Very little is known about the inner lives of mentally retarded persons. It is known that such persons strive continually to enhance their self-esteem, but it is not yet known to what extent their self-esteem and their ability to contribute more positively to society might increase if they had greater access to socially valued activities and relationships. Persons with mental retardation *can* be good citizens, friends, marriage partners, and parents, but too often they find these roles denied to them.

There is general agreement on the factors that limit success in community adaptation. First, there is a lack of opportunity to experience and learn from the challenges and failures of ordinary life. Second, socialization practices that *decrease* the social competence of mentally retarded persons are widespread in many families, schools, and residential settings. So powerful is this process of socialization that persons of normal IQ who are misdiagnosed and socialized as persons with mental retardation also develop low self-esteem, fear of failure, dependency, and poor interpersonal skills (Edgerton, 1986b). Although these practices correlate with failure in community adaptation, the search for variables that will predict successful adaptation continues to be unavailing. No single personal attribute correlates highly with success, nor does any specifiable complex of attributes, although it is generally agreed that emotional and personality attributes have more prognostic relevance than does cognitive ability. It is likely that personality attributes have such limited prognostic value because environments differ so greatly in their demands for competence. Many kinds of social competence are probably setting specific (Alexander, Huganir, & Zigler, 1985), and there has been some promising work in matching persons to environments (Kernan, Begab, & Edgerton, 1983). More research on this issue is needed, but in the author's opinion there is another, still more basic problem that needs to be addressed: very little is known about the "hidden majority" of persons with mental retardation.

THE NEXT STEPS

The findings summarized above are based on research carried out with a small minority of all mentally retarded persons who live in the community. These are persons who were diagnosed as mentally retarded, usually in school, and who have continued to have some contact with the mental retardation service system after leaving school. With a few exceptions in the United States, the United Kingdom, and Sweden (Granat & Granat, 1973, 1978; Richardson, 1978; Ross, Begab, Dondis, Giampiccolo, & Meyers, 1985; Zigler, Balla, & Hodapp, 1984), persons with IQs below 70 who were never diagnosed in their early years or who "disappeared" from the view of the service delivery system have not been studied. These people are a "hidden majority." They are from the lowest socioeconomic strata and from the most deprived ethnic minorities. How they live their lives may differ greatly from the patterns seen in predominantly white, somewhat higher SES populations whose problems and successes fill the pages of our scientific literature.

How this hidden majority of mentally retarded persons adapts to community living raises policy issues about the provisions of services for citizens who may now be neglected, just as it poses more basic scientific questions about the nature of community adaptation among populations whose sociocultural patterns differ greatly from those of the white Euro-American population studied in the past (Koegel & Edgerton, 1982; Mitchell-Kernan & Tucker, 1984). Because the adaptive strategies of the "hidden majority" are unknown and because they may provide new perspectives on abilities of mentally retarded people to cope with environmental demands, priority should be given to research with this population, with special emphasis on ethnic minority populations and the "new immigrant" populations from Asia, Latin American, the Caribbean, and the Middle East. Another promising population for research is the large number of monolingual English-speaking Americans who are illiterate. Instead of using literate nonhandicapped populations as controls for persons with mental retardation, it would be instructive to study illiterate people. One of the major disabilities faced by retarded persons is their relative difficulty with reading and writing (and other "school skills" such as quantitative operations). It might prove instructive to determine whether illiterate but nonretarded people experience problems in community living that are similar to those encountered by persons with mental retardation. All of this proposed research with understudied populations, as well as future research with previously studied populations of persons with mental retardation, should include microanalyses of setting-specific behavior.

Finally, there is a pressing need to examine the full range of effects of various intervention programs. Semi-independent living programs, parental skill training, integrating aging persons into age appropriate community programs for seniors, and supported work programs are a few examples of intervention programs that offer promise for ameliorating life circumstances among persons with mental retardation, yet research on the efficacy of these programs typically lacks time depth and focuses too narrowly on a few outcome measures. Research on supported work programs, for example, should do more than document time spent in competitive employment and employers' ratings of job performance (Wehman & Kregel, 1985). Supported work programs, like other interventions, may have effects that ramify throughout an individual's life. If these programs are to be evaluated, it is important to examine changes in social relationships, life satisfaction, self esteem, and overall quality of life.

LONG-RANGE OPPORTUNITIES

As a result of the aging of the population there is an opportunity to pursue life span studies farther into old age than has been done before. It is generally agreed that knowledge of adaptation is limited because past research has too seldom employed repeated measures over time, relying instead on data that were collected at only one, or at best a few, points in time (Heal, Sigelman, & Switzky, 1978). However, this methodological point aside, the study of community adaptation of older persons with mental retardation has been badly neglected (Seltzer, 1985). Although many aging mentally retarded persons live in restrictive environments (where they are often diagnosed as suffering from dementia), many retarded persons in their 50s and 60s are living in community settings and their needs for services are largely unknown. Moreover, the fact that some of these older people have achieved more positive lives in their later years than they were able to accomplish when they were younger may have significant implications for our understanding of human development (Edgerton, Bollinger, & Herr, 1984).

Important as it is to extend life span studies, the greatest research opportunity, and the greatest need, is the exploration of the association between mental retardation and poverty. By a factor of 10 or 20 to 1, mildly retarded children are born to poor and ethnic minority families. A report by Craig Ramey and his associates (Ramey, Stedman, Borders-Patterson, & Mengel, 1978) has made this point. By showing that it is possible to identify children who will need special educational services before or during grade school by information available on birth certificates—mother's race and education, the month prenatal care began, survivorship of other siblings, and the child's legitimacy—Ramey and his colleagues confront society with the chilling inevitability of the social and cultural creation of mentally retarded children. It need not be added that their mothers were very poor.

Only a charter member of the Flat Earth Society could believe that poverty in the United States is on the wane. Poverty is increasing, and with it the practices and beliefs that are considered to cause mental retardation. Poor nutrition, alcohol and drug abuse, violence, lead poisoning, overcrowding, poor learning environments, lack of prenatal care, teen-age pregnancy, and many other factors combine to put growing numbers of children at risk for mental retardation. How much these factors contribute to the risk equation and how best to combat them is not obvious, and neither the scientific nor the political difficulties that stand in the way of combating this public health crisis should be underestimated. However, neither can one ignore the human tragedy and social dangers that grow every year that the poverty cycle spirals upward. Society faces a moral and scientific imperative to generate research that will lower the risk factor for mental retardation among poor Americans.

BARRIERS

The first and most critical barrier is obvious. The research outline here is personnel intensive, long-term, and therefore very expensive. There is no need to note that worthy competition for research dollars exists, nor is there need to add that there is difficulty in assembling and coordinating interdisciplinary research teams such as those required to study poverty. This is well known by those whose careers go back to the 1960s, when such studies were attempted. There are also conceptual problems regarding such things as the meaning of "independent living," the definition of "quality of life," and the idea of "success." In addition, there is another, less well-recognized barrier that in the author's opinion is not as clearly acknowledged as the others. It is reasonable that greater developmental gains have been expected from children than adults, but it is not reasonable that adult development should be scanted as much as it has been. Adults with mental retardation can and do improve their social competence, if not their IQs (and the latter is an arguable point). This reason alone makes adults worthy of scientific study. The final barrier has to do with the so-called hidden majority of mentally retarded persons. Because they are hidden it is difficult to include them in probability samples, and because they are hidden there is little public concern for their welfare.

REFERENCES

Alexander, K., Huganir, L.S., & Zigler, E. (1985). Effects of different living settings on the performance of mentally retarded individuals. *American Journal of Mental Deficiency, 90*, 9–17.

Bercovici, S.M. (1983). *Barriers to normalization: The restrictive management of retarded persons.* Baltimore: University Park Press.

Bruininks, R.H., Meyers, C.E., Sigford, B.B., & Lakin, K.C. (Eds.). (1981). *Deinstitutionalization and community adjustment of mentally retarded people* (Monograph No. 4). Washington, DC: American Association of Mental Deficiency.

Cobb, H. (1972). *The forecast of fulfillment: A review of research on predictive assessment of the adult retarded for social and vocational adjustment.* New York: Teacher's College Press.

Craft, A., & Craft, M. (1979). *Handicapped married couples: A Welsh study of couples handicapped from birth by mental, physical or personality disorder.* London: Routledge & Kegal Paul.

Edgerton, R.B. (1981). Crime, deviance and normalization: Reconsidered. In R.H. Bruininks, et al. (Eds.), *Deinstitutionalization and community adjustment of mentally retarded people* (Monograph No. 4, pp. 145–166). Washington, DC: American Association on Mental Deficiency.

Edgerton, R.B. (1986a). Alcohol and drug use by mentally retarded adults. *American Journal of Mental Deficiency, 90*, 602–609.

Edgerton, R.B. (1986b). A case of delabeling: Some practical and theoretical implications. In L.L. Langness & H. Levine (Eds.), *Culture and retardation* (pp. 101–126). New York: D. Reidel.

Edgerton, R.B., Bollinger, M., & Herr, B. (1984). The cloak of competence: After two decades. *American Journal of Mental Deficiency, 88*, 345–351.

Graffam, J., & Turner, J.L. (1984). Escape from boredom: The meaning of eventfulness in the lives of clients at a sheltered workshop. In R. Edgerton (Ed.), *Lives in process: Mildly retarded adults in a large city* (Monograph No. 6, pp. 121–144). Washington, DC: American Association on Mental Deficiency.

Granat, K., & Granat, S. (1973). Below-average intelligence and mental retardation. *American Journal of Mental Deficiency, 78*, 27–32.

Granat, K., & Granat, S. (1978). Adjustment of intellectually below-average men not identified as mentally retarded. *Scandinavian Journal of Psychology, 19*, 41–51.

Greenspan, S., & Schoultz, B. (1981). Why mentally retarded adults lose their jobs: Social competence as a factor in work adjustment. *Applied Research in Mental Retardation, 2*, 23–38.

Halpern, A.S., Close, D.W., & Nelson, D.J. (1986). *On my own: The impact of semi-independent living programs for adults with mental retardation.* Baltimore: Paul H. Brookes Publishing Co.

Heal, L.W., Sigelman, C.K., & Switzky, H.N. (1978). Research in community residential alternatives for the mentally retarded. In N.R. Ellis (Ed.), *International Review of research in mental retardation* (Vol. 9). New York: Academic Press.

Johnson & Tucker. (in press). *Human organization.*

Kaufman, S.Z. (1980). A mentally retarded daughter educates her mother. *Exceptional Parent, 10,* 17–22.

Kernan, K., Begab, M., & Edgerton, R.B. (Eds.) (1983). *Settings and the behavior and study of mentally retarded persons.* Baltimore: University Park Press.

Kernan, K.T., & Koegel, P.K. (1984). Employment experiences of community-based mildly retarded adults. In R. Edgerton (Ed.), *Lives in process: Mildly retarded adults in a large city.* (Monograph No. 6, pp. 9–26). Washington, DC: American Association on Mental Deficiency.

Koegel, P., & Edgerton, R.B. (1982). Labeling and the perception of handicap among black mildly retarded adults. *American Journal of Mental Deficiency, 87,* 266–276.

Landesman-Dwyer, S. (1981). Living in the community. *American Journal of Mental Deficiency, 86,* 223–234.

Landesman-Dwyer, S., & Berkson, G. (1984). Friendship and social behavior. In J.W. Wortis (Ed.), *Mental retardation and developmental disabilities: Annual review* (Vol. 13). New York: Plenum Press.

Mitchell-Kernan, C., & Tucker, M.B. (1984). The social structures of mildly mentally retarded Afro-Americans: Gender comparisons. In R.B. Edgerton (Ed.), *Lives in process: Mildly retarded adults in a large city* (Monograph No. 6, pp. 173–192). Washington, DC: American Association on Mental Deficiency.

Ramey, C.T., Stedman, D.J., Borders-Patterson, A., & Mengel, W. (1978). Predicting school failure from information available at birth. *American Journal of Mental Deficiency, 82,* 525–534.

Richardson, S.A. (1978). Careers of mentally retarded young persons: Services, jobs, and interpersonal relations. *American Journal of Mental Deficiency, 82,* 349–358.

Ross, R.T., Begab, M., Dondis, E.H., Giampiccolo, J.S., & Meyers, C.E. (1985). *Lives of the mentally retarded.* Stanford, CA: Stanford University Press.

Seltzer, M.M. (1985). Informal supports for aging mentally retarded persons. *American Journal of Mental Retardation, 90,* 259–265.

Turner, J.L. (1983). Workshop society: Ethnographic observations in a work setting for retarded adults. In K. Kernan, M. Begab, & R. Edgerton (Eds.), *Environments and behavior: The adaptation of mentally retarded persons* (pp. 147–171). Baltimore: University Park Press.

Wehman, P., & Kregel, J. (1985). A supported work approach to competitive employment of persons with moderate and severe handicaps. *Journal of The Association for the Severely Handicapped, 10,* 3–11.

Zigler, E., Balla, D., & Hodapp, R. (1984). On the definition and classification of mental retardation. *American Journal of Mental Deficiency, 89,* 215–230.

22 | Mental Disorders and Psychopharmacology of Retarded Persons

Another Step in Seeing the Whole Person

DONALD J. COHEN
and JOEL D. BREGMAN

Mental illness is an extremely heterogeneous category that covers individuals with impairments affecting the orderly unfolding of development, the regulation and appreciation of feelings and emotions, the logical organization of thoughts, and the adaptive engagement with the social world. However defined, up to 5–10% of all school-age children of normal intelligence suffer from mental disorders. Historically, mental retardation was often included among mental disorders; more modern approaches have separated these two categories for good reasons, including to emphasize the centrality of problems in cognitive development and their various biological and social underpinnings in retardation syndromes. Although the mental versus cognitive distinction has been useful, clinicians and investigators have more recently shown how important it is to approach retarded individuals as whole people; scholars such as Edward Zigler have helped us become aware of how retarded individuals share with all humanity the pain and suffering, the vulnerability to distress, and the confusions that we associate with mental illness (Zigler & Hodapp, 1986). Moreover, the biological handicaps and life situations of retarded individuals place them at higher risk for just those problems of emotional, social, and adaptive functioning that characterize mental illness (Rutter, Graham, & Yule, 1970).

   Thus, over the last decades, we have grown to appreciate that mental illness is far more prevalent among retarded persons (Gillberg, Persson, Grufman, & Themner, 1986; Gostason, 1985; Russell, 1985), and may be a major determinant of the quality of a retarded individual's life, regardless of level of cognitive function. In addition, we also have begun to appreciate that mentally retarded individuals manifest the full spectrum of psychiatric disorders that afflict the general population, suggesting that traditional treatment interventions may produce significant improvements in the emotional and behavioral functioning of those with mental retardation and psychiatric disturbance (Eaton & Menolascino, 1982; Philips & Williams, 1975).

Three major achievements within psychiatry during the last two decades have shaped our understanding of mental illness among retarded persons: 1) multiaxial approaches to diagnosis and classification and a renewed interest in phenomenology; 2) multivariate conceptions of etiology and models of risk and preventive factors based on genetic-environmental interactions; 3) multimodal treatment approaches, including psychosocial, educational, and pharmacological methods.

DIAGNOSIS

The publication in 1980 of the third edition of the *Diagnostic and Statistical Manual of Mental Disorders* (*DSM-III*) (American Psychiatric Association, 1980) brought the multiaxial classification method into the mainstream of American psychiatric epistemology. *DSM-III* encompassed several major shifts: 1) diagnosis of a disorder, not a person; 2) use of specific, operational criteria; 3) use of multiple diagnostic categories for the same individual, to capture the extent of disturbance, rather than hoping to have one term encompass everything; and 4) the need for considering various dimensions or areas of life and experience, and not simply a category. *DSM-III* also attempted to elevate phenomenology and description, and to reduce the role of theoretical understanding, in formulating a diagnosis.

For the retarded individual, this approach has been of great importance. It has helped clinicians and investigators to look specifically at the symptoms and signs, at the behavioral problems and phenomenology, of retarded individuals and to take them seriously. Only a decade ago there was still uncertainty about whether young children could be depressed. Careful clinical studies now reveal that depression in prepubertal children can be a serious problem. Similarly, there is now no longer a question as to whether a retarded individual can suffer depression. The presence of disturbances in mood, appetite, social relations, and motivation that are characteristic of depression are diagnosed readily among retarded individuals (Kazdin, Matson, & Senatore, 1983; Sovner & Hurley, 1983), and often can be attributed to the same types of circumstances of loss and disappointment that are found in those with normal intelligence.

DSM-III's five major axes include specification of the emergent psychiatric disorder, such as depression or anxiety, on Axis I and persistent, underlying problems, such as personality and developmental problems, including retardation, on Axis II. The distinction between Axis I and Axis II was not to diminish the importance of the underlying conditions of Axis II, but to require that they be sought out, regardless of the perhaps more acute and dramatic psychiatric problems of Axis I. *DSM-III* also includes associated biological conditions on Axis III, and for retarded persons this specification is of great relevance, setting the research and clinical goals for much of clinical investigation.

Perhaps of most importance in the understanding of mental illness among retarded persons, *DSM-III* highlights the study of psychosocial stress, on Axis IV, and adaptive functioning, on Axis V, as aspects of diagnosis. Unfortunately, the metrification of stress for retarded as well as nonretarded persons is not well advanced. Yet, in recent years it has become clear that psychiatric disorder may reflect both acute stress (moves, change of caregivers, alterations in vocational setting, advancement and new responsibilities) and persistent, chronic stress (overcrowding, lack of structure, inadequate motivational supports, absence of stimulation). Assessment of mental illness in a retarded individual requires detailed concern for Axis IV issues because they proximally affect the person's daily life.

In contrast, metrification of Axis V (adaptive functioning) has progressed considerably over the past two decades. With the availability of new instruments such as the revised Vineland Adaptive Behavior Scales (Sparrow, Balla, & Cicchetti, 1984), we can specifically assess levels of adaptive functioning in developmentally meaningful ways. Thus, a person's social skills, communication competence, and daily living and motor skills can be operationally defined. Along with rigorous measurements of intellectual and language competence, Axis V thus provides the two major factors used in the definition of retardation—cognition and adaptive abilities—but has been enriched and extended to the understanding of all individuals.

This type of approach to diagnosis, emphasizing a range of possible disorders and multiple dimensions, stands alongside other approaches to diagnosis. The multiaxial categorical approach can be enriched by studies of dimensions of dysfunction, such as disturbances in relation to attention or conduct; and use of statistical clusters, as revealed by factor analytic and similar methods. Importantly, any classification scheme must relate to the broader developmental and clinical issues, in which a person's current problems are placed in the context of lifetime experiences and current life situation and understood in relation to the individual's sense of self and overall motivational and personality organization.

ETIOLOGY/PATHOGENESIS

Along with the major shifts in classification, psychiatry has expanded its range of etiology. Of special relevance to retarded individuals has been the vigorous interest in biological factors as contributing or underlying factors in mental illness, and the interactive relations between genetic or constitutional factors and environmental experiences. Rutter, Tizard, and Whitmore (1970) have demonstrated that the presence of neurological impairment is associated with an increased risk of psychopathology, regardless of intellectual level. On this basis alone, those with mental retardation would appear to be at particular risk for the development of mental illness, since approximately one-third experience abnormalities of the central nervous system.

The importance of biological factors is exemplified in mental retardation by the neuropsychiatric disorders of childhood onset, among the most common mental illnesses of retarded individuals. These disorders share major characteristics: they are of early onset, lifelong duration, and broad range of disability. Unlike many of the disorders of adulthood, where positive and negative symptoms may be relatively discrete and large areas of functioning may remain more or less intact, the neuropsychiatric disorders of childhood tend to be more diffuse and to affect multiple areas of functioning. These areas of behavioral dysfunction include attention, motor activity, cognitive processing, language development, social relations, and emotional development. The categorical diagnoses that are included among the neuropsychiatric disorders are attention deficit disorder with hyperactivity; severe developmental language disorders; chronic multiple tic syndromes; and the pervasive developmental disorders, such as autism. All of these conditions represent in large part disturbances of biological maturation—the organic substrate of competence. To a greater or lesser extent they may also be shaped by a person's experience, and to a great degree they shape the types of experiences a person will be likely to receive.

Retarded individuals are very vulnerable to these neuropsychiatric disorders (Reid, 1980; Rutter, Graham, & Yule, 1970). More than individuals with normal intellectual endowment, they are likely to have attentional and activity regulation difficulties, language disorders, and impairments in the regulation of impulsivity (Philips & Williams, 1977). Autism is particularly a disorder of retarded persons (Gillberg et al., 1986). Although autism is said to occur in 1 in 2,500 individuals, over 85% of autistic individuals are moderately retarded, and it is thus more accurate to convey the epidemiology of autism as occurring in 1:20,000 school-age children and adults with normal intellectual ability and in up to 1:80 individuals with retardation.

Autism thus may serve as a good example of the most serious neuropsychiatric disorder or pervasive developmental disorder of retarded persons. It is currently known that there are multiple possible biological pathways toward autism, including inborn errors of metabolism, malformations of brain development, infections, and toxic factors. Even for autistic individuals without specific syndromes, there are multiple indications of biological involvement. However, the majority of autistic individuals remain without a biological diagnosis that can account for their profound, lifelong disabilities, and are a challenge for future work.

Biological research on psychiatric disorders will be the only way to fundamentally alter the prognosis for the most severe conditions, such as autism. However, contemporary models of etiology also reveal the importance of environmental factors in the pathogenesis, continuation, and determination of severity of mental illness. For retarded persons in particular, environmental adversity and psychosocial factors require careful consideration in understanding mental illness. All too often, retarded individuals are placed under stresses that are not faced by individuals with normal intelligence; their resiliency and coping or defensive skills may be overburdened by situational stresses much less often faced by individuals with normal intelligence, who are more in control of their lives. Such stresses include lack of developmentally appropriate emotional or intellectual stimulation; lack of suitable attunement between the individual's needs and the provisions of the caregivers and family; regimentation and lack of individualization of experiences; disappointments in achieving the normal goals of life; lack of developmentally appropriate channels for expression of sexual and aggressive impulses; unexplained or incomprehensible and repeated changes in teachers and others with whom the person has formed attachments; alterations in life space and circumstances that are not felt to be under the individual's control; and concurrent medical illness and treatment regimens whose purpose cannot be understood. Retarded individuals also have to cope with burdens placed by sensory and motor handicaps and seizure disorders, all of which are deeply stressful, even when more easily understood.

For retarded persons, therefore, it is particularly suitable to use multivariate approaches to etiology—to attempt to integrate underlying vulnerabilities and life experiences, and how they interact, in understanding a current disorder.

TREATMENT

The opening of psychiatric thinking to diversity in relation to diagnosis and etiology has been accompanied by increasing diversity in treatment approaches. The psychiatric treatment armamentarium includes individual psychotherapy, approached from various points of view; behavior modification; group therapies; and various types of activity and psychosocial milieu approaches (Herson, Van Hasselt, & Matson, 1983; Matson & Andrasik, 1983; Sigman, 1985; Stavrakaki & Klein, 1986). Regrettably, these modalities have not been as available or as rigorously studied as they should be with respect to retarded persons. Often, retarded individuals are not included in scientific studies, whose entry criteria specifically may exclude them, and from the educational experiences of psychiatrists in training, who may then be uncomfortable in later extending their knowledge to such individuals.

Of all treatment approaches, the use of medication for mental illnesses has been most dramatically expanded during the past decades, and has most dramatically altered the functioning of individuals with various disorders. There is virtually no dispute about the profound value of psychopharmacological approaches with disorders such as schizophrenia, manic-depressive illness, major depressions, and various anxiety and tic disorders. The use of stimulant medications for hyperactive, inattentive children; lithium for manic-depression; tricyclic antidepressants for depressed children and adults; benzodiazepines for panic and other anxiety disorders; and neuroleptics for individuals suffering from schizophrenia are as well recognized as any drug treatments in general medicine.

Epidemiological research indicates that an appreciable percentage of mentally retarded persons receive some type of psychotropic medication—approximately 40%–50% of those residing in institutions and 20%–30% of those residing in the community (Lipman, 1970). Yet, the use of psychoactive medication among retarded persons has not been without controversy surrounding appropriate use and potential abuse. This controversy, all too familiar to anyone working in the field, has prejudiced the use of medications. Without doubt, retarded and nonretarded individuals have been treated with psychoactive medications inappropriately, and any discussion of drugs must acknowledge this background of concern. Yet, for today, it is as relevant to emphasize the potential benefit of medication and the danger of inappropriate abstention from psychopharmacological approaches. Preliminary studies with mentally retarded patients, for instance, have indicated that neuroleptics are efficacious for those with schizophrenia (Menolascino, Wilson, Golden, & Ruedrich, 1986; Reid, 1972) and pervasive developmental disorders (Campbell, Anderson, Meier, Cohen, & Small, 1978; Campbell et al., 1982; Mikkelsen, 1982); stimulants for those with attention deficit disorders (Gadow, 1985); and lithium carbonate for those with bipolar affective disorders (Naylor, Donald, Le Poidevin, & Reid, 1974; Rivinus & Harmatz, 1979).

Issues in the Use of Psychopharmacology

In light of the apparent efficacy of medications, three issues surrounding the use of psychopharmacological treatment with retarded persons warrant consideration.

First, such treatment rests upon careful assessment and multiaxial diagnosis firmly embedded in a clinical formulation. In this process of diagnosis, the individual's current problems and clinical disorder are contextualized, and related to past experiences, current life situation, and long-term potential.

Second, pharmacological treatment is only one aspect of psychiatric care when a diagnosis is made. All too often, the call for a physician and medication occurs as a last, desperate hope—"after everything else has been tried." When physicians allow themselves to enter into the care of a patient in this way, they are courting trouble; medication will take on the tone of being aversive and the physician's involvement, and the drug, will be conceptualized as extraneous to full programming. Instead, psychiatric concern must be thoroughly integrated in thinking about the lives of retarded persons, and in the process of considering all factors that may be related to emotional or behavioral dysfunction. When mental illness appears, as it will for 30%–40% of retarded individuals, the psychiatric perspective involves thinking about all possible etiologies and approaches to care. Medication thus is part of caring, not an announcement of its failure.

Third, when pharmacological treatment is initiated, it is a dynamic process. Drugs will affect various aspects of behavioral and emotional functioning, and these changes will affect the individual's experience, and so on. The goal of such treatment is to restabilize and facilitate functioning, and careful assessment of the medication's role is needed, along with assessment of the entire life situation. In addition to looking for side-effects and behavioral toxicity, clinical concern requires assessment of the continued need for medication, possible changes in dosage, and relations between medication and other treatments and aspects of the person's vocational and life space.

Barriers to Psychopharmacology

Today, there are barriers—institutional, cultural, disciplinary, even legal—to the easy integration of psychiatric care and psychopharmacology in relation to the mental disorders of retarded persons. Such barriers need to be recognized. They include the continued prejudice that retarded individuals cannot or do not suffer from emotional disorders. Occasionally, one will see a quite severely depressed adult with retardation whose sadness, irritability, tearfulness, anorexia, and insomnia call out for care; if the person were able to speak for himself or herself, his or her internist would have been securing a psychiatric consultation months before. In a group home, the staff may try to cheer the person up with little activities or be perplexed about and angry at his or her lack of interest in self-care. That he or she is depressed—perhaps because of the loss of a friend who was close, perhaps because the move to a nicer home has disrupted his or her connections and associations—will not be taken seriously. Such infantilization and denial of emotional lives may be encouraged by institutional barriers to the use of medication. In other situations, the social phobia and anxiety of an adolescent who is retarded, the panic of a 30-year-old retarded man, or the schizophrenic episode in a young adult may be overlooked or undiagnosed (Matson, 1981; Menolascino et al., 1986). However, one must remember that the probable overuse of psychopharmacology in relation to aggression, self-abuse, and conduct problems has tended to deemphasize the importance of the careful search for environmental triggers to pathology and ameliorating environmental approaches to treatment.

TRENDS AND NEEDS FOR THE FUTURE

Today, we are in a position to reconsider the role of medication in a thoughtful fashion, as one aspect of caring, and to reassess the overuse in certain situations, the dangers of prolonged use, and the various factors that have led to depriving retarded individuals of the highest quality treatment of which we are capable. During the next years, there will be increasing availability of specific pharmacological approaches to mental illness. Drugs are already available, and others in development, that are active at specific neuronal systems and whose mode of action will be better defined. Neurochemical and neuroradiological approaches will provide clinicians with biological data to guide treatment. Advances in neuropsychopharmacology may have potentially great impact on the mental illnesses of retarded persons, and thus on their access to educational and vocational resources and an improved quality of life. Among retarded individuals, clinical investigators and clinicians may find the most dramatic examples of the genetic-environmental interactions and multivariate approaches to etiology.

However, to provide retarded individuals with the benefits of advances in this field, barriers will have to be understood and overcome. Advocates and clinicians concerned with retarded persons will need to redress the balance between protecting them from abuse by psychiatric drugs and encouraging the clinically competent psychiatric care of retarded individuals, including the use of medications. So long as medication is listed among aversive treatments, for example, few physicians will be encouraged to think about psychopharmacological treatment of retarded persons as they do for those in other situations. During their training and in other aspects of their careers, psychiatrists and other physicians involved with psychopharmacology will need to be brought into active clinical work with retarded persons. In research studies, retarded individuals need to be included among the samples studied, so that more can be learned about what is best for them; being protected from research is, in this sense, being deprived of the benefits of research. Epidemiological, diagnostic, phenomenological, and pharmacological research programs are required to better understand the mental disorders of retarded persons, and such work needs to be sensitively attuned to the ecology of their lives.

To see retarded individuals as whole people is to see their functioning as the result of many complex factors—biological and experiential—and to avoid ascribing all aspects of their lives to a single, cognitive variable. To be a whole person, also, is to be vulnerable. The last decades have brought the recognition that because of both their constitution and their life experiences, retarded persons are vulnerable to mental illness to a greater extent than nonretarded persons. No more than for the mental illness of normally intelligent individuals can we hope that mental illness of retarded persons will respond to what is currently available as treatment; decades of systematic research will be needed. Nor will the retarded person's mental illness respond to the well-meaning interventions of ordinary life, the ministrations of parents and caregivers. Love may not be enough. Mental illness will not go away with simple changes in the environment, jollying-up, bullying, or persuasion. It will not go away by mandate or regulation, as important as advocacy may be to protecting retarded individuals from abuse. Instead, seeing retarded individuals as whole people means granting them the right to having mental illness and the rights for careful study and treatment.

Thus, among the highest priorities for the future must be the encouragement of clinical researchers and advocates to move the issues of mental illness of retarded persons into full public and professional awareness. Systematic research on mental illness, from which retarded persons are not excluded, and education of all involved with retardation about mental illness will be essential to improving the quality of the lives of a large number of retarded individuals.

REFERENCES

American Psychiatric Association. (1980) *Diagnostic and statistical manual of mental disorders* (3rd ed.). Washington, DC: Author.

Campbell, M., Anderson, L.T., Cohen, I., Perry, R., Small, A., Green, W., Anderson, L., & McCandless, W. (1982). Haloperidol in autistic children: Effects on learning, behavior, and abnormal involuntary movements. *Psychopharmacology Bulletin, 18,* 110–111.

Campbell, M., Anderson, L., Meier, M., Cohen, I., & Small, A. (1978). A comparison of haloperidol and behavior therapy and their interaction in autistic children. *Journal of the American Academy of Child Psychiatry, 7,* 640–655.

Eaton, L., & Menolascino, F. (1982). Psychiatric disorders in the mentally retarded: Types, problems, and challenges. *American Journal of Psychiatry, 139,* 1297–1303.

Gadow, K. (1985). Prevalence and efficacy of stimulant drug use with mentally retarded children and youth. *Psychopharmacology Bulletin, 21,* 291–301.

Gillberg, C., Persson, E., Grufman, M. & Themner, U. (1986). Psychiatric disorders in mildly and severely mentally retarded urban children and adolescents: Epidemiological aspects. *British Journal of Psychiatry, 149,* 68–74.

Gostason, R. (1985). Psychiatric illness among the mentally retarded. A Swedish population study. *Acta Psychiatrica Scandinavica, 71*(suppl 318), 1–117.

Herson, M., Van Hasselt, V., & Matson, J. (Eds.). (1983). *Behavior therapy for the developmentally and physically disabled.* New York: Academic Press.

Kazdin, A., Matson, J., & Senatore, V. (1983). Assessment of depression in mentally retarded adults. *American Journal of Psychiatry, 140,* 1040–1043.

Lipman, R. (1970). The use of psychopharmacological agents in residential facilities for the retarded. In F. Menolascino (Ed.), *Psychiatric approach to mental retardation* (pp. 387–398). New York: Basic Books.

Matson, J. (1981). Assessment and treatment of clinical phobias in mentally retarded children. *Journal of Applied Behavior Analysis, 14,* 287–294.

Matson, J., & Andrasik, F. (Eds.). (1983). *Treatment issues and innovations in mental retardation.* New York: Plenum Press.

Menolascino, F., Wilson, J., Golden, C., & Ruedrich, S. (1986). Medication and treatment of schizophrenia in persons with mental retardation. *Mental Retardation, 24,* 277-n283.

Mikkelsen, E. (1982). Efficacy of neuroleptic medication in pervasive developmental disorders of childhood. *Schizophrenia Bulletin, 8,* 320–332.

Naylor, G., Donald, J., Le Poidevin, D., & Reid, A. (1974). A double-blind trial of long term lithium therapy in mental defectives. *British Journal of Psychiatry, 124*, 52–57.

Philips, I., & Williams, N. (1975). Psychopathology and mental retardation: A study of 100 mentally retarded children: I. Psychopathology. *American Journal of Psychiatry, 132*, 1265–1271.

Philips, I., & Williams, N. (1977). Psychopathology and mental retardation: A statistical study of 100 mentally retarded children treated at a psychiatric clinic: II. Hyperactivity. *American Journal of Psychiatry, 134*, 418–420.

Reid, A. (1972). Psychoses in adult mental defectives: II. Schizophrenic and paranoid psychoses. *British Journal of Psychiatry, 120*, 213–218.

Reid, A. (1980). Psychiatric disorders in mentally handicapped children: A clinical and follow-up study. *Journal of Mental Deficiency Research, 24*, 287–298.

Rivinus, T., & Harmatz, J. (1979). Diagnosis and lithium treatment of affective disorder in the retarded: Five case studies. *American Journal of Psychiatry, 136*, 551–554.

Russell, A. (1985). The mentally retarded, emotionally disturbed child and adolescent. In M. Sigman (Ed.), *Children with emotional disorders and developmental disabilities: Assessment and treatment* (pp. 111–135). Orlando, FL: Grune & Stratton.

Rutter, M., Graham, P., & Yule, W. (1970). *A neuropsychiatric study of childhood (Clinics in Developmental Medicine, No. 35/36)*. London: Heineman.

Rutter, M., Tizard, J., & Whitmore, K. (Eds.). (1970). *Education, health, and behaviour*. London: Longman.

Sigman, M. (1985). Individual and group psychotherapy with mentally retarded adolescents. In M. Sigman (Ed.), *Children with emotional disorders and developmental disabilities: Assessment and treatment* (pp. 259–276). Orlando, FL: Grune & Stratton.

Sovner, R., & Hurley, A. (1983). Do the mentally retarded suffer from affective illness? *Archives of General Psychiatry, 40*, 61–67.

Sparrow, S., Balla, D., & Cicchetti, D. (1984). *Vineland Adaptive Behavior Scales*. Circle Pines, MN: American Guidance Service.

Stavrakaki, C., & Klein, J. (1986). Psychotherapies with the mentally retarded. *Psychiatric Clinics of North America, 9*, 733–743.

Zigler, E., & Hodapp, R.M. (Eds.). (1986). *Understanding mental retardation*. Cambridge, England: Cambridge University Press.

23 | Long-Term Care Issues in Mental Retardation
MARTY WYNGAARDEN KRAUSS

Long-term care is defined as "the financing, organization and delivery of a wide range of medical and human services to a class of people who are severely disabled and limited in their functional capacities for a relatively long and indefinite period of time" (Callahan & Wallack, 1981, p. 3). The services typically included under the rubric of long-term care are health, residential, day, and social support services.

Although mentally retarded persons of all ages receive long-term care services, the focus of this chapter is on the old or elderly population. Elderly mentally retarded persons are currently enjoying a somewhat privileged status among policymakers, planners, and researchers. We are now acknowledging, somewhat belatedly, that the absolute number of mentally retarded persons aged 55 or over is large and that the numbers are getting larger. Indeed, it is expected that by the year 2020 the size of the general elderly population will double, with a comparable trend for mentally retarded elders (Rice & Feldman, 1985). There is a substantial amount of activity across the country within state mental retardation agencies to *count* aging and aged heads and to *assess* current service patterns. Task forces are being established, special studies are being funded, and new program models or variants are being demonstrated (Janicki, Knox, & Jacobson, 1985).

If one looks critically at information on the number of elderly mentally retarded persons currently served in mental retardation service systems, or at information on their functional characteristics, or at programs in which their observed or inferred needs have served to define program structure, two conclusions are easily reached. First, they are a heterogeneous group of individuals. The range of individual differences among those in their elder years is as impressive as are the differences among younger mentally retarded persons (Janicki & MacEachron, 1984; Krauss & Seltzer, 1986). Second, existing program options may be totally inadequate for the absolute size of this group and for their very diverse needs.

A major concern for policy analysts, planners, and researchers are those elderly mentally retarded persons who are not yet known to the formal service system but who will, in all likelihood, present themselves or be presented for services when a crisis in their current support system occurs. The evidence suggests that this unserved population is at least as large as the number of served elderly mentally retarded persons, and that current resources and program models may not be flexible enough to accommodate their needs. This chapter will briefly address three questions for which there *should* be good empirical answers, but for which there are only tentative findings. This will be followed by a discussion of some areas in which more planning and research is needed to both extend the knowledge base and broaden the scope of policy options in designing a long-term care system responsive to mentally retarded individuals and their families.

QUESTIONS IN NEED OF ANSWERS

What Is the Size of the Elderly Mentally Retarded Population?

Definitionally, the most common chronological demarcation used for identifying this group is age 55, although there is considerable variability on this issue in the literature (M.M. Seltzer & Krauss, 1987).

Using a 1% prevalence rate for mental retardation, it can be estimated that in 1982 there were approximately 490,000 mentally retarded persons age 55 and over. However, estimates based on the served or known mentally retarded population yield less than half of this figure, typically about 200,000 persons (Janicki et al., 1985). Thus, only about 40% of the expected *number* of elderly mentally retarded persons are currently known to the mental retardation service network. Although some in this group may well be receiving services from the aging network of services, the evidence is that this number is miniscule. Obviously, more precise epidemiological studies are needed to provide better estimates of the absolute number of elderly mentally retarded persons, and more research needs to be launched regarding the service patterns of these individuals.

What Is Known about the Functional Characteristics of the Elderly Mentally Retarded Population?

It bears noting that the results described here are not necessarily generalizable to those elders who are not known to the service system and who are consequently not included in analyses based on state registries. With this caveat in mind, there are some important research findings on the functional status of elders with mental retardation.

The evidence derived from the general elderly population is that advancing age is correlated with decrements in health and functional abilities and with more limited family supports. Cross-sectional studies in the field of mental retardation have noted consistent age-related differences among elderly mentally retarded persons in various residential settings (Janicki & MacEachron, 1984; M.M. Seltzer, Seltzer, & Sherwood, 1982). However, other studies have found that, with important exceptions for particular subgroups, older persons with mental retardation function at a significantly higher level than their younger counterparts. For example, Marsha Seltzer and I compared persons ages 22 to 54 with those age 55 and over who were receiving state-supported services in Massachusetts (Krauss & Seltzer, 1986). We found that elderly mentally retarded persons in both institutional and community-based settings were *less impaired* than their younger adult counterparts in functional and cognitive abilities, and in medical needs.

Similarly, Bruininks and his colleagues at the University of Minnesota reported that almost two thirds of persons age 62 or over living in community-based residences and over a quarter (28.9%) of those living in institutional settings were able to care for themselves relatively independently with only minimal staff assistance (Hauber, Rotegard, & Bruininks, 1985). Compared to younger persons living in these settings, the older cohort consistently demonstrated greater levels of functional and behavioral independence. Bruininks's research also found that among older cohorts living in community-based settings, two thirds (68.8%) of those age 62 and over had no chronic health disorders.

There are two plausible explanations for these unanticipated findings. First, the elderly cohort includes persons who would not today be labeled mentally retarded—persons previously labeled borderline retarded. Second, the younger cohort receiving services includes a disproportionate number of severely and profoundly retarded persons who are unlikely to live to old age and who are not represented in the older cohort. The importance of these findings is that there is a large group of older retarded persons who function at a comparatively high level, and whose capacities to engage in social and domestic activities are not rated as major impediments despite their advancing age.

What Is Known about Current Service Delivery Mechanisms for This Older Population?

There are three general service strategies for elderly mentally retarded persons (M.M. Seltzer & Krauss, 1987):

1. To include elderly mentally retarded persons in programs for younger retarded adults (called the *age-integrated option*).
2. To include elderly mentally retarded persons in programs for nonhandicapped elderly persons (called the *generic services integration option*).
3. To develop specialized programs for elderly mentally retarded persons (called the *specialized service option*).

By far the most common approach identified in the research and practice literature is the age-integrated option. Bruininks and his colleagues (Hauber et al., 1985) reported that in 1982 almost a quarter (23.3%) of the persons in residential facilities for retarded persons were ages 40–62 and another 5% were age 63 or older. They also reported an almost 4% increase between 1978 and 1983 in the percentage of residents between the ages of 40 and 62. These data suggest that residents are "aging in place."

The facilities with the highest percentage of residents in the 62 and older category were the personal care homes (17% of residents in this age category), followed by boarding homes (15.3%). Interestingly, these two types of facilities are characterized by the minimal amount of supervision and training provided.

The second option, the generic services integration option, is probably the least common option for a mentally retarded person's *day* program but among the most common options for *residential* programs. With respect to residential services, a commonly utilized "generic" service program is the nursing home that serves both retarded and elderly persons. Data from the 1977 National Nursing Home Survey indicated that approximately 42,000 persons whose primary diagnosis was mental retardation lived in nursing homes (Lakin, 1985). Over half of these residents were age 55 or older. Although studies (G. Seltzer & Wells, 1986; M.M. Seltzer & Krauss, 1987) indicate that there are generic senior citizen programs that accept mentally retarded clients, and indeed have positive experiences to report, the absolute number of mentally retarded persons involved in such programs is very small.

The third service option, specialized programs for mentally retarded elders, is capturing considerable attention among researchers, planners, and program developers. The National Survey of Programs Serving Elderly Mentally Retarded Persons (M.M. Seltzer & Krauss, 1987) located 202 institutionally based programs and 327 community-based programs in which at least 50% of the mentally retarded participants were age 55 or above. Considerable diversity was found among programs with respect to client characteristics, program structure, content, staffing, and organizational auspices. Despite the laudable innovation evident in these programs, they serve a relatively small percentage of the elderly mentally retarded population.

One could add a fourth service option to the three described above. Many mentally retarded persons continue to live with their natural family throughout their lives (M.M. Seltzer, 1985) or, as studies by Edgerton, Bollinger, and Herr (1984) and Zetlin (1986) describe, to live somewhat independently with considerable assistance from family members such as siblings, parents, or other relatives. Although there are few good data sets on the prevalence of lifelong family care, consider the findings from Meyers, Borthwick, and Eyman (1985) in their analysis of mentally retarded persons known to the California state system. They found that over half (52.2%) of the approximately 59,000 mentally retarded persons receiving some services lived in their natural family home. This proportion varied with ethnicity, severity of retardation, and age of the person. However, at age 55, about one quarter of all mildly retarded persons, one fifth of moderately retarded persons, 8% of severely retarded persons, and about 3% of profoundly retarded persons were still living with their natural family. Other studies indicate that about 13% of those retarded persons between the ages of 55 and 64 in Massachusetts and 10% of those in New York live with their natural family (Jacobson, Sutton, & Janicki, 1985). Furthermore, data showed that elders living with their family were more capable in terms of adaptive, motor, emotional, cognitive, and social skills than were elders living in other types of residential settings (Jacobson et al., 1985).

PROPOSALS FOR PLANNING AND RESEARCH

What do these findings with respect to the size of the elderly mentally retarded population, their functional characteristics, and the current service options suggest for the future? In the author's view, two major points warrant discussion and further investigation.

First, the evidence suggests that there are at least an equal number of elderly mentally retarded persons who are not known to the mental retardation service network as there are individuals who are served by these systems. These "unknown" people may be living with family members, residing in residential settings outside the purview of the mental retardation services network, or living independently with no formal contact with the service sector. However, virtually nothing is known about the characteristics, needs, and functional status of these unserved or underserved persons. This is an area in which considerable research needs to be done. Studies of the strength and durability of the informal support systems of elders, particularly those living with relatives or friends, will be very important to the development of sound long-term care policy (M.M. Seltzer, 1985).

Second, a serious and open-minded look needs to be given to the range of program options supported by public and private sector funds. The current community system is based on the principle of dispersion. It is structured so that mentally retarded persons, as do nonhandicapped persons, access residential, health, social, and day services from many different service providers. This structural feature was intentionally designed to prevent any one service sector from exercising total control over mentally retarded persons, as was and is typically true in institutional settings. One acknowledged result of this feature, however, is the ongoing challenge of coordinating various service providers to meet clients' needs.

Studies in gerontology have demonstrated that a substantial number of elders prefer to live in age-segregated settings in which there is a concentration of needed services (Huttman, 1985). These settings—such as life care communities and congregate care settings—typically provide a wide range of services to residents within a single location. The National Survey mentioned above (M.M. Seltzer & Krauss, 1987) uncovered scores of age-segregated residential programs; however, the extent to which these programs provided comprehensive care within a single site varied considerably. Most continued to rely on externally based day programs and health care services for their clients, and many elders living within these settings continued to attend traditional, age-integrated day programs that were not specially geared for a geriatric population.

Obviously, the results of many studies have indicated that not all persons with mental retardation who are over 55 need or want to "retire" from traditional day programs or move to age-segregated housing. However, we have been sluggish in developing comprehensive care systems that are particularly suited for mentally retarded elders whose needs increasingly reflect the impacts of aging. We need to evaluate the types of innovative care models being developed to meet the long-term care needs of the general elderly population and draw from these models those components that are transferable to this group.

Two recent long-term care innovations are particularly interesting for the population with mental retardation. The first is called the social/health maintenance organization (S/HMO). As Greenberg and Leutz (1984) described, this model "attempts to extend the HMO acute-care model of case management and capitation to encompass long-term care" (p. 57). The model is based on three concepts: 1) the acute and chronic care systems should be *integrated* into a single system, 2) the care of the individual should be *managed* across the system, and 3) providers should work in the context of *controls and/or incentives* to be efficient in their use of limited resources. The applicability of this model to mentally retarded persons of all ages, but particularly for those in their middle-age adult years who will be the next and larger generation of elders, deserves consideration. The S/HMO may well ensure the type of coordinated, long-term health and therapeutic services that are so often lacking in today's delivery system and that have been implicated in precipitous moves of elders from their current residential settings to nursing home facilities.

The second service innovation for the general elderly population is the life care community or continuing care retirement community. These communities "attempt to combine residential retirement living with the availability of health care services" (Pies, 1984, p. 41).

These communities, generally associated with elders of considerable means, offer a prototype for consideration in the field of mental retardation. They are designed to support the elder's ability to live independently with the assured backup of skilled nursing and medical services should they be necessary. There *are* a handful of facilities currently serving mentally retarded persons that could be roughly categorized as life care communities (M.M. Seltzer & Krauss, 1987). These programs warrant more research to determine their impacts on the resident's quality of life and appropriateness of services.

CONCLUSIONS

There are three central challenges for researchers, policymakers, and practitioners in the immediate future with respect to elderly persons with mental retardation. First, consensus must be achieved regarding the chronological demarcation by which to define "elderly" and to study the prevalence and characteristics of the elderly mentally retarded population. Specifically, longitudinal studies are needed to track the aging process among this group and to distinguish significant cohort effects from individual differences.

Second, the relationship between different environmental structures, contexts, and service models in relation to client outcomes must be carefully examined. This area of research will require what Landesman (Landesman, 1986; Landesman-Dwyer, 1985) has been consistently advocating for a number of years, a more rigorous taxonomy of environments. However, it will also require that the goals, or the desired client outcomes, be defined. Client outcomes relevant for elders with mental retardation are very likely to be different than those identified for younger retarded persons.

Third, researchers in the field of mental retardation will have to join with others in the long-term care policy field in designing new models of service that effectively couple financing structures with service structures. The fragmentation between funding and services that has characterized the community-based system will be increasingly dysfunctional for older persons with retardation. Innovative experiments are being tested for the frail elderly (such as S/HMOs) and for the nonfrail elderly (such as life care communities). A similar spirit of innovation and experimentation is needed in order to broaden the range of options for mentally retarded persons.

REFERENCES

Callahan, J., & Wallack, S. (Eds.). (1981). *Reforming the long-term care system.* Lexington, MA: Lexington Books.

Edgerton, R.B., Bollinger, M., & Herr, B. (1984). The cloak of competence: After two decades. *American Journal of Mental Deficiency, 88*, 345–351.

Greenberg, J., & Leutz, W. (1984). The social/health maintenance organization and its role in reforming the long-term care system. In P. Feinstein, M. Gornick, & J. Greenberg (Eds.), *Long-term care financing and delivery systems: Exploring some alternatives* (HCFA Pub. No. 03174). Washington, DC: U.S. Department of Health and Human Services.

Hauber, F.A., Rotegard, L.L., & Bruininks, R. (1985). Characteristics of residential services for older/elderly mentally retarded people. In M.P. Janicki & H. Wisniewski (Eds.), *Aging and developmental disabilities* (pp. 327–350). Baltimore: Paul H. Brookes Publishing Co.

Huttman, E.D. (1985). *Social services for the elderly.* New York: The Free Press.

Jacobson, J., Sutton, M.S., & Janicki, M. (1985). Demography and characteristics of aging and aged mentally retarded persons. In M.P. Janicki & H.M. Wisniewski (Eds.) *Aging and developmental disabilities* (pp. 115–142). Baltimore: Paul H. Brookes Publishing Co.

Janicki, M., Knox, L.A., & Jacobson, J. (1985). Planning for an older developmentally disabled population. In M.P. Janicki & H. Wisniewski (Eds.), *Aging and developmental disabilities* (pp. 143–160). Baltimore: Paul H. Brookes Publishing Co.

Janicki, M., & MacEachron, A.E. (1984). Residential, health, and social service needs of elderly developmentally disabled persons. *The Gerontologist, 24*, 28–37.

Krauss, M.W., & Seltzer, M.M. (1986). Comparison of elderly and adult mentally retarded persons in community and institutional settings. *American Journal of Mental Deficiency, 91*, 237–243.

Lakin, K.C. (1985). *Estimated mentally retarded population in nursing homes according to the National Nursing Home Survey of 1977* (Brief No. 26). Minneapolis: Department of Educational Psychology.

Landesman, S. (1986). Toward a taxonomy of home environments. In N.R.

Ellis & N.W. Bray (Eds.), *International review of research in mental retardation* (Vol. 14, pp. 259–289). New York: Academic Press.

Landesman-Dwyer, S. (1985). Describing and evaluating residential environments. In R.H. Bruininks & K.C. Lakin (Eds.), *Living and learning in the least restrictive environment.* Baltimore: Paul H. Brookes Publishing Co.

Meyers, C.E., Borthwick, S.A., & Eyman, R. (1985). Place of residence by age, ethnicity, and level of retardation of the mentally retarded/developmentally disabled population of California. *American Journal of Mental Deficiency, 90,* 266–270.

Pies, H.E. (1984). Life care communities for the aged—an overview. In P. Feinstein, M. Gornick, & J. Greenberg (Eds.), *Long-term care financing and delivery systems: Exploring some alternatives* (HCFA Pub. No. 03174). Washington, DC: U.S. Department of Health and Human Services.

Rice, D.P., & Feldman, J.J. (1985). Living longer in the United States: Demographic changes and health needs of the elderly. In M.P. Janicki & H.M. Wisniewski (Eds.) *Aging and developmental disabilities: Issues and approaches* (pp. 9–26). Baltimore: Paul H. Brookes Publishing Co.

Seltzer, G., & Wells, A. (1986). *Generic day programs for seniors: An untapped resource?* Paper presented at the 110th annual meeting of the American Association on Mental Deficiency, Denver, CO.

Seltzer, M.M. (1985). Informal supports for aging mentally retarded persons. *American Journal of Mental Deficiency, 90,* 259–265.

Seltzer, M.M., & Krauss, M.W. (1987). *Aging and mental retardation: Extending the continuum* (Monograph No. 9). Washington, DC: American Association on Mental Retardation.

Seltzer, M.M., Seltzer, G.B., & Sherwood, C.C. (1982). Comparison of community adjustment of older versus younger mentally retarded adults. *American Journal of Mental Deficiency, 87,* 9–13.

Zetlin, A. (1986). Mentally retarded adults and their siblings. *American Journal of Mental Deficiency, 91,* 217–225.

24 | Applications of Research in Programs for Aging Mentally Retarded Persons

MARY C. HOWELL

The author is the director of a small project established and funded by the Kennedy Foundation and the Department of Mental Health of the Commonwealth of Massachusetts to teach health professionals about the problems and care of persons who are both mentally retarded and elderly. This teaching occurs in a context of provision of clinical services. Health is defined broadly, to include a range of concerns: medicine and nursing, of course, but also social work, clinical psychology, the law, leisure activities and sports, and ministry.

Work such as that of this project is founded on the demographic and service surveys described in the preceding chapters in this section (e.g., Janicki & MacEachron, 1984; Krauss & Seltzer, 1986). Their careful and sophisticated analyses help those working in the project to fine-tune their clinical work. Also, Leventhal and Schaefer (in preparation) and others have found that with advancing patient age the distinction between those with Down syndrome and those without Down syndrome is of central importance. Down syndrome significantly affects the pace of physiological aging, the risk of dementia, and withdrawal from social intercourse.

In general, however, those persons with mental retardation who live into old age are quite healthy and sturdy. They are indeed survivors. Their problems of medical care are for the most part problems of access, for they tend to be not much valued as individuals by generic service providers. Nor do community physicians feel that they are adequately rewarded by Medicaid for provision of service to this group of patients.

There is, it is true, a small proportion of adults with mental retardation (and an even smaller proportion of those with mental retardation who live into old age) who have complex problems requiring sensitive and attentive medical management. An example is seizures that are intractable to ordinary measures of anticonvulsant medications. Too little primary care may be given in the community setting by providers who are not willing to take time to listen, and to perform examinations and medical procedures at a slow enough pace and with enough explanation to elicit maximal understanding and cooperation from the patient.

RESEARCH AREAS USEFUL IN CLINICAL CARE

Having said that the medical problems are the least of the worries of these clients, the author hastens to say that their problems of health *in a broad sense* are many and complex. This can be illustrated by citing five lines of research that have been useful to the project in the provision of clinical care. These are not the only research studies that are relevant, nor are they necessarily the most important. They have been chosen simply to give a sequencing of problems.

Family Relationships

First, there are studies on family relationships. For instance, Heller and Factor (1986) and Lutzer and Brubaker (in press) have learned that in families with a mentally retarded adult who is growing older as the parents and siblings themselves grow older, it is extraordinarily difficult to make and put into action workable plans for care of the child or sibling who is retarded.

What would these parents, who have taken care of their retarded child for so many years, like to see happen to the child? One of the investigators told the author that what they really want is some kind of fictional resolution in which, minutes before the parent dies, the child dies of some natural cause. The parents cannot imagine the child being able to go on and be well cared for after they are dead.

The author and her colleagues find this also in their clinical work. Families come complaining that things are not working well at home, the parents are getting older, the retarded family member is having difficulties with workshop, with friends, with behavior problems— and when the suggestion is made that they could look at a variety of alternative options, the family says, "No, none of that will work." Obviously, they have a need to go on just as they have been doing.

One of the devices that has been successfully used is to offer some legal services, for instance estate planning and will writing, which often help the family begin to think and talk about issues involved with death and dying, their own and also that of the retarded family member. Staff members must stay in touch with families over long months and keep checking back with them; ultimately they may be willing to look at a few community residences as possibilities for their retarded child.

Deterioration of Client Behavior

Another frequent problem is related to deterioration of the client's behavior, either actual or anticipated. A common scenario is that a bed in a group home is needed, or a place in a workshop is needed, and the client *begins* to show some small behavior change. Then the caregivers, or administrators (perhaps the area office), begin to ask "Are these the first signs of Alzheimer's disease?" or "Is this patient becoming demented?" The underlying questions are "Is this hopeless? Should we transfer this patient out of the group home? Should we transfer this client out of the workshop?" Workshop places and beds in group homes are in short supply, so those are momentous questions. Transfer may mean moving to a nursing home.

As in the work of Harper and Wadsworth (1986), the author and her colleagues have focused on the clients' learning capacity as a critical marker of the difference between dementia and other kinds of maladaptive behavior. For instance, the client may be grieving because of the death or absence of a parent or sibling or a staff member or a friend. The client might be mourning some changes in residence or workshop. The client might be showing a behavioral reaction to physical changes, such as a decrease in exercise tolerance, an increase in arthritic pain, or a decrease in sensory acuity. The client may be attention-seeking as staff attention shifts to other clients, or as family attention shifts to other family members. In fact, more often than not the client is not showing early signs of dementia but is having other kinds of behavior problems. The ability to learn, as revealed by both clinical psychological testing and careful history-taking, and particularly the maintenance of short-term memory function, seems to be a key to the possibility of shaping behavior to more adequate adaptive behavior forms. Therefore, the ability to learn is key to the client's being able to continue on in the same residence and the same work situation.

Translocation Trauma

It is known from the work of Heller and Factor (1986) and others that changes in residence, workshop, or caregiving staff can be very deleterious to the maintenance of function in people who are retarded and also old. Benz' (1986) study emphasized that with increasing age the client's greatest worries are "Who is going to take care of me as I get older? What is going to happen to the people who are now taking care of me? Am I going to have to move from where I am now living? Where am I going to be able to find care as I get older and less able to function on my own?"

Maintenance of Function

There is a line of research, primarily in the gerontology literature (e.g., Granger, Seltzer, & Fishbein, 1987) on maintenance of function. This is a major problem for clients with mental retardation who are also old. Medicaid regulations require that patients receiving services at home continue to improve. It is sometimes difficult to focus on maintenance of function in old age, and especially in frail old age, when the language of the individual service plan relates to learning new skills. Such constructs do not allow a focus on maintaining function at its present level: maintenance of physical function, which primarily means continuing to walk; maintenance of cognitive function, which means continuing to have access to stimulating and interesting experiences; maintenance of social function, which means continuing to be in contact with people who can be friends and with whom one can have an interpersonal exchange; and also maintenance of spiritual function. (In the author's program an assessment of the client's spiritual life is always made and the program works with community churches to help them welcome these clients more into the life of the church.)

Learned Helplessness

Edgerton (1986) wrote that a concomitant of being subject to public service systems is a demand for dependency. The preliminary results of some of the most recent work from Anderson, Bruininks, and Hill (1987) show that among clients living in foster homes, those in homes where there is the least cost of care, the least formal programming, and the lowest educational level of the caregiver have the best integration of community life. This gives one pause for consideration. The idea that less money should be spent on the provision of services to clients who are old and retarded should not be promoted, but perhaps some kind of a voucher system that allows clients to purchase services might be more helpful than giving the money directly to professionals.

PROPOSALS FOR FUTURE RESEARCH

From the perspective of clinical care, there are three lines of research that need to be pursued. First, models of assessment techniques must be developed for provision of care that emphasizes autonomy and self-esteem, without imposing undue dependency or a learned helplessness. This relates to the consideration of whether the care needs to be less professionalized, rather than more.

Secondly, there must be a sophisticated analysis of work. More weight and value must be given to activities that are generally productive, for instance, washing windows. Such work is very productive, can serve as a source of self-esteem and social interaction, and can be rewarded in the fashion in which society usually rewards work, by appropriate amounts of money. Clients in the author's program who are old and retarded want to work. They do not want to retire. Those who say they would like to retire frequently mean that they would like to retire to more interesting jobs rather than stop working. A very close look must be taken at what is meant by "work" in this society.

Finally, guidelines must be developed for the assessment of situation-specific competencies so that individuals with mental retardation can take maximal control of their lives, and can at the same time be protected from neglect or abuse and be assured of advocacy for access to needed services.

REFERENCES

Anderson, D., Bruininks, R., & Hill, B. (1987). *National study of residential and support services for elderly developmentally disabled people* (Report No. 22). Minneapolis: University of Minnesota, Center for Residential and Community Services.

Benz, M.R. (1986). *Factors affecting the well-being of elderly mentally retarded persons.* Unpublished raw data, National Institute of Handicapped Research (now known as National Institute for Disability and Rehabilitation).

Edgerton, R.B. (1986). A case of delabeling: Some practical and theoretical implications. In L.L. Langness & H.G. Levine (Eds.), *Culture and retardation* (pp. 101–126). New York: D. Reidel.

Granger, C.V., Seltzer, G.B., and Fishbein, S. (1987). *Primary care of the functionally disabled: Assessment and management.* Philadelphia: Lippincott.

Harper, D., & Wadsworth, J. (1986, November). *Cognitive/behavioral decline in elderly mentally retarded persons.* Paper presented at the meeting of the American Association of University Affiliated Programs, Boston.

Heller, T., & Factor, A. (1986, November). *Development of a transition plan for persons with developmental disabilities residing with their elderly parents.* Paper presented at the meeting of the American Association of University Affiliated Programs, Boston.

Janicki, M.P., & MacEachron, A.E. (1984). Residential, health, and social service needs of elderly developmentally disabled persons. *Gerontologist, 24,* 128–137.

Krauss, M.W., & Seltzer, M.M. (1986). A comparison of elderly and adult mentally retarded persons in community and institutional settings. *American Journal of Mental Deficiency, 91,* 237–243.

Leventhal, E., & Schaefer, P. (in preparation). *Aging in the developmentally disabled: An assessment of Down syndrome and non-Down syndrome adults.* Madison: University of Wisconsin.

Lutzer, V., & Brubaker, T. (in press). Differential respite needs of aging parents of individuals with developmental disabilities. *Mental Retardation.*

EPILOGUE

Epilogue
FELIX DE LA CRUZ

While earning about $100 a month as a resident in pediatrics in the state of Washington in 1958, I supplemented my income by providing inpatient and outpatient medical care in an institution for mentally retarded persons every other weekend. Medical records at the institution, located in a small town 45 miles from Seattle, were at best sketchy, and the reasons for institutionalization were frequently obscure for the 2,000 residents—the term used to describe the individuals residing in the institution. The residential facilities were large and overcrowded, and the spectrum and quality of care the residents received were unsatisfactory. The employees were, by and large, overworked and inadequately trained. Some of the more capable residents provided basic care such as feeding, bathing, and personal hygiene assistance to the less capable residents. Laboratory and x-ray facilities were inadequate and the drugs available in the hospital pharmacy were limited.

This woeful scenario changed dramatically when a young and caring physician fresh out of pediatric training was employed to be the medical director of the institution. A research program, with a strong emphasis in cytogenetics, was initiated. There soon followed a long list of students and professional groups—dental, medical, nursing, dental hygiene—who made field trips to the institution to hear lectures and see demonstrations from the clinical staff about the nature and scope of mental retardation and its multifaceted etiologies. Pediatric residents from the University of Washington School of Medicine spent 2–3 months of their training working in the hospital, and a full-time psychology research laboratory was established in the institution by the University. The man who was primarily responsible for instituting these changes became the first director, in 1963, of the Mental Retardation Program in the newly established National Institute of Child Health and Human Development (NICHD), and the Institute's third director.

Much has transpired in research and in the law since the early 1960s, most of which benefited mentally retarded persons. The most significant event occurred on October 31, 1963, when the 88th Congress passed Public Law 88-164, the Mental Retardation Facilities and Community Mental Health Centers Construction Act. This enabling legislation provided assistance in combating mental retardation through grants for construction of Centers for Research on Mental Retardation and Related Aspects of Human Development (MRRCs) as well as University Affiliated Facilities (UAFs). The MRRCs, to be administered by NICHD, were constructed to facilitate "research, or research and related purposes relating to human development, whether biological, medical, social, or behavioral, which may assist in finding the causes, and means of prevention, of mental retardation, or in finding means of ameliorating the effects of mental retardation" (Public Law 88-164). In fiscal year 1964, support provided by NICHD for research on mental retardation amounted to $3 million, which represented 11% of the Institute's budget. In fiscal year 1986, support for mental retardation-relevant research totaled $47 million, or 18% of NICHD's research budget.

Some of the major research accomplishments in the biomedical and behavioral sciences in the past 25 years have been presented in this volume, along with speculations on future research efforts on behalf of mentally retarded individuals. Several future research trends are of note. Barring catastrophic reduction of support for research, the human genome will be mapped, cloned, and sequenced. Early and noninvasive prenatal diagnostic techniques will be developed, such as using fetal cells obtained from maternal peripheral blood or cervical secretions. Abortion will no longer be the only alternative for families in whom a defective fetus is diagnosed prenatally. Various genetic therapies will be attempted for inherited neurological diseases. These therapies will rely upon cell or tissue transplants or the direct use of genes or gene products. Designer drugs will continue to be developed for ameliorating various retardation-related problems.

Corresponding advances will be achieved using animal models, in which preliminary investigations of the safety and efficacy of genetic procedures must be demonstrated before studies in humans can be morally and ethically initiated. Information from such studies will provide a resource for the study of genetic defects resulting in neurobiological deficits. Early in this century, genetics and embryology diverged. Geneticists did not appreciate that Mendelian inheritance concepts must ultimately be interpretable in embryological terms. The next few decades will witness a reconciliation of the rapidly advancing fields of genetics and embryology. This reconciliation will represent the cutting edge of developmental biology, and its impact on mental retardation research, as well as in other areas, will be tremendous.

There will be a continued influx of researchers into the neuro-sciences as a result of rapid advances in neurobiology, the application of molecular biology to neurobiology, and the intriguing relationship between mind and brain. Over the next several years, a major effort will be made to determine what controls the assembly of the brain. Research projects will be developed to discover what is the driving force for the development of brain structures, the organization of these structures, and how they account for function.

Research on the effects of prenatal exposure to noxious agents has up to now been concentrated on the morphological consequences. Future research will be devoted to the behavioral, psychological, and learning sequelae of environmental agents. Research on how to enhance in utero development of the fetus, morphologically and behaviorally, will flourish.

Technical advances in molecular biology and genetics will continue to make the study of inherited neurological diseases practical. These technical advances, which will range from the development of more sensitive assays and physiological procedures to the development of new drugs for the ablation of specific brain nuclei, may help reduce the prevention and treatment problems associated with the complexity of the central nervous system.

In the years and decades ahead, significant advances will be made in the study of mental retardation. These advances will be realized only if public support for research does not diminish. In fact, several investigators have already expressed concern about the diminishing federal support for mental retardation–relevant research. In research in general, it is axiomatic that some of the significant achievements were the product of serendipity. Thus it is often difficult to ascertain which research is relevant to mental retardation. It therefore behooves research administrators to be more liberal in their interpretation of research project relevancy, if significant progress is to be achieved on behalf of mentally retarded persons. Judging from the research trends reported in the chapters in this volume, there is plenty of room for optimism in the years ahead. However, success in preventing mental retardation or in mitigating its consequences will occur only if government officials and private citizens work in concert and with unwavering determination to achieve this goal.

REFERENCE

Public Law 88-164. (1963, October 31). 88th Congress, §1576.

Index

Developmental neuroscience
research findings in, 81–83
see also Prenatal
neurodevelopment
Developmental outcome, neonatal
intensive care and, 171–177
see also Low birth weight
Developmental patterns, cognitive
research and, 258–259
see also Cognitive development
Development quotient (DQ), birth
weight and, 172–173, 176
Diagnosis, *see* Neonatal screening;
Prenatal diagnosis; *specific
disorder*; *specific method*
*Diagnostic and Statistical Manual of
Mental Disorders (DSM-III)*,
320–321
Diaphragmatic hernia, fetal surgery
for, 96
Diet
food additives in, toxicity of,
67–69, 70–71
see also Nutrition
Differential gene expression, 81–82
Diphtheria-tetanus-pertussis (DPT)
vaccine, Hib vaccine and,
242–247
Discrimination, visual, 210
Disruptive behavior, 267–275
biobehavioral research on,
272–273
future research on, 273–275
Dissociated cell culture system,
83–88
DNA
CMV strain, restriction enzyme
analysis of, 143–145
restriction endonuclease cleavage
of, 11
see also Molecular biology
Dopamine, self-injurious behavior
and, 273
Doppler ultrasound analysis,
pulsed, fetal assessment with,
100–101
Down syndrome
as "atheroma-free model," 292
incidence of, 29–30
projected, 31

infant-parent interactions and,
224–225
premature aging and, 291–292
risk factors for, 29–30, 31
DQ (developmental quotient), birth
weight and, 172–173, 176
Drugs
mental illness treatment with,
324–326
during pregnancy, 109–111
reduction of, 117–118
see also Teratogenicity
*DSM-III (Diagnostic and Statistical
Manual of Mental Disorders)*,
320–321
DTP (diphtheria-tetanus-pertussis)
vaccine, Hib vaccine and,
242–247

Early experience paradigm,
278–280
Early intervention, 277–285
candidates for, 281–282
cost of, 284
methods of, 282–284
policy implications of, 284–285
program evaluation in, criteria
for, 285
rationale for, 277–281
Education, compensatory, 283
Educational level, maternal, low
birth weight and, 26, 27, 29,
125
Educational theories, critical period
research and, 278–279
EEG, *see* Electroencephalogram
Elderly, *see* Old age
Electrical activity
brain, 181–190
see also Brain electrical activity
mapping (BEAM)
neuronal, nervous system
development and, 83–89
Electroencephalogram (EEG),
181–183
BEAM and, 183–185
see also Brain electrical activity
mapping
limitations of, 183